Attention in Vision

Attention in Vision is an important work which aims to identify, address and solve some major problems and issues in the psychology of visual perception, attention and intentional control. The central aim is to investigate how people use their visual perception in the performance of tasks and to explore how the intentional control of action is achieved. Through an extensive review of the philosophy of psychology, the history of ideas and theories of intentional control, and an analysis of various tasks, a new theory is developed which argues that there is an important difference between report tasks and act tasks.

The first part of the book introduces the issue of the use of visual perception in a historical context and outlines van der Heijden's theory. The theory is developed in the second and third parts talk performance by analysing the findings from some of the main experimental paradigms of cognitive psychology and applying the theory to report tasks and act tasks. Finally, the epilogue skilfully draws together the theory into an explanation of important issues on the borderline between philosophy and psychology.

This book will be invaluable to researchers and high-level undergraduates in the field of visual perception and attention.

A. H. C. van der Heijden is a Professor from the Department of Psychology at Leiden University in The Netherlands. He has previously authored *Short-term Visual Information Forgetting* and *Selective Attention in Vision* (both published by Routledge), which have been widely cited by researchers in the field and which have also been used as high-level textbooks in graduate courses.

Attention in Vision

Perception, Communication, and Action

A. H. C. van der Heijden

Psychology Press
Taylor & Francis Group

HOVE AND NEW YORK

First published 2004 by Psychology Press Ltd
27 Church Road, Hove, East Sussex, BN3 2FA

Simultaneously published in the USA and Canada
by Taylor & Francis Inc
29 West 35th Street, New York, NY 10001

Psychology Press is an imprint of the Taylor & Francis Group

Copyright © 2004 Psychology Press Ltd

Typeset in Times by Graphicraft Limited, Hong Kong
Printed and bound in Great Britain by Biddles Ltd, King's Lynn
Cover design by Jim Wilkie
Cover painting by Lisa van der Heijden

British Library Cataloguing in Publication Data
A catalogue record for this book is available
from the British Library

Library of Congress Cataloging-in-Publication Data
Heijden, A. H. C. van der.
    Attention in vision : perception, communication, and action /
A.H.C. van der Heijden. – 1st ed.
        p. cm.
Includes bibliographical references and index.
    ISBN 1-84169-348-0
    1. Visual perception. 2. Selectivity (Psychology). 3. Attention. I.
Title.
    BF241.H42 2003
    152.14—dc21

                                                    2003010585

ISBN 1-84169-348-0

For Lisa

... the best that any individual scientist, especially any psychologist, can do seems to be to follow his own gleam and his own bent, however inadequate they may be ... In the end, the only sure criterion is to have fun.

(Tolman, 1959, p. 152)

... theory should not start with stimulation, but somewhere else; and this is where the difficulties begin.

(Broadbent, 1993, p. 876)

Contents

Foreword

Attention in Vision: Perception, Communication, and Action is a research monograph presenting a selective review of empirical findings on visual attention and a new theoretical account of the findings. It is the third book authored by Lex van der Heijden, and like his previous books, *Short-term Visual Information Forgetting* (1981) and *Selective Attention in Vision* (1992), it is a major contribution to the study of attention. Let me sketch the essence of Van der Heijden's work and place it in a historical context.

The first modern theory of attention was the selective-filter theory proposed by Donald Broadbent in his book entitled *Perception and Communication* (1958). In this theory, information flows from the senses through many parallel input channels into a short-term memory buffer. Further processing is done by a perceptual categorisation system whose capacity is much smaller than the total capacity of the parallel input channels. Therefore, a selective filter operates between the short-term buffer and the perceptual categorisation system. The filter acts as an all-or-none switch, selecting information from just one of the parallel input channels at a time. Thus, in Broadbent's theory, selection is *early* in the sense that it is *precategorical* (i.e., occurring before perceptual categorisation). Perceptual processing capacity is regarded as a limited resource, and perceptual attention as a mechanism for allocating the capacity to selected inputs to the system. Attentional selection of inputs is *selection for perception*, and it protects the *limited-capacity* system for perceptual categorisation from informational overload.

Broadbent's selective-filter theory of attention accounted for the main results of early studies on selective listening, but the theory was soon challenged by experimental findings showing that certain categories of stimulus material (e.g., subjectively important stimuli such as the subject's own name) tend to be recognised even if presented on a channel to be ignored. Such findings suggested that attentional selection is *late* in the sense that it is *postcategorical* (i.e., occurring after perceptual categorisation). The late-selection view of attention was introduced by J. Anthony Deutsch and Diana Deutsch in 1963 and developed by a few prominent theorists including Richard M. Shiffrin, Donald Norman, John Duncan, and Lex van der Heijden. In this view, all sensory messages that impinge upon the organism are perceptually analysed and categorised at the highest level. Thus, attended and unattended messages receive the same amount of analysis by the system for perceptual categorisation, so attentional selection has no effect on perceptual categorisation. However, after a stimulus has been categorised, the importance of the stimulus is evaluated (retrieved), and the stimulus with the greatest importance is selected for further processing including conscious awareness.

The contrast between early- and late-selection theories of attention has dominated the psychology of attention for nearly half a century, and the late-selection view of attention got major impetus from the early work of Van der Heijden. In his 1981 book, *Short-term Visual Information Forgetting*, Van der Heijden analysed performance in visual whole- and partial-report experiments and argued forcefully that 'selection in whole and partial report experiments is postcategorical selection' (p. 7). He also explicated the notion of postcategorical selection: The perceptual categorisation system is effectively *unlimited in processing capacity*, so perceptual categorisation is not selective. However, visually guided actions are typically directed against one or a few objects at a time, so regardless of any limitations in our capacity for processing of perceptual information, some selective process is needed to map the visual representations of just the target objects onto parameters controlling the action. This selective process is attentional selection. Thus, with an expression later coined by Alan Allport, attentional selection is *selection for action*.

In the empirical sections of his 1992 book, *Selective Attention in Vision*, Van der Heijden took the reader on a systematic tour de force through the wealth of empirical findings from 'single-item detection and recognition tasks with accuracy as the dependent variable', 'single-item detection and recognition tasks with latency as the dependent variable', 'multiple-item detection and recognition tasks with accuracy as the dependent variable', and 'multiple-item detection and recognition tasks with latency as the dependent variable'. In the theoretical sections of the book, he further developed his theory of visual attention but made a sharp distinction between the capacity issue and the selection issue. He argued that the visual system for perceptual categorisation is *unlimited in processing capacity*, and attentional selection is selection for action. However, the selection is done by feeding position information back via top-down connections to an *early*, *precategorical* level of processing.

The new version of the theory was built around a selective attention model (SLAM) proposed by R. H. Phaf, Lex van der Heijden, and P. T. W. Hudson in 1990. SLAM is a neural network model, so information processing consists in a flow of activation through a network of neuron-like units, which are linked together by facilitatory and inhibitory connections. The network is capable of both object selection and property selection. Object selection is implemented by arranging the connections so that (a) units representing mutually compatible categorisations of the same object facilitate each other, but (b) units representing incompatible categorisations inhibit each other, and (c) units representing categorisations of different objects also inhibit each other. Selection of a red target, for example, can then be done by providing a unit representing redness with extra activation. If a red target is present, the extra activation will directly facilitate the correct categorisation of the target with respect to colour. Indirectly the activation will facilitate categorisations of the target with respect to other properties than colour, but inhibit categorisations of any other objects than the target. Thus, the theory offered a truly computational account of selective attention in vision.

The present book by Van der Heijden builds on his previous works. The basic assumption that the perceptual categorisation system is unlimited in processing capacity is more or less taken for granted rather than argued anew. SLAM is reviewed, but the focus is on higher-order control processes and overarching theoretical issues. In the terminology used in the book, Van der Heijden attempts to explain how the Intending Mind uses Visual Perception for generating propositions (in report tasks) and moving the body (act tasks) in the physical world. Inspired by Turing's description of a universal machine, the Intending Mind is explicated as a sequence of states in an intentional machine. In report tasks, the Intending Mind goes through successive cycles of selecting an object (filtering) and determining the value of an attribute to be reported (pigeon-holing). In act tasks, the Intending Mind goes through successive cycles of selecting an object and extracting those parameters of the object that are needed for action. Complex behaviour is generated by organising such cycles hierarchically.

The overall structure of the book is exceedingly clear and logical. The prologue and the first main part of the book introduce the problem and the approach in a historical setting. The second main part of the book develops and applies the general theory by analysing extant findings from some of the main experimental paradigms of cognitive psychology: paradigms with accuracy of performance as the dependent variable and paradigms with speed of performance as the dependent variable. The third main part of the book further develops the theory by applying it to 'act tasks'. Most interesting, I think, is the theoretical treatment of processing of spatial position and the treatment of cognitive control of saccadic eye movements. The epilogue rounds off the book by applying Van der Heijden's theoretical account to issues on the borderline between philosophy and psychology such as the mind–body problem and the freedom of the will.

The book is both learned and provocative. In classical academic style, the book is extremely systematic. It also has plenty of endnotes, which form an essential part of the book. In a more personal style, the system is unorthodox, and the notes are anything but predictable. Lex has followed his own gleam and his own bent.

Claus Bundesen

Prologue

In the chapter 'On Being a Person: Problems of Self' of his book *The Singular Self*, Harré (1998, p. 1) starts with visiting a bookstore. He tells us that

> Drifting from genre to genre one is struck by the number of books with 'self' in the title or subtitle . . . Books with 'consciousness' in the title or subtitle are almost as common . . . We can be sure in these too the 'self' will figure prominently. Yet neither selfhood nor consciousness are clear, univocal or straightforward notions. What is it to be a human being is what is really at issue of course . . .

Under 'Free Will' in *A Companion to Metaphysics*, Watson (1995, p. 177) explains the differences in views of Hobbes and of Reid. He concludes that

> We come here to a fundamental divergence of outlook between Hobbes and Reid as between compatibilists and 'libertarians' more generally. [Compatibilists believe that free will is compatible with determinism.] (Libertarians are those who insist that human beings are free in a way that precludes determinism.) Their dispute is not just about freedom but about what a human being is.

And of course in the end, for psychology – and not only for psychology – what is always really at issue is 'What is it to be a human being?', and in psychology ultimately the scientific dispute has to be about 'what a human being is'.

When I started the work presented here, however, I had no intention whatsoever of writing about topics like 'the self' and 'free will', topics that inevitably immediately lead to the most basic questions about human existence. In fact, what I planned to do was exactly the opposite – to try to get rid of these and similar concepts as fast as possible and to replace them by something better. What I then intended to do, I can best further introduce by quoting Broadbent (1987, p. 73) who, in my view, after a lifetime of reading, experimenting, and theorising, correctly diagnosed that

Psychological opinion tends to sway between a view that people are almost infinitely flexible and a view that there are definite and unchangeable fundamental mechanisms that always work in the same way and set limits to flexibility. A popular compromise has been to suppose that 'lower' mechanisms are as determinate as type-writers, while 'higher' ones are unanalysable, autonomous, and perhaps even beyond scientific enquiry.

My opinion then was that contemporary experimental psychology – information processing psychology, cognitive psychology and/or cognitive neuroscience – did not need such a 'popular compromise'.[1] In particular, my opinion was that the 'higher', unanalysable and autonomous, mechanisms Broadbent referred to, are basically the 'selves' with 'free wills' and that these unanalysed autonomous agents show up in a variety of disguises in the theorising in experimental psychology. And, again, my opinion was that contemporary experimental psychology did not need that kind of ghosts in the machine.[2] My intention was to track down and to unmask that spook and to replace it by a decent 'lower' information processing mechanism – a mechanism as determinate as a type-writer.

In my view then, the chances of succeeding in this endeavour – replacing a spook by a mechanism in the theorising in experimental psychology – were not bad at all. My reasoning ran approximately as follows. I assumed that Broadbent's (1987) unanalysable, autonomous, 'higher' mechanisms were indeed nothing more, and nothing less, than 'selves' with 'free wills'. Complete embodied and situated 'selves' with 'free will', as met in streets, stations, and stores, seem indeed unpredictable systems beyond scientific enquiry. However, those are not the situations in which we meet and address the same 'selves' with 'free wills' when they perform as subjects in a laboratory experiment. In that situation their 'self' is neither of relevance nor of importance, and their 'free will' is not only not required but is even not welcome. In that situation, not the 'self' and the 'free will' of the subject but the 'self' and the 'free will' of the experimenter determine what has to be done, how that has to be done, where that has to be done, and when that has to be done. In a sense, the subjects are 'hypnotised', losing their selves, their free wills, their responsibility and dignity. But then, in that situation, the 'unanalysable, autonomous, "higher" mechanisms' of the subject are eliminated, or, at least, made irrelevant. What then, in that situation, remain in operation are only the 'lower' mechanisms 'that are as determinate as type-writers'.

In this work on *Attention in Vision: Perception, Communication, and Action*, I present the results of my attempts to replace the ghost in the machine.[3] The work is primarily concerned with the problem of how people use their visual perception and their attention in the performance of tasks. The tasks I am first and foremost concerned with are, of course, simple laboratory tasks.[4] They are, however, tasks in which, in one way or another, the 'subject' is in control, not tasks in which only the visual world is in control; tasks involving 'voluntary', 'controlled' processes, not tasks involving only 'involuntary', 'automatic' processes (see Shiffrin & Schneider, 1977, for the distinction between 'controlled' and 'automatic' processes).[5]

In Part I, Considerations, the considerations are presented that led me to my solution of the ghost in the machine problem. In Part II, Report tasks, first that solution is elaborated, and then its viability is investigated for tasks in which subjects have, for instance, to name objects or attributes of objects, or to read letters or words; that is, tasks in which subjects report about what they see. In Part III, Act tasks, first visual perception is elaborated and then the viability of the solution is investigated for tasks in which subjects have, for instance, to make a saccadic eye movement to a position or to hit an object at a position; that is, tasks in which subjects do something with regard to what they see. These types of tasks, the report tasks and the act tasks, are studied with great success in the visual branch of the information processing approach within contemporary experimental psychology.

As will become clear in the main parts of this study, for the solution of my problem of how people use their visual perception and attention in the performance of tasks, I use two major explanatory ingredients or components. One is Visual Perception, and the other I call, for want of a better term, Intending Mind. Visual Perception is the visual perception as investigated and modelled in contemporary information processing psychology. Intending Mind is, of course, my own invention and, even worse, Intending Mind is the explanatory ingredient that I need for solving my problem of how people use their visual perception and attention in the performance of tasks. Intending Mind is a new theoretical entity, invented to replace Broadbent's (1987) unanalysable, autonomous 'higher' mechanisms by a 'lower' mechanism that is as determinate as a type-writer.

It is, of course, completely up to the reader to decide whether this replacement of the 'higher', autonomous mechanisms by a 'lower', determinate mechanism is justified and/or successful. The reader has to decide whether the considerations, presented in Part I, are valid, and whether the elaborations, extensions, and tests, presented in Parts II and III, are appropriate. For making a final decision, however, the following additional information is possibly of some help.

Intending Mind, as used in the present work, was invented just for the purpose of explaining task performance in laboratory tasks involving vision without invoking unanalysable, autonomous 'higher' mechanisms. Intending Mind is not conceived as a fixed structure whose architecture can be mapped, but as a flexibly functioning entity that can be characterised in terms of 'units of analysis'.

Once upon a time, units of analysis or 'basic units' were the theoretical entities looked for and fostered in experimental psychology. They were used for characterising complex internal and external states of affairs, and for a good scientific reason. In several places, G. A. Miller was explicit about these units of analysis and about that scientific reason. Miller, Galanter, and

Pribram (1960), for instance, have a chapter titled 'The Unit of Analysis' that starts with:

> Most psychologists take it for granted that a scientific account of the behavior of organisms must begin with the definition of fixed, recognizable, elementary units of behavior – something a psychologist can use as a biologist uses cells, or an astronomer uses stars, or a physicist uses atoms, and so on. Given a simple unit, complicated phenomena are then describable as lawful compounds. That is the essence of the highly successful strategy called "scientific analysis." (p. 21)

And, in his evaluation of S–R theories, Miller (1964, pp. 202–203) writes:

> Some proponents of S–R theories assume that the conditioning experiment is the prototype of all learning. For more complex situations the theoretical task is to discover how the behavioral processes can be analyzed into these basic components . . . "After all," they might say, "analysis into basic units is essential to all scientific progress: look at the analysis of matter into atoms, or the analysis of organisms into cells. Everywhere in science it is the same. We must find the proper elements and then discover the laws of their combination. That was, after all, what Wilhelm Wundt wanted to do; the trouble with Wundt was that he chose the idea instead of the S–R bond as his element."

It will be clear that my Intending Mind is a complex internal state of affairs. And, to bring this state of affairs within the reach of scientific enquiry, I chopped it up into manageable bits and pieces, into its units of analysis, its atoms, cells, or stars.

The important point is now that this divide-and-conquer technique brought not only the expected theoretical results but also a number of quite unexpected ones. The expected results are presented in Parts II and III of this study. The unexpected results, which became clear only after the main work was done, are presented in the Epilogue. There it is shown that the units of analysis are not only adequate for explaining how subjects use their visual perception and their attention in the performance of tasks, but also are useful theoretical entities for (a) elucidating what experimental psychologists have been doing, contributing, and accumulating during the last 120 years, (b) elucidating and approaching some of the problems surrounding the elusive concept of 'self', which we indicate with terms like 'I', 'me', and 'you', (c), elucidating and approaching some of the problems with the intangible concepts 'freedom' and 'free will', and (d) elucidating and approaching the mind–body problem and some of the problems concerning the planning, structuring, and executing of goal-directed behaviour.

So, after the main work was done, it appeared that ultimately I had not really been successful in completely avoiding and evading the basic questions

'What is a human being?' and 'What is it to be a human being?'. For the final decision about the work presented here, I invite the reader also to take this shortcoming into account.

Notes

1 In this work, I use the terms 'information processing psychology' and 'cognitive psychology' interchangeably. For a possible distinction in terms of 'explaining behaviour' and 'explaining mind' see Van der Heijden (1996b).
2 The expression 'ghost in the machine' comes from Gilbert Ryle (1949), *The Concept of Mind*, London: Hutchinson.
3 One remark and apology is in order here. Because of the topic I am concerned with,

> The text will often seem inconsistent. English, like all languages, is full of prescientific terms which usually suffice for purposes of casual discourse. No one looks askance at the astronomer when he says that the sun rises or that the stars come out at night, for it would be ridiculous to insist that he should always say that the sun appears over the horizon as the earth turns or that the stars become visible as the atmosphere ceases to refract sunlight. All we ask is that he can give a more precise translation if one is needed.
>
> (Skinner, 1972, p. 21)

4 Because I am mainly concerned with simple laboratory tasks and not with real-life tasks, Chomsky's (1959) devastating critique of behaviourism seems, at first sight and with some changes in wording, to apply equally to the work here presented:

> The notions of "stimulus," "response," "reinforcement" are relatively well defined with respect to the bar-pressing experiments and others similarly restricted. Before we can extend them to real-life behavior, however, certain difficulties must be faced. We must decide, first of all, whether any physical event to which the organism is capable of reacting is to be called a stimulus on a given occasion, or only one to which the organism in fact reacts; and, correspondingly, we must decide whether any part of behavior is to be called a response, or only one connected with stimuli in lawful ways. Questions of this sort pose something of a dilemma for the experimental psychologist. If he accepts the broad definitions . . . he must conclude that behavior has not been demonstrated to be lawful. In the present state of our knowledge, we must attribute an overwhelming influence on actual behavior to ill-defined factors of attention, set, volition, and caprice. If we accept the narrower definitions, then behavior is lawful by definition (if it consists of responses); but this fact is of limited significance, since most of what the animal does will simply not be considered behavior.
>
> (From Chomsky's review of B. F. Skinner's *Verbal Behavior*, in *Language*, 1959, *35*, 26–58; taken from Miller, Galanter, & Pribram, 1960, p. 23.)

Two points are of importance, however. The first is, that the present work is concerned with the 'ill-defined factors of attention, set, volition, and caprice'. The second point is elaborated later in this Prologue.
5 The tasks I am concerned with are tasks in which, according to Descartes, the soul, *res cogitans*, is involved ('attention'), not tasks in which only the body, *res extensa*, is involved ('admiration'); see Descartes (1650/1973), *Les Passions de L'âme*.

Part I
Considerations

1 The problem and the approach

1.0 Introduction

This work is primarily concerned with the problem of how people use their visual perception in the performance of tasks. The tasks with which this work is first and foremost concerned are simple laboratory tasks, in which subjects have to name objects or attributes of objects, or have to read letters or words; that is, tasks in which people report about what they see (Part II), and tasks in which subjects have to make a saccadic eye movement, or have to hit an object at a position; that is, tasks in which subjects do something with regard to what they see (Part III).[1] Via an analysis of internal task performance in this type of tasks, I hope to find out what kind of machines human beings basically are.

To reach my main aim, the characterisation of *Man a Machine*, I need more than what is offered by contemporary information processing psychology.[2] The reason is that in the past task performance has been approached from different directions by different psychologies that all have something of relevance to tell. Of special interest and importance for me are early 'subjective' introspective experimental psychology, with its centres of gravity in Germany and the USA, the psychology preceding and wiped out by behaviourism, and, of course, contemporary 'objective' information processing psychology, with participants and schools in Europe and North America, the psychology that followed and wiped out behaviourism. The two psychologies agree in the conviction that in task performance the involvement of attention is of crucial importance.

In Section 1.1, I briefly introduce early introspective psychology and contemporary information processing psychology. I argue that these two psychologies neatly complement each other because they refer from different points of view to the same state of affairs; introspective psychology describes the states and contents of the mind, and information processing psychology infers the structure and processes of the mind. My conclusion is that the combination of these two psychologies allows a more complete view on how people use their visual perception for task performance than either psychology alone.

Sections 1.2 and 1.3 are concerned with specifying what is presently the main problem in an account of how people use their visual perception in the performance of tasks. Section 1.2 is concerned with William James's (1890/ 1950) *The Principles of Psychology*. James rejected the 'sensationalism' of mainstream introspective psychology and theorised in terms of 'objects'. He emphasised the distinction between 'thought' and 'object thought of'; that is, he recognised that 'intentionality' is an essential characteristic of the mind. Specifying 'intentionality' in information processing terms and introducing the resulting 'intentionality' in the theorising of the information processing approach, can be regarded as my main aim in this book.

In Section 1.3, the visual perception and attention branch of the information processing approach is briefly introduced. It is argued that in the theorising in this branch two components can be recognised, an unproblematic component, concerned with perception and attention, and a problematic component, postulating a 'subject' as an agent. Specifying this 'subject' in information processing terms and introducing the resulting 'subject' in the theorising in the information processing approach can be regarded as my main aim in this book.

In Section 1.4, the two main aims specified in the foregoing sections – the aim with regard to 'intentionality' (Section 1.2) and the aim with regard to the 'subject' (Section 1.3) – are related and combined. The central aim in this book is to replace the 'subject' in the information processing theories by one or another form of James's (1890/1950) 'intentionality'.

1.1   Two psychologies

James (1890/1950) starts *The Principles of Psychology* by proclaiming:

> Psychology is the Science of Mental Life, both of its phenomena and their conditions. The phenomena are such things as we call feelings, desires, cognitions, reasonings, decisions, and the like . . . (p. 1)

and he declares further on:

> *Introspective Observation is what we have to rely on first and foremost and always.* The word introspection need hardly be explained – it means, of course, the looking into our own minds and reporting what we there discover. (p. 185)

James was not an enthusiastic experimentalist – a method that, in his view, 'taxes patience to the utmost, and could hardly have arisen in a country whose natives could be *bored*' (p. 192). Nevertheless, he knew perfectly well what was going on in the laboratories of the early German experimental psychologists such as Wundt and Münsterberg and Müller. In their experiments these investigators studied, for instance, visual perception as subjectively experienced. Introspection was the method, and the data, obtained under well-controlled conditions, consisted of descriptions of experienced phenomena or of what was seen and felt. As is well known, this psychology flourished between about 1880 and 1920 and thereafter virtually completely disappeared from the psychological scene. The introspective method yielded only unreliable data and the theoretical controversies remained unresolved – so, at least, the story goes.

Present-day information processing psychology can proclaim:

> Psychology is the Science of the Mind, both of its operations and their conditions. The operations are such processes as we call perceiving, selecting, attending, storing, retrieving, remembering and the like . . .

and can further declare that

> *Analysis of behavioural data is what we have to rely on first and foremost and always.* The expression analysis-of-behavioural-data need hardly be explained – it means, of course, the looking at reaction times and percentages correct and the figuring out what those data tell us about the operations of the mind.

And, just like the grand old men such as Broadbent, Haber, and Sperling, who started the information processing approach in the 1960s, all current information processing psychologists are experimental psychologists. They firmly believe that "What generous divination, and that superiority in virtue which . . . give a man the best insight into nature, have failed to do, their spying and scraping, their deadly tenacity and almost diabolic cunning, will doubtless some day bring about" (James, 1890/1950, p. 193). This approach started around 1960 and is still flourishing. The behavioural experiments deliver reliable data and theoretical progress is steadily made – so, at least, the story goes.

This brief introduction makes clear that there are two psychologies that both possibly have something of relevance to tell about how people use their visual perception in the performance of tasks. Because in studies concerned with vision the introspective psychologists tried to describe what they saw and the subjects in the information processing experiments try to report what they see, both psychologies investigate, in one way or another, how people use their visual perception in the performance of tasks. Moreover, in their studies exploring vision, the two psychologies were often concerned with the same topics and even often used the same tasks. For instance, at the start of the information processing approach Von Helmholtz's (1871, 1894) visual attention tasks were reinvented and reintroduced by Sperling (1960) and Averbach and Coriell (1961) and are still used nowadays; see Van der Heijden (1992) for details. Kuelpe's (1904) visual set experiments were reintroduced by Harris and Haber (1963) and subsequently thoroughly elaborated and analysed; see Haber (1966) for an overview. And the visual backward masking paradigm of Exner (1868) and the metacontrast paradigm of Stigler (1910) were reintroduced by Sperling (1960) and Averbach and Coriell (1961) and are still, as I write, often used; see Neumann (1990b) for details.

As already indicated, however, the two psychologies differ vastly in their presuppositions with regard to a viable and productive psychology; in their presuppositions about the proper data (features of mind versus features of behaviour), about the proper method (subjective introspection versus objective response registration), and about the ultimate goal of their scientific enterprise – the characterisation of states and contents of the mind versus the characterisation of the structure and the processes of the mind.[3] Moreover, as I have already said, early introspective psychology fully failed and disappeared completely from the scene while information processing psychology currently flourishes. Therefore, a question that we need to consider first is: Do we, information processing psychologists or cognitive psychologists, nowadays still need some of the data and some of the insights of the rejected introspective past? This question deserves two answers, one for introspective psychology in general and one for James's (1890/1950) idiosyncratic version of introspective psychology.

With regard to introspective psychology in general, my view is that selected bits and pieces can certainly improve and enhance the theorising in the information processing approach (see also Van der Heijden, 1992). In general, my conviction is that a combination of, at the first sight, different stories with regard to one and the same state of affairs can often provide a much better starting point for understanding that state of affairs than either individual story alone. And, in my view, this is particularly true for the combination of early systematic introspective psychology and contemporary information processing psychology. Here I can only briefly indicate why, in my view, this combination can be a 'winning couple'; the rest of this book also serves to further substantiate this point.

In my view, early systematic introspective psychology and current information processing psychology neatly *complement* each other in a theoretically highly desirable way.

- Early introspective psychology is concerned with aspects of the subjective question of what it is to be a human being. This psychology looks from the inside at the inside. This approach is good at description of the contents and states of mind; these are the givens that are accessible to introspection. This psychology, however, has virtually nothing to say about internal processes or functions; this is because these processes or functions are *Unanschauliche*/impalpable givens that mainly elude systematic introspection (see, e.g., Boring, 1950, p. 451). When introspective psychology reigned, there were attempts to investigate processes and processing times with reaction time methods, but these were soon generally regarded as complete failures (see Boring, 1950, p. 149).

• Information processing psychology is concerned with aspects of the objective question of what a human being is. This approach looks from the outside at the outside. This approach is good at inferring internal structures and processes or functions from features of behavioural data; these are the information processing operations or functions that produce these data features. This psychology, however, has virtually nothing to say about the contents of states; states and changes of states are not sufficiently constrained by the behavioural data, the reaction times, and the percentages correct, that are used (see, e.g., Van der Heijden, 1996b, for an extensive discussion of this issue).[4]

So, it seems that only a proper combination of early introspective psychology and current objective psychology can yield a complete psychology that sheds light on both states and contents, and structures and processes. A proper combination of the two approaches can provide an information processing psychology enhanced with introspected states and contents and/ or an introspective psychology enhanced with inferred structures and functions. And, of course, to really shed light on my problem, the problem of how people use their visual perception in the performance of tasks, I need a psychology that is as complete and as enhanced as possible.

A first, provisional, answer to the question of whether we, information processing psychologists or cognitive psychologists, nowadays still need aspects of James's introspective psychology we can, for the moment, fortunately take from James (1890/1950) himself; again, the rest of this work serves to further substantiate this point. For James

> The conception of consciousness as a purely cognitive form of being . . . is thoroughly anti-psychological . . . Every actually existing consciousness seems to itself at any rate to be a *fighter for ends*, of which many, but for its presence, would not be ends at all. Its powers of cognition are mainly subservient to these ends, discerning which facts further them and which do not. (p. 141)

So, by introducing the relevant aspects of James's introspective psychology, it is possible to transform the 'anti-psychological' information processing psychology or 'cognitive psychology' into a psychological psychology. By injecting the relevant aspects of James's views into the current theorising of the information processing approach, 'interests' and 'ends' are introduced on the theoretical scene. And, it will be clear, for my problem, the problem of how people use their visual perception in the performance of tasks, a 'fighter for ends' with 'interests' comes in very handy.

In general, my conviction is that experimental psychology – the proper combination of early subjective psychology and current information processing psychology – has much more to tell about important questions with regard to the human mind and human behaviour than is generally known or

surmised.[5] That this combination has something of relevance and importance to tell, I hope to make clear in the process of answering the question of
how people use their visual perception in the performance of tasks. In the
attempts to answer that question, I use the fortunate given that the two
psychologies often refer from *different points of view* to *the same state of
affairs.*

Let us now turn to James's (1890/1950) views and his 'attention' (Section 1.2) and to contemporary information processing psychology and its
'attention' (Section 1.3) to find out what presently the main theoretical problem is in an account of how people use their visual perception in the performance of tasks, and how that problem can possibly be solved (Section 1.4).

1.2   James, attention, and intentionality

James (1890/1950) is clear about the influence of presuppositions in psychology in general and about one presupposition in particular.

> It is astonishing what havoc is wrought in psychology by admitting
> at the outset apparently innocent suppositions, that nevertheless con-
> tain a flaw. The bad consequences develop themselves later on, and are
> irremediable, being woven through the whole texture of the work. The
> notion that sensations, being the simplest things, are the first things to
> take up in psychology is one of these suppositions. The only thing
> which psychology has a right to postulate at the outset is the fact of
> thinking itself, and that must first be taken up and analyzed.
>
> (James 1890/1950, p. 224)

And, for James, the word *thinking* stands for every form and state of consciousness indiscriminately; for perceiving, recognising, judging, remembering,
thinking, feeling, etc.

From this quotation it will be clear that James's theoretical position within
early introspective psychology was very unusual. Just like the later Kuelpe,
and just like the Gestalt psychologists that followed Kuelpe, he rejected the
'sensationalism' of the mainstream introspective psychology of, for instance,
Wundt and Titchener.

> William James . . . had no patience with Wundt's narrow definition of
> psychology and held that awareness of objects is what you find in
> consciousness . . . Titchener is said even to have ruled James out of psy-
> chology, on the ground that James was dealing with the knowledge of
> objects and therefore with epistemology. At any rate, Titchener ignored
> James when he was writing about functional psychology and presumably
> on this ground.
>
> (Boring, 1950, p. 610;
> see also Note 8 in this chapter and the Epilogue.)

James was a Gestalt psychologist *avant la lettre*. Just like Wertheimer (1923/
1958), he could have exclaimed:

> I stand at the window and see a house, trees, sky. Now on theoretical
> grounds I could try to count and say: "here there are . . . 327 brightnesses
> and hues." Do I *have* "327"? No, I see sky, house, trees . . .
> (Wertheimer, 1923/1958, p. 115)

And, just because James was convinced that objects, things, and events, not
sensations, were the contents of consciousness, he could come up with the
now well-known characterisation of attention:

> Every one knows what attention is. It is the taking possession by the mind,
> in clear and vivid form, of one out of what seem several simultaneously
> possible objects or trains of thought. Focalization, concentration, of
> consciousness are of its essence. It implies withdrawal from some things
> in order to deal effectively with others . . .
> (James, 1890/1950, pp. 403–404)[6]

What, as far as I know, is nowadays appreciably less well-known is that this
characterisation of attention, as well as James's further thoughts about how
these attentional phenomena arise, are completely consistent with and fit in
perfectly well with James's general views on what one finds in the human
mind. To appreciate the consistency and adequacy of James's views, it is
worthwhile to first look at what he says about thought in general and then
turn to attention again.

In the chapter 'The Stream of Consciousness', James (1890/1950) presents
'a painter's charcoal sketch' of how 'thought goes on' (and, please, remember
here that James uses the word *thought* for every form of consciousness
indiscriminately). James assumes that we immediately notice five important
characters in the process. The first three – thought is personal, always changing, and sensibly continuous – I leave without discussion. For the present
work the last two are of great importance. They read – and please also note
the 'objects' and 'parts of objects' in these quotations:

> (4) It always appears to deal with objects independent of itself.
> (p. 225)
> (4) Human thought appears to deal with objects independent of
> itself; that is, it is cognitive, or possesses the function of knowing.
> (p. 271)
> (5) It is interested in some parts of these objects to the exclusion of
> others, and welcomes or rejects – *chooses* from among them, in a word
> – all the while. (p. 225)
> (5) It is always interested more in one part of its object than in another,
> and welcomes and rejects, or chooses, all the while it thinks. (p. 284)

These two characteristics – which are certainly related in one or another way, a relation that theory has to make clear – deserve our special attention because they are going to figure prominently in this work (that is why I have quoted them twice).[7] Let us here briefly consider the first one: thought deals with objects independent of itself. What characteristic of thought or consciousness is James trying to express here?

In my view, in his chapter on thought, James (1890/1950) is not too clear about what property of thought he is pointing to and trying to express. There we find remarks like:

> The judgement that *my* thought has the same object as *his* thought is what makes the psychologist call my thought cognitive of an outer reality. The judgement that my own past thought and my own present thought are of the same object is what makes *me* take the object out of either and project it by a sort of triangulation into an independent position, from which it may *appear* to both. (p. 272)

We find much clearer remarks in several places earlier in his text. For cognitive psychologists the clearest one is:

> *The psychologist's attitude towards cognition ... is a thoroughgoing dualism.* It supposes two elements, mind knowing and thing known, and treats them as irreducible. (p. 218)

And, for cognitive psychologists in the English-speaking part of the world, James is kind enough to be extra clear when, while discussing the misleading influence of speech as a source of error in psychology, he remarks in a footnote:

> In English we have not even the generic distinction between the-thing-thought-of and the-thought-thinking-it, which in German is expressed by the opposition between *Gedachtes* and *Gedanke*, in Latin by that between *cogitatum* and *cogitatio*. (p. 195; see also his pp. 245–246.)

In short, James (1890/1950) emphasises the, in his view indisputable, given that in introspection two elements are always encountered, 'The Thought Studied' and 'The Thought's Object' (p. 184). (And, again, remember that for James the word *thinking* stands for any form or state of consciousness indiscriminately.) This 'observation', expressed in the quotations, is the observation that states of consciousness are characterised by 'intentionality' (see Flanagan, 1991, pp. 28–29).

The concept 'intentionality' (from the Latin word *intendo*; 'to aim at' or 'to point to') stems from Aristotle and was elaborated and (re)introduced in German psychology by Brentano (1874). Brentano distinguished between mental acts and mental contents, with the contents having their existence in the acts ('intentional inexistence').

> We say that people desire that [. . .], hope that [. . .], expect that [. . .], perceive that [. . .], and so on, where whatever fills in the blank is the intentional content of the mental act. Intentionality, then, refers to the widespread fact that mental acts have meaningful content.
>
> (Flanagan, 1991, p. 29)

'Brentano's thesis' is that intentionality is the ineliminable mark of the mental (see also Note 8 in this chapter).

Just because intentionality is such a difficult concept, it is good to hear what Boring (1950, p. 360) says:

> Brentano defined psychical phenomena by their possession of *immanent objectivity*. Phenomena possess immanent objectivity when they refer to a content – are directed upon an object, have that object 'inexisting intentionally' within them. These phrases become intelligible only when it is realized that psychical phenomena are to be thought of as *acts*. When one sees a color, the color itself is not mental. It is the seeing, the act, that is mental. There is, however, no meaning to *seeing* unless something is seen. The act always implies an object, refers to a content. The color as content of the act, 'seeing', thus 'inexists' by intention within the act. A psychical act is therefore not self-contained but contains its object within itself intentionally; that is to say, it is characterized by immanent objectivity. Physical phenomena, on the other hand, are self-contained because they do not refer extrinsically to objects.

While Brentano's (1874) psychology was organised in terms of mental acts, and not in terms of mainstream Wundtian and Titchenerian elements such as sensations and feelings, and while the introspective analysis of acts in laboratory experiments appeared to be virtually impossible, his distinction between 'act' and 'content of the act' was nevertheless picked up later in early German experimental psychology by Stumpf, who distinguished 'phenomena' and 'psychical functions' and later still by Kuelpe, who recognised 'content' and 'function' (see Boring, 1950).[8] Both Stumpf and Kuelpe emphasised that the two 'horns' of the mental are independently variable:

> If the reader does not understand the difference between a psychical function and a phenomenon, Stumpf gives him examples of their independent variability. The function changes without the phenomenon, when an unnoticed phenomenon becomes noticed without change in itself, as when a musical chord or a touch blend or a taste blend is analyzed. The phenomenon changes without a change in the function, when the room gets darker at twilight without the change being noticed,

or when sensations change continuously but we notice the change abruptly and only at intervals of the just noticeable difference.

(Boring, 1950, p. 369)

. . . Kuelpe's argument runs thus . . . the two are independently variable. Content changes without function when one perceives one sense-object and then another, keeping on perceiving all the time. Function changes without content when one successively perceives, recognizes and judges the same sensory content.

(Boring, 1950, p. 451)

James knew Brentano's (1874) book (see, for instance, the footnotes in James, 1890/1950, on pp. 160, 240, & 547) and he visited Stumpf in Germany a couple of times (see Boring, 1950, p. 364). So he knew perfectly well what was going on in the field of content and act.

Let us now return to James's (1890/1950) attention. The important point to know now is that James recognises only one central mechanism of attention. That one and only central mechanism is: 'The anticipatory preparation from within of the ideational centers concerned with the object to which the attention is paid' (p. 434).

James struggles to find the appropriate words for expressing the content of this preparatory state of mind that precedes, causes, and contributes to attentive perception. He comes up with terms like 'reinforcing imagination', 'inward reproduction', 'ideational preparation', 'anticipatory thinking', 'premonitory imagination', 'anticipatory imagination', 'creation of an imaginary duplicate of the object in the mind', 'ideal construction of the object', 'mental duplicate', and 'reproduction of the sensation from within'. He concludes that 'preperception' seems the best possible designation for this anticipatory state. 'The image in the mind *is* the attention; the *preperception* . . . is half of the perception of the looked-for thing' (p. 442).

When watching for the distant clock to strike, our mind is so filled with its image that at every moment we think we hear the longed-for or dreaded sound. So of an awaited footstep. Every stir in the wood is for the hunter his game; for the fugitive his pursuers. Every bonnet in the street is momentarily taken by the lover to enshroud the head of his idol.

(James, 1890/1950, p. 442)[9]

In Chapter 3 (see Section 3.1: Early systematic introspective psychology) we turn to one of the reasons why James faced severe difficulties in finding an adequate expression for the conscious anticipatory states that ensure that objects or events are subsequently thought about or attended. The 'Wuerzburg school' of Kuelpe, Ach, and Watt studied preparatory thought with introspection and discovered the paucity of conscious content in thought (*unanschauliche*/impalpable contents); there was not much to introspect. Here two further points are worth noticing.

The first is that what James is trying to express in understandable concrete detail are the phenomenal characteristics of intentional states of the type 'expect that [. . .]', 'imagine that [. . .]', or 'preperceive that [. . .]', which precede intentional states of the type 'perceive that [. . .]' or 'observe that [. . .]' or 'notice that [. . .]'. So, James's view on the central mechanism underlying the phenomena of attention fits in perfectly well with his general dualistic attitude towards cognition. Also with regard to attention, with something like 'expect that [. . .]' as its central mechanism, and something like 'perceive that [. . .]' as the outcome, he consistently supposes two elements, mind knowing and thing known, and treats them as irreducible.

The second point to be noticed is, of course, that for James this variety of intentionality, this 'expect that [. . .]' intentionality, is all that is required for producing the phenomena that go under the term *attention*. Paying attention to something, for instance for using that attended something for the performance of one or another task, consists of the intentional state 'perceiving that [. . .]', preceded and caused by an appropriate 'expecting that [. . .]'. For attending for task performance, nothing further is required. In James's intentional explanation 'attending to something' for one or another purpose is the result of a correct internal anticipation or expectation.[10]

Intentionality is certainly not a worn-out old-fashioned concept. In the contemporary philosophy of mind the concept is still around and flourishing in various versions and variants (see, e.g., Garfield, 2000; Lycan, 1996; Rosenthal, 1996, see Güzeldere, 1996, for an excellent overview.) In his *Concepts: Where cognitive science went wrong*, Fodor (1998) presents as the first thesis of the representational theory of mind:

> *Psychological explanation is typically nomic and is intentional through and through.* The laws that psychological explanations invoke typically express causal relations among *mental states that are specified under intentional description*; viz. among mental states that are picked out by reference to their contents. (p. 7)

And he comments:

> I'm aware there are those (mostly in Southern California, of course) who think that intentional explanation is all at best pro tem, and that theories of mind will (or anyhow should) eventually be couched in the putatively purely extensional idiom of neuroscience. But there isn't any reason in the world to take that idea seriously . . . (p. 7)

Although, since Brentano (1874), within the philosophy of mind intentionality has been regarded as an, or possibly better, as *the* essential characteristic of mind and mental life, this characteristic has, to the best of my knowledge, never found a decent place in the models proposed by mainstream information processing psychology. In the next section, I attempt to show that the theorising in the branch of the information processing approach with which I am mainly concerned, is badly in need of one or another kind of information processing mechanism – one or another kind of Intending Mind – that can perform the function that intentionality performs in James's (1890/1950) theorising.

This brings me to a position to make clear what I am looking for in the present work. The two basic issues I am concerned with are:

•   The issue of how Brentano's and James's intentionality can be interpreted in useful information processing terms.
•   The issue of how the resulting 'intentionality' can be introduced into the theorising of the information processing approach.

1.3   The information processing approach, attention, and the subject

During the last 40 years, the information processing approach to perception and cognition has been by far the most dominating and, as far as productivity and usable results are concerned, the most successful approach within general experimental psychology. Crudely stated, this approach tries to infer the internal structure and functioning of a behaving organism from the overt behaviour of that organism, so that it becomes possible to explain the organism's behaviour in terms of its internal structure and functioning. The exact style of the theorising in the information processing approach will become abundantly clear further on in this work. Here it suffices to quote Palmer and Kimchi (1986, p. 42) who term these theories 'functional theories' and explain:

> Theories at the functional level are concerned directly with neither material substances nor subjective experiences, but rather with how the brain or mind *works* or *behaves* within the context of the environment.

The precise nature of the data used in the information processing approach will also become abundantly clear in the rest of this work. Here it suffices to say that these data mainly consist of simple, quantifiable, aspects of observed 'objective' behaviour such as (reaction) times (RTs) between stimulus onset and start of overt action (latency) and percentages correct and/or incorrect responses (accuracy).[11]

An important feature of the information processing approach is that in principle it is self-correcting. The approach needs an initial theory as a starter that can be confronted with data. Where that initial theory comes from is not of great importance.

... many I[nformation] P[rocessing] psychologists use personal introspection as a source of ideas and hypotheses about cognitive events. Of
course, these must then be subjected to more rigorous evaluation by
measuring observable behavior in others to be scientifically respectable,
but this is a standard procedure for much I[nformation] P[rocessing]
work in cognitive psychology.

(Palmer & Kimchi, 1986, p. 60)

Whether the initial theory comes from introspection, from a good friend, or
from the blue sky is not that important. What is important is that the initial
theory can be tested and be pushed and shaped in the right direction by the
pertinent experimental data.

There are several branches of information processing psychology, even in
the part concerned with vision (see Chapter 2). For my problem – the problem of the use of visual perception for the performance of tasks – the branch
concerned with the role of attention in visual perception is of prime importance. In this 'perception-for-perception' branch, the initial theories came
mostly from introspection and intuition (see also Section 1.1).

A central assumption in most of the initial theories was that the hypothetical information processor suffered from severe central capacity limitations. Another central assumption was that in the processing of (visual)
information in one way or another 'attention' was involved (see, e.g.,
Broadbent, 1958, 1971; Kahneman, 1973; Neisser, 1967; see Van der Heijden,
1996a, for a detailed overview of the start of visual information processing
psychology). Subsequently, nearly all theorists adopted these points of
view. As a result, nearly all visual information processing theories that
have been proposed, and that are currently in the running, are two-stage,
limited-capacity models. They postulate an initial pre-attentive stage of
information processing which processes all the visual information available,
but only partly, and a subsequent attentive stage of information processing
which processes part of the pre-processed information, but that part completely. (See Van der Heijden, 1996b, for a critical overview of these limited-
capacity two-stage models; see also Chapters 5 and 6 for a more detailed
description and evaluation.)

In the next chapter I return to this 'perception-for-perception' branch
of the information processing approach. In the present context, and just
to clarify in what direction the present work will move, the important point
to know is that, from the starting point on, in nearly all proposed varieties
of the two-stage theories, two components or explanatory ingredients can be
distinguished – one component that is unproblematic and that was, and still
is, further and further elaborated, and another component that is nowadays
quite often regarded as highly problematic but has remained virtually in its
initial problematic state.

The first, unproblematic, component concerns 'visual perception' and
'the role of attention in visual perception'. Neither the existence of 'visual

perception' and 'attention' nor 'some role of attention in visual perception' can be denied. And, from the 1960s on, aspects of this component have been intensively studied, often with ingenious paradigms, by the information processing approach. This work has resulted in a great number of productive methods, reliable results, and important insights, and in elaborated, detailed, information processing models, specifying the role of 'information processing', 'selective attention', and 'selection of information'. In their excellent review with regard to this component, Egeth and Yantis (1997, p. 294) indeed rightfully say: '. . . many empirical details have been clarified, richer theoretical frameworks have evolved, and important new ideas . . . have been advanced and developed.' In further chapters I return to and use this component.

The second, problematic, component concerns 'the subject' who is 'controlling, guiding, and using selective attention'. Of course, the existence and importance of 'subjects' can hardly be denied.[12] From the 1960s on, however, this component, sometimes in the open as 'the subject' and sometimes in disguise as 'she', 'he', 'we', 'the man', or 'a person', has appeared as an unstructured, unanalysed blob in the information processing literature. In note 13 are a couple of examples to consider.[13] In the visual perception and selective attention literature of the information processing approach thousands and thousands of similar statements can be found.[14] And of course, it is this problematic, unstructured, and unanalysed component, this 'subject', that we now have to consider further.

Clearly, this component 'instantiates' or 'materialises' a basic intuition that stems from common-sense 'folk psychology'. Skinner (1972, p. 177) summarises this wisdom as follows:

> A[n . . .] example, a "cognitive activity", is *attention*. A person responds only to a small part of the stimuli impinging upon him. The traditional view is that he himself determines which stimuli are to be effective by "paying attention" to them. Some kind of inner gate keeper is said to allow some stimuli to enter and to keep all others out. A sudden or strong stimulus may break through and "attract" attention, but the person himself seems otherwise to be in control.

And, according to Skinner, that inner gate keeper has to be replaced by contingencies of reinforcement to which an organism has been exposed.

In several works I have pointed out that the 'person', the 'subject', a 'you', a 'he', or a 'she' is a highly problematic information processing component (see, e.g., Van der Heijden, 1992, 1996b; Van der Heijden & Bem, 1997).[15] Here, however, I have to admit that I did not really understand the further implications of my critical views. Fortunately, I need not repeat my arguments – others voice them better. Fernandez-Duque and Johnson (1999), for instance, evaluated the use of attention metaphors in the information processing approach concerned with vision. In a metaphor, knowledge of a known (source) domain is applied to an unknown (target) domain.[16] What follows is what they say about the metaphor that is nowadays most frequently used in information processing psychology – the spotlight metaphor of attention.[17]

> According to the Spotlight metaphor, a spotlight is a device separate from the field upon which it sheds light, and separate from the agent that controls it. . . . In the Attention Spotlight metaphor the spotlight is controlled by an executive system, which is also in charge of detecting verbal targets, initiating volitional acts, etc. The positing of an all powerful executive system gains its appeal from the structure of the source domain of the Spotlight metaphor, in which there is an agent who is in control of the spotlight.
>
> Consequently, the logic of the Spotlight metaphor raises the crucial question of who or what is controlling the attention spotlight. . . . In the source domain the question reads: how does the spotlight choose its next location? How does the spotlight choose its next target? The obvious answer is that it does not. The choice is made by the human controlling the spotlight. . . . Asking about the reasons for choosing the next object equates to asking about the reasons the controller of the spotlight might have for moving it to a new object. This already takes the emphasis away from the attention mechanism and puts it onto the executive control mechanisms. Moreover, we usually do not ask for mechanistic explanations of free actions, like choosing where to move the spotlight. Transferred to the target domain, scientists did not ask for mechanistic explanations of voluntarily choosing a new object of attention.
>
> (Fernandez-Duque & Johnson, 1999, pp. 95–96)[18]

In short, just because the spotlight metaphor inevitably introduces a 'controller' in charge of directing the spotlight and just because about that controller – about you and me and she and he – no further questions are asked, the important questions about the control of attention for perception and for appropriate task performance are not formulated and, consequently, do not even receive the beginning of an answer.[19] In other words:

> . . . one of the central problems of the Attention As Spotlight metaphor remains unsolved, namely, what is the nature of the control system for the attention spotlight. Although the Spotlight metaphor has been remarkably robust in generating attention research, one of its core concepts remains highly problematic.
>
> (Fernandez-Duque & Johnson, 1999, p. 96)[20]

This problematic state of affairs is not only encountered with the Attention As Spotlight metaphor (see van der Heijden & Bem, 1997, for other examples). Within the information processing approach, Bundesen (1990), for instance, presented one of the most complete and powerful information processing and selective attention theories that is certainly not simply a single spotlight model (see Section 3.3 for details of Bundesen's model). He is clearly aware of a theoretical problem, and explicitly admits that in his theory

> No attempt is made to discard the notion that attentional selection is controlled by an intelligent agent, but a serious attempt is made to relieve the burden on the agent by placing a powerful mechanism at its disposal.
>
> (Bundesen, 1990, p. 523)

But an 'intelligent agent' is an information processor; intelligence is the ability to cope with a variety of situations on the basis of information about these situations. Therefore, especially in the information processing approach to perception and cognition, serious attempts should be made to do something about that notion of an 'intelligent agent', which is nowadays variously named the 'subject', the 'person', the 'man', 'she/he', and 'we', and which is in charge of guiding or directing attention and of a lot of other things besides.[21]

Allport (1980b, pp. 122–123) already wondered what an expression like '... *activated under control of, and through attention by, the subject*' can mean, and asked 'Is "the subject" equivalent to the whole system ...? ... Or does "the subject" refer to some sub-part of the system, a ghost-in-the-machine?' This remark, when properly interpreted, makes clear that there are at least two ways to proceed; either one can regard 'the subject' as equivalent to the whole system or one can regard 'the subject' as some sub-part of the system, a ghost in the machine, a Cartesian soul in the body. Let us have a brief look at the two alternative ways.

On the first way, one chooses to regard 'the subject' as equivalent to the whole system. Fernadez-Duque and Johnson (1999, p. 96) looked at and evaluated this route:

> Of course, the difficulties with the Spotlight model of attention have become evident to many researchers, and alternative models without a central executive system [a subject] have been proposed (Allport, 1993; Johnston & Hawley, 1994; Dennett & Kinsbourne, 1992; Desimone & Duncan, 1995). Such models, in which perceptual inputs compete for resources, solve the infinite regression problem of having a volitional executive system, but they create a similar problem by postulating perceptual inputs that have agent-like properties. Moreover, competition models usually beg the difficult question of top-down, volitional selection, that is central to the idea of agency.[22]

On the second way, one chooses to regard 'the subject' as some sub-part of the system. With this route, the task faced by theorists in the information processing approach is not to get rid of the notion of 'the subject' in theoretical accounts and statements. The task is to maintain 'the subject' in an adequate form; that is, to replace 'the subject' by a decent, structured, information processing component that is neither a ghost in the machine nor invites an infinite regression problem. One then has to search for a theoretical entity that can perform the job done nowadays by the 'subject' and by 'you' and by 'me'.

In my view, the second way, Allport's (1980b) ghost-in-the-machine way or Descartes' soul-in-the-brain way, is the way to go.[23] Here I can only briefly indicate why I think this is so; the remainder of this work serves to further substantiate this point. Two points are worth considering. The first is that not only common, everyday language, but also the language of the introspection psychologists, the language of the information processing approach, and many other special languages, abundantly and convincingly show that terms like 'the subject', 'the agent', 'the person', and terms like 'I', 'you', 'she' and 'he' (that is, terms that refer to an inner agent) simply cannot be avoided. I, at least, can hardly avoid the word *I* and I am in good company.[24] By talking one or several of these languages, everybody implicitly admits that she/he assumes that such inner agents do indeed exist and are causally effective. But then one had better have that skeleton out of the closet and see what can be done with it in an information processing theory.

A second point is that 'postulating perceptual inputs that have agent-like properties', or better, postulating *entities* that have agent-like properties, is not a prerogative alone for theorists who choose to regard 'the subject' as equivalent to the whole information processing system. Further theoretical analysis might very well show that this is also the way to go for theorists who regard 'the subject' as part of the system and try to replace that 'subject' by a decent information processing component. Upon proper analysis, it might turn out that 'inputs that have agent-like properties' or 'entities that have agent-like properties' or 'an entity that has agent-like properties' can, at least in some cases, replace in an adequate way 'the agent' or 'the subject' or 'the ghost in the machine' in the theorising in the information processing approach. To say the least: The search for a structured, causally effective, agent that exerts top-down volitional control is certainly worth some effort.

At this point, I am again in a position to further clarify what I am looking for. As will appear further on, the basic issues I am concerned with are:

• The issue of how 'the subject', 'the agent', etc., might be interpreted in useful information processing terms,
• The issue of how the resulting 'subject' might be introduced into the theorising of the information processing approach.[25]

1.4 The approach

As I have already stated, the present work is first and mainly concerned with the problem of how people use their visual perception for the performance of tasks. In this work, I am going to use the fortunate fact that there are two main approaches to the problem – the approach of early introspective psychology and the approach of contemporary information processing psychology.[26]

Of course, it can be stated, and indeed often has been stated, that neither early introspective psychology nor current cognitive psychology has anything of importance to say about the problem of how people use their visual perception in the performance of tasks. For instance, it can and often has been said that both approaches studied 'visual perception as such' or 'visual perception as a subjective experience', not 'the use of visual perception for task performance'. However, that position is very hard to defend because it is simply wrong. The early introspective psychologists '*looked at*' what was going on when they perceived and they *reported* what they saw. So, they literally used their visual perception for subsequent verbal report. And the strength of the information processing approach lies exactly in the fact that it uses objective *tasks* for obtaining the critical data. So, what the data reflect is the subject's (!) use of visual information for task performance, not visual perception as such.[27] The results of early introspective psychology and the data of current information processing psychology are exactly the results and the data that are required for answering the question with which this work is concerned; the question of how people use their visual perception in the performance of tasks. What these results and data teach us about 'visual perception as such' and about 'visual perception as subjectively experienced', I leave to others to decide.

The two psychologies are going to serve somewhat different functions in the present work. A slight repetition of what was said in Section 1.1 might make these different functions clear. The early experimental psychology was a *mind* psychology. Systematic introspection in well-controlled settings was its method, descriptions of experiences formed its data, and empirical generalisations were its theoretical aim. In this psychology professionals studied states of mind and changes of states of mind. This psychology can serve as a source of initial ideas and hypotheses about cognitive events. The current experimental psychology, the information processing psychology, is a *behaviour* psychology. The registration of aspects of overt objective behaviour in well-controlled settings is its method, quantitative summaries of observed behaviour form its data, and the construction of a hypothetical information processor which produces that behaviour is its theoretical goal. This approach has produced a wealth of important data that, in my view, can certainly serve to test any initial ideas and hypotheses about cognitive events.

Of course, now I have to show that early introspective psychology can indeed serve as a source of ideas and hypotheses about cognitive events.

Well then, as stated in Section 1.3, within the theorising in the information processing approach two components or ingredients can be distinguished – an unproblematic and a problematic component. The unproblematic component consists of a large collection of 'clarified empirical details', 'richer theoretical frameworks', and 'important new ideas' in the fields of visual perception and attention. The problematic component, which seems to be unavoidable and therefore shows up time and again, is 'the subject' or 'the agent'. That global blob, that ghost in the machine, has to be replaced by a decent, still unknown, detailed, and effective information processing component. Let us, for the moment, call this theoretical entity that has to be found component Q (for Quest). What we need is an appropriate initial hypothesis or idea for this mysterious component Q, the Q that is capable of making sure things get done.

Decent initial hypotheses or ideas about how to replace 'the subject' by a detailed and effective information processing component, Q, are very difficult to come by. Especially for my topic – the use of visual information for task performance – the user, in experiments 'the subject', is the first and only candidate for the role of Q that immediately and convincingly suggests itself. A 'central executive' with the properties and the functions of the 'subject' – controlling attention, detecting and recognising targets, initiating actions, etc. – brings us, however, not very much further here. And, unfortunately, neither our own introspection, nor the 'introspections' and 'intuitions' provided by the information processing approach, provide much further usable detail (see Section 1.3).

Here then, for the first time, early introspective psychology can help me to find the required intuition. It can provide me with a decent initial hypothesis about the searched-for Q, which can be refined and elaborated later on and can be tested. What I have to do is to take early introspective psychology seriously and to adopt the psychologist's attitude towards cognition:

> *The psychologist's attitude towards cognition . . . is a thoroughgoing dualism.* It supposes two elements, mind knowing and thing known, and treats them as irreducible (see Section 1.2).

With this attitude in place, it is easy to see that Q, the problematic component, is 'mind knowing', and the rest, the unproblematic component, is 'thing known'. The problem of how the mind uses visual perception for task performance is the problem of how 'mind knowing' uses 'thing known' for task performance. My task, as an information processing psychologist, is to find one or another specification of 'mind knowing' that can use visual perception, 'thing known', for the performance of tasks. I have to show that 'the subjects' and 'the agents' of Section 1.3 can be interpreted in useful information processing terms by interpreting 'mind knowing' and 'intentionality' of Section 1.2, in useful information processing terms. And I have to show that the resulting subject, the resulting 'mind knowing' or Intending

Mind, when inserted in the theorising of the information processing approach, provides the required insight in the problem of how people use their visual perception in the performance of tasks.[28] In Brentano's and James's intentionality I have found a first important clue.

In this context it is worthwhile to see that the 'to perceive that [. . .]' format is only one way to express the basic idea underlying intentionality. Remember that the single important point of the idea of intentionality is that a distinction can and has to be made between the act (perceiving, remembering, expecting, thinking, etc.) and the content of the act (the cat, the colour, the choir, the chaos, etc.). That basic idea is possibly better expressed with the format 'to [. . .] : [. . .]'. This format expresses that at each moment in time from all possible acts one act has to be selected, and that from all possible contents one content has to be selected. This format also allows me to express an, in my view crucial, distinction between two different contents of acts in the same format. This example makes this clear:

'to [perceive] : [the apple]'.
'to [perceive] : [the apple is red]'.

The relevance of this distinction will become clear further on in this work.

As a last point, it is worthwhile to note that my way of working is fully in line with the spirit and method of attack of the information processing approach. I derived my initial theoretical view from introspection by good old friends, in particular from the introspective work of James and Brentano. In subsequent chapters this initial theoretical view will be further structured and developed with pertinent available introspective and objective information and will subsequently, in Parts II and III, be tested through a confrontation with the pertinent objective data of the information processing approach.

Notes

1 See Chapter 2 for this classification of laboratory tasks.
2 *Man a Machine* is the translation of Jullien Offray de la Mettrie's (1748) *L'homme Machine*, which was published in 1912, so just before the start of American behaviourism, in La Salle, 100 km west of Chicago.
3 To really see the correspondences and differences between the two psychologies one needs a theory that specifies how people use their visual perception in the performance of tasks, i.e., the theory I am looking for. In the Epilogue, in Section E.1, I return briefly to this issue.
4 Information processing psychologists might object here that their objective methods do provide important and sufficient information about states and changes of states. It is worthwhile, however, to realise that in *information processing terms* proper not much more than distinctions like 'not processed', 'partly processed', and 'processed', or 'selected' and 'not selected', can be expressed.

   Of course, it is true that information processing psychologists use many more terms to indicate states and properties of states. They use terms like 'see', 'clearly see', 'consciously perceive', and even 'the conscious awareness of the experience of perceiving'; and, in their experiments, they present 'bright', 'coloured' shapes and 'loud', 'high' tones. These 'terms' are indeed subjective mind terms. However, the terms get their content from casual introspection by the experimenter. Just because early systematic introspective psychology had professionals, trained at characterising and describing these internal states of affairs, I prefer to turn to them when 'subjective' assistance or information is useful or required. (See also Van der Heijden, 1996b.)

5 As will appear further on in this work, selected bits and pieces from other psychologies (behaviourism, ecological psychology, etc.) and from other disciplines (the neurosciences, philosophy, phenomenology, etc.) are also often very useful.

6 In a recent thesis (June 2001) a section titled 'Capacity Limitations' starts with: 'The times in which a scientist could get away with stating "everyone knows what attention is" (James, 1890/1950) are gone forever.' This is a nice example of what havoc is wrought in psychology by admitting at the outset apparently innocent suppositions. In *The Principles* there is not only a chapter on 'Attention' of about 60 pages, in several other chapters the concept attention is further elaborated, analysed, and generalised.

7 It is of importance to note the distinction between 'objects' and 'parts of objects' that James here introduces. A related distinction will return repeatedly further on in this work.

8 Even Titchener (1898) had some use for Brentano's distinction. He distinguishes between an experimental psychology concerned with structure trying to analyse the *structure* of mind (bare sensations and bare feelings, etc.) and a complementary descriptive functional psychology trying to characterise the *functions* of the total organism (recognition, imagination, etc). With regard to Brentano's (1874) views he states:

> Brentano's principal criterion of psychical, as contra-distinguished from physical phenomena, is that of 'intentional inexistence' or 'immanent objectivity', which we may paraphrase as reference to contents, direction upon something as object. 'Every psychical phenomenon contains in it something as object, though not every one in the same way. In ideation something is ideated, in judgement something is admitted or rejected, in love and hate something loved and hated, in desire something desired, etc.' This is evidently the language of function, not of structure.

Titchener clearly recognises the importance of a functional psychology. In his view, however, '. . . there is still so much work to be done in the field of analysis . . . that a general swing of the laboratories towards functional work would be most regrettable', and '. . . the mental elements of the experimentalists, the bare sensation and the bare feeling, are abstractions, innocent of any sort of reference.'

9 Dewey (1896, p. 361) voices a related point of view where he warns against ignoring the status of the observer prior to hearing a loud unexpected sound:

> If one is reading a book, if one is hunting, if one is watching in a dark place on a lonely night, if one is performing a chemical experiment, in each case, the noise has a very different psychical value; it is a different experience.

10 However, see also James (1890/1950, pp. 447–454) on attention as a resultant or a force.

11 The observed behaviour is 'objective' behaviour because subjects are concerned with what is there in the outer world, not with what is going on in their inner

minds. In this respect, information processing psychology differs in an important way from early introspective psychology. In early introspective psychology no agreement could be reached over what was exactly experienced (to the description 'I experience here a vague diluted kind of yellowish red', the words 'correct' and 'incorrect' can hardly be applied). In information processing psychology full agreement can be reached about what is there in the outer world (the statement 'that square that was just presented was red' can be evaluated with 'correct' or 'incorrect').

12 For reasons that are not clear to me, 'the subject' is nowadays called 'the participant'. As will become clear further on, this change of name has not elucidated important aspects of the problematic component in the information processing theories.

13 In the following quotations all underlines are mine.

> Thus a man listening to a voice from the right and ignoring voices from the left is filtering; when he decides to change over and start listening to the left, this decision is an instance of filter-setting.
>
> (Broadbent, 1971, p. 15)

> Thus, the page, the line, the word, or the individual letter may be the relevant units, among which we select that word or that letter to which most attention will be paid.
>
> (Kahneman, 1973, p. 68)

> Subjects can strategically control visual *selection* by varying the span of spatial attention in the visual field. Dependent on the task demands, attention can be spread out over the entire visual field . . . or be focussed on a specific location.
>
> (Theeuwes, 1993, pp. 143–144)

> . . . the occasionally found almost flat search functions are obtained because subjects adjust the attentional beam, which allows a strategy in which a conjunction target occasionally will pop out . . .
>
> (Theeuwes, 1993, p. 144)

> If subjects were indeed controlling which set of dots they tracked by selectively attending to the dots . . . then one would expect this to have perceptual consequences.
>
> (Pashler, 1998, p. 86)

> It has often been suggested that location knowledge permits a person to allocate processing capacity to a location . . . in advance of the stimulus, and that doing so enhances perception.
>
> (Pashler, 1998, p. 168)

14 Sometimes this problem appears in disguise. Consider the following examples:

> Attention . . . can sometimes . . . be called to a particular location from a particular feature map . . . The target feature activates its reciprocal link to the master map and allows attention to home in on its location.
>
> (Treisman, 1990, p. 460)

> Suppose that each parallel feature map excites all of the spatial locations of candidate targets in a map . . . If the "spotlight of attention" is directed to

the point of maximum excitation, it will find the target without the necessity of conducting a random, serial search.

(Wolfe et al., 1989, p. 428)

With this type of formulation the question arises: Who 'directs the "spotlight of attention"' and who makes that 'attention home in'?

15 See also Johnston and Dark (1986, p. 68) who notice that the ease with which a number of theories

> . . . can account for the known phenomena of selective attention betrays a serious metatheoretical problem with the view that selection of stimulus information is controlled by an active mental agent . . . a processing homunculus . . . if a psychological construct is to explain the intelligent and adaptive selection powers of the organism, then it cannot itself be imbued with those powers.

16 Fernandez-Duque and Johnson (1999, p. 84) explain:

> Technically, a conceptual metaphor consists of a conceptual mapping of entities, properties, relations, and structures from a domain of one kind (the source domain) onto a domain of a different kind (the target domain).

In science, metaphors are generally used when the 'source domain' is well known and the 'target domain' is not well known. The knowledge of the 'source domain' is then applied to and used for structuring and talking about the 'target domain'. Because the information processing approach tries to infer hidden internal structures and processes from behavioural data, metaphors come in very handy. (See also Van der Heijden, 1996b, pp. 334–335, for the use of metaphors to structure the theoretical concept of attention.)

17 I turn in later chapters to other metaphors that Fernandez-Duque and Johnson (1999) discuss; see, for instance, the filter metaphor of attention in Section 3.3.

18 Possibly a little repetition does no harm here:

> A spotlight implicitly presupposes an 'operator' and 'user' equipped with eyes and a visual system, 'looking' at the regions he deals with by using the spotlight. This homunculus is simply smuggled in, hidden in the package containing the spotlight, and seems to provide the answers to nasty questions like 'who operates the spotlight?', 'where does the operator get its instructions from?', and 'how does the operator perform its job?'. But even if one answers these questions with, for instance, 'from the thalamus' . . . these questions remain unanswered.

(Van der Heijden, 1992, p. 251)

19 This is really a remarkable state of affairs, because the information processing approach has literally and explicitly set itself the task of finding out what 'you and me and she and he' (or 'the subject' and 'the person'), as information processors, consist of.

20 It is worthwhile to note that in this quotation the 'problematic' and 'unproblematic' components, mentioned earlier in this section, are explicitly recognised.

21 The important point is here not so much that the theories contain an unanalysed 'blob'. The important point is that this 'blob' performs information processing operations that are not really specified. After specifying these operations, it might appear that among the operations are some that are nowadays assigned to other theoretical entities or system components. In other words, after specifying these

operations it might appear that some of our current views on perception and the role of attention in perception are simply wrong. In still other words, the 'blob problem' is not a 'local' problem. It is a 'global problem', the solution of which can have implications for our view on the total human information processing system.

22 With his 'integrated competition hypothesis', Duncan (1996) presents a model of this type that adequately deals with 'the difficult question of top-down, volitional selection'. In that model, which is mainly based on neuropsychological data, competition is top-down controlled by task-dependent advance priming of units in one or more subsystems.

23 The fact that models postulating 'perceptual inputs that have agent-like prop-erties' have not been capable of replacing 'the subject' in mainstream theorising supports this position.

24 Gibson (1979, p. 286), one of the greatest experts in vision, for instance writes:

> It has been generally believed that even adults can become conscious of their visual sensations if they try. You have to take an introspective attitude, or analyze your experience into elements, or pay attention to the data of your perception, or stare at something persistently until the meaning fades away. I once believed it myself. I suggested that the "visual field" could be attended to, as distinguished from the "visual world," and that it was *almost* a flat patchwork of colors, like a painting on a plane surface facing the eye. . . . The awareness of depth in the scene could not be wholly eliminated, I thought, but it could be reduced. The similarity to a painting could be enhanced by not rotating the head and not displacing it, by closing one eye, and by avoiding any scene with motion. I recognized even then that the normal field of view of an ocular orbit is continually changing and that an arrested pattern is exceptional.
>
> My comparison of the visual field to a perspective painting, although guarded, now seems to me a serious mistake . . . What one becomes aware of by holding still, closing one eye, and observing a frozen scene are not visual sensations but only *the surfaces of the world that are viewed from here* . . . One's attention is called to the fact of occlusion, not to the pseudo-fact of the third dimension. I notice the surfaces that face me, and what I face, and thus where I am.

It is also of interest here to note that Gibson inspects and reports about his visual perception and assumes that we can do the same.

25 In other quarters of information processing psychology, for instance in the area of memory research, top-down control mechanisms are recognised (see, e.g., Baddeley, 1986; see also Norman & Shallice, 1986). Also, properties of 'executive control mechanisms' are actively investigated in 'task-switching' tasks (for some recent work see, e.g., Allport, Styles, & Hsieh, 1994; Meiran, 1996, 2000; Monsell, Yeung, & Azuma, 2000; Rogers & Monsell, 1995; Wylie & Allport, 2000). This work, on existence and properties of a 'central executive', is certainly related to the work I am going to present here. As already might be clear, and as will become clearer further on, however, a main difference is that my work is con-cerned with the characterisation of a 'central executive' in 'visual perception' where, up to now, because of the assumption of bottom-up processing, no role for such an agent has been recognised (see the 'perception for perception' approach in Chapter 2).

26 Where needed, I also use other psychologies and other disciplines.

27 Neumann (1990a, p. 232) points to the same interpretation issue in the theoretical context of 'central processing' and 'action control':

... there is a difference between the processes and factors that are *explicitly addressed* by experimental research and those that are *actually involved* in the experiments. While the large majority of experimenters ... have been interested in central selectivity ..., the experimental paradigms that they have typically used nevertheless involved action control. The simple reason is that, in behavioral research, one has to ask the subject to perform some action in order to get some performance measure. The theoretical analysis usually stopped at some point where 'information processing' was thought to be completed, but the experimental situation involved the whole process of the sensory control of action.

28 To distinguish the theoretical entity I am looking for from James's 'mind knowing', from now on I use for that looked-for entity the term Intending Mind.

2 Types of tasks and instructions

2.0 Introduction

This work is primarily concerned with the problem of how people use their visual perception in the performance of tasks, or, formulated better, the problem of how Intending Mind uses Visual Perception in the performance of tasks, with Intending Mind and Visual Perception referring to different components of the human information processing system. And, of course, the first place to look for a solution of this problem is the theoretical work of contemporary information processing psychology.

Within the branch of the information processing approach concerned with vision, a distinction between two theoretical camps can be made. One camp, the major mainstream 'perception for perception' camp, is concerned with and theorises about the role of attention in perception and cognition. The other camp, the minor dissident 'perception for action' camp, is concerned with and theorises about the role of attention and perception in action.

The perception for perception camp I have already briefly introduced in Section 1.1. In their experiments, members of this camp mainly use tasks in which subjects report what they see, i.e., name objects or attributes of objects, or read letters or words. This camp has produced a wealth of appropriate, important, and useful data. Because this camp theorises about the role of attention in perception and cognition, and not about the use of vision for task performance, not much assistance for the solution of my problem is to be expected from here.

The perception for action camp has still to be introduced. In their theorising, members of this camp look at tasks like walking around, picking up objects, driving cars, and riding bicycles. Up to now, this camp has not generated that much research. Because this camp theorises about the role of attention and perception in action, the theoretical framework developed in this camp seems to offer me a natural and adequate starting point for the solution of my problem.[1]

In Section 2.1, the theorising in the perception for action camp is introduced. It is shown that the theory developed there in its present form is applicable to only a limited range of tasks. The theory cannot account for the important results reported by the perception for perception camp. It is concluded that a disciplined distinction between tasks is badly needed, because without such a distinction theorising only leads to confusion and ends up in frustration.

In Section 2.2, a classification of tasks is derived. A disciplined distinction between tasks requires a theory of internal task performance, a theory that provides the theoretical means and concepts that can express the relevant differences and similarities between the tasks in terms of internal operations. That theory is, however, the theory I hope to develop in this work.[2] In this section I have therefore to rely on other information sources to arrive at a workable tentative classification. The main distinction arrived at is the distinction between 'act' tasks and 'report' tasks, with within the 'report' tasks the further distinction between 'name' tasks and 'read' tasks.

In Section 2.3, we visit a laboratory in the perception for perception camp in order to hear and see what happens there when subjects have to perform a 'report' task using vision. That field research reveals not only that impressive results are obtained but also that there is a serious discrepancy between the experimental practice and the theoretical work. The experimenter uses stimuli and instructions but the theorist emphasises stimuli and internal processes and forgets the instruction. Therefore, the theoretical accounts are incomplete.

In Section 2.4, I indicate how this discrepancy points to the way to proceed. A structured, causally effective, internal representation of the instruction can and has to replace 'the subject' in information processing theories. Here the usefulness of the concept of intentionality, introduced in Chapter 1, becomes more clear.

2.1   Selection for action

Within information processing psychology, the term 'attention' refers to a mechanism that selects a spatially coherent subset of sensory information from among all information available (see the 'Attention as Spotlight' metaphor in Section 1.3). With regard to the function of attention, two different theoretical camps can be distinguished – a major perception for perception camp and a minor perception for action camp.

Theorists in the perception for perception camp, for instance Bundesen (1990), Eriksen (1990, 1995), and Treisman (1988; see also Treisman & Gelade, 1980), seem to answer the question 'What is (visual) perception for?' with the straightforward answer 'For (visual) perception!'. This answer leads directly and immediately to the conviction that the study of the human visual information processing system and visual cognition

> . . . deals with the processes by which a perceived, remembered, and
> thought-about world is brought into being from as unpromising a

beginning as the retinal patterns. Similarly, auditory cognition is concerned with transformation of the fluctuating pressure pattern at the ear into the sounds and the speech and music that we hear.

(Neisser, 1967, p. 4)

Just because perception is for perception, the processes that lead to perception and cognition are the processes the experimental research has to be concerned with.

Pashler (1998, p. 13) is clear about this point. In comparing early introspective psychology and information processing psychology, he states:

One change . . . was methodological: from theories based primarily on introspective observation to theories based on various kinds of behavioral data. A second change reflected the emergence of new concepts that permitted the events that make up perception to be fractionated. Writers such as James and Titchener spoke of the conscious percepts elicited by stimuli and speculated on how attention might affect different attributes of the percepts, such as clarity or intensity. They did not, however, view perception as a process of achieving successively more elaborated and defined internal descriptions of a stimulus.

And describing perception as a process of achieving successively more elaborated and defined internal descriptions of a stimulus is the goal of the perception for perception camp in the information processing approach.

Treisman has offered a consistent series of intriguing suggestions about these processes for visual cognition. In her theorising, the modularity of the visual system – in the visual brain, object features like colour, shape, and position are represented in different regions or modules – and 'attention' play a prominent role:

Stimulus locations are processed serially with focal attention. Any features which are present in the same central "fixation" of attention are combined to form a single object. Thus focal attention provides the "glue" which integrates the initially separable features in unitary objects. Once they have been correctly registered, the compound objects continue to be perceived and stored as such.

(Treisman & Gelade, 1980, p. 98; see also, e.g., Treisman, 1988, p. 201)

So, in this theory the 'glue' explains visual perception.

As stated in Section 1.4, in my view the information processing approach to visual perception and cognition studies the use of visual perception for task performance and not perception as such, as the theorists in the perception for perception camp suggest. And, as will become apparent further on, it is beyond any doubt that exactly the perception for perception camp with its many eminent contributors has done the bulk of the relevant experimental work and has produced a wealth of important data pertaining to the use of visual information for task performance. These data deserve an appropriate theoretical framework. A type of theory such as Treisman's theory, however, does not help me very much further with my problem of how the Intending Mind uses Visual Perception for task performance.[3]

As already stated in Section 1.3, the basic assumption in the theorising of the perception for perception camp is that the human information processing system has severe central capacity limitations. In line with this assumption of limited central capacity, perception is generally construed as a two-stage, limited-capacity process. In the first, 'pre-attentive', stage, all information receives a preliminary, superficial evaluation. In the second, 'attentive' stage, only a part of that pre-processed information is selected and subjected to a definitive, complete interrogation. Limited central capacity is regarded as the basic functional characteristic of the human information processor and attentional selection and processing as a secondary functional consequence.

There are several reasons to doubt the limited capacity assumption. A theoretical reason is that in this theorising an observed phenomenon – people show overt performance limitations – is simply translated into an explanatory construct: people suffer internal capacity limitations.[4] An empirical reason is that the behavioural experiments concerned with visual perception have not convincingly demonstrated these central capacity limitations. And an extraneous reason is that also neurophysiology and neuroanatomy do not really support the assumption of insufficient computational power in the brain (see also Van der Heijden & Bem, 1997). In Chapter 5 I return to the problematic aspects of this limited capacity assumption.

Because of the problems with the assumption of limited central capacity, and for a variety of other reasons, theorists in the perception for action camp, Allport (see, e.g., 1987, 1989) and Neumann (see, e.g., 1987, 1990a) for instance, reject the assumption of limited central capacity. They answer the question 'What is visual perception for?' with the equally straightforward answer 'For action!' In their view, visual perceptual systems, just as all other '. . . perceptual systems have evolved in all species of animals solely as a means of guiding and controlling action . . .' (Allport, 1987, p. 395) And indeed,

> A strong argument can be made that vision evolved in vertebrates and other organisms, not to provide perception per se, but to provide distal sensory control of the movements that these organisms make in living their often precarious lives . . . Natural selection operates at the level of overt behavior: it cares little about how well an animal "sees" the world, but a great deal about how well the animal forages for food, avoids predators, finds mates, and moves efficiently from one part of the environment to another.
>
> (Milner & Goodale, 1993, p. 317)[5]

In their theoretical treatments, Allport and Neumann have presented consistent analyses and systematic views in which perception, action, and selection play a prominent role.

In the perception for action views, two control problems are recognised – the problem of effector recruitment (the available effectors can be used for a range of different actions and one of the actions has to be selected) and the problem of parameter specification (a selected action can be executed in a number of ways and one of these ways has to be selected). For solving these problems *selection for action* is required. In these views, this selection for action is regarded as the basic functional characteristic of the human information processor and overt behavioural limitations are regarded as a functional consequence.

In correspondence with the two control problems, in the perception for action views two selection mechanisms are distinguished. The first mechanism is in charge of determining which *action* – or, more precisely, which category or mode of action out of the total repertoire of actions – is given temporal priority at a certain moment in time (Allport, 1987, p. 395). This mechanism determines which skill is allowed to recruit which effectors now (Neumann, 1987, p. 376). The introduction of a mechanism for skill or action selection is the unique feature of the perception for action approach.

The second mechanism is in charge of determining which *object* is acted upon at a certain moment in time, or, where the action has now to be directed (Allport, 1987, p. 395). This mechanism determines from what region in space the parameters are taken that are allowed to specify a selected action in detail at a certain moment in time (Neumann, 1987, p. 376). The assumption that there is a mechanism for object or region selection is one that the perception for action camp has in common with the perception for perception camp (see, e.g., the 'Attention as Spotlight' metaphor in Section 1.3).

In my view, this perception for action approach presents a convincing functional analysis at a general level (see Van der Heijden, 1992, Ch. 8). Especially attractive and important is the idea that the control structures that serve to guide the selected actions, e.g., walking, picking up, throwing, or catching, have built-in, hardware, causal selective capacities; that is, have the causal power to select and extract the subset of parameters that is required to specify the selected action in detail. Therefore, besides 'action selection' and 'object selection', no further 'parameter selection' is required. Devoted control structures take care of 'direct parameter specification'.

The clearest statement about this direct or automatic parameter specification is in Neumann (1990a, p. 235; see also 1990a, p. 242.)

> . . . there is some (possibly complex) stimulus property . . . that specifies the required parameter(s), but it is not the stimulus as an object, with its particular combination of properties (shape, size, color, etc.) that enters into action control . . . this type of selection-for-action takes place within,

and is controlled by, specific control structures, or skills . . . systems that, by means of specific neuronal connections, translate specific stimulus properties into specific action parameters . . . Stimulus processing within such a control structure is, of course, highly selective. But this selectivity is not the work of a selection mechanism that exists *in addition* to the control structure. Rather, this structure itself provides the required selectivity through the way in which sensory neurons and motor neurons are connected.

The selected act 'switches in' the 'specific control structures' that select the parameters required for the act, or, action selection consists of the 'switching in' of the 'specific control structures' that select the required parameters for the act.

Of course, for the solution of the problem I am concerned with in this work, each attempt to put functions like perception and attention in an action framework is welcome. Nevertheless, a serious problem arises here. Because the perception for perception camp has done the bulk of the relevant experimental work and has produced a wealth of important data, the problem I have first and foremost to be concerned with is that of how the Intending Mind uses Visual Perception in the tasks used in the perception for perception camp. And here it has to be admitted that the perception for action camp has not been able to contribute to the theorising in the perception for perception camp. The prime reason for this lack of influence has, in my view, to be found in the fact that the mainstream perception for perception approach is not really helped by the theoretical insights and contributions of the perception for action camp. Why this is so, is not too difficult to see.

As already stated, the perception for action camp distinguishes between object selection and skill or action selection. It is of importance to see that with regard to object selection, the two approaches do not really differ, so the perception for action camp has nothing of importance to contribute here. The two approaches differ with regard to skill selection and here the perception for action camp has something of relevance to say. The perception for perception camp, however, is not concerned with the skills and the behaviour that animals and humans have in common; with how they forage for food, avoid predators, find mates, and move efficiently from one part of the environment to another. The experiments performed within the perception for perception camp nearly always capitalise upon a uniquely human capability: the use of language or a related symbolic behaviour; subjects have to name objects, colours, or positions, or to read letters or words.

With regard to this language behaviour used in the perception for perception camp, the theoretical analysis presented by the perception for action camp is incomplete and still needs to be further developed. Indeed, for the actions that humans share with animals, the hardware control structure of

the selected act might always determine and extract the required set of parameters from a selected object. This is, however, generally not the case with
language behaviour, i.e., with 'the act of speaking'. Consider an experiment
with coloured letters as stimuli, e.g., one stimulus with a red A, another with
a blue B, and another with a green C, and with 'the act of speaking' as the
selected skill. In this situation, after object selection, 'the act of speaking'
does not have the power to determine what task will be performed and what
the overt response will be. The letter can be read and the colour – and a lot
of other aspects of the object, e.g., its position, size, and brightness – can be
named.

Even when in 'the act of speaking' a distinction is made between 'the act
of naming' and 'the act of reading', the selected act does not have the power
to determine what task will be performed and what the overt response will
be. Two groups of problems have to be considered, one group for the act of
naming and another group for the act of reading.

First, 'the act of naming' cannot select the required parameters. When the
selected object is, for instance, a small, bright, homogeneous, red triangle
on the left, 'the act of naming' insufficiently constrains the overt verbal
behaviour that has to occur. The size, brightness, texture, colour, form,
position, and many more properties can be named. Of course, the introduction of 'size naming', 'brightness naming', 'texture naming', 'colour
naming', 'form naming', and 'position naming' as independent, autonomous
acts, with their own devoted internal control structures, is not of real help
here. That trick deprives the perception for action theories of their parsimony
and elegance.

Second, 'the act of reading' cannot select all required parameters. When
the selected object is, for instance, the capital letter A, 'the act of reading'
insufficiently constrains the overt verbal behaviour that has to occur. Subjects need in no way respond with 'a' when that A is presented and when
they have to read that A. Subjects can, for instance, simply refrain from
responding – this is an adequate reaction under the instruction: Say 'b'
when there is a B and 'c' when there is a C but refrain from responding
when there is an A. Subjects can also respond with 'yes' (and 'no') – these
arc adequate reactions under the instructions: Say 'yes' ('no') when there is
a vowel (consonant) and 'no' ('yes') when there is a consonant (vowel).
Subjects can also respond with 'one' – this is an adequate reaction under the
instruction: Name the serial position of the letter in the alphabet. Subjects
can also respond with 'ape' (or 'cat') – these are adequate reactions under
the instruction: Give an animal name that begins (or not) with an A. In
short, to explain a subject's task performance, more than a control structure
concerned with 'the act of reading' is required.

Three conclusions are in order here:

- The perception for action theorists have failed up to now to generalise
  and elaborate their views in such a way and in such detail that 'the act

of speaking', encountered in most experiments in the perception for perception camp, can also be adequately dealt with. This explains why their important insights failed to have real impact.

- The bulk of the appropriate, relevant, and important data pertaining to the use of visual information for task performance are produced by the perception for perception camp. Because these are the data I want to explain first and above all, I am not very much helped by the perception for action views and have to look for a starting point elsewhere.

- To find an appropriate starting point and prevent the theoretical confusions pointed to above, a disciplined classification of (laboratory) tasks is badly required. Without such a classification, theorising only leads to confusions and frustrations and ends up in an ever-expanding, inextricable mess.[6]

2.2   Two types of tasks

As just stated, to solve my problem of how the Intending Mind uses Visual Perception for the performance of tasks, a disciplined classification of tasks is badly needed. Without such a classification, essential distinctions are neglected, issues are confused, and a theoretical muddle is the result. But here for me two problems arise – a minor one and a major one.

The minor problem arises because in the daily activities of human beings an endless variety of tasks and combinations of tasks can be distinguished. This diversity defies any classification. This problem is, however, easily solved by restricting the classification to simple laboratory tasks.

The major problem arises because for a devoted information processing psychologist a disciplined classification of tasks is a classification in terms of internal processes and operations. For such a classification an appropriate theory is required, a theory that provides the theoretical means and concepts to express the relevant differences and similarities between tasks in terms of internal operations. That theory is not, however, at this point available; it is the theory I hope to derive, to introduce, and to develop in the following chapters. In this section, I therefore have to rely on authorities.

In this section I present two classifications – one in terms of three types of stimuli and one in terms of two types of acts. Not without some wisdom of hindsight, I then argue that, in terms of internal processes, a distinction between two types of tasks has to be made – a distinction between 'act' tasks and 'report' tasks, with within the 'report' tasks a further distinction between 'name' tasks and 'read' tasks. In Chapters 6 and 9, I return to the viability of this distinction.

Gibson's (1960, 1979) empirical and theoretical work is of great importance to the search for a disciplined distinction between types of tasks. In 'The Concept of the Stimulus in Psychology', Gibson (1960) convincingly argues that psychology has to develop a 'science of stimuli':

... we will have to develop the needed discipline on a do-it-yourself principle. It might be called ecological physics, with branches in optics, acoustics, dynamics, and biochemistry. We cannot wait for the physical scientists to describe and classify potential stimuli. The variables would seem to them inelegant, the mathematics would have to be improvised, and the job is not to their taste. But it is necessary. And if successful, it will provide a basis for a stimulus–response psychology, which otherwise seems to be sinking in a swamp of intervening variables.

(Gibson, 1960, p. 701)

Under 'Some positive hypotheses' he proposes a classification:

A systematic study of the specifying power of stimuli will put the problem of meaning in perception on a new footing. It will take several forms, depending on the kinds of relations discovered. My guess is that there will be at least three, corresponding to stimuli from things, from pictures, and from words. It is true that men, besides learning to perceive objects, also learn to apprehend things by way of perceiving pictures and words. These mediated perceptions get mixed with direct perceptions in the adult. But we shall have to disentangle them before we can have a complete theory of human perception.

(Gibson, 1960, p. 702)

In Gibson's (1979) *The Ecological Approach to Visual Perception*, it does not become fully clear where, for him, the big and major divide is. In *theory*, it is between (the direct perception of) 'things' on the one hand and (the indirect or mediated perception of) pictures and words on the other:

The world does not speak to the observer. Animals and humans communicate with cries, gestures, speech, pictures, writing, and television, but we cannot hope to understand perception in terms of these channels; it is quite the other way around. Words and pictures convey information, carry it, or transmit it, but the information in the sea of energy around each of us . . . is not conveyed. It is simply there.

(Gibson, 1979, p. 242)

In *practice*, however, the major divide is between stimuli from 'things' and 'pictures' on the one hand and stimuli from 'words' on the other. In Gibson's (1979) work, most of the chapters are devoted to 'things' and two chapters are devoted to 'pictures'. There are, however, no chapters about 'words'. This fact as such already indicates that an appropriate classification of stimuli is not a trivial matter.

Of course, a 'science of stimuli' – and possibly also a 'science of responses' – is badly needed.[7] And, of course, Gibson is right when he, for instance, says that an apple can be picked and named but not read, that a word can be read and possibly be named but not picked, and that a colour can be named and possibly be pointed at but not read.[8] Nevertheless, in my view, the important distinction is not between types of stimuli, and also not between types of responses. In my information processing point of view, the important distinction is exactly in what Gibson called the 'swamp of intervening variables'.

That, *pace* Gibson (1960, 1979), the important distinction is not between types of stimuli as such, already follows from what was said in Section 2.1. A small, bright, homogeneous, red triangle on the left as a stimulus in no way constrains the overt behaviour – not even when (a) that stimulus is selected from among all stimuli that can be selected, and (b) the task of naming is selected from among all tasks that can be performed. And the capital letter A as a stimulus in no way constrains the overt behaviour, not even when (a) that stimulus is selected and (b) the task of reading is selected from among all tasks that can be performed. It is simply not true that

> In a system of psychology completely worked out, given the response the stimuli can be predicted; given the stimuli, the response can be predicted.
>
> (Watson, 1913, p. 168, in Vanderplas, 1966, p. 77)

That, *pace* Gibson (1960, 1979) and Watson (1913) with his simple stimulus–response psychology, the relevant distinction has to be found in the 'swamp of intervening variables' had already been demonstrated with objective methods in early introspective experimental psychology. Lange (1888), working in Wundt's laboratory in Leipzig, introduced a distinction between *muscular* and *sensorial* reaction times. In Lange's experiments, subjects had simply to press a single response key in response to a single (auditory) stimulus (later on the same results were found and reported with a light stimulus; see, e.g., Angell & Moore, 1896). In the two conditions in his experiments, Lange induced in his subjects one of two sets (or '*Einstellungen*'). The subjects had to perform the task either with a muscular set, i.e., to attend to the motor response that had to be performed, or with a sensorial set, i.e., to attend to the auditory stimulus that was going to be presented. Lange found that the 'simple reaction times' were appreciably smaller when the task was performed with a muscular set (an average RT of about 130 ms) than with a sensorial set (an average RT of about about 220 ms). In replications, a difference in mean simple reaction times of about 100 ms was consistently found (see Titchener, 1895a, for an overview).[9]

> Moreover, introspection indicated a qualitative difference between the two cases. Subjects reported that under sensorial set the stimulus was first consciously perceived ("apperceived" in Wundt's terminology) before there was a voluntary impulse to react. By contrast, with a muscular set, there was the experience of reacting before having consciously

perceived the stimulus . . . From this Lange and Wundt concluded that there are two ways in which a sensory stimulus can trigger a motor response. Normally, responding requires that the stimulus be apperceived and that there is a conscious decision to react. This is what Wundt termed the complete reaction. With simple, well-practiced actions there is, however, the alternative possibility that the stimulus triggers the motor response directly in a kind of short circuit. This is what Wundt called the shortened reaction.

(Neumann, 1990b, p. 211)

So, in Lange's (1888) research one and the same simple stimulus (a sound or a light) and one and the same response (a button push) were used in two different tasks that provided different results. This indicates that neither 'type of stimulus' nor 'type of response' is the critical factor. So, from Lange's research, but also from other research to which I turn further on, it appears that the important distinction is neither between 'stimuli as such' nor between 'responses as such'. The important distinction must be in what Gibson calls the 'swamp of intervening variables', or in what Lange calls the '*Einstellungen*'. What we clearly need is a cognitive psychology that specifies what happens in the information processing system, a theory that at this point we still do not have.

In this context it is interesting to know that Dennett (1992), a philosopher of mind, is well aware of the fact that there are more types of button pushing:

Typically, pushing a button is a way of performing some conventionally fixed speech act, such as *asserting that* the two seen figures appear superimposed to me right *now*, or answering that *yes*, my hurried, snap judgment (since you have told me that speed is of the essence) is that the word that I have just heard was on the list I heard a little while ago. For many experimental purposes, then, we will want to unpack the meaning of these button-pushes and incorporate them as elements of the text. Which speech act a particular button-pushing can be taken to execute depends on the intentional interpretation of the interactions between subject and experimenter that were involved in preparing the subject for the experiment. (Not all button-pushing consists in speech acts; some may be make-believe shooting, or make-believe rocket-steering, for instance.)

(Dennett, 1992, p. 77)

So, Dennett distinguishes between button pushing as a 'speech act', as a 'report' from subject to experimenter meant to communicate what is seen and known, and button pushing as a 'world act', as an 'act' from the subject in his or her visual world meant to do something or to change something in the outer material world.

At this point in my search for a tentative classification of tasks, Bridgeman's (1992, 1999a) empirical and theoretical work becomes of great importance. This is because Bridgeman and associates provide important empirical evidence, i.e., behavioural dissociations, to support the same distinction between types of tasks that Dennett's (1992) arguments and my arguments presented up to now are leading me to.[10] (For related neuropsychological evidence see, e.g., Goodale & Milner, 1992, and Milner & Goodale, 1993, 1995.) Moreover, the theorising and the evidence Bridgeman presents are concerned with the perception of spatial position, a central topic in the information processing approach to perception and cognition (see Chapter 7).

Bridgeman's (1992) empirical and theoretical work started with a paradox or dissociation. Evidence indicated that '. . . perception can suffer spatial illusions that are not shared in spatial behavior, and visually guided behavioral orientation can be modified without affecting perception' (Bridgeman, 1992, p. 79).

> In an attempt to resolve this paradox, [Bridgeman] noted that the two conflicting observations use different response measures. The [perception] experiments requires a non-spatial verbal report or button press, both symbolic responses. [The behavioral orientation experiments], in contrast, requires quantitative spatial information with a 1:1 correspondence between stimulus position and motor output.
>
> (Bridgeman, 1992, p. 79)

So, two different types of tasks are distinguished, 'perceptual tasks with a symbolic output', and behavioural tasks 'with isomorphic motor responses' (Bridgeman, 1992, p. 79) – 'report' tasks and 'act' tasks, in short.

In a 'report' task or 'perceptual' task, the subject is asked to tell what he or she sees. The performance of these tasks requires a categorisation in which the relation between what is seen, e.g., the target position, and behaviour, e.g., the verbal response, is arbitrary. In an 'act' task or 'behavioural' task, the subject is asked to act. These tasks require a 1:1 relationship between behaviour, e.g., pointing at a target, and stimulus information, e.g., position (see Bridgeman, 1992, p. 83). In terms of acts, instead of tasks, the distinction is between 'communicatory' acts, through which subjects are 'offering their opinion', and 'instrumental' acts, in which subjects 'do something to the world' (Bridgeman, 1999a, p. 7).[11]

Bridgeman and associates provide substantial evidence to support the adequacy and validity of their distinction. Because I have no reason whatsoever to doubt this evidence, I confine myself to one 'double dissociation', reported by Bridgeman, Kirch, and Sperling (1981). In this study

> . . . a fixed target was projected in front of a subject, with a background behind it . . . When the background was displaced left or right, subjects experienced the illusion of stroboscopic induced motion – the target

appeared to jump in the opposite direction. Target and background were then extinguished, and the subjects pointed to the last target position. Despite the induced motion, they pointed to the same location whether the target had appeared to jump to the left or the right. The illusion did not affect pointing . . .

[In] Another condition . . . Each subject adjusted the real target motion until the target appeared stationary. When properly adjusted the target's real motion, in phase with the background, exactly matched the induced motion, out of phase with the background. . . . Nevertheless, subjects pointed in different directions when the target was extinguished in the left or the right positions . . .

This is a double dissociation because in the first condition the apparent target displacement affected only the cognitive measure, while in the second condition the real displacement affected only the sensorimotor measure.

(Bridgeman, 1999a, p. 5)

This double dissociation, and related observations, are explained by Bridgeman (1992, 1999a) in terms of 'two visual systems', a 'cognitive' system and a 'sensorimotor' system (see also Goodale & Milner, 1992, and Milner & Goodale, 1993, 1995). At the basis of the explanation is the hypothesis that in humans and primates two quasi-independent visual systems with independent representations of visual space, i.e., independent 'maps', can be distinguished (see Bridgeman, 1992, for excellent overviews of the physiological evidence and of the history of the distinction). Bridgeman (1999a, pp. 3–4) briefly characterises the two systems in anatomical and functional terms. The two systems have a common input but diverge in the cortex. The cognitive (or 'what') system, containing the information for pattern recognition and underlying visual experience, follows a course into the inferior temporal cortex of the temporal lobe. Its space representation is experienced. The sensorimotor (or 'how') system, containing information for controlling visual guided behaviour, follows a course into the posterior parietal areas. Its space representation is not experienced.

Of course, armed with this distinction an explanation of the behavioural evidence and of the dissociations is not difficult to find:

An interpretation of the [behavioural evidence] that is consistent with cortical neurophysiology, as well as the literature . . . , is that the cognitive and motor measures access information from different maps of visual space. The motor map is accessed by a pointing measure that requires a 1:1 relationship between stimulus position and behavior . . . The cognitive map, in contrast, requires a categorization in which the relationship between target position and behavior is arbitrary.

Thus the normal human possesses two maps of visual space. One of them holds information used in perception: if a subject is asked what he sees, the information in this 'cognitive' map is accessed. This map can obtain great sensitivity to small motions or translations of objects in the visual world by using relative motion as a cue . . .

The other visual map drives visually guided behavior, but its contents are not necessarily available to perception. This map does not have the resolution and sensitivity that the cognitive map has, but it is not required to: a small error in pointing, grasping or looking is of little consequence.

(Bridgeman, 1992, pp. 83–84)

In Chapter 9, I return to this explanation.

Neumann (1987, 1989, 1990a, 1990b) presents and elaborates a distinction between two types of tasks/actions that is very close to and supports Bridgeman's classification. This convergence of opinions is not too surprising because what we basically meet here is the distinction between perception and action.[12]

I am now in the position to present a preliminary and tentative classification of tasks. First, following Bridgeman, Dennett, and Neumann, I distinguish two different cases.

* The first is the case of perceiving and 'acting', the case the perception for action camp is concerned with (see Section 2.1). In this case, the selection of an object to act upon or a region to act in is almost always required. With Neumann (1989, 1990a, 1990b), I assume that for the 'acting' itself no 'cognition' is required (nobody 'knows', for instance, the details of 'riding a bike').[13] What is required is that the parameters needed to guide the action are available (i.e., are specified in the light), are extracted, and are used in the performance of the action. A devoted, special-purpose, action module can perform that extraction and guide the action. Because the parameter extraction requires no 'cognitive' mediation, there is direct or automatic parameter extraction/specification for action.[14]

* The second case is the case of perceiving and 'reporting', the case the perception for action camp is not concerned with (see Section 2.1). Also in this case, the selection of an object or region about which something is going to be reported is almost always required. After Gibson (1960), I distinguish within this case two sub-cases (see also Section 2.1 for this distinction).

The first sub-case is the case of perceiving and 'naming'. Gibson (1979) is of help for further clarifying this case. He first recognises that

It is surely true that speech and language convey information of a certain sort from person to person . . . But we should never forget that this is information that has been put into words. It is not the limitless

information available in a flowing stimulus array . . . The human observer
can verbalize his awareness, and the result is to make it communicable.
But my hypothesis is that there has to be an awareness of the world
before it can be put into words. You have to see it before you can say it.
Perceiving precedes predicating.

(Gibson, 1979, p. 260)

And he then elaborates:

Consider an adult . . . who sees the cat on the mat. He knows *that* the
cat is on the mat and believes the proposition and can say it, but all the
time he plainly sees all sorts of wordless facts . . . The parts of it he can
name are called concepts, but they are not all of what he can see.

(Gibson, 1979, p. 261)

So, according to Gibson, in this case in parameter extraction 'perception'
('you have to see it') and 'cognitive mediation' ('parts . . . called concepts')
are involved in the selection of the to-be-reported information from all that
is perceived (one 'plainly sees all sorts of wordless facts' that do not enter in
report). Just because this parameter selection requires 'awareness' and 'cognitive mediation', there is indirect, non-automatic, parameter extraction for
naming.

The second sub-case is the case of perceiving and 'reading'. This is a case
pointed to by Gibson (1960), but neglected by Bridgeman and Neumann
because in their crucial experiments no reading was involved. Also in this
case, the selection of an object or a region that is going to be read is almost
always required.

The exact status of this case is, at this moment, difficult to specify. The
case of 'reading' has possibly something in common with the case of
'acting', because in both cases something like 'devoted control structures'
are involved (direct parameter specification). Nevertheless, the 'reading' case
has to be distinguished from the 'acting' case because in 'reading' the relation between stimuli and responses is fully arbitrary and has therefore to be
acquired in a long-term learning process. (When in Japan, I can walk on the
streets and pick and eat the apples, I can also name the colours, positions,
and shapes, but I cannot read the texts.)

The 'reading' case certainly has something in common with the 'naming'
case because the relation between (attributes of) stimuli and responses is
fully arbitrary and has to be learned. Nevertheless, the 'reading' case has
to be distinguished from the 'naming' case because, after object selection,
the parameters for reading are fixed while for naming a further specification is required. (When presented with the word WORD in red and after
selecting that WORD, only 'word' can be read but the colour, size, position, etc., can be named. Stated otherwise, after selecting the object with
the task of naming an additional choice is required that is not required

with the task of reading[15]).[16] In Chapters 6 and 9 I return to the status of reading.

At this point it is of interest to note that in my classification of tasks into 'act' and 'report' tasks, with within the 'report' tasks the 'name' and 'read' tasks, the important differences are neither in the stimuli nor in the responses, but in the information processing operations in between. In this classification, the difference between the three types of tasks is not in what I called object or region selection. All three types of tasks require object or region selection.[17] The difference between the three types of tasks is in what further happens with the selected object or selected region. In 'act' tasks something like an inborn, hardware, devoted action module extracts the parameters required for action; in 'read' tasks an acquired, over-learned, devoted reading routine performs this job; and in 'name' tasks one or another form of 'cognitive mediation', possibly working with Gibson's 'concepts' and 'perception', takes care of this task.

I am now in the position to specify further the tasks with which the present study will be concerned. Part II of this work is concerned with the 'report' tasks, the 'name' tasks, and the 'read' tasks, as specified above, the perceptual tasks with a symbolic output. These are the tasks most often used in the perception for perception camp within the information processing approach. The evidence produced by this camp gives me the opportunity to test my initial theoretical propositions. Part III of this work is concerned with some selected 'act' tasks, the perceptual tasks with direct parameter specification. These are the tasks favoured and emphasised by the perception for action camp within the information processing approach. The evidence considered in this part provides me with the opportunity to elaborate and expand my theoretical position.

Let us now look at an important 'report' task to find out how to proceed.

2.3   Stimuli and instructions

Now the time has come to visit the laboratories to see what happens there. There it readily appears that a great diversity of visual information processing tasks are used. Given the versatility of the human visual information processing system and its action possibilities, this does not come as a surprise. We all know that an apple or a pear can be picked and pointed at, named and categorised, and that the colour, shape, position, etc., can be named. We also all know that a picture of a car or a bike can be picked and pointed at, that the object displayed can be named and categorised, and that the object's colour, shape, size, etc., can be named. And we also know that the word RED in blue or the word BLUE in red can be read or spelled, that the number of letters or vowels can be counted, and that the word's colour, size, position, etc., can be named. And after what was said in the preceding section, we now also know that all these tasks, and variations and modifications of these tasks – and many other tasks besides – can be used in experiments in the laboratory to study how people use their visual perception in the performance of tasks.

At this point it is important to see that in all such experiments two experimental 'factors' are involved.

- The first experimental 'factor' consists of the stimuli that are presented in an experiment. This factor determines/specifies the visual world in which the subject has to operate.
- The second experimental 'factor' consists of the instruction given to the subjects to act or perform in a specified way. This factor determines/specifies the operations the subject has to perform in that visual world.

Clearly, the instruction and the stimuli are of equal importance. The instruction specifies the task to be performed and the action to be executed. The stimuli provide the task-relevant objects and deliver the required visual details. And of course, each experimenter knows that no experiment will work without one or another kind of stimuli. Equally, each experimenter knows that no experiment will work and produce interpretable behavioural data without one or another kind of instruction that specifies what object has to be selected, what task has to be performed, and what kind of response is required. So, in *practice*,

> The psychologist's attitude towards experimenting . . . is a thoroughgoing dualism. It supposes two elements, task instruction and set of stimuli, and treats them as irreducible.

In *theory*, however, a completely different attitude is found. In the theorising in the perception for perception camp – and not only in the theorising in this camp – the importance of the instruction is generally not recognised. With few exceptions, to which I will turn later in this work, researchers are mainly concerned with the automatic, bottom-up, two-stage processing of stimulus information.

Reasons for this remarkable state of affairs are not too difficult to find.

- A first reason is, of course, that within the perception for perception camp *perception* is emphasised, not task performance (see also Sections 1.4 and 2.1); the investigators are almost exclusively interested in the effect of the stimulus, in how it is initially processed and ultimately perceived.
- A second related reason is that, in line with this main interest, in nearly all experiments the stimulus varies from trial to trial and produces an interesting detailed pattern of results that invites a detailed explanation,

while the instruction remains the same and therefore can play no role in that explanation of detail. (See also Van der Heijden, 1992.)

Just because of its importance, it is worthwhile to illustrate this second point with a concrete example. Let us therefore visit a laboratory in the perception for perception camp and consider in more detail a task that was first used by Von Helmholz (1894). Von Helmholtz looked at briefly presented arrays of letters. With introspection he investigated the possibility of selecting and seeing a voluntarily chosen part of the visual field in the absence of overt eye movements (see Section 3.1 for a further description). Von Helmholtz noted and reported that this central selection of a subset of the information was indeed possible. In the early 1960s this paradigm was rediscovered and brought into the laboratory as an objective information processing experiment by Sperling (1960) and Averbach and Coriell (1961). For our present purposes, a brief look at a simplified version of Averbach and Coriell's paradigm, the partial-report bar-probe task, suffices. Here are the stimuli and the instruction.

The stimuli

In the partial-report bar-probe paradigm in each of the, say per subject 200, experimental trials a single row of, say, eight letters is presented. For each trial a different row of eight randomly selected letters is used. At the top of one of the letters is a bar marker. The position of the bar marker varies from trial to trial so that in the course of the experiment all positions are indicated equally often. Figure 2.1 presents two examples of the kind of stimuli used. In the upper one the bar is on top of the letter A in position two and in the lower one the bar is on top of the letter Z in position 5. Before the experiment proper, the subjects are allowed to inspect a couple of the stimuli at leisure. During the experiment proper, the subjects have first to fixate a central fixation point. When correctly fixated, one of the stimuli is presented with an exposure duration that makes useful (saccadic) eye movements from the fixation point to the letter indicated by the bar marker impossible (exposure times of less than about 150 ms suffice for this purpose).

|
XAZNOVPT

|
QRLNZXAV

Figure 2.1 Examples of stimuli used in the partial-report bar-probe task (see text for further explanation).

The instruction

In the partial-report bar-probe paradigm the subject is instructed to name the letter indicated by the bar marker.

When 200 experimental trials are used, each letter position is probed 25 times. This number of observations makes it possible to calculate per subject reliable percentages or proportions correct per position. The main result revealed by this calculation is that subjects can perform the task quite well; for all positions their performance is much better than to be expected with pure random guessing (i.e., for all positions the proportions correct are much larger than .04). In this way, this objective behavioural experiment with proportions correct per position as the dependent variable fully corroborates Von Helmholtz's important basic introspective observation: It is possible to select a subset of the visual information by purely internal means, i.e., without any external 'accommodation or adjustment of the sensory organs' (James, 1890/1950, p. 434).

Some further findings, obtained with the objective behavioural method and not noticed by Von Helmholtz with his subjective introspective method, deserve to be mentioned. The first finding is sketched in Figure 2.2. With the linear arrays used, there are spectacular differences in performance per letter position. The observed percentages correct are much higher in the middle (positions 4 and 5) and at the end (positions 1 and 8) than in the positions in between (2 and 3 at the left and 6 and 7 at the right); the function relating percentages correct to letter positions is clearly W-shaped. After the introduction of this selection paradigm by Averbach and Coriell (1961), this intriguing pattern of results has often been confirmed and reported in the literature.

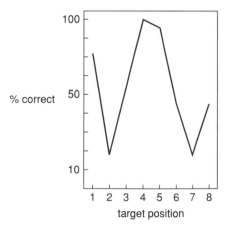

Figure 2.2 Accuracy of report as a function of target position observed with Averbach and Coriell's (1961) partial-report bar-probe paradigm (linear eight-letter arrays).

Initially, this pattern of results was explained in terms of ease of identi-fication. According to Estes (1978, p. 188), for instance, there are two factors that, in combination, are responsible for this W-shaped position function. The first is 'retinal acuity' and the second is 'lateral masking'. Retinal acuity, sharpness of vision, is highest in the fovea and decreases progressively and dramatically towards the periphery. This explains the high level of perform-ance at the middle positions as compared to the more peripheral positions. Lateral masking, the adverse effect on identification of a letter caused by a letter in close spatial and temporal proximity, is greatest in the interior of the array where each letter has two neighbours, and least at the ends where a letter has only a single, foveal, neighbour, and empty space at the peri-pheral side. This explains the high level of performance at the end positions as compared to the central positions. In combination, these two factors explain the W-shaped position function (see Van der Heijden, 1992, Ch. 5, for the strength of this explanation).

Unfortunately, or better, fortunately, for the information processing approach, percentages or proportions correct do not reveal everything of importance. A further analysis of the *errors* revealed a number of unexpected results and provided important information for a correction and refinement of Estes' (1978) explanation. Mewhort, Campbell, Marchetti, and Campbell (1981) observed that the bulk of the errors consisted of *localisation* errors, not of identification errors, and that the bulk of these localisation errors consisted of *near* localisation errors; that is, consisted of the report of the name of a letter that was in a position adjacent to the target letter. Further experiments and analyses by Hagenaar and Van der Heijden (1997) con-firmed these results. Their research revealed in addition that the majority of the near localisation errors consisted of *central near localisation* errors; that is, reports consisted of the name of the letter adjacent to and at the foveal side of the target letter. Moreover, their analyses revealed that central near location errors occurred about equally frequently with pre-exposure as with post-exposure of the bar marker and appreciably less with simultaneous presentation of indicator and linear array.[18]

The latter experiments and analyses clearly show that, contrary to what was initially thought, in the performance of the partial-report bar-probe task with linear arrays as depicted in Figure 2.1, identification is not the only internal operation of importance. Localization of the to-be-selected information is also a factor determining task performance. This information led to improved and refined explanations of the W-shaped position curve for correct reports (see, e.g., Mewhort et al., 1981; Hagenaar & van der Heijden, 1997; Van der Heijden, 1992; see Section 7.2). At this point, the details of these explana-tions are not of importance. Two points are, however, of importance:

•   The first point is that, over the years, the quality and the detail of the explanations of performance in the partial-report bar-probe task have steadily improved.[19]

- The second point is that this progress was achieved with a great variety of stimuli and with only *one single, simple, invariant instruction: Name the letter indicated by the bar marker.*

Small wonder that in the information processing approach to perception and cognition the importance of the instruction is virtually never recognised.[20]

But recognised or not, in all experiments there *is* always an instruction that specifies what has to be done. Before each experiment, all experimenters make sure that their subjects receive the appropriate instruction and understand that instruction. During the experiment the experimenters generally rely upon the 'given' that subjects still 'remember' that instruction and 'use' that instruction. And in the evaluation and interpretation of the data, the background conviction is that the subjects at least attempted to perform according to the instruction – that they attempted to select the object or region they were instructed to select and that they attempted to 'treat' what they selected in the way they were instructed to 'treat' what they selected.

So, there is a huge and remarkable discrepancy between theory and practice. In the experimental practice in the information processing approach the importance of the instruction is nearly always recognised, but in the theorising the importance of this factor is nearly always neglected. Of course, this discrepancy has to be eliminated. What has to be recognised within information processing psychology is that the instruction is not merely an 'outside' trick for ensuring that one gets the results one wants and that one can then forget. What the experiments show is that an instruction, when appropriate and effective, has resulted in an 'inside' mental representation of that instruction that is appropriate and effective. That 'inside' mental representation of the instruction is 'part' of the total information processing system with which the information processing approach is working, is interested in, and wants to disentangle. That internal representation – which, as all experiments show, undeniably has the causal powers that make the subjects perform according to the instruction and the experimenters obtain the interesting patterns of results they are looking for – cannot remain outside the theorising in the information processing approach. When it remains outside, explanatory fictions and illusions, for instance, a 'subject', an 'agent', a 'he', or a 'she', stay in.

For the moment, after Neumann (1987, pp. 380–381), the internal representation of the instruction can be called an 'action plan'.

> . . . action planning enables combining skills without any training. This is the basis of almost every psychological experiment. For example, when we instruct subjects to press a button if two briefly presented letters are identical, and to press another button if they are different, we ask them to construct and execute an action plan that combines perceptual, cognitive, and motor skills that they have, if they are naïve subjects, never before used in this combination.

In current theorising in the information processing approach, the important theoretical issues with regard to such 'action plans' – how they are derived from instructions, how they are structured, how they are implemented in the information processing system, and how they can exert their causal effects – are generally neglected. Therefore, the theoretical accounts are incomplete. Indeed, the internal representation of a single fixed instruction cannot contribute to the explanation of the interesting *detailed pattern* of results obtained in an experiment such as the partial-report bar-probe task. Without that representation with its causal powers, however, the results that exhibit that interesting pattern of detail would never have been produced in the first place.[21]

2.4   The subject is the instruction

As stated in Section 1.3, nearly all visual information processing and selective attention theories produced by the information processing approach to perception and cognition are two-stage theories. And, as stated and demonstrated in Section 1.3, in nearly all two-stage theories and two-stage theorising two components or ingredients can be distinguished, an unproblematic component and a problematic component. The unproblematic component concerns 'visual perception' and 'the role of attention in visual perception'. The problematic component concerns 'the subject' or 'the agent' who is 'controlling, guiding, and using selective attention'. And, as argued in Section 1.3, the latter component, which sometimes appears in the open and sometimes appears in disguise, has to be eliminated by replacing it with a decent, structured, causally effective information processing component.

As stated in Section 2.3, in nearly all experiments in experimental psychology in which human beings serve as subjects – in the experiments of the early subjective introspection psychology and in the experiments of the current objective cognitive psychology – two experimental 'factors' can be distinguished. The first 'factor' consists of the stimuli presented in the experiment. This factor determines the visual world. The second 'factor' consists of the instruction. This factor determines how to perform and how to respond. Both 'factors' have to be acknowledged because they jointly determine task performance, but in theories the 'factor' of instruction is generally neglected. And, as argued in Section 2.3, that factor has to be introduced into the theorising by specifying it as a decent, structured, causally effective information processing component.

At this point, I am sure that the reader knows already in what direction my argument is going to proceed. Nevertheless, I summarise that argument in terms of what I regard as three 'basic facts':

• In the experiments in the information processing approach, the *subjects* generally perform according to the *instruction*; on nearly all trials *they* do what they are *instructed* to do. To perform according to the *instruction*, the *subjects* must have 'picked up' and 'understood' the *instruction* and must have applied what *they* 'picked up' and 'understood' in one way or another, to what *they* visually experienced or what *they* saw. So, somewhere in the *subject* there is 'something' derived from an *instruction* with regard to 'what to do', then a visual stimulus is briefly presented, and then, without very many noticeable problems, that 'something' makes the *subject* reliably respond according to the *instruction*.

• In the theorising in the information processing approach, the *subject* and the *instruction* is one too many. One's theory can either contain a *subject*, who does the required work, or it can contain an internal representation of the *instruction*, which does the required work. When the theorising contains a *subject* there is no further need for a representation of an *instruction*. In such a theory, the *subject* takes care of the instruction-induced appropriate task performance. When the theorising contains an internal representation of the *instruction*, there is no further need for a *subject*. In such a theory, the internal representation of the *instruction* can take care of appropriate task performance. So, in the theorising one has to choose between the *subject* and the internal representation of the *instruction*.

• The *subject*, as an unanalysed blob, is a dispensable information processing component, an illusion, an explanatory fiction, which has to be eliminated by replacing it with a decent, structured, causally effective information processing component. The internal representation of the *instruction* is an indispensable information processing component, a reality, an explanatory necessity, which has to find its place in the theories after developing it into a decent, structured, causally effective information processing component. If developed and elaborated in the appropriate way, the internal representation of the *instruction* can replace the *subject*. After all, from the *subjects* in the information processing experiments not much more is expected than to perform according to the *instruction*. Stated otherwise, just because the experimenter, not the *subject*, determines what has to be done and when that has to be done, for the purpose and the duration of the experiment the *subject* is nothing more or less than the internal representation of the *instruction*.[22]

So, the question that I am going to consider is the question of *how* to replace 'the subject' by an effective representation of the instruction, an 'action plan'. And the answer I am going to develop is: That is possible by replacing 'the subject' of the information processing approach by James's (1890/1950) 'mind knowing', conceived as an internal representation of the instruction, by introducing what I prefer to call an Intending Mind concerned with the required instruction-induced internal and external task performance.

This answer brings the concept 'intentionality', introduced by Brentano (1874) and emphasised by James (1890/1950) as one of the important

characters of 'thought', on to the theoretical scene of the information processing approach. It introduces there the distinction between a mental act and
the content of that act, with the content existing within the act – [desire] :
[. . .], [expect] : [. . .], [perceive] : [. . .], etc., are the examples (see Sections
1.2 and 1.4). In the answer I am going to develop, the mental *acts* required
for internal and external task performance are specified in and derived from
the instruction and stored in or as the Intending Mind. The *contents* of the
mental acts required for internal and external task performance are specified
in and derived from the stimulus and represented in or as Visual Perception
in feature modules. In this way my answer recognises the important fact that
in all experiments two factors determine task performance – the instruction
given and stored in or as the Intending Mind, and the stimuli presented and
stored in or as Visual Perception.

It is not difficult to see *that* a structured, causally effective instruction-
derived action plan can be characterised in intentional terms. From the
instruction, an action plan can be derived that consists of and specifies:
[remember] : [. . .], [expect] : [. . .], [detect] : [. . .], [perceive] : [. . .], and
[report] : [. . .]. The problem of the implementation, structure, and causal
powers of the instruction-derived action plans *is* the problem of the implementation, structure, and causal powers of the act component implied by the
concept intentionality. The real problem is, of course, *how* such an action
plan has to be characterised. To solve that problem we have to look for suggestions in the literature and to try to find an appropriate characterisation,
a decent unit of analysis, for the Intending Mind.

Notes

1 This was what I thought and defended in much of my earlier work (see, e.g., Van
   der Heijden, 1992).
2 Please remember that we met exactly the same problem in Chapter 1, where I
   tried to distinguish between early introspective psychology and current information
   processing psychology (see Chapter 1, Note 3).
3 Because the perception for perception approach assumes that in their experiments visual perception as such is studied, no need is felt for the explicit introduction of a 'user' of that visual perception (for the implicit introduction of the
   'user' see Section 1.3, the 'subject'). As soon as it is acknowledged that what is
   studied is the use of visual information for task performance, the explicit recognition of one or another 'user' becomes unavoidable.
4 Neumann (1991) named the fictitious explanations based on this type of assumption *Virtus Dormitiva* explanations, after Molière's pun. Molière put a candidate
   doctor on the stage who gave a mock explanation of the soporific working of
   opium: because it has a *virtus dormitiva*, a power that puts one to sleep.
5 At this point it is already worthwhile to see that there is a difference between
   'how something initially evolved' and 'how something is used later on'.
6 The behaviourists Watson and Tolman, for instance, also emphasised that a
   distinction between types of tasks has to be made (see Section 3.2). However,
   from their work it does not become clear exactly what the classification has to be.
7 Information processing psychologists often present stimuli that they describe
   with terms like 'red' and 'bright'. The qualities 'red' and 'bright' are, however,

the outcome of the information processing, not the inputs to the information processing system.

8 It is not clear whether a colour can be pointed at because then inevitably the whole coloured object is pointed at (see Skinner, 1972, in Note 11).

9 After Lange (1888), the muscular–sensorial paradigm was used in a great number of laboratories and studies. In *Mind*, Titchener (1895a) summarised the results obtained up to then. In Titchener's view, the assessment of the simple reaction time – 'the interval elapsing between the mental "receiving" of a sense impression and the execution of a movement in response to that impression' – is of importance because 'The reaction is the simplest type of voluntary action' and 'therefore, is the material which must be employed in the teaching or acquiring of introspective control of this combination of conscious processes.' At the end of his paper he appends 'as postscript a table of introspective differences between the two forms of the simple reaction, as taught in the Leipsic institute. *Muscular* (I) Motor attention . . . (III) Reflexlike, spasmic movement. (IV) Simple perception of impression, with previous act of will . . . *Sensorial* (I) Sensory attention . . . (III) Willed, slow movement. (IV) Apperception of impression, with consequent act of will . . .'

10 Bridgeman (1999a, p. 7) correctly notes the critical point. He states: 'Even if both the stimuli and the movements themselves are identical, behavior with a purely instrumental goal might follow different rules from behavior with a communicatory goal.'

11 Skinner (1972, pp. 179–180) points to a related distinction:

> We react to an object in many practical ways because of its color; thus, we pick and eat red apples of a particular variety but not green. It is clear that we can "tell the difference" between red and green, but something more is involved when we say that we *know* that one apple is red and the other green . . . When someone asks about the color of an object which he cannot see, and we tell him it is red, *we* do nothing about the object in any other way . . . Only under verbal contingencies can a speaker respond to an isolated property to which a nonverbal response cannot be made. A response made to the property of an object without responding to the object in any other way is called *abstract*.

12 Neumann (1990b) starts with an obvious but important distinction and an obvious but important question:

> Stimuli that reach the sensory surface may result in perception, or serve to guide action. How are these two potential consequences of sensory stimulation related? (p. 207)

The firmest answer to the perception–action relation question is given in Neumann (1989). In the empirical part of that study he presents a broad range of evidence that, in his view, shows that for vision, the two consequences of stimulation can be, and often are, dissociated in the sense that a given stimulus can specify action parameters in a way that is not (fully) compatible with the experienced mental representation of that stimulus; evidence which suggests that what is done does not square with what is perceived. Neumann (1989) arrives at the theoretical conclusion that *direct parameter specification* is possible (see Section 2.1 for a definition of direct or automatic parameter specification). In his view, the data indicate that it is possible to use visual information for the guidance of action without (at least, before) the experienced mental representation corresponding with this information being established.

13 The exact underlying principle is: "Adjust the curvature of your bicycle's path in proportion to the ratio of your unbalance over the square of your speed" (Miller et al., 1960, p. 87). Most of us do not even know that during cycling we turn the handlebars in the direction we are falling.

14 It is of importance to see that in direct parameter specification tasks visual perception and attention is also involved. The answer to the question of how perception and attention is involved can be found in Neumann (1990a, p. 234):

> In man, property selection for automatic parameter specification has been investigated in various kinds of visually guided behavior, such as controlling body balance . . . pointing to an object . . . car driving . . . hitting a ball . . . and jumping . . .

Neumann (1990a, p. 257) is, however, well aware that

> . . . actions such as walking through a room or driving a car . . . require spatial selection as much as the action of picking an apple does; hence . . . they are under attentional control.

And of course, in the laboratory one has to point at the light, not at the experimenter or at the door, on the road home one has to drive on the right (left) side, not on the left (right), and to get home one has to turn to the left etc., not to the right etc., etc. And, in Neumann's view (1990a, p. 249), this

> . . . attentional selection takes place within the functional framework of [comprehensive and cumulative] internal representations [of the visual environment]; i.e., the internal representation guides selection . . .

So, in actions involving direct parameter specification *not only* direct parameter specification is involved. In these actions two stages have to be distinguished – a first stage concerned with the (attentional) selection of an object or region from within a mental representation and a second stage concerned with the (non-attentional) selection for action by a devoted, action-specific, control structure or skill concerned with direct or automatic parameter specification.

15 The fact that after object selection the required parameters are fixed for reading but not for naming, where a further choice is required, can possibly explain the often reported differences between reading and naming (see, e.g., Fraisse, 1969). However, see also Chapter 6.

16 I neglect here some peculiarities, such as, e.g., that an 0 can be read as a letter and as a digit, and that, e.g., a word like ROT is pronounced differently and means something different in different languages.

17 Just because all types of tasks require object or region selection, Dennett (1992, pp. 328–329) can rightfully explain:

> In general, when subjects comply with their instructions in an experiment, this is seen as unproblematic evidence that they have been able to comply with the instructions because they have *consciously experienced* the relevant stimulus events. That's why the following preparatory instruction would be viewed as nonsensical:
>
> > Whenever you are conscious of the light going on, press the button on the left; whenever the light goes on but you are *not* conscious of it going on, press the button on the right.

How on earth could a subject comply with this? You would be asking the subject to do the impossible: to condition his behavior on occurrences that are inaccessible to him. It would be like saying "raise your hand whenever someone winks at you without your knowing it." An experimenter wouldn't feel the need to insert the adverb "consciously," as in

> Whenever you consciously hear a tone, make a guess

since the standard assumption is that one can't condition one's policies on unconscious experiences, even if such things occur. To adopt the policy

> Whenever x happens, do y

you have to be able to be conscious of x happening.

18 With circular arrays, as used by Eriksen and associates, a different outcome is obtained (see, e.g., Eriksen & Collins, 1969; Eriksen & Rohrbaugh, 1970). With circular arrays the letters are projected on retinal positions of equal acuity and all letters have an equal number of neighbours (see Estes', 1978, explanation in the text). With this variant, the proportions correct as a function of position in the array show nothing of importance; performance is virtually the same at all positions and very few localisation errors are observed. Moreover, accuracy of report declines monotonically from pre-exposure via simultaneous exposure to post-exposure of the indicator (see also Section 7.2).

19 The information processing approach is self-correcting; see also Section 1.3.

20 The causal effect of instructions is, of course, clear in experiments comparing situations with identical stimuli and different instructions. Recently, the importance of the instruction was discovered and investigated in the research field concerned with 'task switching' (see, e.g., Allport et al., 1994; Meiran, 1996, 2000; Monsell et al., 2000; Rogers & Monsell, 1995; Wylie & Allport, 2000). In the experiments, two conditions are compared: (1) a condition in which subjects switch between two tasks on successive trials and (2) a condition in which subjects perform the same task on successive trials. Of course, in this field of research the differences in performance in the two conditions are explained in terms of what distinguishes the two conditions, i.e., in terms of instructed 'switch' and 'no switch'. It is worthwhile to note, however, that only differences in internal performance are explained, not complete internal task performance.

21 For the partial-report bar-probe task the internal representation of the instruction has to explain how subjects can report the letter indicated by the bar marker, not the W-shaped function or the location errors.

22 It is worthwhile to note here that the experimenter makes the action *choice* and that only the action *execution* is left for the subject.

3 The internal representation of the instruction

3.0 Introduction

In experiments in the information processing approach, subjects always receive an instruction and generally perform according to that instruction. For theory, this raises the problem of the implementation, structure, and causal powers of the internal representation of the instruction, i.e., of what I called the instruction-induced action plan. As argued in Section 2.4, this problem *is* the problem of the implementation, structure, and causal powers of the act component of intentionality, of James's (1890/1950) 'mind knowing', and of what I prefer to call the Intending Mind. So, what I have now to look for is an adequate characterisation of 'mind knowing'. What I want to find is a decent 'unit of analysis' for the Intending Mind.

To find an entrance to the solution of this problem, it is of importance to scrutinise the literature and to learn what has been said in the past about the internal effects of verbal task instructions. That task is, however, far beyond my central and peripheral capacities. According to Dewey, in 1896 the cabinets of the science of psychology had already broken under their own dead weight.[1] Therefore, the present chapter can only be concerned with some selected bits and pieces of what has been stated, suggested, or implied about the effect of verbal task instructions. Most evidence comes from and concerns tasks requiring selection within a single eye-fixation and verbal responding. Some additional evidence from unexpected, suspected, and unsuspected sources, is also included. The guided tour of the literature proceeds as follows.

In Section 3.1, we turn to the early systematic, introspective, experimental psychology, the psychology that reigned from about 1880 until 1920. In that psychology, subjects had to describe what they heard, saw, and did. Therefore, from this psychology we can learn what *subjects* had to say about the internal representation and the internal effects of a task instruction. One school, the Wuerzburg school, is of special interest and importance here. That school was explicitly concerned with the implementation and effect of the instruction, and came up with the concept 'determining tendency'.

In Section 3.2, we turn to the objective, behaviourist, experimental psychology, the psychology that flowered from about 1920 until 1960. This psychology mainly used animals as subjects. Of course, the rats and pigeons used did not understand, and therefore did not receive, verbal task instructions. Nevertheless, the animals performed tasks and the theorists attempted to account for task performance. Therefore, this psychology also has something to say of relevance for our problem. An important immediate 'cognitive' successor, Miller et al.'s (1960) theory concerned with 'plans' and 'the structure of behaviour', is also briefly considered.

In Section 3.3, we look at current information processing psychology or cognitive psychology, which started around 1960 and is still booming. In this psychology, subjects perform objective tasks and produce latency distributions and percentages correct as data. The theorists under the investigators use these data for modelling the subject as an information processor. In these information processing models, the structure and the causal effects of the instruction are hidden somewhere. So, from these models we can learn what *theoreticians* have, implicitly or explicitly, to say about the implementation, structure, and causal effects of verbal task instructions.

In Section 3.4, we return to introspection. Turing invented the basic principles of the computer by introspecting how a computation on a sheet of paper is performed. The abundant presence of computers, which perform a great variety of calculations, proves that his introspective analysis was not that far from the mark. For me, what Turing detected and described is of great importance. His introspective observations provide important hints for a systematic and disciplined solution of the problem I am concerned with; the problem of finding a proper characterisation or decent 'unit of analysis' for the Intending Mind.

3.1   Early systematic introspective psychology

In the history of experimental psychology the current information processing approach to perception and cognition is not the only psychology that in its theories consistently neglected the instruction. Prinz (1997b) aptly noticed and showed that the effect of instructions, or more in general and in his words, the issue of the control of action through action goals and/or intentions, forms a major problem for and is dealt with in a highly superficial way in experimental psychology in general. He points out that this problem can already be noticed in Donders' (1868) 'On the Speed of Mental Processes', a paper that was translated in 1969 and served as one of the foundations of modern work on choice reaction tasks. In this seminal work, Donders treated 'voluntary' responses as stimulus-provoked reflexes.

In his attempts to sketch the architecture of the mind, Donders (1868/ 1969) employed a method developed by Von Helmholtz for the measurement of nerve conduction velocity (see Prinz, 1997b). A critically important feature of Von Helmholtz's reaction time method is that it can only be used under conditions where the stimulus is a necessary and sufficient condition for the response to occur, i.e., in situations where the response occurs as a reflex. In Von Helmholtz's physiological work this was certainly the case; an efferent nerve was isolated and stimulated and the time until the response, e.g., a muscle twitch, was measured. Donders used this reaction time method in simple reaction time tasks and choice reaction time tasks for measuring the time required for the execution of mental operations. But, in these tasks, the stimulus was only a necessary and not a sufficient condition for responding. For a response to occur, two conditions had to be fulfilled: there had to be an appropriate stimulus *and* the subject had to be instructed in order to respond in the way required. Donders' experiments required stimuli and instructions. In his theorising, however, Donders had no place for an internal representation of the instruction (or for action goals and/or intentions). In his theoretical interpretations, the response is completely determined by the stimulus.

In the flourishing period of early systematic introspective psychology, which reigned from about 1880 until 1920, there were, however, also invest-igators who clearly recognised that, besides the internal representation of the stimulus, another internal factor is involved in task performance. These investigators had great difficulty in specifying what that internal factor exactly comprised. Nevertheless, a suggestion that repeatedly appears is that this factor is closely related to, and has something to do with, language. Of course, this suggestion is not too surprising given a verbal instruction. Let us have a look at a few examples.

Von Helmholtz was one of the investigators who clearly recognised the importance of the internal representation of the task to be performed. He studied important aspects of the selection of visual information within a single eye fixation; that is, the *internal* selection of visual information in the absence of any usable eye movements (see also Section 2.3). In the experiments, in which he served himself as a subject, he used a

> ... completely darkened field on which was spread a page with large printed letters ... the observer saw nothing but a slightly illuminated pinhole in the paper. He fixed his gaze rigidly upon it ... [Then an] electric discharge illuminated the printed page for an indivisible instant ... Eye movements of a measurable magnitude could not be executed within the duration of the spark ... I found it possible to decide in advance which part of the ... field ... I wanted to perceive, and then actually recognized ... groups of letters in that region of the field ... With a subsequent electric discharge I could direct my perception to another section of the field, while always fixating the pinhole, and then read a group of letters there.
>
> These observations demonstrated, so it seems to me, that by a volunt-ary kind of intention, even without eye movements, and without changes of accommodation, one can concentrate attention on the sensation from a particular part of our peripheral nervous system and at the same time exclude attention from all other parts.
>
> (Von Helmholtz, 1894; Warren & Warren, 1968, translators)

For Von Helmholtz, the finding that '. . . our attention is quite independent of the position and accommodation of the eyes . . . is one of the most important observations for a future theory of attention' (Von Helmholtz, quoted in James, 1890/1950, p. 438). And, according to Von Helmholtz, besides the stimulus, a 'voluntary kind of intention' is involved. That 'intention' effectuates that one can 'concentrate attention' and 'direct perception'.

In relation to another type of selection experiments, Von Helmholtz elaborates:

> The natural tendency of attention when left to itself is to wander to ever new things; and so soon as the interest of its object is over, so soon as nothing new is to be noticed there, it passes, in spite of our will, to something else. If we wish to keep it upon one and the same object, we must seek constantly to find out something new about the latter, especially if other powerful impressions are attracting us away.
>
> . . . *we can set ourselves new questions about the object, so that a new interest in it arises, and then the attention will remain riveted.* The relation of attention to will is, then, less one of immediate than of mediate control.
>
> (Von Helmholtz, Physiol. Optik, par. 32,
> in James, 1890/1950, pp. 422–423)

It is hard to believe, however, that, after a couple of trials, subjects in a standard selection experiment are still really interested in, and really try to find out something new about, the stimuli they receive. Nevertheless, even when the interest is over, they perform according to the instruction. Is some kind of verbal activity, some neutral kind of 'asking and answering questions', a viable description of the process that an instruction induces? (Lots of people ask questions about issues they are not really interested in, for instance: "How are *you* today?".)

Angell and Moore (1896) also clearly recognised the importance of the instruction. In their research they used variants of Lange's (1888) task, in which subjects had to press a single response key in reaction to a single auditory (or visual) stimulus under two different instructions, a 'sensorial' instruction and a 'muscular' instruction (see Section 2.2 for Lange's tasks).[2] They explain:

> Not to go into too great detail, the process of attention in its essential outlines in, say, the auditory–hand reaction, appears something as follows: As the reagent [the subject] receives his instructions for the reaction, he formulates in imagination what he is going to do. This formulation, the getting in mind what he is to do, is his attention to the act. Whatever may be the detail of imagery involved in this formulation, it involves primarily the coördination of two groups of incoming

sensations, one from the ear, the other from the hand, started by the operator's [the experimenter's] descriptions.

The 'reaction' as meaning the whole act to be performed is not the mere response of the hand to the ear, but the act of attention in coördinating the incoming stimuli from *both* the hand and the ear.

(Angell & Moore, 1896, in Vanderplas, 1966, p. 168)

So, in their view, besides the stimulus, a 'formulation in imagination', for getting in mind what to do and for coordinating ear and hand, is also involved.

In the work of early systematic introspective psychology more incidental remarks about instructions and the internal effects of instructions hinting at the involvement of language – 'asking and answering questions', 'formulation in imagination' – can be found. For our purposes, however, the systematic work of the Wuerzburg School of Kuelpe, Watt, and Ach, around the turn of the nineteenth century, is especially highly relevant.[3] That school attempted to study thought with introspection.

The experimental study of thought by the Wuerzburg School resulted in two important, connected, discoveries. First, there was the discovery of the paucity of conscious content in thought or the discovery that thought is not really accessible to introspective observation (image-less thought; *unanschauliche*/impalpable, and therefore indescribable states that fell outside the then accepted categories of sensation, image, and feeling). Second, there was the discovery of the importance of tasks; that is, the discovery of the importance of the instructions given to the subject in an experiment and of the subject's preparation for the task to be performed.

Both Kuelpe (1904) and Watt (1904) demonstrated that tasks were at least as important as the stimuli in determining a subject's response. In their experiments, a number of different tasks were presented to the subject in the form of (auditory) instructions in the same way as a number of different stimuli were presented in the form of (written) nonsense syllables or words. In the present context, Kuelpe's (1904) *Versuche ueber Abstraktion* are the most relevant.

Kuelpe (1904) presented his subjects with brief-duration displays containing differently coloured three-letter nonsense syllables. Prior to stimulus exposure, the subject received either one of four tasks or no task at all (the tasks were: name the colours and their approximate positions, name the spatial arrangement of the syllables, name the total number of visible letters, and name the individual letters and their approximate positions). The tasks were labelled with a catchword. When a task instruction was given, subjects had first to answer according to that instruction but were subsequently also questioned about the other stimulus properties. The main finding was that the subjects were substantially more accurate and complete about the stimulus aspect emphasised in the instruction (and reported first) than about the other three stimulus aspects. Later replications with improved paradigms showed essentially the same results (see Haber, 1966, for an overview).

In his attempt to describe what exactly happens with the instruction, Kuelpe (1904) distinguishes between what occurs before stimulus exposure and what happens during and after exposure. The introspective reports revealed that the subjects had something to tell about the period of getting ready (preparation) but not about the subsequent processes dealing with the stimulus and the reaction itself (execution). With regard to the preparation, Kuelpe remarks:

> The preparation when there was a task consisted most of the time of an acoustical-motorical repetition of the catchword, with one of my subjects only in a passive expectation and approximately in such a way that she knew what had to be done . . .
>
> (Kuelpe, 1904, p. 65; my translation)

So, Kuelpe also hints at the involvement of language.

With regard to the execution Kuelpe remarks:

> It is not possible to give a nearer description of the execution of the task . . . The determination of the data relevant for the task was accomplished first . . . One subject declared that for her it seemed as if the process of determination was completely de-coupled from the process of visual perception. Another said more than once that she had seen/ known more than she was later capable to report . . .
>
> (Kuelpe, 1904, p. 66; my translation)

So, about the execution not much can be said. It is nevertheless interesting to note that in this quotation Kuelpe finds it worthwhile to mention that one subject reports a 'process of determination' that is separate from a 'process of visual perception'; that is, she distinguishes between two internal processes, between something like James's (1890/1950) 'mind knowing' and 'thing known' or between something like my Intending Mind and Visual Perception.

On the basis of the thought experiments in Watt (1904), in which words were presented and subjects had to perform under a variety of instructions such as 'name an example', 'name a part', and 'name another of the same class', Watt (1905–1906) tries to answer the question:

> How does any one particular reaction come about and not another? The *first influence* at work on the subject is the given *task*. This he hears spoken by the experimenter, and generally repeats to himself in words, *e.g.*, "find a part!" "name an example!" or he may exemplify the experiment to himself, *e.g.*, "animal-dog," and so on. The scanty description of the preparation for the experiment given in the subject's account of it does not help us to form a very clear idea of what the process itself is.
>
> (Watt, 1905–1906, in Mandler & Mandler, 1964, p. 191)

So, again, the results indicated that in task preparation some verbal activity was reported.[4] Task preparation was efficient, but how this preparation was further accomplished and especially how this preparation was effective during the execution of the task remained obscure. About the execution of the task nothing was reported.

Despite this paucity of introspective data, Ach (1905) made a next step. He firmly and decidedly moved the external tasks inside, where from then on they did their work as 'determining tendencies'. Exactly the Wuerzburg atmosphere made this outside → inside move possible and acceptable. The investigation of thought had already led to indescribable dispositions of consciousness (image-less thought). So, in Wuerzburg there was nothing revolutionary about an indescribable, task-derived determining tendency, given the paucity of conscious content in thought and the inaccessibility to introspective observation of higher mental processes in general.

In a further elaboration of how tasks exert their effects, Ach (1905) distinguishes two (re)presentations, a 'goal-presentation' and a 'referent-presentation' and states:

> Influences, arising from the goal-presentation and directed toward the referent-presentation, which determine the course of events so as to accord with the goal-presentation, are called determining tendencies.
>
> (Ach, 1905, in Mandler & Mandler, 1964, p. 206)

He clarifies:

> It is due to determining tendencies that, of all the tendencies readied by the perception of the stimulus, those will become reinforced to over-valence which are associatively coordinated with a presentation corresponding to the given intention . . .
>
> (Ach, 1905, in Mandler & Mandler, 1964, p. 206)[5]

And he concludes:

> *Thus, the ordered and goal-directed course of mental happening is the effect of determining tendencies.* The independence of goal-directed mental happening from incidental external stimuli, and from the customary associative course of presentations, is due to the influence of these determining tendencies . . .
>
> (Ach, 1905, in Mandler & Mandler, 1964, p. 207)

For Ach and for us, the distinction between a 'goal-presentation', 'intention', or 'goal-directed mental happening' on the one hand, and a 'referent-presentation', 'perception of the stimulus', or 'incidental external stimuli' on the other, is of great theoretical importance. For Ach the distinction is of importance because it allows him to define 'determining tendencies' as 'influences from the goal-presentation directed toward the referent-presentation'.

For us, the distinction is of importance because here we meet Brentano's (1874) act–object distinction and James's (1890/1950) 'mind knowing'–'thing known' distinction again in explicit form, albeit in a different terminology.

In Kuelpe (1904), the expression 'determining tendencies' is still nowhere to be found. Some 10 years later, however, Kuelpe (1912, 1922) accepts, agrees with, and propagates Ach's theorising.

> The subject receives a task, a direction or instruction as to the point of view he must adopt toward the presented stimulus . . . All such tasks, if they are willingly undertaken and remembered, exercise a great determining force upon the behavior of the subject. This force is called the determining tendency.
>
> (Kuelpe, 1922, in Mandler & Mandler, 1964, p. 215)

With regard to the tasks and their internal equivalents, Kuelpe (1912, 1922) looks back and sketches where exactly, in his view, the theoretical renewal of the Wuerzburg school was.

> . . . No psychological experiments are imaginable without tasks! The tasks must, therefore, be considered just as important an experimental condition as the apparatus and the stimuli that it presents. A variation in the task is at least as important an experimental procedure as a change in external experimental conditions.
>
> This importance of the task and its effects on the structure and course of mental events could not be explained with the tools of association psychology . . . The force with which a determining tendency acts is not only greater than the familiar reproductive tendencies, it also derives from a different source and its effectiveness is not tied to associative relations.
>
> (Kuelpe, 1922, in Mandler & Mandler, 1964, p. 216)

Indeed, the tasks must be considered just as important an experimental condition as the apparatus and the stimuli that it presents (see Section 2.3). And indeed, a theoretical elaboration in terms of two different 'sources', two interacting representations, is highly likely to be the right way to go (see Section 1.4). But how to conceive and model the content and structure of the 'goal-presentation' ('some verbal activity'?) and how to conceive and model the content and the structure of the 'referent-presentation' (the stimulus as perceived?)? And how do 'determining tendencies', interpreted as associations, perform the required explanatory job? Here we clearly reach the limits of early introspective psychology.

In this context, it is worthwhile to return briefly to James (1890/1950). In Section 1.2, we saw that James faced great difficulties with characterising, in introspective terms, the central mechanism of attention ('reinforcing imagination', 'anticipatory thinking', etc.). The work of the Wuerzburg School makes clear why James was faced here with such a difficult job. The extensive experimental research of this school showed that these central mechanisms are not really accessible to introspective observation (image-less thought).

At this point, it is also worthwhile to see that the Wuerzburg School tested James's (1890/1950) general empirical views with regard to selection with adequately controlled and standardised introspective laboratory experiments. The members of the Wuerzburg School must have been convinced that what James's generous divination had failed to do, their spying and scraping, their deadly tenacity and almost diabolic cunning, would doubtless some day bring about.

> . . . James laid down as an essential characteristic of consciousness – the fact that it is selective, that it "chooses." . . . It is plain that only a small part of the potentially effective world of stimulus comes to consciousness, and the principle of selection is, James thought, "relevance". Hence, consciousness selects so that it tends to run in logical grooves, and trains of thought arrive at rational ends . . . Of special interest to us is that James in this concept of relevance anticipates the Wuerzburg concept – Watt, Ach, Kuelpe – of set and determining tendency.
>
> (Boring, 1950, p. 514)

And, as we have now seen, James's empirical views passed the experimental tests. The attitude towards cognition the Wuerzburg School ultimately arrived at, is indeed James's thoroughgoing dualism. It supposes two elements, a 'goal-presentation' ('mind knowing') and a 'referent-presentation' ('thing known') and treats them as irreducible. But the details of what I prefer to call the Intending Mind and Visual Perception still remain to be filled in.

3.2 Behaviourism

Behaviourism reigned from about 1920 until 1960. Positively stated, the basic conviction of the behaviourists, Watson, Tolman, Lashley, and Skinner, to name a few, was that it was profitable and interesting to study behaviour for its own sake. Negatively stated, the basic conviction was that introspection did not work and was therefore useless. The struggle with the introspectively inaccessible 'determining tendencies' in the Wuerzburg School was one of the factors that led to the shift from subjective introspection of what was experienced to objective observation of what was done.

> It seems strange to say that Kuelpe's Wuerzburg school of imageless thought, the school which argued so vigorously for "systematic experimental introspection" . . . played a rôle in the history of objective psychology; yet, such was the case . . . Kuelpe's final judgment about the work of that school was that contents of thought are conscious but impalpable (*unanschaulich*), that they do not stand up to introspection

but can be described in retrospection. What is, however, of still more importance . . . is the finding of Watt and Ach that the key to thought and action lies in the predetermination (in the set, *Aufgabe* or attitude) which carries on through the thought or action, determining its course without remaining conscious. Really the most important contribution of the Wuerzburg school was the discovery that the determining tendencies which control thought and action do not appear as such in consciousness and must be known by other means than introspection.

(Boring, 1950, p. 640)

And, observation of behaviour is certainly another means, or so at least it seems.[6]

At first sight, it might seem that for my problem, the problem of the implementation, structure, and causal powers of the instruction, the behaviourists with their animal research do not have much of relevance to tell. In looking back, Watson (1936, p. 276) even remarked:

I never wanted to use human subjects. I hated to serve as a subject. I didn't like the stuffy, artificial instructions given to subjects. I always was uncomfortable and acted unnaturally. With animals I was at home. I felt that, in studying them, I was keeping close to biology with my feet on the ground. More and more the thought presented itself: Can't I find out by watching their behavior everything that the other students are finding out by using *O*'s [subjects].

Nevertheless, in his 'Psychology as the Behaviorist Views It', Watson (1913) had something of interest about instructions to say. In Watson's view

The man and the animal should be placed as nearly as possible under the same experimental conditions. Instead of feeding or punishing the human subject, we should ask him to respond by setting a second apparatus until standard and control offered no basis for a differential response. Do I lay myself open to the charge here that I am using introspection? My reply is not at all . . . be it understood that I am merely using this second method as an abridged behavior method.

(Watson, 1913, in Vanderplas, 1966, p. 80)

In a footnote, Watson adds:

I should prefer to look upon this abbreviated method, where the human subject is told in words, for example, to equate two stimuli; or to state in words whether a given stimulus is present or absent, etc., as the *language method* in behavior. It in no way changes the status in experimentation. The method becomes possible merely by virtue of the fact that . . . the experimenter and his animal have systems of . . . signs (language), any one of which may stand for a habit belonging to the repertoire both of the experimenter and his subject. To make the data obtained by the language method virtually the whole of behavior – or to attempt to mould all of the data obtained by other methods in terms of the one which has by all odds the most limited range – is putting the cart before the horse with a vengeance.

(Watson, 1913, in Vanderplas, 1966, p. 80)

These remarks are of interest, because they show that Watson makes a distinction between something like 'good' 'animal' tasks and 'bad' 'language' tasks, a distinction not unlike my 'act' task – 'report' task distinction, and warns against attempting to mould all data in terms of one (see also Note 7).

In the behaviourist era, the determining tendencies were not completely forgotten. In 'A Behavioristic View of Purpose', Perry (1921, p. 97) writes:

The central feature of this conception of human behavior is that general state of the organism which has been termed a determining tendency. The organism as a whole is for a time preoccupied with a certain task which absorbs its energy and appropriates its mechanisms.

In 'A Critical Review of the Concept of Set in Contemporary Experimental Psychology', Gibson (1941) presented a thorough analysis of the concept of determining tendency and related it to attention, intention, and expectation. And Lashley (1951, p. 117) in 'The Problem of Serial Order in Behavior', finds in determining tendencies a good start for his theoretical speculations (see later).

Here, however, I am not concerned with types of tasks that have to be distinguished or with the issue of what happened with determining tendencies in the behaviouristic period. There is another, closely related, point in the theorising of some of the behaviourists that has to be mentioned here. That point is that, just like Brentano, James, Kuelpe, and Ach, these theorists recognised that two different types of internal 'processes', 'variables', 'systems', or 'representations' have to be postulated that, in interaction, explain the observed behaviour. Tolman's (1932, 1959) and Lashley's (1951) theoretical work serves here to illustrate this point.

In his *Purposive Behavior in Animals and Man*, Tolman (1932) was concerned with the explanation of *molar* behaviour, the total action of a whole organism. In subsequent papers, he elaborated that explanation and summarised the results of his thinking in 'Principles of Purposive Behavior' (Tolman, 1959). His system is far too complex to be summarised here. The essence of his view is that behaviour, the consequence C, is a function of the situation and other antecedent causes, the antecedents A, and that between A and C there may be *intervening variables*, hypothetical constructs that Tolman invented to fill in the correlations observed between C and A. Tolman explains:

> My intervening variables are generally speaking mere temporarily
> believed-in, inductive, more or less qualitative generalizations which
> categorize and sum up for me (act as mnemonic symbols for) various
> empirically found relationships. They do not lead to any then-and-there
> precise further quantitative predictions. They do, however (when mixed
> with a healthy brew of intuition, common sense, and phenomenology),
> lead to suggestions for further empirical relations to be tested.
>
> (Tolman, 1959, p. 97)[7]

In the present context, it is important to know that Tolman (1959) divides
his intervening variables into two groups. One group contains perceptions,
representations, expectations, and valences, particular internal events which
are conceived to be present only on the individual occasion (p. 107). The
other group consists of means–end readinesses.

> These acquired dispositions or readinesses can be thought of as
> dispositional sets for certain types of (stimulus – response > stimulus)-
> sequences or for certain types of (stimulus – stimulus)-sequence.
>
> (Tolman, 1959, p. 105)

While Tolman (1959) struggles with the exact specification of means–end
readinesses (also called beliefs), and especially with the difference between
beliefs and expectations, the distinction between means–end readinesses
on the one hand and perceptions, representations, expectations and valences
on the other is nevertheless of fundamental importance. For Tolman, the
means–end readiness introduces an order in time, a temporal sequence, that
the other group of intervening variables lacks. For us the distinction is of
importance because here something like a distinction between two representations seems to emerge, one concerned with 'what is here now' and one
concerned with 'what can be done'.

Lashley, a physiological psychologist and student of Watson, worked for
several years on the 'logical and orderly arrangement of thought and action',
i.e., on temporal aspects of internal and external behaviour. He described
the insights he arrived at in 'The problem of serial order in behavior' (Lashley,
1951). His general and central point is

> . . . that the input is never into a quiescent or static system, but always
> into a system which is already excited and organized. In the intact
> organism, behavior is the result of interaction of this background of
> excitation with input from any designated stimulus. Only when we can
> state the general characteristics of this background of excitation, can we
> understand the effects of a given input.
>
> (Lashley, 1951, p. 112)

So, what we encounter here is a clear distinction between 'background of
excitation' and 'input from any designated stimulus'. And, in Lashley's view,

the determining tendency of the Wuerzburg school provides a good starting point for understanding this background of excitation (1951, p. 117).

In the present context, Lashley's speculations about the interaction of a spatial and a temporal system are of particular importance. His discussion is primarily concerned with memory, but is readily applicable to vision. Here is how Lashley (1951, p. 128) introduces his space–time problem:

> Since memory traces are, we believe, in large part static and persist simultaneously, it must be assumed that they are spatially differentiated. Nevertheless, reproductive memory appears almost invariably as a temporal sequence, either as a succession of words or of acts. Even descriptions of visual imagery (the supposed simultaneous reproductive memory in sensory terms) are generally descriptions of sequences, of temporal reconstructions from very fragmentary and questionable visual elements . . . The translation from the spatial distribution of memory traces to temporal sequence seems to be a fundamental aspect of the problem of serial order.[8]

And of course, the translation from the spatial distribution in visual perception to the temporal sequence in reporting and acting seems to be a fundamental aspect of the problem of how people use their visual perception in the performance of tasks.

Lashley (1951, p. 129) speculates:

> There are indications that one neural system might be held in [a] state of partial excitation while it is scanned by another. Here is an example. A series of four to six numbers is heard: 3–7–2–9–4 . . . While it is retained in this unstable way . . . the order of the numbers can be reassorted: 3–7–2–9–4, 3–2–7–9–4, 4–9–2–7–3, and the like. It is as if, in this case, a rhythmic alternation can suppress alternate items, or a direction of arousal can be applied to the partially excited system . . . In attempts to play a melody backward, we have a further illustration. I find that I can do it only by visualizing the music spatially and then reading it backward. I cannot auditorily transform even "Yankee Doodle" into its inverse without some such process, but it is possible to get a spatial representation of the melody and then to scan the spatial representation. The scanning of a spatial arrangement seems definitely to determine, in such cases, the order of procedure. Two assumptions are implied by this. First, the assumption is that the memory traces are associated, not only with other memory traces, but also with [a] system of space coordinates . . . Second, the assumption is that these space characters of the memory trace can be scanned by some other level of the coordinating system and so transformed into succession.

In general, he concludes:

> This is as far as I have been able to go toward a theory of serial order in action. Obviously, it is inadequate ... such determining tendencies as the relation of attribute to object, which gives the order of adjective and noun, do not seem to be analyzable into any sort of spatial structure or for that matter, into any consistent relationship.
>
> (Lashley, 1951, pp. 129–130)

And for the selective mechanism of grammatical form in speech he adds:

> The real problem, however, is the nature of the selective mechanism by which the particular acts are picked out in this scanning process, and to this problem I have no answer.
>
> (Lashley, 1951, p. 130)

Clearly, postulating two 'neural systems', 'levels', or representations, one spatial (memory, imagery, or perception) and one temporal (a scanning device or a direction of arousal) is an important step. And clearly, this important step is a step in the direction of recognising something like Brentano's (1874) distinction between 'content' and 'act', James's (1890/ 1950) distinction between 'thing known' and 'mind knowing', and Ach's (1905) distinction between 'referent-presentation' and 'goal-presentation' – the distinction I prefer to indicate with the terms Intending Mind and Visual Perception. But again, specifying what that spatial system consists of, and especially specifying what that temporal system consists of, how it is structured, how it works and how it interacts with the spatial entity, is quite another.

At the end of the behaviourist era and the beginning of the cognitive era in experimental psychology, the distinction between two processes, representations, or systems, one spatial and one temporal, introduced and elaborated in behaviourism by Tolman and Lashley, showed up in a very explicit form. In their *Plans and the Structure of Behavior*, Miller et al. (1960) distinguished between a spatial Image and a temporal Plan.

> The Image is all the accumulated, organized knowledge that the organism has about itself and its world. The Image consists of a great deal more than imagery, of course. What we have in mind when we use this term is essentially the same kind of private representation that other cognitive theorists have demanded. It includes everything the organism has learned – his values as well as his facts – organized by whatever concepts, images, or relations he has been able to master. (pp. 17–18)

> A Plan is any hierarchical process in the organism that can control the order in which a sequence of operations is to be performed. A Plan is, for an organism, essentially the same as a program for a computer ... (p. 16)

In their chapter 'The unit of analysis', Miller et al. (1960) explain that their plans are structured in such a way that the interaction of a plan with an image results in fixed, recognisable units of behaviour. The structures in the plans and the units of behaviour are called Test-Operate-Test-Exit units or TOTE units; the unit starts with a test, T, which assesses whether an operation, O, has to be performed. If so, the operation is performed and a next test is performed. If not, the plan and the action are terminated: Exit, E. In this theory, TOTE units of a control structure or plan, in interaction with the image, produce TOTE units as units of behaviour.[9]

When Tote units are written as >T>O>T>E> units, the question arises of where the arrows, >, stand for; the question of what could flow along the arrows. Miller et al. (1960, pp. 27–29) discuss three alternatives – energy, information, and control. They remark:

> A third level of abstraction, however, is extremely important for the ideas we shall discuss. It is the notion that what flows over the arrows . . . is an intangible something called *control*. Or perhaps we should say that the arrow indicates only succession. This concept appears most frequently in the discussion of computing machines . . . But the idea is certainly not limited to computers.
>
> (Miller et al., 1960, p. 28)

Clearly, for the problem of how people use their visual perception in the performance of tasks, a 'plan' that controls and interacts with an 'image' is certainly an important theoretical proposal. Moreover, with their TOTEs, Miller et al. propose a decent unit of analysis for plans and for behaviour. But is a plan for an organism essentially the same as a program for a computer? And what do the plans for 'report' tasks, 'read' and 'name' tasks, look like? What is tested and what is the operation when the task is 'Name the letter indicated by the bar marker' and what is tested and what is the operation when the task is 'Name the colour of the square'? Especially for the 'report' tasks, but also for the 'act' tasks, the details of Intending Mind and Visual Perception still remain to be filled in.

Here it is still of interest to know that, with Miller et al. (1960), the importance of language, hinted at in early introspective psychology but neglected by mainstream behaviourism, reappears on the theoretical scene. Miller et al. (p. 38) explain:

> In lower animals it appears that the pattern of their behavior is normally constructed more or less fortuitously by the environment . . . That is to say, the environment provides stimuli that "release" the next stage of the animal's activity . . .
>
> As we ascend the evolutionary scale we find in mammals an increasing complexity in the kind of tests the animals can perform. In man we have the unique capacity for creating and manipulating symbols, and

when that versatility is used to assign names to TOTE units, it becomes possible for him to use language in order to rearrange the symbols and to form new Plans. We have every reason to believe that man's verbal activities are very intimately related to his planning abilities. And, because human Plans are so often verbal, they can be communicated, a fact of crucial importance in the evolution of our social adjustments to one another.

Experimenters in the information processing approach working with human subjects are well aware of the importance of language. They provide verbal instructions because they know that their verbal activities are very intimately related to what subjects plan and do in the standard laboratory experiments. Let us now look at how the theorists in the information processing approach deal with this knowledge in their information processing theories, in their models of the human information processor.

3.3   The information processing approach

The information processing approach to perception and cognition began in about 1960 and is up to now the dominant theoretical stream in experimental psychology. The approach tries to infer the internal structure and functioning of a behaving organism from the overt behaviour of that organism, so that it becomes possible to explain the organism's behaviour in terms of its internal structure and functioning (see Section 1.3). The inferred internal structure and functioning are often represented in a flowchart, a boxes and arrows model of the human information processor. In one way or another in the representations (in the boxes) and/or the processes (the arrows between the boxes) in these models, the internal representation of the instruction is incorporated. So, to find information about the implementation, structure, and causal powers of the internal representation of the instruction, we have to look at the models produced by the information processing approach.

Broadbent (1958) was one of the first to present an information processing theory as looked for by the information processing approach. In the last chapter of his pioneering work *Perception and Communication*, he offered a detailed account of observed behaviour in, e.g., 'shadowing' tasks and 'split-span' tasks, in which the subjects had to select one of two auditory information streams. In the theory, Broadbent brought together his main theoretical conclusions with regard to the processing and selection of auditory information. He summarised that theory in a flowchart and in a summary of principles.[10]

The first principle in Broadbent's list of principles reads: 'A nervous system acts to some extent as a single communication channel,' so that it is meaningful to regard it as having a limited capacity.' (Broadbent, 1958, p. 297). This 'limited-capacity channel' is, as shown in the flow chart

Figure 3.1 The core of Broadbent's filter model. (Adapted from Broadbent, 1958, p. 289, fig. 7.)

in Figure 3.1, the core of Broadbent's information processing model. Its function is to categorise, recognise, or identify the information. This core is protected by a 'selective filter', which has the ability to select a 'sensory channel' (in a 'short-term store' or 'buffer') on the basis of simple 'physical' properties – e.g., information from the left or from the right, or with a certain pitch or loudness – and to allow all information with this property access to the limited-capacity channel. How this 'selective filter' knows what it has to select and how to 'set' itself, and how the 'limited-capacity channel' knows what categories to apply, remains obscure in the theory. Stated otherwise, in this model we miss an instruction-derived internal representation of the instruction that ensures that the system is performing the task-relevant internal and external operations. This state of affairs, of course, invites the introduction of a 'subject' or an 'agent'.

Broadbent's (1958) main concern was with the 'filtering' tasks I briefly described above. In the present context, it is of importance to know that soon afterwards, a number of theorists recognised that not all selection tasks are 'filtering' tasks. They emphasised that different selection tasks have to be distinguished and that in these tasks different selection mechanisms are operative. Treisman (1969), for instance, distinguished four types of tasks: selection of inputs, selection of targets, selection of attributes, and selection of outputs. However, it can be argued that tasks requiring selection of inputs and tasks requiring selection of targets are closely related, and also that tasks requiring selection of attributes and tasks requiring selection of outputs are closely related (see, e.g., Kahneman, 1973; Phaf, Van der Heijden, & Hudson, 1990). So, it can be argued that only two main types of tasks have to be distinguished, something like 'input selection' tasks (with selection performed by 'settings' of the 'selective filter' in Broadbent's model) and 'output selection' tasks (with selection performed by the 'categories' in the 'limited-capacity channel' in Broadbent's model). Broadbent (1970, 1971) proposed exactly this distinction. Moreover, and of great importance in the present context, Broadbent explicitly recognised the importance of instructions.

The title of Broadbent's (1970) paper and of the relevant section in Broadbent's (1971) book is 'Stimulus set and response set: Two kinds of selective attention'. In terms of his two-stage conceptualisation, Broadbent (1971, p. 177) explains:

... subjects may, when the experimental situation allows it, use either of two processes for selecting material for transfer from the buffer to subsequent stages. One process corresponds to what we have been calling filtering, and one to what we have been calling pigeon-holing ... In the case of perceptual selection, we may ... treat them as equivalent to stimulus set and response set. Filtering or stimulus set is the selection of certain items for analysis and response, on the basis of some common characteristic possessed by the desired stimuli. Pigeon-holing or response set is the selection of certain classes of response (category states) as having a high priority for occurrence even if the evidence in their favour is not especially high. In concrete terms, stimulus set is obtained by the instruction "Listen to this voice and repeat whatever it says, regardless of any other sounds you hear". Response set is obtained by the instruction "Listen to this medley of voices and repeat any digits you may hear". The first instruction controls the source of the stimuli controlling response, but not the vocabulary used in response; the second controls the vocabulary of responses but not the source of stimuli.

So, here we have different tasks and different instructions that control what task is going to be performed![11]

Of course, the distinction between 'stimulus set' and 'response set' is not only applicable to auditory selection tasks (see Broadbent, 1970, 1971). With visual information, 'stimulus set' is investigated with a task instruction like 'Name the upper row of letters, not the lower row' (from a display containing two rows of letters) or 'Name the red digits, not the black ones' (from a display with red and black digits). 'Response set' is investigated with a task instruction like 'Name the digits, not the letters' (from a display containing digits and letters) or 'Name the vowels, not the consonants' (from a display containing vowels and consonants).

According to this 'stimulus set – response set' analysis, Kuelpe's (1904) tasks (see Section 3.2) are classified as 'response set' tasks and Von Helmholtz's (1894) task and Averbach and Coriell's (1961) task (see Sections 3.1 and 2.3) as 'stimulus set' tasks (see Broadbent, 1970, p. 54; however, see also Kahneman, 1973). Possibly, as a first approximation, there is not very much wrong with this classification of tasks. Broadbent, however, also held that 'stimulus set' (or 'filtering') was sufficient for performing 'stimulus set' tasks and that 'response set' (or 'pigeon-holing') was sufficient for performing 'response set' tasks. Remember, he postulated 'Two kinds of selective attention', one for each type of task and stated '... subjects may ... use either of two processes for selecting material ...' (see the quotation above).

This interpretation in terms of two kinds of attention, one for each type of task, is, however, very difficult to defend. For instance, what about the subjects in Averbach and Coriell's (1961) task? These subjects not only selected stimuli; they also named (shape-derived) letters, not colours, sizes, or positions, so a response set was also involved. And what, for instance, about the subjects in Kuelpe's (1904) task? These subjects not only selected responses; they also derived their colour responses from the nonsense syllables, not from the background or from the border or the rest of the visual field, so a stimulus set was also involved. (See Van der Heijden, 1992, for a review of this 'stimulus set' – 'response set' theorising.)

The point that in all these selection tasks at least two selective operations – 'two kinds of selective attention' – are involved was clearly recognised by Treisman (1960, 1964). She proposed an information processing and selection theory with two simultaneously operating selection mechanisms; a selective filter, with about the same properties as Broadbent's filter, and a set of 'central structures', with variable thresholds reflecting importance or relevance. Unfortunately, this theory was never really seriously considered (however, see Broadbent, 1971).

Subsequently, Kahneman and Treisman (1984; see also Kahneman, 1973, p. 69) again emphasised that the distinction between 'stimulus set' or 'filtering' tasks and 'response set' or 'pigeon-holing' tasks is not as straightforward as was initially thought. They write that, for example, with a stimulus containing a small, blue disk at the left and a large, red square at the right and the task instruction 'Name the colour of the square',

> ... two distinct functions ... are controlled by different aspects of the information presented ... : *stimulus choice*, the segregation of relevant items from irrelevant ones, must be guided by some identifying property ... ; *response choice* is controlled by other properties ...
> (Kahneman & Treisman, 1984, p. 31)[12]

So, within such a task, two 'choices' have to be distinguished, one concerned with the 'defining attribute' (the 'square' in the example) and the other with the 'reported attribute' (the 'colour' in the example) (see also Duncan, 1985, for this distinction).

Not very much later, the correctness of the point of view that in (nearly) all visual selection tasks (at least) two different selective operations are involved was forcefully demonstrated by Bundesen (1990) with a mathematical model of visual selective attention, and by Phaf et al. (1990) with a connectionistic model of selective attention in vision. The force of both demonstrations derives from the fact that both models had to produce specific responses – Bundesen's mathematics had to produce responses like 'e', 'z', and 'f', and Phaf et al.'s connections had to come up with answers like 'red', 'blue', and 'green'. So, with these models, sets of required selective operations could not be hidden behind sequences of words.

For ease of exposition it is, for the moment, appropriate to regard Bundesen's (1990) mathematical model as being especially concerned with 'stimulus set' or 'object selection' tasks, e.g., tasks with the instruction: 'Name the red letters, not the blue ones'. In Bundesen's terms:

The theory contains two mechanisms of attention: a mechanism for selection of elements and a mechanism for selection of categories. Following Broadbent (1971), I refer to a selection of elements as *filtering* and to selection of categories as *pigeonholing*.

(Bundesen, 1990, p. 525)

And, in this mathematical model, only the combined operation of filtering ('stimulus set'), selecting elements or inputs, and pigeon-holing ('response set'), selecting categories or responses, leads to performance that is in accord with the (implemented or simulated) task instruction.

Also for ease of exposition, it is, for the moment, appropriate to regard Phaf et al.'s (1990) connectionist model as being especially concerned with 'response set' or 'attribute selection' tasks, e.g., tasks with the instruction: 'Name the colours, not the forms'. In Phaf et al.'s terms:

. . . two selective processes and their corresponding mechanisms may be necessary and sufficient to perform selective attention tasks in vision: (1) object selection controlling the source of stimuli and (2) attribute selection controlling the vocabulary of responses. One mechanism is needed for object selection; we call this mechanism *object set*. The other is needed for attribute selection; we call this mechanism *attribute set*. They cooperate in nearly all selective attention tasks.

(Phaf et al., 1990, p. 278)

Again, in this connectionist model, only the combined operation of object set ('stimulus set'), selecting objects or inputs, and attribute set ('response set'), selecting attributes or responses, leads to performance that is in accord with the (implemented or simulated) task instruction.[13]

Despite the chaotic terminology we are now confronted with, it is not too difficult to sketch in broad lines what the common basis is of Bundesen's (1990) successful mathematical model and Phaf et al.'s (1990) successful connectionist model. Figure 3.2 presents what I regard as the essence of both models. In the figure, Visual Perception is modelled with a set of dedicated maps or modules (see, e.g., Schneider, 1999; Treisman, 1988; Van der Heijden, 1992; Wolfe, 1996, for similar models). Information enters the information processing system in an Input Map (IN). From there the information is sent on to a Colour Map, (C), where colour information is made explicit, to a Shape Map, (S), where the shapes are made explicit, and to a Position Map, (P), where the positions are made explicit. Information for responding is collected in an Output Module, (O). In Figure 3.2 it is assumed that the system is confronted with a stimulus with a large, red square at the right and a small, blue disk at the left. So, C has codes for red (at the right) and blue (at the left), S has codes for large square (at the right) and small disk (at the left) and P has codes that indicate that the left position is occupied and that the right position is occupied.

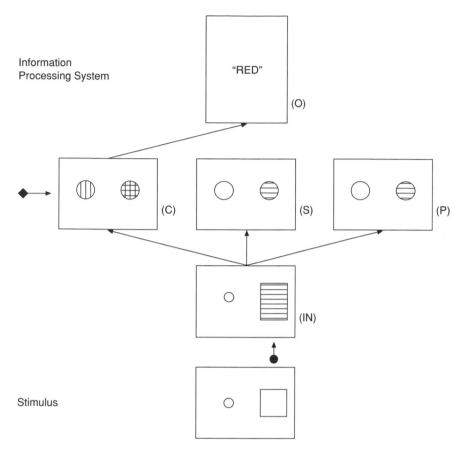

Figure 3.2 The common basis of Bundesen's (1990) and Phaf et al.'s (1990) visual information processing and selection models. (See text for further explanation.)

Let us now consider how, in essence, the instruction 'Name the colour of the square' has its appropriate selective effects in this information processing model.

- In one way or another, the instruction part 'of the square' has as a result that the appropriate object or input is selected – see the arrow pointing at module (IN). This is Bundesen's (1990) 'filtering' or Phaf et al.'s (1990) 'object set'. As a result of this selective operation, all attributes of the selected object are selected in modules (C), (S), and (P). This result is indicated in the figure with horizontal lines in the selected representations.
- In one way or another, the instruction part 'Name the colour' has as a result that the appropriate dimension or category is selected – see the

arrow pointing at module (C). This is Phaf et al.'s 'attribute set' and this takes care of Bundesen's 'pigeon-holing'. As a result of this selective operation, all the representations in the colour module, (C), are selected. This result is indicated in the figure with vertical lines in the selected representations.

As can easily be seen in the figure, from all attributes from all objects presented and internally represented, only the colour of the square is selected by both selection mechanisms, by 'filtering' or 'object set' and by 'pigeon-holing' or 'attribute set'. By using this intersection and additive interaction of the two selective operations, Bundesen's (1990) mathematical model and Phaf et al.'s (1990) connectionistic model are capable of 'producing' the wanted, instructed, response. So the postulated mechanisms are indeed capable of performing the required selection job.

In my view, what we encounter here is a major achievement of the information processing approach to perception and cognition. Remember that James got no farther than 'objects' and 'parts of objects', i.e., object selection (see Section 1.2). And remember that Von Helmholz talked about 'new questions about the object', without specifying the nature of those questions (see Section 3.1). Remember also that Lashley (1951, p. 130) had to admit explicitly that

> . . . such determining tendencies as the relation of attribute to object, which gives the order of adjective and noun, do not seem to be analyzable into any sort of spatial structure or for that matter, into any consistent relationship.

Lashley could only handle object selection; attribute selection was outside his theoretical reach (see Section 3.2). The information processing approach, with its objective experimental methods and detailed way of modelling, attacked exactly this object–attribute problem and converged upon a theoretical outcome that delivers what it suggests.

It is, however, of importance to note that what the Broadbent, Treisman, Bundesen, and Phaf et al. line of theorising delivers is not the 'fractionation of perception', as assumed in the perception for perception camp in the information processing approach. The 'fractionation of perception', as shown in Figure 3.2 into IN, C, S, and P, is simply borrowed from the neurosciences. What this line of theorising delivers is the *'fractionation of attention'*. It recognises two kinds of attention, 'filtering', 'stimulus set' or 'object set', and 'pigeon-holing', 'attribute set' or 'response set', and demonstrates with calculations and simulations their crucial importance for the understanding and explanation of internal task performance. That is a result that, as far as I know, neither early introspective psychology nor later behaviourism could ever deliver (see above).

Figure 3.2 presents the unproblematic component of the theorising in the information processing approach I referred to in Section 1.3. The figure, however, also makes immediately clear the problematic component of the present state of affairs with regard to the selection of information in the information processing approach. It shows in an impertinent way in what respects Bundesen's (1990) mathematical model and Phaf et al.'s (1990) connectionist model are incomplete and where the work is waiting. In the figure, we find two arrows, one pointing at (IN) and another pointing at (C), that both come from nowhere. This is a fair representation of the essence of both models. In Bundesen's model it is Bundesen who sets the parameter values in the equations, not the information processing model that is characterised with the equations (and, for obvious reasons, I refrained from including Bundesen as a 'subject' in the model in Figure 3.2 and preferred to let the arrows come from nowhere). In Phaf et al.'s model it is Phaf et al. who determine the activation values in the nodes, not the information processing model that is characterised with connected nodes and activations (and, again, for obvious reasons, I refrained from including Phaf et al. as 'agents' in the model in Figure 3.2 and preferred to let the arrows come from nowhere). So, in these models, the ultimate *effects* of the instruction are implemented. The *source* of these effects, the internal representation of the instruction that can produce these effects, however, remains completely obscure (see Chapter 1 for a general description of this state of affairs: 'the subject'). Indeed, in these models:

> No attempt is made to discard the notion that attentional selection is controlled by an intelligent agent, but a serious attempt is made to relieve the burden on the agent by placing a powerful mechanism at its disposal.
>
> (Bundesen, 1990, p. 523)

There is Visual Perception, there are task-required operations in Visual Perception, but a decent specification of the intelligent agent, of what I prefer to call the Intending Mind, is simply missing.[14]

One last point is still of importance here. It is that there is an arbitrary and, as will also appear further on in this work, problematic, assumption in Bundesen's (1990) and Phaf et al.'s (1990) successful selection models. In my representation of these models in Figure 3.2, there are two arrows coming from nowhere, one implementing 'stimulus set' (the selection of the relevant object) and the other implementing 'response set' (the selection of the relevant attribute). The arbitrary and problematic assumption is that the arrows are always *simultaneously* operative.

This assumption is arbitrary because, as I will show further on in this work, a *successive* operation of 'stimulus set' and 'response set' will also lead to the required result. Here it suffices to note that in Broadbent's (1958) filter model, depicted in Figure 3.1, information first enters a filter, which takes care of 'filtering' or 'object selection', and then enters the limited-capacity channel, which takes care of 'pigeon-holing' or of 'categorisation'. I see no reason whatsoever for replacing the rigid assumption of sequentiality by the equally rigid assumption of simultaneity. In my view a better assumption is that what exactly happens is task-dependent.

The assumption of simultaneous selection is problematic because, just as a result of this simultaneous operation, the to-be-'reported attribute' is emphasised and the 'defining attribute' is to a large extend neglected. [Note that in Figure 3.2, at the level of the Shape Map (S) and the Position Map (P), there is no difference whatsoever between the representation of 'square' and the representation of 'right'; so already at this level the system has completely lost the information that the 'red' is 'of the square'.][15] One can avoid this kind of problem and do justice to the intuition that under the instruction 'Name the colour of the square' first the square is selected and only then the colour, with a *sequence* of, possibly partially overlapping, selective mechanisms – first 'stimulus set' working with the 'defining attribute' and then also or only 'response set' concerned with the to-be-'reported attribute'. For other problems with this simultaneity assumption, see Sections 8.3 and 9.4.

3.4   Towards a unit of analysis

In Section 2.4, I expressed my conviction that the concept of 'intentionality', emphasised by James (1890/1950) and still abundantly used in the contemporary philosophy of mind, can be of great help in elucidating important aspects of the problem of the structure, implementation, and causal powers of instruction-induced action plans, or of what I called the Intending Mind. I am now in the position that I can further elaborate my view and can indicate how I am going to proceed. That elaboration and choice of route are determined by four important points, suggested by the guided tour of the literature presented in this chapter.

•   The first point is that the format of intentional talk – e.g., [see] : [. . .], [remember] : [. . .]; in general the '[act] : [object]' format – shows up repeatedly in the texts of early, systematic, experimental introspective psychology, albeit often in disguise (see Section 3.1). The theorists even express their theoretical views in an intentional terminology. Von Helmholtz, for instance, says that [we can set ourselves questions about] : [the object]. Kuelpe talks about [the process of determination . . .] : [the process of visual perception]. And in Ach we read about [influences arising from the goal-presentation and directed toward] : [the referent-presentation] and about [goal-directed mental happening] : [incidental external stimuli . . .]. So early systematic introspective psychology seems to agree with my point of view that the concept 'intentionality' is useful and shows that intentional talk can hardly be avoided in the search for and formulation of a theory that can provide a solution for the problem of an effective instruction.

- The second point is that many theorists suggest that this 'intentionality' can be realised in the information processing system with two independent, but interacting, representations, one for the task to be performed and one for the information required for task performance. In early introspective psychology, Ach in particular, with his interacting 'goal-presentation' and 'referent-presentation', is explicit about this point. In behaviourism Lashley in particular, with his two neural systems – a temporal one that scans a spatial one – is explicit about this point. And, at the end of the behaviourist era, Miller et al. emphasise the same two-representations solution with their theorising in terms of the 'image' and a 'plan' that uses that image.

- The third point is that behaviourism and early cognitive psychology are explicit about what kind of representation is missing in a purely bottom-up approach, or stimulus–response approach to perception and action. They largely agree about what the second representation – the representation responsible for the proper execution of the task that has to be performed – has to be concerned with. They convincingly show that, for explaining observed goal-directed behaviour, besides a representation originating from the stimulus and containing a structured representation of *space*, a 'representation', 'structure', or 'system', derived from the task to be performed and taking care of an appropriate structure in *time*, is also required. Tolman, for example, emphasises 'sequences'; Lashley postulates a serial 'scanning device'; and Miller et al. introduce sequential plans. So a second representation taking care of temporal aspects, of the order in time, has to be added.

- The fourth important point is that for selection experiments of the type 'Name the colour of the square' (or 'Read the letter indicated by the bar marker') – and certainly not only for selection experiments of this type – the Broadbent, Treisman, Bundesen, and Phaf et al. line of theorising in the information processing approach has been successful in making explicit what the effective [objects] are in the intentional '[act] : [object]' format. As stated and demonstrated in Section 3.3, within such a task two 'choices' have to be distinguished – one working with the 'defining attribute' of an object (the 'square') and the other concerned with the to-be-'reported attribute' (the 'colour'). So, in intentional vocabulary, with the stimulus of Figure 3.2 and with the task 'Name the colour of the square', subjects have, in one way or another, first [to remember] : [to name the colour of the square] and upon stimulus presentation they have [to perceive] : [the square] and [to perceive] : [the colour] and subsequently they have [to report] : [that colour].

At this point, with this summary of results of the guided tour in the back of our minds, it is worthwhile to turn briefly to the observations and insights of the mathematician Allan Turing, the inventor of the computer. Turing (1936) was concerned with the problem of 'computability'. With introspection he tried to find out how a computation on a sheet of paper is performed. Before making any suggestions about the construction of a machine that can do the computational work, he talks in general and intuitive terms about himself as a 'computer', looking at a tape. So, Turing adopted the psychologist's attitude, and started his introspective observations with a thoroughgoing dualism. He supposed two elements, the computer and the tape, and treated them as irreducible.

In Turing's story, the tape is divided into squares and each square contains one out of N symbols. At each moment in time, the computer is in one out of N 'states of mind' and 'observes' one square with a symbol. The computer can perform either of two simple actions or 'changes' – (a) it can change (or not change) the symbol in the observed square, and (b) it can change to another square and observe the symbol it contains.

Just because in Turing's story there are 'states of mind' on the one hand and 'symbols in squares' on the other, the relation and interaction between the two has to be specified. With regard to this relation and interaction, Turing (1936, p. 238) states:

> The most general simple operation must therefore be taken to be one of the following:
> A.   A possible change (a) of symbol together with a possible change of state of mind.
> B.   A possible change (b) of observed squares, together with a possible change of state of mind.
> The operation actually performed is determined . . . by the state of mind of the computer and the observed symbols.

Given these specifications, it is not too difficult to see that (1) because the computer is always in one of the 'states of mind' and (2) a 'change of square' and a 'change of symbol' can always involve a 'change of state of mind', the computer can run in a sequence of steps of the following general form:

$$> (x) \text{ (square)} > (x+1) \text{ (symbol)} > (x+2) \text{ (square)} > (x+3) \text{ (symbol)} > \text{ etc.}$$

Here the (x)s stand for the 'states of mind', the >s for the transitions between 'states of mind', the (square)s for the selection of a square with a symbol, and the (symbol)s for the 'treatment' of the symbol.

This sequence can be read as: The computer is in state x and selects a square with a symbol, then it moves into state x+1 and 'treats' the symbol, then it moves into state x+2 and chooses another square with a symbol, then it moves into state x+3 and 'treats' the symbol, etc.

Given this format and interpretation, it is also not too difficult to see that in this sequence sub-sequences can be distinguished:

>> (x) (square) > (x+1) (symbol) >> >> (x+2) (square) > (x+3) (symbol) >> etc.

In the computer in each sub-sequence >> . . . > . . . >>, the first part, >> . . . >, is concerned with the choice of a square with a symbol, and the second part, > . . . >>, is concerned with the 'treatment' of the symbol. So, the computer in Turing's story runs in a series of sub-sequences of the general form:

>> X > Y >>

with X and Y standing for two different 'states of mind' that take care of two different 'mental operations', state X selects a square with a symbol and state Y takes care that something is done with that selected symbol. With >> X > Y >> we have the 'unit of analysis' of Turing's (1936) computer which looks at and works with the tape.

I started this section by listing four important points for our problem of the implementation, structure, and causal powers of the instruction, suggested by the guided tour of the literature. At this point it is of importance to see that all four points are 'realised' or 'implemented' in Turing's (1936) complete computer-plus-tape machine.

• The first point is that Turing's computer is just the intentional part of a complete 'intentional machine'. In the computer there are 'states of mind' that deal with 'squares' and 'symbols' on a tape. The computer [selects] : [the square] and [observes] : [the symbol] and treats the symbol in the appropriate task-required way.
• The second point is, of course, that Turing's complete 'intentional machine' works with two different 'representations'; one, the sequence of 'states of mind' in the computer, for the task to be performed, and one, the tape with symbols, for the information required for task performance.
• The third point is that this 'intentional machine' makes clear what kind of representations are required for adequate task performance. The 'intentional machine' needs a spatial representation, the tape with symbols, and a temporal representation, the successive states of mind.
• The fourth point is that the two 'changes' that the states of mind of Turing's machine can bring about – (a), a change of square (the selection of another square with a symbol) and (b), a change of symbol (the treatment of the symbol in the selected square) – are very close to (a) stimulus or input selection (the selection of a complete object) and (b) response set or attribute selection (the selection of one aspect of that selected object). In Chapter 4, I return to this close correspondence.

From Turing's 'intentional machine' one can move in two directions. One can move in the direction of the modern, very fast, 'computers'. The omnipresence of these 'computers', and the great variety of tasks these 'computers' can perform, proves that Turing's introspective analysis was not that far from the mark. However, one can also move in the direction of the ancient, very slow, human mind, and this is, of course, the direction I am going to take in the rest of this work. As just shown with the four main points, the important characteristics of Turing's (1936) 'intentional machine', with $>> X > Y >>$ as the 'unit of analysis' of its computer, are very close to the main characteristics of the human information processor, as emerged from the brief review of the experimental literature presented in this chapter. This close correspondence invites the conclusion that one or another slow version of Turing's 'intentional machine' is the kind of machine I am looking for and that something like the 'unit of analysis' of Turing's computer is also the appropriate 'unit of analysis' for James's (1890/1950) 'mind knowing' and for what I prefer to call the Intending Mind.

Let us now see how this conclusion can be further worked out in the context of 'report' tasks (Part II) and of 'act' tasks (Part III).

Notes

1   Dewey starts his famous 'The Reflex Arc Concept in Psychology' with:

> That the greater demand for a unifying principle and controlling working hypothesis in psychology should come at just the time when all generalizations and classifications are most questioned and questionable is natural enough. It is the very cumulation of discrete facts creating the demand for unification that also breaks down previous lines of classification. The material is too great in mass and too varied in style to fit into existing pigeon-holes, and the cabinets of science break of their own dead weight.
>
> (Dewey, 1896, p. 357)

Dewey finds in the "'reflex arc' concept" his 'unifying principle' or 'unit of analysis'.

2   In the USA a highly unpleasant quarrel about the interpretation of Lange's (1888) simple reactions and reaction times arose between Baldwin (see, e.g., Baldwin, 1896) and Titchener (see, e.g., Titchener, 1896). Baldwin observed and reported that with some unpractised observers faster sensorial than muscular reactions are found. He proposed a distinction between 'sensory' and 'motor' observers ('sensory and motor types'). He accused the 'Leipsic' school of using only highly practised subjects who showed the difference in reaction times required by the 'Leipsic' theory. Titchener argued that psychology is only concerned with the laws of the generalised mind, not with individual differences. He argued that practice is required in order for these laws to exhibit themselves. He regarded as a 'grave defect' that Baldwin did not first and independently test his subjects for 'type'. In his view 'The obvious plan would surely be to make certain of the type first, and then obtain reactions' (Titchener, 1895b, p. 510).

    In 'a paper which merits an important place in the history of experimental psychology because it performed a Hegelian synthesis between Titchener's thesis and Baldwin's antithesis' (Boring, 1950, p. 555), Angell and Moore (1896) 'settled' the issue. In their view the basic problem the observer is confronted with is the problem of the coordination of ear (or eye) and hand. The interpretation in terms of 'habit' and 'attention' they arrive at combines

> . . . elements from both sides of the 'type discussion'. On the [Baldwin] side it would say: (1) that the 'type' of attention and its accompanying time are determined by the relation between the individual's stock of coördinations, inherited and acquired, already on hand, and the particular coördination required by the reaction; (2) . . . On the [Titchener] side it would say that under practice, in both forms, upon the same coördination, the sensory phase passes more completely under the control of habit and thus leaves the faster time to the motor form.
>
> (Angell & Moore, 1896, p. 258)

This 'synthesis' shows that some theoretical work still has to be done here. In Chapter 9, I therefore return to Lange's task.

3 Wundt also recognised the existence of a goal-directed inner activity that he called *apperception* and which resulted in apperception (in Wundt's theorising apperception is a process and also the outcome of a process). He distinguished apperception as a process from association because, in his view, apperception occurs in logical connections between mental contents whereas associative connections are not logical. For our problem, Wundt's rather vague notion of 'an inner activity' called apperception and resulting in apperception is not of much help because here, of course, a serious difficulty arises:

> Difficulty arises . . . when activity is taken as implying an active agent. Wundt would of course have denied the imputation of an external free active apperception . . . But did he let the concept in surreptitiously? Perhaps. Even the zealot can not get more than just so far ahead of his *Zeitgeist*.
>
> (Boring, 1950, p. 339)

4 What we find in the quotations is 'acoustical-motorical repetition of the catch-word', 'knew what to do', and 'repeats [the task] to himself in words, e.g., "find a part", "name an example" . . . "animal-dog" '.

5 It is worthwhile to note that, according to Ach, these influences are realised by means of associations (the two 'presentations' are 'associatively coordinated').

6 It is worthwhile to note here that the behaviourists used their visual perception for task performance, e.g., for observing and reporting the behaviour of pigeons and rats that, in their turn, used their visual perception for task performance, e.g., for running through a maze or for picking at a light. I return to this point in the Epilogue.

7 Tolman (1936) asks:

> But what about introspection? Is not introspection after all, at least in the case of men, a significant method by which one can get at and define these intervening variables in a direct and really reliable fashion?
>
> (in Marx, 1951, p. 100)

Because of my concern with an appropriate classification of tasks in Chapter 2, Tolman's answer to this question is highly relevant. That answer shows that, just as I argued in Chapter 2, he is convinced that a distinction between two different tasks has to be made.

> . . . the validity of introspection is, as I see it, restricted to one special type of investigation – the type of investigation where what we are primarily

concerned with are those intervening variables (whatever they may be) which underlie the ability or nonability of being able "to talk about it." But in the other, far greater majority of psychological investigations, this ability or nonability "to talk about" is not important or determinative. And, indeed, when it is called into play, it is apt to lead to decided errors relative to the other types of intervening variable with which, in such cases, we are concerned.

(in Marx, 1951, p. 101)

This answer shows that Tolman's distinction is close to my distinction between 'report' tasks and 'act' tasks.

8 It is worthwhile to note in this quotation the 'succession of words or of acts'. So, for Lashley (1951) too, reports and acts are not the same.

9 In this theorising, internal operations (Tests) and external operations (Operate) are not clearly distinguished. Miller et al. also do not make the, in my view, essential distinction between 'act' tasks and 'report' tasks (see Chapters 2 and 9). As a result, with regard to internal operations, their treatment is quite shallow. For these reasons, I position Miller et al. (1960) at the end of behaviourism, not at the beginning of information processing psychology. (For yet another reason, see Chapter 9.)

10 Broadbent (1971) extended and generalised the theory in such a way that the results obtained in visual information processing tasks could also be accounted for.

11 It is worthwhile to note that according to Broadbent '. . . subjects may . . . use either of two processes . . .'. This formulation raises, of course, the problem of what those 'subjects' are.

12 It is worthwhile to try to figure out what controls what in this quotation. Here not 'the subject', but 'aspects of the information presented' control the choices. It remains completely unclear, however, how these 'aspects of the information presented' know that they have to control and how they can exert that control.

13 I am well aware that the terminology becomes chaotic here. This chaos arises because Bundesen (1990) emphasises selection of *categories* and Phaf et al. (1990) emphasise selection of *attributes*. In my view, for task performance besides object selection both attribute selection and category selection are required. An example can make this clear. Consider an experiment in which the subject has to name the colour of a light that can be red or blue. To perform this task the subject has to select the colour attribute of the light, not its position or brightness. However, the selected attribute does not completely determine the category or response. The colour of that light can be categorised as 'red' or 'blue' but also as 'warm' or 'cold' (subjective impression) and as 'long' or 'short' (objective wavelength).

14 With his 'integrated competition hypothesis' Duncan (1996) makes clear where the solution for this problem has to be sought. In this model, which is mainly based on neuropsychological data, competitive brain systems are controlled by advance priming of units in higher brain systems. These higher brain systems then function as 'the intelligent agent' or 'the Intending Mind'. In this context the task I set myself in the present work can be described as: Finding a proper characterisation of the operations of the 'higher brain systems' in terms of units of analysis.

15 This problematic assumption becomes especially worrying under the, nowadays virtually generally accepted, interpretation that these models model the processing/perception/recognition of visual information. To see this, let us consider what logic forces Bundesen (1990) to conclude. For producing the correct answer to the question 'Name the colour of the square' – required answer 'red', not 'square' or 'right' – the theory uses 'response set' as a selection mechanism.

This mechanism speeds up the processing/recognition/perception of the attribute required for responding (the colour) relative to *all* other attributes of the selected object (the form and the position). This, however, has as a result that under this instruction the subject first processes/recognises/perceives 'it is red', and only afterwards processes/recognises/perceives 'that red is of a square'. The theory does even not exclude the possibility that subjects, when asked the question 'Name the colour of the square', come up with an incoherent answer like 'the square is red, but I did not process/perceive/recognise that the square is a square' (see Bundesen, 1990, p. 525: 'To recognize . . . rather than other attributes . . .').

Part II
Report tasks

4 An intentional machine

4.0 Introduction

In this chapter, I outline my answer to the question of how people use their visual perception in the performance of report tasks. In answering this question, I use the fortunate fact that there is a close correspondence between what has been said in the experimental literature of the past about the implementation of an instruction for task performance and what Turing (1936) has said about the performance of a computation on a sheet of paper (see Chapter 3, especially Section 3.4). The exposition presented in this chapter is not intended to be complete nor even to be correct in all theoretical details and for all experimental circumstances; in further chapters my answer is refined, elaborated, and extended. The purpose of this chapter is mainly didactic. It presents the core of my answer plus some further theoretical arguments that, in my view, strengthen my theoretical position.

In Section 4.1, the two components required for an intentional machine performing a report task are introduced – a 'computer', the Intending Mind that runs in a series of >> object selection > attribute selection >> steps, and Visual Perception, consisting of localised activations in a set of maps or modules. The Intending Mind is derived from Turing's (1936) analysis. Visual Perception is borrowed from the information processing approach to perception and cognition. By means of a logical analysis, it is shown how these two components of the intentional machine, Intending Mind and Visual Perception, in interaction can produce and/or account for task performance in a simple, standard selective attention task – the report task: name this A(attribute) of that O(object).

In Section 4.2, it is shown that the internal information processing steps involved in the performance of this report task can be made explicit in such a way that it becomes possible to conceive and devise a 'connectionist machine' that can perform the task. The vague and general term 'processing', used in the information processing approach, is replaced by three more specific, neuronal realisable operations or relations: 'concatenation' within the Intending Mind, 'propagation' within Visual Perception, and 'association' connecting Intending Mind and Visual Perception.

In Section 4.3, Logan and Zbrodoff's (1999) view on 'selection for cognition' is introduced. It is shown that this view is addressing the same topic as the view elaborated in this work and that it comes up with about the same answer – the interaction of a 'conceptual representation' and a 'perceptual representation' for the production of 'propositions'. The two views start from different, high-level and low-level, tasks. The convergence of the two views strongly suggests that with this type of two-representations approach a broad range of tasks can be dealt with. The distinction between 'report' tasks and 'act' tasks is further elaborated.

In Section 4.4, it is shown that the assumption of two interacting representations is compatible with what is nowadays known about the localisation of functions in the human brain. The functions performed by the Intending Mind can be localised in the anterior part of the brain. This part interacts with Visual Perception, localised in the posterior part of the brain, for task performance.

4.1   An intentional machine

In contemporary standard experiments investigating selection within a single eye fixation, the subject first receives an instruction and is then confronted with a series of visual stimuli. Figure 4.1 shows one of the stimuli that can be used, a stimulus with a large, red square on the right and a small, blue disk on the left (often black letters, instead of coloured shapes, are presented, but in the present context that is irrelevant). Each stimulus is presented very briefly, e.g., for 150 ms, to ensure that the subjects cannot make useful saccadic eye movements during stimulus presentation. To ensure that subjects indeed fixate in advance in the middle of the stimulus, a small digit (or letter) can be presented that can only be read and reported when it is fixated. (In the figure this is a 3.) Subjects can then be instructed to name first that letter or digit and then one or more other aspects of the stimulus presented. Let us assume that this stimulus is presented under appropriate

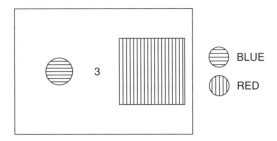

Figure 4.1 A stimulus with a large, red square on the right, a small, blue disk on the left, and a small digit, a 3, in the centre. (See text for further explanation.)

conditions, i.e., that the subject fixates where the (very) small digit is going to appear and that the exposure duration is such that during stimulus exposure no useful eye movements can be made.

With this type of stimuli a variety of selective instructions can be given. To name just a few: name first the digit and then the colours (or the shapes, or the sizes), or name first the digit and then the colour (or the shape, or the size) of the left object, or name first the digit and then the position (or the shape, or the size) of the red object, etc. Let us assume that the instruction given to the subjects is:

> First name the digit in the middle,
> then name the colour of the square.

And, let us analyse how this report task can be performed.

The first analysis of 'internal' task performance I am going to present is a logical analysis in Turing's (1936) terms, not an information processing model. The analysis postulates a series of 'states of mind' with 'contents' in a 'computer' that interact with the stimulus in order to bring about the desired result – first the name of the digit in the middle and then the name of the colour of the square.[1]

In this preliminary analysis I distinguish six steps:

1   The verbal instruction is transformed in the computer into a sentence, or better an internal sequence, of the form:

> \>\> MIDDLE > SHAPE \>\> \>\> SQUARE > COLOUR \>\>.

    This step can be regarded as a transformation of the instruction from a 'surface structure' into a 'deep structure'. That sequence, with MIDDLE as the starting point, is stored in the computer until stimulus presentation. The onset of the stimulus triggers the temporal development of the sequence.[2]

2   Upon stimulus presentation, the computer moves into the sequence state MIDDLE and the state MIDDLE selects the object in the middle with all its properties in the stimulus.

3   The computer then moves into the sequence state SHAPE and the state SHAPE selects the digit, i.e., the form aspect, of the selected object in the middle.

4   The computer then moves into the sequence state SQUARE and the state SQUARE selects the square with all its properties in the visual stimulus.

5   The computer then moves into the sequence state COLOUR and the state COLOUR selects the attribute 'red', i.e., the colour aspect, of the selected square.

6   The computer stops.

What was selected, the 'object in the middle', the '[3]', the 'square', and the '[red]' has to be retained in one way or another and has now to be reported; for instance, 'in the middle was a 3 and the square was red'. I return to this storage and report later.

In Section 3.4, I showed that Turing's (1936) computer runs in a series of subsequences of the general form $>> X_i > Y_i >>$. This format can be used to code the six steps I have just distinguished. In the following series of six steps, the state the computer is in is shown in **bold** face and <u>underlined</u>.

1 **(Start)** $>> X_1 > Y_1 >> >> X_2 > Y_2 >>$
2 $>>$ **<u>X1</u>** $> Y_1 >> >> X_2 > Y_2 >>$
3 $>> X_1 >$ **<u>Y1</u>** $>> >> X_2 > Y_2 >>$
4 $>> X_1 > Y_1 >> >>$ **<u>X2</u>** $> Y_2 >>$
5 $>> X_1 > Y_1 >> >> X_2 >$ **<u>Y2</u>** $>>$
6 $>> X_1 > Y_1 >> >> X_2 > Y_2 >>$ **(Stop)**.

Inspection of this series shows that, given that the required 'selections' are realisable, this *is* one specific instantiation of the computer in Turing's machine. This 'special purpose' computer can 'compute' (i.e., select) the 'parameters' required for responding, given instructions of the type 'name this A(ttribute) of that O(bject)'. So, what we have here, is a mechanistic, instruction-derived, selection device. For task performance in this report task not a subject or an agent, only a computer, is required.

For the moment, in this computer a sub-part

$$>> X > Y >>$$

can be regarded as the 'unit of analysis' of its internal operations. In such a unit, there are two terms with contents, with different functions.

•   The first term, X, is the 'sending' term. The content of term X – the instruction- and task-derived representation of the 'defining attribute' (Duncan, 1985) – has to pick out or select the required object from among all available objects. This 'sending' term initiates and takes care of Bundesen's (1990) and Phaf et al.'s (1990) 'filtering', 'stimulus set', or 'object set' (this function is often called 'selection').
•   The second term, Y, is the 'receiving' term. The content of term Y – the instruction- and task-derived representation of the to-be-'reported attri-bute' (Duncan, 1985) – has to pick out or select the required attribute from among all available attributes. This 'receiving' term initiates and takes care of Bundesen's and Phaf et al.'s 'pigeon-holing', 'response set', or 'attribute set' (this function is often called 'processing').

So, in this computer, each unit of analysis coordinates, controls or guides the operation of two selective operations – object selection and attribute selection. The unit of analysis can therefore be written as

>> OBJECT > ATTRIBUTE >> .

The two selective operations are the selective operations that were already recognised and specified by the Broadbent, Treisman, Bundesen, Phaf et al. line of theorising in the information processing approach (see Section 3.3).[3] In Chapter 5, I return to these selective operations.

In Turing's (1936) 'intentional machine' and in the analysis just presented, a computer runs through a sequence of 'states of mind'. For the human information processor as an intentional machine, I need a theoretical term for the computer and for such a sequence of 'states of mind'. Let us, from now on, call such a sequence of 'states of mind' in the computer for the human information processor a Verbal Intention in an Intending Mind.

In Turing's (1936) 'intentional machine' and in the analysis just presented, the 'states of mind' in the computer interact with an external tape with squares with symbols, and with an external stimulus with objects with attributes. For the human information processor confronted with visual information processing tasks, a Verbal Intention in an Intending Mind cannot interact directly with an external state of affairs such as a tape with squares with symbols, or a stimulus with objects with attributes. For such an interaction, a mediating internal representation is required. For the human information processing system, that mediating internal representation is in his or her visual system. For the human information processor as an intentional machine I need a theoretical term for that representation. Let us, from now on, call that mediating representation in the visual system Visual Perception.

So, from now on, my human information processor as an intentional machine, designed for performing report tasks of the type 'name this A(ttribute) of that O(bject)', consists of a Verbal Intention in an Intending Mind, interacting with Visual Perception in the visual system. The verbal instruction, given by the experimenter, has to induce or implement a Verbal Intention in the Intending Mind that is compatible with and can interact with Visual Perception with objects with attributes. The intentional sequence, the sequence of 'states of mind' of the Verbal Intention, has to use the results offered by Visual Perception in such a way that the required, i.e., instructed, task performance can appear as a result.

From this human information processor, we have already considered the Verbal Intention part, with >> object > attribute >> as its unit of analysis. Now we must have a closer look at the visual system with Visual Perception. And, with regard to the implementation of Visual Perception, the information processing approach can help us further. The study and analysis of Visual Perception – the 'fractionation' of perception – has been one of the most important topics with which the approach has been concerned up to now (see Section 2.1). So, at this point in the theorising, I can simply take what I regard as the relevant results and findings of the information processing approach with regard to Visual Perception and confront these results and findings with the Verbal Intention. With such a confrontation we can see whether, and if so, how, my intentional machine – the Intending Mind

with its Verbal Intention as defined above and Visual Perception as conceptualised in the information processing approach – can together produce the
required task performance.

As 'states of mind' in this confrontation, I again use the sequence derived
from the instruction: first name the digit in the middle and then name the
colour of the square, i.e., the Verbal Intention

>> MIDDLE > SHAPE >> >> SQUARE > COLOUR >>.

With regard to Visual Perception, a choice has now to be made. The information processing approach has produced more models of perception and
selection, not just one. A main distinction is between models that regard all
attributes – colour, shape, position – as equal (the 'all equal' models; see,
e.g., Bundesen, 1990; Kahneman, 1973; Phaf et al., 1990) and models that
recognise a special, dominant role for the attribute position (the 'position
special' models; see, e.g., Treisman, 1988, 1993; Van der Heijden, 1992,
1993, 1996a). At this point, however, because I only want to illustrate the
interaction of the Verbal Intention and Visual Perception, the choice of
the 'correct' model is not really crucial. I therefore choose the simpler of the
two, the symmetrical type with all attributes with an equal status (in Section
5.1, I return to this choice of model). This model is also the one I illustrated
and used in Section 3.3, to explain the effective selective operations in
Bundesen's (1990) and Phaf et al.'s (1990) models (see Figure 3.2). For
implementing selection without 'loose ends', (symmetrical) 'top-down' connections are added.[4]

In Figure 4.2, the Verbal Intention is represented as a sequence of states
in the Intending Mind, and Visual Perception is represented as localised
patterns of activation in an input module (IN) and three feature modules
(C: Colour; S: Shape; P: Position). The stimulus activates its corresponding
representations from IN upwards. This information processing is indicated
by the upward pointing arrows. The Verbal Intention in the Intending Mind
develops or unfolds as already described. Its states have their initial selective
effects by activating top-down relevant localised representations via the downwards pointing arrows ('sending' or 'selection') and their ultimate selective
effects via enhanced activation in the upward pointing arrows ('receiving' or
'processing'). In this framework, the interaction between the Verbal Intention and Visual Perception proceeds as follows.

First, the Verbal Intention in the Intending Mind is in the state MIDDLE
and, after a short while, moves to the state SHAPE. The attribute shape
of the object in the middle is selected because MIDDLE in the Verbal
Intention provided top-down enhanced activation on the position of the
representation of the middle of the stimulus in module P.[5] From there, this
enhanced activation propagates further downwards to the corresponding
position in module IN and then propagates upwards to the corresponding
position in module S (and in modules C and P, but that is not of importance

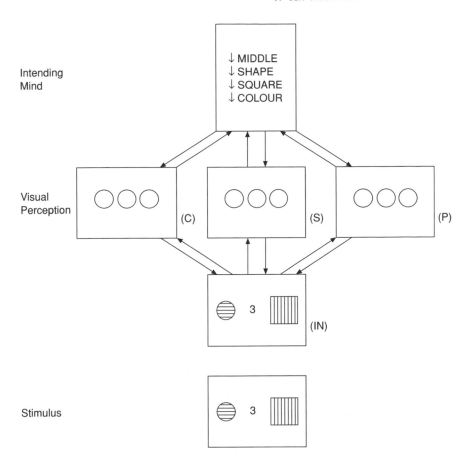

Figure 4.2 Visual information processing and selection model consisting of an Intending Mind (upper box) interacting with Visual Perception (activations in modules). (See text for further explanation.)

because the sequence is in the state SHAPE and can only select the shape, i.e., the form aspect). The form aspect of the object in the middle is now selected by Verbal Intention state SHAPE.[6]

The second selection proceeds in the same way. The Verbal Intention moves to the state SQUARE and, after a short while, moves to the state COLOUR. The colour aspect is selected because state SQUARE of the Verbal Intention provided top-down enhanced activation on the position of the representation of the square in module S. From there this enhanced activation proceeds further downwards to the corresponding position in module IN and then upwards to the corresponding position in module C (and in modules S and P, but that is not of importance because the sequence is in the state COLOUR and can therefore only select the colour aspect).

Module C then provides the colour attribute for Verbal Intention state COLOUR.[7]

So, what happens in this conceptualisation is that the Verbal Intention initiates top-down the appropriate object selections (in the example this is accomplished by states MIDDLE and SQUARE). Shortly after the selection is initiated, two simultaneously operating 'mechanisms' or 'operations' make the selection a success:

(a) In IN, the complete representation of the task-relevant object is singled out or selected with enhanced activation.
(b) In the Intending Mind, from among all 'enhanced' attributes of the task-relevant object, the Verbal Intention singles out the task-relevant attribute (in the example states SHAPE and COLOUR accomplish this).

In this conceptualisation there is a succession of states in the Intending Mind that induces a simultaneous operation of two selective 'mechanisms' or 'operations, as specified by Bundesen (1990) and Phaf et al. (1990); 'filtering', 'stimulus set' or 'object set', and 'pigeon-holing', 'response set' or 'attribute set'.

One important problem still has to be solved. My intentional machine must not only select the required information but also retain that information and report the information later on. In this section we have a brief look at the retaining. For the reporting we need some further information and I return to this in Chapter 9.

In Turing's (1936) complete computer-plus-tape machine, the results of the operations, the 'changes', are retained on the tape. The 'symbol' in the square 'observed' is either altered or left unchanged. In my complete Intending Mind – Visual Perception machine, the internal representation Visual Perception plays the role of Turing's tape. To change or alter Visual Perception in the course of *internal* task performance is, however, not a very attractive proposition. In my view, Visual Perception can best be regarded as providing a veridical representation of the world that is not altered or changed by the internal performance of one or another report task. But then, my view leaves me with no other possibility than to change or alter the content of (some of) the states of the Verbal Intention in the Intending Mind during internal task performance – besides Visual Perception and Intending Mind, I have nothing else that can be changed in the intentional machine.

It is not too difficult to elaborate the suggestion that the content of (some of the) states of the Verbal Intention in the Intending Mind are changed during internal task performance and thereby retain the selected information. Let us consider again the task 'Name the digit in the middle and the colour of the square', performed with the Verbal Intention presented at the beginning of this section as the initial sequence. The Verbal Intention in the Intending Mind is first in the state MIDDLE and selects the middle of the representation of the stimulus. The content of the state and the selected information corres-pond and nothing has to change. Then the Verbal Intention is in the state SHAPE and the form aspect is selected. Here the selected form aspect provides information that is not yet available in the Verbal Intention in the Intending Mind; it provides a detailed specification of the shape currently present in the middle of the stimulus representation. This makes it possible to change or alter the general state SHAPE in the Verbal Intention into a more specific state, i.e., in our example into something like the state '[3]'. Again, for the state SQUARE the content of the state and the selected information correspond and no change is invited. The state COLOUR, however, receives more precise information about the actual colour of the square and can therefore be altered or changed accordingly, i.e., in our example into something like the state '[red]'.[8]

So, in more general terms, my proposal is that internal task performance of the Intending Mind starts with an *initial* intentional sequence or Verbal Intention [select] : [ ], of the form specified at the beginning of this section. During internal task performance, this initial Verbal Intention is changed or altered into a *resulting* intentional sequence or Verbal Intention [report] : [ ], retaining or storing the selected information. For our example, the content of this resulting Verbal Intention [report] : [ ] is of the form

[>> MIDDLE > '[3]' >> >> SQUARE > '[red]' >>].

Upon reporting, the state '[3]' can pick out the required response, 'three', from among the set of available/allowable digit responses and the state '[red]' can pick out the required response, 'red', from among the set of available/allowable colour responses.[9] After the internal task performance, the resulting intention [report] : [ ] can be developed 'in real time', resulting in: 'in the middle was a 3 and the square was red'. This reporting can be regarded as consisting of a transformation back from a 'deep structure' into a 'surface structure'.[10]

At this point, it is worth noting that the intentional machine we have now arrived at is consistent with the findings, feelings, and theoretical views put forward in the history of experimental psychology (see Chapter 3). Four points are of importance.

- The machine is an intentional machine. Before stimulus presentation, the machine has to [remember] : [ ]. Upon stimulus presentation the system has to [perceive] : [ ] and to [notice] : [ ]. After stimulus presentation the system has to [remember] : [ ] and to [report] : [ ]. The machine runs through a sequence of intentional states as defined and described by James and Brentano. The complete Intending Mind – Visual Perception machine is in clear agreement with James's 'prescription':

> *The psychologist's attitude towards cognition . . . is a thoroughgoing dualism.* It supposes two elements, mind knowing and thing known, and treats them as irreducible.
>
> (James, 1890/1950, p. 218)

- In the intentional machine the intentionality, required for internal task performance, is realised with two independent but interacting representations, the Verbal Intention in the Intending Mind and the visual world in Visual Perception. This way of realisation had already been suggested by Ach and Kuelpe, who recognised two independent but interacting representations, a 'goal-presentation' and a 'referent-presentation'. The same suggestion was put forward by Tolman and especially by Lashley and by Miller et al. (see Section 3.2).
- The intentional machine derives one representation, the one in Visual Perception, from the visual stimulus and the other, the Verbal Intention in the Intending Mind, from the verbal instruction. Visual Perception displays objects with attributes in space. The Verbal Intention in the Intending Mind controls task performance in time. The Verbal Intention is essentially a sequence of states, in charge of introducing a task-induced and task-required temporal order in the machine. The Verbal Intention produces Ach's 'determining tendency' – it *is* the internal 'causal structure' that, by its temporal development and contents, determines the sequence of internal information manipulations required for adequate task performance. The necessity of introducing a representation or subsystem in charge of regulating the order in time was also recognised and emphasised by Tolman (sequences), Lashley (a 'scanning device'), and by Miller et al. (plans).
- In the Verbal Intention in the Intending Mind, the effective [acts] in the '[act] : [object]' format specify a concrete 'defining attribute' for object selection in the X part and an abstract to be 'reported attribute' for attribute selection in the Y part of the unit of analysis >> X > Y >>.[11] That for report tasks the internal states have to be characterised in terms of *content*, had already been recognised by, e.g., Von Helmholz (questions), James (objects and parts of objects), and Gibson (concepts). That *objects* and *attributes* are essential, is the major discovery of the information processing approach (see Section 3.3).

The interaction of the 'states of mind' of the Verbal Intention in the Intending Mind with the contents in Visual Perception has as a result that the 'focus of consciousness' moves from state to state. This aspect of the theorising is, of course, compatible with James's description of consciousness and thought as a stream with 'substantive parts' and 'transitive parts' (James, 1890/1950, p. 243.) In the Verbal Intention in the Intending Mind the 'substantive parts', which interact with visual perception, are indicated by words (MIDDLE, RED, etc.), and the transitive parts, which interact with nothing, are indicated by > and >>. James explains why it is so difficult to see the transitive parts for what they really are: '. . . stopping them to look at them . . . is really annihilating them' (p. 243). In my view, there is simply nothing to see (see Section 3.1).

4.2 Three relations

By now it will be clear what is the kernel of my solution to the problem of how people use their visual perception in the performance of report tasks. Somewhere in the information processing system is a representation, which can be called a Verbal Intention. That Verbal Intention consists of a concatenation of Turing units, $>> X_i > Y_i >>$.[12] That Verbal Intention interacts with another representation which can be called Visual Perception. The interaction of Verbal Intention and Visual Perception produces the required task performance.

Of course, the analysis presented in the preceding section leaves a lot of questions unanswered and a great number of details to be filled in. At this point, however, I am not yet really interested in how far the details of this conceptualisation are correct, in the exact temporal properties of the operations, in the question of parallel and serial processing, in the problem of the neuronal realisation, etc. Most of these issues will be addressed in later chapters. What is of importance here and now is the successful combination of the new, the Verbal Intention, and the old, Visual Perception. When viewed broadly, it appears not to be too difficult to combine the Verbal Intention, interpreted as an instruction-derived internal sequence, and Visual Perception, interpreted as activated representations in a connected set of modules, and produce the required task performance. My Verbal Intention, derived from Turing, plus the Visual Perception, borrowed from the information processing approach, appear to be a promising couple.

One issue, however, deserves some further consideration. My intentional machine contains the representation 'visual perception', specified by the information processing approach, as one of its two components. It therefore cannot be excluded that I not only import the virtues, but also some of the vices of that approach. In the past, I have pointed out several of those vices (see, e.g., Van der Heijden, 1992, 1995, 1996b; Van der Heijden & Bem, 1997). And before sending the intentional machine into the wilderness of experimental designs and results, one of these vices has to be dealt with. That vice concerns the story the limited-capacity perception theories in the information processing approach tell about the 'attentive processing' of the information – about the transition from a first, preliminary stage of information processing to a second, definitive stage of information processing resulting in full perception (see Section 2.1 for this two-stage theorising).

Inspection of the literature shows that, with regard to the processing operations performed during attentive processing and which are assumed to result in full perception and categorisation/identification, the information processing theories do not have very much of relevance to tell.[13] In specifying what 'a more detailed analysis' means, most theorising is nowadays not much further on than in 1967, when Neisser wrote:

> It seems to me, therefore, that attention is not a mysterious concentration of psychic energy; it is simply an allotment of analyzing mechanisms to a limited region of the field. To pay attention to a figure is to make certain analyses of, or certain constructions in, the corresponding part of the icon.
>
> (Neisser, 1967, pp. 88–89)

(It is interesting to know that Neisser, 1976, p. 17, summarised this type of characterisation with 'processing → more processing → still more processing'.) The attention literature is full of statements like:

> The benefits of processing are attributed to the alignment of the attentional spotlight on the appropriate location of the visual field, so that processing can begin more quickly when the stimulus occurs than if attention direction had to await the occurrence of the stimulus.
>
> (Eriksen, 1990, p. 11)

Cave and Wolfe (1990), for instance, correctly and honestly remark, with regard to their computer simulation of visual search:

> The simulation says little about how the serial stage operates, except that it is capable of deciding conclusively whether or not an element is the target. The serial stage is undoubtedly a large collection of complex processing mechanisms. For present purposes, the important aspect of these mechanisms is that they operate over a limited part of the field at any one time, and that they use the quickly-prepared evidence from the parallel stage to decide what to process next.
>
> (Cave & Wolfe, 1990, p. 237)

With one exception – the feature integration theory of Treisman which assumes that attention locally completes perception by gluing separate features into objects (see, e.g., Treisman, 1988; see also Section 2.1) – the issue of what the 'processing' actually consists of or what 'processing' attention actually does is not really made explicit.[14] To the starting assumption in Treisman's theory, I briefly turn in Chapter 7.

The important point now is that there is no reason whatsoever for assuming that I have to import this problematic aspect of the theorising in the information processing approach. The analysis presented in the preceding section nowhere requires some kind of unspecified processing. Let me be crude here and state this point bluntly: It is possible to make all required steps, listed in the preceding section, explicit in such a way that it is possible

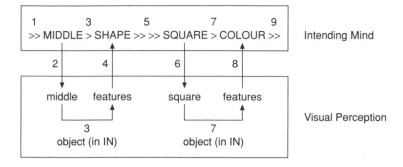

Figure 4.3 The interaction between the successive states in the Intending Mind and the activations in the feature modules and in IN in Visual Perception. (See text for further explanation.)

to conceive, devise, and program a 'connectionist machine' that can perform the task of the intentional machine in the way I sketched. This point certainly deserves some further consideration and elaboration.

With regard to such an operational 'connectionist machine', one theoretical point is of importance. That point is, that matters are considerably simpler than up to now it might possibly appear. A closer inspection shows that in the whole analysis presented up to now, basically three and only three different, neuronal realisable kinds of relations or kinds of operations are involved. Figure 4.3 serves to illustrate this point. In this figure there are two representations, one in the upper box labelled Intending Mind and one in the lower box labelled Visual Perception.

The first type of relation, the relation indicated with the upper row of digits 1, 3, 5, 7, and 9, is found within the upper box labelled Intending Mind. It is a verbal–verbal relation (or a category–category, concept–concept, symbol–symbol, or type–type relation; see Note 20) and has to do with time. It is the timing relation found in and imposed by the instruction-derived sequence called the Verbal Intention. That sequence begins to unfold or develop upon stimulus presentation (1), it moves one step (3) and waits until it receives the appropriate information, it then again moves one step (5) and still another step (7), and again waits for the appropriate information and then returns to its starting point (9). Within each unit of analysis, there is always an >> object > attribute >> order but the contents of each unit and the sequence of units are task- or instruction-dependent and therefore short-term and arbitrary.[15] The (sequence of) unit(s) cannot therefore be reduced to long-term associations.[16] For this relation I used the verb 'to move'. For the moment I prefer to summarise this type of time relation within the box labelled Intending Mind with the neutral term 'concatenation'.

My interpretation of this time relation is the same as Miller et al.'s (1960, pp. 27–29) interpretation of the >s in their >T>O>T>E> units (see Section

3.2). Remember that they discuss three alternatives, energy, information, and control, and remark:

> A third level of abstraction, however, is extremely important for the ideas we shall discuss. It is the notion that what flows over the arrows . . . is an intangible something called *control.* Or perhaps we should say that the arrow indicates only succession. This concept appears most frequently in the discussion of computing machines . . . But the idea is certainly not limited to computers.
>
> (Miller et al., 1960, p. 28)

The second type of relation, the one indicated with the lower row of digits 3 and 7, is found within the lower box labelled Visual Perception. It is a visual–visual–visual relation (or exemplar–exemplar–exemplar or token–token–token relation; see Note 20) that uses connections between positions in maps.[17] Through enhanced activation, it temporally connects the representation of a position on a position (middle in our example; 3) or of another feature on a position (square in our example; 7) with a representation that still contains all object features (in IN), and connects that representation (in IN) with all its features in the feature modules. This position–position–position relation was not explicit in Section 3.4, because Turing's (1936) computer-plus-tape machine involves no within-tape operations. (In Turing's machine, a change of symbol in a square has no consequences – effects on – connected symbols in other squares.) It was introduced in Figure 4.2, as enhanced activation propagating downward from a position in a feature module (P, S, or C) to the corresponding position in the input module, IN, and from that position in IN upward to the corresponding positions in all feature modules. The operation is task-dependent, and therefore arbitrary and short-term.[18] For this relation I used the verb 'to connect'. For want of a better term, I call this type of position relation 'propagation'.

This operation uses the hardware connections between representations in the visual system. There is abundant evidence that the visual information processing systems of higher animals are modular systems; that is, systems consisting of relatively isolated networks that take the visual world apart. The primary visual cortex – a kind of 'map' containing all the information from the whole visual field – distributes its information over a surprisingly large number of higher-order visual areas. Felleman and van Essen (1991) distinguish more than 30 of these regions, and more than 300 bundles of connections among these regions. Within the visual areas, the anatomical positions separate the pieces of information. Between the visual areas, bundles of position–position connections form a network that can be used for interactions between modules. So, the modularity of the visual system and the abundant connectivity in the visual system makes the 'propagation' relation between attributes of objects and objects possible. In Chapter 9, I return to this relation.

The third type of relation, indicated with the middle row of digits 2, 4, 6, and 8, connects the upper box labelled Intending Mind and the lower box labelled Visual Perception. It is a verbal (visual) – visual (verbal) relation (or a type (token) – token (type) relation; see Note 20) and has to do with content. It is the relation that brings the system from MIDDLE in the intentional sequence to the middle of the visual stimulus (2) and from SQUARE in the intentional sequence to the square in the visual stimulus (6), indicated with downward pointing arrows ('sending' and 'selecting'). It is also the relation that connects the form aspect of the object in the middle with SHAPE in the intentional sequence (4) and that connects the colour aspect of the square with COLOUR in the intentional sequence (8), indicated with upward pointing arrows ('receiving' and 'processing'). This type of relation is based on or uses learned long-term associations. For this relation I used the verb 'to select'. I prefer to summarise this type of content relation with the term 'association'.[19]

In my 'connectionist machine', the 'associations' via upward pointing arrows come closest to the unspecified 'processing' of the information processing approach. Unfortunately for theory, nowadays information processing psychology concerned with vision has not very much use for the concept of association and favours talking in terms of 'the processing of visual information' (see above). Once upon a time, however – or better, once upon more times – association appeared as a core concept in philosophy and psychology. The concept was elaborated and investigated by the British empiricists (Locke, Berkeley, Hume), by the early German experimental psychology (Ebbinghaus, Wundt, Mueller), and by the behaviourists (Watson, Thorndike, Skinner).

One of the formerly almost generally accepted laws of association is the law of contiguity – events get connected or associated when they frequently co-occur or occur close together in time and/or space. For instance, when a visual shape, e.g., the shape {square}, and an auditory string, e.g., the string 'square' – two perceptual 'objects' that have nothing in common and that therefore cannot be matched or compared – have frequently occurred and been experienced together, then upon presentation of one of the two, the {square} or the 'square', its internal representation will call or evoke the internal representation of the other, of the 'square' or the {square}. For bridging the gap between Intending Mind and Visual Perception, my 'connectionist machine' makes use of exactly this type of association.

It is not clear why presently the empty term 'processing' is mainly used. In his *Textbook*, in explaining a figure, Hebb (1966, pp. 111–112) remarks:

> . . . it is worth observing that [the figure] simply diagrams what used to be called the *association of ideas*. Though this term has disappeared from psychology, as a result of the house cleaning by Watson that got rid of all "mentalistic" terms . . . , it has meaning again now we have found out how to deal with mental or cognitive processes behavioristically.

We have already seen that "idea" is not a precise term, so "association of ideas" is not likely to be precise either, but it does refer generally to the common experience that some things occur together in thought because they have been perceived together in the past . . . Whether it is called the "association of ideas" or "connections between mediating processes," this tendency of simultaneously active central processes to become capable of exciting one another appears fundamental to the existence of organized thought.

As stated, in the model depicted in Figure 4.2 exactly this type of symmetrical verbal (visual) – visual (verbal) or type (token) – token (type) association is presupposed (see Note 20). So, in this model, 'sending' or 'selection' and 'receiving' or 'processing' basically means: exploiting the availability of strong, multiple, upward, bottom-up, and downward, top-down connections produced by earlier repeated encounters. Along the available connections the Verbal Intention in the Intending Mind sends (selects) and receives (processes) enhanced activation to effectuate the internal information processing that is required for adequate and successful task performance. An associatively rich, structured, temporal intentional sequence interacts with an associatively rich, structured, visual spatial representation.

In this connectionist machine, this interaction has as a result that

> . . . of all the tendencies readied by the perception of the stimulus, those
> will become reinforced to overvalence *which are associatively coordinated*
> with a presentation corresponding to the given intention . . .
>
> (Ach, 1905, also quoted in section 3.1; italics mine)

And it can do that because:

> To a first approximation, computations are those causal relations among
> symbols which reliably respect semantic properties of the relata. Association, for example, is a bona fide computational relation within the
> meaning of the act. Though whether Ideas get associated is supposed to
> depend on their frequency, contiguity, etc., and not on what they're
> Ideas *of*, association is none the less supposed reliably to preserve
> semantic domains . . .
>
> (Fodor, 1998, p. 10)

In Chapters 6 and 9, I return to associations.

Taken all together, it seems that only three different relations or operations are involved in my 'connectionist machine' (see also Table 4.1); one within the box Intending Mind (concatenation), one in the box Visual Perception (propagation), and one connecting the boxes Intending Mind and Visual Perception (association). For adequate task performance the system seems to have 'to move' (concatenation) 'to connect' (propagation), and 'to send'

Table 4.1 Summary of the characterisation of the operations within the Intending Mind, within Visual Perception, and the relation or interaction between the two

Intending mind	Interaction	Visual perception
(Concatenation)	(Association)	(Propagation)
(Time)	(Content)	(Position)
Verbal → Verbal	Verbal ←→ Visual	Visual → Visual
Type → Type	Type ←→ Token	Token → Token
Category → Category	Category ←→ Exemplar	Exemplar → Exemplar

(See text for further explanation.)

and 'to receive' (association). And, in my view, a machine that can perform these functions can be devised and properly programmed, i.e., can be built.[20]

4.3 Thought and propositions

As a summary and an extension of the theoretical elaborations presented in this chapter, I now briefly introduce and discuss Logan and Zbrodoff's (1999) theoretical work on 'selection for cognition'. This introduction and discussion will show, I hope, that the ideas presented in the preceding two sections are not as idiosyncratic and weird as might possibly seem up to now. In fact, while Logan and Zbrodoff neglect the, in my view essential, order in time aspect, it will appear that the main ideas introduced in the foregoing sections were already around, albeit in a somewhat different and less elaborated form.

Logan and Zbrodoff (1999) convincingly argue that current theories of perception and attention (i.e., information processing theories) are incomplete. In their view:

> There is more to human attention than perception and action. Humans think, and there is more to thought than the simple stimulus-to-response mappings that are investigated in experiments on attention. Theories of attention may provide a complete account of behaviour in such experiments, but the behaviour in those experiments is not representative of the cognitive capacities manifest in everyday thought and language . . . a complete theory of attention must also explain significant aspects of thought and language. (p. 57)

They argue that, in addition to selection for perception and selection for action (see Section 2.1. for this distinction), selection for cognition has to be recognised.[21]

In Logan and Zbrodoff's (1999) view, the primary function of attention (i.e., of information processing) in selection for cognition is to create or construct propositions, structured (compositional) representations called predicates, with truth values. And of importance in the present context is that this creation or construction of propositions is conceived in almost exactly the same way as I conceived the use of visual information for task performance in report tasks. There are two striking points of correspondence.

First, just like the view on the use of visual information for task performance presented here, Logan and Zbrodoff's (1999) view on selection for cognition postulates (at least) two separate representations:

- A conceptual representation (i.e., a structured predicate) which contains symbols that represent perceptual objects and the relations among them. Of course, in my conceptualisation this is the representation called 'Verbal Intention', with >> X > Y >> as its basic structure.
- A perceptual representation which contains modality-specific information about objects that impinge on sensory surfaces. Of course, in my conceptualisation this is the representation called 'Visual Perception', with activations in an input module (IN) and in feature modules (C, S, and P).

Second, just as in my conceptualisation of the use of visual information for task performance, in Logan and Zbrodoff's (1999) view on selection for cognition the appropriate 'connection', 'coordination', or 'interaction' between elements of the two different representations is regarded as the essence of the internal information processing operations. In their view, for selection for cognition:

> Perceptual objects corresponding to the arguments of the predicate have to be selected; interpretations of, or identities for, the selected objects have to be chosen; and the identified objects have to be connected or bound to symbols that represent the arguments. (p. 64)

> For example, in apprehending "the dog is beside the fireplace", an object corresponding to the dog and an object corresponding to the fireplace must be selected and identified. The object corresponding to the dog must be bound to the argument, *dog*, in the predicate *beside(dog, fireplace)*, and the object corresponding to the fireplace must be bound to the argument, *fireplace*, in the same predicate. (p. 67)

And in my view, for answering the question 'Where is the dog?' or for obeying the instruction 'Name the position of the dog', that question or instruction is first translated into what I called an initial Verbal Intention [to select] of about the form

>> (our) DOG > POSITION (in house coordinates) >>.

The concept '(our) DOG' interacts with Visual Perception and selects the dog with all its properties and the concept 'POSITION (in house coordinates)' picks from all these properties the property 'beside the fireplace'. This results in what I called the resulting Verbal Intention [to report]

>> (our) DOG > BESIDE THE FIREPLACE >>,

that is transformed and uttered as 'The dog is beside the fireplace' (see Section 4.1). I briefly return to this analysis at the end of this section.

The quotations and the example show the close correspondence of the view presented here and Logan and Zbrodoff's (1999) view. That Logan and Zbrodoff's view and my view are so close together is not really surprising. In '[see] : [the square is red]', the [the square is red] is the intentional object of the act '[see] : [. . .]'. That intentional object is an internal proposition. When that intentional object is overtly expressed as 'the square is red' or as 'red', we have an overt proposition, a statement or assertion that expresses a judgement or opinion about a state of affairs in the outer world that can be true or false. And, in [perceive] : [the letter indicated by the bar marker is a Z], the intentional object [the letter indicated by the bar marker is a Z] is an internal proposition. When that intentional object is overtly expressed as 'the letter indicated is a Z' or as 'Z', we have an overt proposition, a statement or assertion that expresses a judgement or opinion about a state of affairs in the world that can be true or false. So, just like Logan and Zbrodoff's work, my work was concerned with propositions. The main difference between Logan and Zbrodoff's work and the work presented here is not in the resulting theory, but in the starting point. Logan and Zbrodoff seem to suppose that in experiments on attention only 'simple stimulus-to-response mappings' are involved (see the quotation above; see, however, also their pages 62–63). I am convinced that in nearly all these experiments 'propositions' are involved.[22] Because the subjects express propositions, judgements, or opinions about states of the world that can be false or true, the percentages correct and errors, the basic data obtained in experiments with 'simple stimulus-to-response-mappings', can be calculated. Chapters 5 and 6 also serve to support my position.[23]

The fact that the two views, one starting with and concerned with the use of visual information for task performance and the other starting with and concerned with selection for cognition, are so close together strongly suggests that they are closing in on a general information processing theory that can deal with a broad range of tasks – from tasks involving 'simple stimulus-to-response mappings that are investigated in experiments on attention' to tasks involving 'the cognitive capacities manifest in everyday thought and language'. Of course, what these tasks have in common is that language, in one form or another, e.g., as a 'structured sequence' or as a 'structured predicate', directs attention, i.e., controls the internal information processing operations required for adequate task performance.

One difference between Logan and Zbrodoff's (1999) theorising and the theoretical view developed in this chapter remains to be discussed. It concerns the conceptualisation of the 'connection', 'coordination', or 'interaction' between the two postulated representations – the relation between Verbal Intention and Visual Perception, which I called 'association'.

In Logan and Zbrodoff's (1999) view, representations by themselves do not do anything.[24] Additional processes are required for relating or 'binding' the two representations. For the above dog–fireplace case, in their view:

> Selection of objects for these bindings may involve a search process, in which candidate objects are selected and compared iteratively with conceptual representations of *dog* and *fireplace* until appropriate matches are found. (p. 67)

Theoretical concepts like 'compare' and 'match', however, introduce insurmountable theoretical difficulties. In Logan and Zbrodoff's (1999) theoretical work, for instance, someone or something has to compare or match elements of representations that cannot be compared because they have nothing in common (modality-specific information about objects in the perceptual representation has to be compared with symbols that represent perceptual objects in the conceptual representation). Therefore this aspect of their theorising has to be rejected (see Van der Heijden & Van der Velde, 1999, p. 85, for further details). The alternative for 'matching' and 'comparing' is 'association' (see Section 4.2).

I end this section with five brief remarks. The first concerns selection and language. As stated, what the tasks considered by Logan and Zbrodoff (1999) and the report tasks I am concerned with here have in common is that language, in one or another form, e.g., as a 'structured sequence' or as a 'structured predicate', directs attention, i.e., controls the internal information processing operations required for adequate task performance. In my view, the idea that in some types of tasks 'language', in one form or another, is in control is fully consistent with the development during human evolution. There are two important points here. The first is that initially during that evolution not only did visual perception as such and auditory perception as such evolve, but also, of course, their communication and interaction. The second important point is that, with this communication and interaction already in place, during and after the development of auditory language not very much more had to happen for 'language' to be in control.

The second remark concerns selection without language. It must be clear that, in my view, for the operation of an Intention in $\gg X > Y \gg$ steps, neither an explicit overt verbal instruction (or an overt question) nor an explicit overt verbal report is required. It is highly likely that the information processing system often spontaneously investigates and scrutinises the visual environment without any accompanying report or other overt action, i.e., for the purpose of acquiring information only (see, e.g., Neumann,

1990a, on 'updating the internal representation'). My contention is, however, that this spontaneously looking for learning what is out there also proceeds in >> object > attribute >> steps, and that in this case not language, but the perceived world most often suggests or triggers the 'types' or 'concepts' (see also Logan & Zbrodoff, 1999, pp. 63–64).

The third remark concerns the number of maps or modules that are required for accounting for performance in report tasks. With few exceptions, in this part of the work I will mainly work with the Intending Mind and the Visual Perception modules in Figure 4.2, plus some additional action modules. It will be clear, however, that for an adequate and realistic account of task performance many more maps and modules are required. This is not only so at the Visual Perception side; remember that Felleman and Van Essen (1991) have already distinguished more than 30 regions (and more than 300 connections between regions) in the visual system (see Section 4.2). This is also true for the Intending Mind side (see also Section 4.4). At that side, we now have only a Verbal Intention, conceived as a concatenation of units of analysis, >> . . . > . . . >>. Additional modules concerned with language and with language transformations are certainly required. Also modules concerned with the general orientation in space and in time, and with the general orientation in content, i.e., modules providing the required contexts or 'frames of reference', are certainly required. That such modules are missing, however, I do not see as damaging or problematic for the views presented in this work. This lack of modules simply points to topics in need of further experimental investigation in, I hope, the near future.

The fourth remark concerns the number of units of analysis that are required for accounting for performance in report tasks. In this work, I will consistently assume that for report tasks, one or a series of units of analysis of the >> object > attribute >> type suffice (see Section 9.4 for extensions and generalisations and for the power of this format).[25] Logan and Zbrodoff's (1999) analysis in terms of *beside(dog, fireplace)*, however, at least suggests that alternative proposals are possible.[26] Moreover, my analysis of their example might not be that convincing; an analysis in terms of two 'basic' propositions, >> dog > position >> and >> fireplace > position >>, and their combination into a 'complex' proposition 'higher on' in the information processing system, is possibly a better alternative.[27] These and related issues, however, I do not see as damaging or problematic for the views presented in this work. Again, these problems simply point to topics in need of further experimental investigation in, I hope, the near future.[28]

The last remark concerns 'types of tasks' (see Chapter 2). The important point is that, with the information provided in this section, a principled distinction between types of simple laboratory tasks comes within reach. The report tasks can be defined as tasks in which subjects express propositions, i.e., express a judgement or opinion about a state of affairs in the world. The reports are evaluated by the experimenter in terms of 'true' or 'false' (not as 'good' or 'bad'). The act tasks can be defined as tasks in which subjects do something to, in, or with the world. The performance is evaluated by the experimenter in terms of 'good' and 'bad' (not with 'true' or 'false'). The report 'the colour is red' while the patch is blue is a false report, not a bad report. Failing to catch a ball is a bad performance, not a false performance.

4.4   Programs and brains

What is the task of an information processing psychologist? To answer this question

> ... let us consider the familiar parallel between man and computer ... The task of a psychologist trying to understand human cognition is analogous to that of a man trying to discover how a computer has been programmed. In particular, if the program seems to store and reuse information, we would like to know by what "routines" or "procedures" this is done. Given this purpose, he will not care much whether his particular computer stores information in magnetic cores or in thin films; he wants to understand the program, not the "hardware" ... He wants to understand its utilization, not its incarnation.
>
> (Neisser, 1967, p. 6)

Indeed, the information processing approach is concerned with a functional analysis of perception, cognition, and action, not with their implementation. By using behavioural experiments, the approach attempts to learn how the information processing system functions when a task is performed (see Section 1.4). For the approach as such, it is not of much importance to know either how exactly the brain performs the postulated functions or where exactly in the brain the postulated functions are located. What is important to know is whether the postulated functions are realisable, and if so, whether it is reasonable to assume that they are indeed realised somewhere in the human brain.

In the previous sections of this chapter, all my efforts were directed at defining internal operations that could indeed perform the required job. And, as demonstrated in Section 4.2, there are not very many reasons to assume that the 'connectionist machine', derived from a variety of suggestions in early and contemporary psychology and from 'Turing's machine', is not realisable. In this section I briefly turn to the issue of whether it is also reasonable to assume that the postulated functions are indeed realised somewhere in the human brain. And of course, with regard to this issue the question of the viability of my core assumption – the assumption that in the performance of report tasks two interacting representations, one in the Intending Mind and one in Visual Perception, are involved – is of particular importance. The adequacy of my unit of analysis for report tasks is considered in the next two chapters.

Until recently there was an almost complete lack of knowledge about where and how cognitive operations are implemented in the brain. Recently developed and improved brain-imaging techniques – positron emission tomography (PET), functional magnetic resonance imaging (fMRI), and the recording of event-related potentials (ERPs) – have made it possible to study aspects of these operations in the brain in real time. Within the branch of experimental psychology I am concerned with, the pioneers Posner (see, e.g., Posner & Badgaiyan, 1998, for a recent overview) and LaBerge (see, e.g., LaBerge, 1995, for an extensive overview) have made particularly impressive contributions in this advanced field of research. Nominally their work is concerned with 'attention in vision' (see the titles of their works), but factually their work is concerned with all cognitive operations involved in the performance of (report) tasks (see the contents of their work). What follows is a short summary of their main relevant findings and interpretations. Readers who are not interested in this 'hardware' stuff can simply skim or skip this section.

Posner's work led him to a general theory of attention involving three brain networks, a 'vigilance network', an 'orienting network', and an 'executive network'. The vigilance network is responsible for the maintenance of the alert state of the brain and is a *conditio sine qua non* for the execution of cognitive operations. For our purposes, only the executive network (in the front or anterior part of the cortex) and the orienting network (in the back or the posterior part of the cortex) are of importance. And the questions that have to be answered are: Can the 'executive network' be equated with the Intending Mind, and how is the 'orienting network' related to Visual Perception?

With regard to the executive network in the front of the cortex, Posner and Badgaiyan (1998, p. 65) remark:

> An anteriorly located attentional network is involved in attentional recruitment and it controls the brain areas that perform complex cognitive tasks. It exerts general control over the areas involved in target detection and response. This network is more active when the task involves complex discrimination . . . and the degree of activation depends on the number of targets presented . . . The network is also responsible for anticipation of the target location . . . Areas involved in this network are the midprefrontal cortex, including the anterior cingulate gyrus and supplementary motor area . . .

And, with regard to the anterior cortical areas, LaBerge (1995, p. 220) remarks:

> The dorsolateral and ventrolateral areas have been shown to contain neurons that specialize in spatial location and in attributes such as color and shape, and these neurons discharge during delays between a cue

and a target, suggesting that they serve as working memory for location and shape attributes. The anterior cingulate area is particularly active when novel combinations of actions are required . . . , and it would appear that this area may store a sequence of actions, somewhat like the dorsolateral and ventrolateral prefrontal areas store location and shape attributes of an object.

From these quotations it will be clear that there are no arguments that prevent me from assuming that the anterior network – the 'working memory' that 'store(s) a sequence of actions', 'is . . . responsible for anticipations', and 'exerts general control over the areas involved in target detection and response' – can play the role of the Intending Mind with its Verbal Intention.

With regard to their orienting network in the back of the cortex, Posner and Badgaiyan (1998) remark;

Anatomically, this network is located posteriorly, and for the visual system it is largely responsible for operations needed to bring attention to a location or object and to shift attention from an unattended to a target location. It serves to enhance information at the attended location in comparison with that that occurs at relatively unattended locations . . . In terms of cognitive theories, this network mediates disengagement, engagement, and amplification of the attentional target. (p. 62)

When a target is attended, activity of the brain areas which specialize in its processing are selectively enhanced. Thus, in a Pet study, wherein the subjects were required to attend to different aspects of a stimulus – its motion, form, or color – different prestriate brain areas were activated in each condition . . . In general, attention to sensory information appears to increase blood flow in the specific brain areas which process that event. (p. 64)

These quotations make clear that, according to Posner and Badgaiyan (1998), the posterior part of the cortex, which houses the visual system, also contains an 'orienting network', a network that 'shift(s) attention from an unattended to a target location', 'bring(s) attention to a location or object', and 'enhance(s) information at the attended location'.

This hypothetical 'orienting network' produces all the effects I have to expect in Visual Perception. It will be clear, however, that in my view there is no posterior orienting network in the visual system with causal powers on its own.[29] According to my analysis, what is observed in the visual system in the posterior part of the brain are the *effects caused* by the executive network in the frontal part of the brain working with the current Verbal Intention. Fortunately, here I find LaBerge (1995) at my side. He clearly and adequately distinguishes between the location where control *originates* and the location where control is *expressed*. In his view, in the visual cortex, or more generally in the brain structures subserving visual perception,

> Attention may be expressed in many different cortical areas simultaneously, as happens when a subject is attending to a particular object . . . and attending to its location . . . The expression of attention in a brain area appears to be described effectively as an enhancement of activity in the attended set of pathways relative to the activity in the unattended set of pathways . . . Anterior cortical areas that serve working memory for object locations, object attributes, and operations on object representations are assumed to control the expression of attention in the cortical areas . . .
>
> (LaBerge, 1995, p. 139)

So, according to LaBerge, control originates anteriorly and is expressed posteriorly.[30] And, clearly, for the question of whether the functions I postulated are indeed realised somewhere in the brain, no answer suits me better than: *Anterior cortical areas that serve working memory for object locations, object attributes, and operations on object representations are assumed to control the expression of attention in the cortical areas . . .* (LaBerge, 1995, p. 139)

Of course, quite a lot of questions still remain open in this intriguing field of research. Nevertheless, my interpretation of internal performance in report tasks – an interaction between a Verbal Intention, conceived as a developing sequence in the Intending Mind, and Visual Perception, conceived as activations in a set of maps – seems not at variance with what recent advanced brain-imaging techniques are indicating. The operations I postulated are not only realisable in a 'connection machine', they also seem to be actually implemented in the human brain as orderly activity originating in an anterior system, which interacts with and therefore is expressed in a posterior system, concerned with visual perception.

Let us turn next to the viability of my unit of analysis for report tasks, >> X > Y >>.

Notes

1 In this analysis I simply assume that subjects select and process the verbal task instruction. It seems that this starting point is inadequate and begs the question. How subjects use their *auditory* perception for task performance is simply neglected. In Chapter 9, Section 9.4, I briefly return to this issue.

2 For the moment, the terms MIDDLE, SHAPE, etc., can be regarded as Gibson's (1979) 'concepts' (see Section 2.2).

3 It possibly worthwhile to note that this conceptualisation *is* Broadbent's (1958) structure, depicted in Figure 3.1 (filter > channel), in terms of functions of a sequence (>> X > Y >>) instead of structures. See also Chapter 9.

4 For such downward connections, see, e.g., De Kamps and Van der Velde (2001) and Van der Velde and De Kamps (2001).

5 This enhanced activation comes back immediately, i.e., bounces via the upward pointing arrow. However, that is not important because the sequence has moved to the state SHAPE and therefore cannot accept position information. (Theoretically even more interesting is the possibility that exactly this 'feedback' makes the sequence move to the next stage.)

6 The sequence is in the state SHAPE. The state SHAPE, or possibly better, the meaning of the state SHAPE, can be considered as consisting of all possible shapes plus, possibly, some related information. Only the shape aspect of the selected visual object – that is, of the small, black digit in the middle – is compatible with this meaning of SHAPE. Therefore, only this aspect of the selected object is selected by (the meaning of) the state SHAPE.

7 It is worthwhile to note that this conceptualisation, this serial selection of attributes of different objects for report, is consistent with findings on parallel and serial processing. There is substantial evidence indicating that, when features that belong to dimensions of different objects have to be reported, a severe capacity limitation and interference is found. Features that belong to different dimensions of the same object can, however, be processed simultaneously without apparent capacity limitation and interference (for relevant research see, e.g., Allport, 1971; Biederman & Checkosky, 1970; Duncan, 1980, 1983, 1984; Saraga & Shallice, 1973; Treisman, Kahneman, & Burkell, 1983; see also Neumann, 1987, pp. 366 & 385, and Pashler, 1998, pp. 124–134). After reviewing the relevant empirical evidence, Pashler (1998, p. 132) concludes:

> If the task requires reporting more than one attribute from a display . . . interference is usually found if the reported attributes reside in different objects. This interference seems to be avoided when the attributes are part of a single object.

8 The essential point here is that the 'sending' state, which 'selects', is specific/ detailed/certain, while the 'receiving' state, which 'processes', is general/global/ uncertain.

9 It is worthwhile to note that in this conceptualisation the Verbal Intention selects attributes of objects and that the selected attributes pick out the responses from among the set of available/allowable responses. By distinguishing between attributes and responses, the problem mentioned in Note 13 in Chapter 3 is solved. What responses are used in a colour-naming task – red/blue, warm/cold, long/short – depends on what set of responses is specified in the instruction.

10 It is possibly worthwhile to note that this conceptualisation presents a starting point for explaining 'repetition' and 'alternation' effects, i.e., effects of preceding trials.

11 It is of importance to note that the $\gg X > Y \gg$ unit is the unit of analysis of the Verbal Intention in the Intending Mind. For the complete intentional machine, i.e., for the Verbal Intention in the Intending Mind interacting with the visual world in Visual Perception, the unit of analysis can be written as $\gg [X] : [\ ] > [Y] : [\ ] \gg$, with [X] and [Y] referring to states of the Verbal Intention and [ ] and [ ] referring to contents in Visual Perception.

12 The units can also be seen as Miller et al.'s (1960) TOTE units interpreted as $\gg$ OBJECT $\gg$ ATTRIBUTE $\gg$ units (see Section 3.3).

13 This problem is directly connected with the problem that information processing psychologists also have no ideas about what information is, i.e., about what has to be processed, what is processed, and what the result of that processing is. Pashler (1998, p. 37) can serve to illustrate this point. The introductory paragraph to selective attention reads (italics mine):

We are almost always subjected to a barrage of different sources of *sensory information* at any instant. You can verify this by pausing and trying to survey the various *sensations* impinging upon you at this very moment. You will probably find some *auditory stimuli* (an *airconditioner*?) and *kinesthetic stimuli* (the *back of the chair*?), as well as many *visual inputs* originating in this text, but also more *peripheral visual stimuli*. Probably you would agree that you were not aware of more than a few of these *stimuli* at the moment you began trying to enumerate them . . . The process of selecting from among the many *potentially available stimuli* is the clearest manifestation of selective attention.

14 It is interesting to note that the two-stage theories simply postulate that the first stage of processing results in a preliminary form of perception. For instance, the problem of how to get from wavelengths or photons to perceived colour is simply neglected. The assumption is that subjects are presented with coloured stimuli and that they process the colours. The subjects 'process' what the experimenters 'see'.

15 That the content of each unit of analysis and the sequence of units is short-term and arbitrary, i.e., task- or instruction-dependent, is easy to see by playing around with instructions and sequences. For instance, at the same moment in time and without changing the stimulus, the instruction could have been 'Name first the position of the red object and then name the colour of the digit in the middle' with as sequence:

>> RED > POSITION >> >> MIDDLE > COLOUR >>

So the instruction temporarily induces an arbitrary sequence.

16 This 'control' operation cannot be reduced to long-term associations for the report tasks we are concerned with here. However, this is not so for all tasks (see Chapter 9, Section 9.4).

17 In Chapter 7 I turn to the relation between positions in maps or modules and the representation of position in external space.

18 That this relation is short-term and arbitrary is easy to see. The connections used are fixed, hardware connections in the visual system. What position–position–position connections are used, however, is completely task- or instruction-dependent.

19 In a sense, the system has to 'know' what MIDDLE means in order to select the middle and not the left or the red object in the representation of the visual stimulus, and the system has to 'know' what SHAPE means in order to select the shape and not one of the other attributes of the visual object in the middle. The term MIDDLE is long-term associated or connected with something triggered by or related to the 'middle of the representation of the stimulus', and the 'shape of the object in the middle' is long-term associated or connected with something triggered by or connected with SHAPE.

20 There is still another way to characterise or elucidate the differences between the three different relations or operations, namely in terms of 'types' and 'tokens'.

A *type* . . . can be defined . . . as any class of things – physical objects, numbers or whatever – organized in terms of some essential property shared by all members of the class. For example, the class of chairs is a type, defined (very roughly) as the class of artifacts that you can sit on. A *token* is an individual member of a type. Thus the chair you are now sitting on is a token of the type, chair. Tokens can differ dramatically in terms of their

> contingent properties . . . Tokens of a type, however, cannot differ in terms
> of their essential property(ies) . . .
>
> (Flanagan, 1991, p. 14)

(It is interesting to note that tokens occupy positions and types do not.) Given this terminology, the elements of the intentional sequence can be regarded as types, and the representation of the middle of the visual stimulus, the representation of the shape corresponding with that position, the representation of the square in the visual stimulus, and the representation of the corresponding colour, can be regarded as tokens.

With this terminology, the temporal relations within the sequence consist of type–type relations (concatenation), the content relations between the elements of the sequence and the relevant parts of the visual representation and between the parts of the visual representation and elements of the sequence are type–token and token–type relations (association), and the spatial relations between the representation of the middle of the stimulus and the representation of the shape in the middle and the representation of the square in the visual stimulus and the representation of the colour are token–token relations (propagation). In other words, 'to move' (concatenation) is 'to move from type to type', 'to select/receive' (association) is 'to select with a type a token or with a token a type', and 'to connect' (propagation) is 'to contact a token starting with another token'.

21 There are a number of problematic points here that, however, I do not want to emphasise. One is that, in my view set out in this chapter, the stimulus-to-response mappings investigated in experiments on attention are not really that simple; see also Chapters 5 and 6. Another is that, in my view, the information processing approach is not concerned with the role of attention in perception but with the role of attention and perception for task performance (see Section 1.4). Still another is that, in my view, neither the role of attention in perception nor the role of attention in action control is really clarified.

22 In the objective experiments used in the information processing approach the subjects have to report something about the state of affairs in the outer world. It is difficult to see how they can do that without expressing, in one way or another, a proposition.

23 It can be stated that it appears that, after all, my theorising is concerned with 'thought'. It must then be realised, as will be demonstrated in the next two chapters, that this 'thought' is then the 'thought' that is generally encountered in the experiments performed in the perception for perception camp in the information processing approach.

24 In my view, 'connectionism' has shown that the idea that representations by themselves do not do anything is simply wrong. Connectionist representations consist of activation patterns in networks of homogeneous processing units in which 'activation' passes along connections with 'connection weights'. In such a network, activated units relay their activation to the units they are connected or associated with. So, in these networks the causal power of a representation derives from the sole fact of its being activated, without an additional process operating on it. The presence of an activation ensures that it exerts an appropriate causal effect, given the appropriate connectivity pattern or pattern of associations (see, e.g., Scheerer, 1992).

25 See Logan and Zbrodoff (1999, p. 70) for a distinction between 'reference object selection' and 'reference frame selection', a distinction close to 'object selection' – 'attribute selection'. Logan and Zbrodoff's theory therefore directly leads to a >> reference object > reference frame >> unit of analysis that is compatible with my >> object > attribute >> unit of analysis.

26 See also, however, Hurford's 'The Neural Basis of Predicate–Argument Structure' (in press).

27 It is worthwhile to see here that there is a difference between the selection of information for task performance (proposed format: $\gg X > Y \gg$) and the expression of what is selected with this format in language (a great variety of formats).

28 It is interesting to know that the issue of what basic propositions are and what complex propositions are has been intensively investigated in the past in analytic philosophy by, for instance, Russell, Wittgenstein, and the members of the Wiener Kreis. In my view, time has come for experimental psychology with its powerful objective methods to take up this issue.

29 It is important to note that Posner and Badgaiyan (1998) ascribe selective functions to this orienting network. So, within visual perception a network performing selections is postulated. What is problematic, of course, is how this network knows what to select.

30 In a later part of their chapter, Posner and Badgaiyan (1998) express a similar point of view when they try to answer the crucial question:

> What is the cingulate activation actually doing? According to our analysis the cingulate is involved in producing the local amplification in neural activity that accompanies top-down selection of items. It is easiest to understand this function in the domain of processing words. It is well known from cognitive studies that a target word is processed more efficiently following a related prime word . . . A portion of this improvement occurs automatically . . . However, another portion of the activation is top-down because attention to the prime word leads the subject to expect a particular type of target . . . We believe that the cingulate is responsible for these top-down effects by providing a boost in activation to items associated with the expectation. (p. 71)

> We also believe that cingulate activation is involved when elements of a thought are ordered in time. By increasing activation of the brain area that performs a specific computation, one can change the time course of the organization of the component operations . . . (p. 72)

5 Paradigms with accuracy as the dependent variable

5.0 Introduction

In Section 2.3, we visited the laboratory to see what happened there. Now, after two chapters of indoctrination, the time has come to return there and have a closer look at what happened and happens there. This chapter is concerned with evidence produced by paradigms with accuracy, proportions correct, as the dependent variable – paradigms that require subjects to express propositions that can be scored as true or false.[1] Chapter 6 is concerned with evidence produced by paradigms with latency as the dependent variable – paradigms that require subjects to express these propositions as fast as possible. In both chapters, only research using exposure conditions that make useful (saccadic) eye movements impossible (or irrelevant) is considered.

In Section 5.1, we start with Broadbent's research on stimulus set and response set. It is shown that, as argued in Section 3.3, in both tasks (a series of) the couple of selective operations 'object selection' and 'attribute selection' is repeatedly involved. Broadbent's work is mainly concerned with the effectiveness of the 'sending' term, X, in the unit of analysis $\gg X > Y \gg$. Recent research on the effectiveness of X, research using 'visual search' tasks, is briefly referred to. Then an intriguing variant of the stimulus set task with a forced-report part and a free-report part is introduced. The free-report part of that task provides strong support for the view of attention in terms of content as developed in this work and against the conceptualisation of attention in terms of space, that is, as a kind of 'spotlight' or 'zoom lens'.

In Sections 5.2 and 5.3, research involving experimental manipulations in the time domain is discussed. In Section 5.2 we have a closer look at experiments in which a series of visual information is presented in rapid succession (RSVP, rapid serial visual presentation tasks). Because the Verbal Intention or intentional sequence in the Intending Mind also develops in time, the sequence and the visual information can be in step and out of step. It is shown that the $\gg X > Y \gg$ approach can handle the major results obtained in this field of research in a natural way. As a matter of fact, the approach predicts the phenomena that at the time of their discovery were completely unexpected.

In Section 5.3, we have a closer look at the results obtained with position cueing experiments with central symbolic cues and peripheral location cues, and with varying cue–target intervals. The difference in results obtained in tasks with location cues and with symbolic cues is explained in terms of the number of units of analysis involved. It is argued and shown that selection experiments with less than 100% validity conditions reveal to only a limited extent the internal effects of the position cues. The results obtained with a 100% validity condition are completely in accord with the $>> X > Y >>$ approach.

In Section 5.4, the 'capacity issue' – the basic intuition that the human information processor has severe central capacity limitations – is critically discussed. It will appear that my conceptualisation is in accord with this intuition; the conceptualisation has the same predictive power as Broadbent's (1958) limited-capacity information processing model and only a reinterpretation of that model is required. This reinterpretation does not run into the theoretical difficulties faced by the classical capacity views. Moreover, this reinterpretation makes clear why capacity is limited in the way it is: to ensure adequate task performance.

5.1   Stimulus set, response set, and free report

Broadbent (1970, 1971) distinguished between two types of tasks, stimulus set tasks and response set tasks (see Section 3.3). For at least three reasons it is worthwhile to have a closer look at Broadbent's empirical research using these tasks. First, this research deals with the extremes of the spectrum of selection tasks, very easy 'stimulus set' tasks and very difficult 'response set' tasks. Second, this research allows me to demonstrate that in both tasks the same two selective operations are (repeatedly) at work. And third, this research allows me to introduce some other important fields of research.

In Section 3.3, I described the stimulus set task and the response set task, so here a short summary suffices. In a stimulus set task

> ... the irrelevant stimuli are perfectly appropriate to the allowable re-sponses, but are distinguished by some other feature which has in itself no connection with the class of responses allowed. For example, a man might be asked to report the red digits in a mixed array of red and black digits, where the black stimuli are then irrelevant only by their colour.
>
> (Broadbent, 1970, p. 51)

In a response set task

> ... the vocabulary of responses determines the selection, because the irrelevant stimuli are not appropriate to any one of the allowable responses. For example, a man may be asked to report only the digits in

a mixed array of letters and digits, and each letter stimulus then has no corresponding member of the allowable class of digit responses.

(Broadbent, 1970, p. 51)

Broadbent (1970) used both tasks. In the stimulus set task, the stimuli contained a mixed array of red digits and black digits and the instruction was 'Name the red digits, not the black ones'. In the response set task, the stimuli contained a mixed array of letters and digits and the instruction was 'Name the digits, not the letters'. Broadbent used the two tasks in two conditions – one in which the instruction was given before stimulus presentation and one in which the instruction was given after stimulus presentation. In the present context, only the results obtained in the condition with the instruction before stimulus presentation are of importance. In this condition, appreciably better performance was observed with the stimulus set instruction than with the response set instruction.

Broadbent's (1970) stimulus set findings fit in perfectly well with other evidence reported in the literature. There is abundant evidence that selection of objects on the basis of colour, i.e., selection with colour [red, not black] as the 'defining attribute', is easy (see, e.g., Bundesen, Pedersen, & Larsen, 1984; Bundesen, Shibuya, & Larsen, 1985; Francolini & Egeth, 1980; Humphreys, 1981; Kaptein, Theeuwes, & Van der Heijden, 1995; Nissen, 1985; Snyder, 1972; Tsal & Lavie, 1988; Van der Heijden, Kurvink, De lange, De Leeuw, & Van der Geest, 1996; Von Wright, 1968, 1970).

Given this information and given the analysis presented in Chapter 4, it will be clear that, in my view, this stimulus set task is performed with the intentional sequence or Verbal Intention

>> RED1 > SHAPE >> >> RED2 > SHAPE >> >> RED3 > SHAPE >> >> RED4 > SHAPE >> etc.

The assumption here is that the red items are selected one after another (X: 'sending' or 'selection') and that for each red item the shape aspect is assessed (Y: 'receiving' or 'processing').[2]

Broadbent's (1970) response set findings also fit in well with other evidence reported in the literature.[3] There is abundant evidence that selection of objects on the basis of subtle differences in shape, i.e., selection with shape [digit, not letter] as the 'defining attribute' is very difficult/impossible (for relevant research see, e.g., Sperling, 1960; Von Wright, 1968, 1970; see also Duncan, 1983; Merikle, 1980; see Van der Heijden, 1992, for an overview).

Given this information and given the analysis presented in Chapter 4, it will be clear that, in my view, this response set task is performed with the intentional sequence or Verbal Intention

>>OBJECT1 > SHAPE >> >> OBJECT2 > SHAPE >> >> OBJECT3 > SHAPE >> >> etc.

The assumption here is that the intentional sequence or Verbal Intention is not capable of initiating top-down the orderly selection of the digits and therefore selects 'objects' on positions. The objects are selected one after another (X: 'sending' or 'selection'), from each object the shape is selected (Y: 'receiving' or 'processing'), and, on the basis of this shape information, the digit/letter aspect is assessed (I return to this assessment in Chapter 6).

Broadbent's (1970) main result – appreciably better performance in the stimulus set task than in the response set task – follows, of course, immediately from the two hypothesised intentional sequences or Verbal Intentions. Under the stimulus set instruction, each initiated 'red object' selection and 'shape' processing is a 'hit' resulting in a required digit name. Under the response set instruction, however, only about half of the initiated 'object' selections and 'shape' processings result in a 'hit', delivering a required digit name. In the other half of the trials, time and effort are wasted because, after 'object' selection and 'shape' processing during letter/digit assessment, it appears that what is selected is not a digit, as required by the instruction, but a letter, which has to be rejected.

In Section 3.3, I mentioned that Broadbent (1970, 1971) assumed that, with advance instructions, the stimulus set task and the response set task had their own, dedicated, selection mechanisms; 'stimulus set' or 'filtering' in the stimulus set task and 'response set' or 'pigeon-holing' in the response set task. There I also mentioned that Bundesen (1990) and Phaf et al. (1990) showed with calculations and simulations that in both types of tasks two (simultaneously operating) selective operations are required for adequate task performance. It will be clear that the analysis presented here corroborates and extends Bundesen's and Phaf et al.'s contention. It corroborates this contention because it demonstrates that in both types of tasks two different selective operations are (repeatedly) involved – for both tasks all sub-sequences involve 'object set' or 'filtering' terms and 'attribute set' or 'pigeon-holing' terms, i.e., are all of the form >> object > attribute >> or >> X > Y >>. It extends this contention by the introduction of a Verbal Intention or intentional sequence in an Intending Mind that initiates and controls these selective operations.

What the analysis just presented also shows is that Broadbent's (1970) stimulus set and response set research is basically concerned with the effectiveness of the 'sending' term, X, of the basic unit >> X > Y >>.[4] And what Broadbent found was efficient selection in the stimulus set task and inefficient selection in the response set task. Looking at this research in this way reveals that, for investigating this effectiveness question, Broadbent's stimulus set task and response set task are complicated in an unnecessary way. In both tasks the same internal operations are repeated a great number of times. Moreover, also in both tasks the 'receiving' term, Y, is massively and repeatedly involved. For assessing the properties of a particular term X, such an involvement of term Y is undesirable and unnecessary.[5]

The effectiveness of various types of the sending term, X, of the unit of analysis >> X > Y >> has been, and presently still is, intensively and more appropriately investigated with a simpler type of task, the *visual search* task. In this type of task, the subjects are presented with stimuli with varying numbers of items (e.g., letters, coloured letters, letters and digits). They are instructed to say '*yes*' (or press a 'yes' button) when there is a pre-specified item (e.g., a red E) and to say '*no*' (or press a 'no' button) when there is not. In this field of research, the existence and influence of top-down factors in task performance is not only simply acknowledged, but also explicitly recognised and modelled.[6] Because this research is mainly concerned with spatial properties of attention, and not with the temporal properties I am primarily concerned with in this work, I will not review or interpret it further.[7] For excellent recent overviews of this research the reader is referred to Egeth and Yantis (1997) and Yantis and Egeth (1999).[8]

In Section 4.1, I stated that in my conceptualisation state X picks out or selects the required object from among all available objects – my conceptualisation is 'object-based'. However, the 'spotlight', 'zoom-lens', and 'gradient' models of attention of, e.g., Eriksen and St. James (1986) and LaBerge and Brown (1989), assume that not objects but regions in visual space are picked out or selected – these conceptualisations are 'space-based'. Duncan (1984) designed a simple and appropriate experimental situation for deciding *what* is selected in selection experiments, an object or a region. Duncan presented stimuli consisting of two overlapping objects, a (small or large) box with a (dotted or dashed) line. The box had a gap on the right or the left and the line slanted to the right or the left. From the values on the four variables (small–large, gap right–left, dotted–dashed, slanted right–left) the subjects had to report two at a time. Duncan (1984, p. 501) found

> . . . that two judgements that concern the same object can be made simultaneously without loss of accuracy, whereas two judgements that concern different objects cannot. Neither the similarity nor the difficulty of required discriminations, nor the spatial distribution of information, could account for the results. The experiments support a view in which parallel . . . processes serve to segment the field into separate objects, followed by a process of focal attention that deals with only one object at a time.

So, Duncan's results clearly support my 'object-based' view. (For further supporting evidence see, e.g., Baylis, 1994; Baylis & Driver, 1993; see also Luck & Vogel, 1997.)

In general, simple experimental tasks, as used for instance by Duncan (1984), have to be preferred over complicated experimental tasks. There is, however, one complicated, but highly intriguing 'stimulus set' task that still needs to be discussed because it provides important information about *how* the selection process works. The task was introduced by Tsal and Lavie (1988) and later on used by Van der Heijden et al. (1996) and Tsal and Lamy (2000). First I introduce the theoretical context, then the stimuli and the task, and then the relevant results.

In Chapter 4, I described how the information processing approach to perception and cognition has produced more models of perception and selection, not just one. A main distinction is between models that regard all attributes – colour, shape, position – as equal (see, e.g., Bundesen, 1990; Kahneman, 1973; Phaf et al., 1990) and models that recognise a special, dominant role for the attribute position (see, e.g., Treisman, 1988, 1993; Van der Heijden, 1992, 1993, 1996a). My >> X > Y >> approach, as presented up to now, is a clear example of an 'all-equal' model. There is no attribute with a privileged status (see also Figure 4.2). It is worthwhile to remember here, however, that for my purposes in Chapter 4 the choice of the 'correct' model was not crucial. I therefore chose the simplest of the two main types of models, the symmetrical type with all attributes with an equal status (see Section 4.1). The data produced with the paradigm that I am now going to introduce show that this choice of model was not that unreasonable.

Tsal and Lavie (1988, Experiment 1) presented their subjects with a circular array containing a mixture of three red, three green, and three brown letters. Letters of the same colour were never adjacent. The subjects were instructed to first report a single letter of a given colour, for example, a red one, and then any other letters they could identify. So, each trial consisted of a 'forced-report' part (a red one) and a 'free-report' part (any other letters). Tsal and Lavie considered the free-report part as the important part of the experiment. This part was intended to reveal which attribute of the letter named first was attended to. In Tsal and Lavie's view, if attention is allocated to the location of this letter, adjacent letters should be reported more frequently than other letters in the display. If, however, attention is directed to the colour of the letter named first, letters of the same colour should be reported more frequently than other letters in the display (see Tsal & Lavie, 1988, p. 16).

That 'position-special' models have to predict that the 'free-report' part mainly consists of spatially adjacent letters is not difficult to see. These theories assume, explicitly or implicitly, that the instruction 'Name first a red one' guides the spotlight or zoom lens of attention to the *position* of one of the red letters. It is reasonable to assume that, after processing that red letter, it is easiest to move attention to an adjacent position for processing letters for free report. That 'all-equal' models have to predict that the 'free-report' part mainly consists of same-colour letters is also not difficult to see. These theories assume that the instruction 'Name first a red one' makes the colour *red* relevant or salient. It is reasonable to assume that, after processing that red letter, the system goes on processing red letters, i.e., does not change from defining attribute. (See Van der Heijden et al., 1996, p. 1225, for the derivation of this prediction in terms of Bundesen's, 1990, 'all-equal' model.)

My $\gg$ X $>$ Y $\gg$ conceptualisation, introduced in Chapter 4, is a particular version of the all-equal conceptualisations (see later). In line with what has just been said, in terms of my conceptualisation, it is reasonable to assume that the system attempts to perform this task with a 'simple', unchanging Verbal Intention of the form

$$\gg \text{RED1} > \text{SHAPE} \gg \gg \text{RED2} > \text{SHAPE} \gg \gg \text{RED3} > \text{SHAPE} \gg \tag{1}$$

(all units of analysis work with the same defining attribute) and not with a 'complex', changing Verbal Intention of the form

$$\gg \text{RED1} > \text{SHAPE} \gg \gg \text{POS2} > \text{SHAPE} \gg \gg \text{POS3} > \text{SHAPE} \gg \tag{2}$$

(after the first unit of analysis, the intentional sequence switches to a different defining attribute in the following units of analysis).

Tsal and Lavie (1988, Experiment 1) reported results obtained with their paradigm that clearly supported the 'position-special' models – in the 'free-report' part the subjects reported more 'adjacent' letters than 'colour' letters. However, their experiment lacked the required fixation controls. Van der Heijden et al. (1996, Experiment 1) introduced these controls in Tsal and Lavie's paradigm; to ensure correct fixation the subjects had first to name a small digit that appeared in the middle of the stimulus. The results obtained with this improved research clearly favoured the 'all-equal' models – in the 'free-report' part, in the standard paradigm and in minor variations of that paradigm, the subjects consistently reported significantly more letters of the same colour as the first letter than letters adjacent to the first letter. This outcome clearly favours the 'all-equal' models. This shows that, after all, my choice of model in Chapter 4 was not that unreasonable.

In Tsal and Lavie's (1988) paradigm, the instruction is: 'Name one letter in colour x, and then as many other letters as you can identify'. Tsal and Lavie's idea was that with this ingenious instruction a property of the information processing system could be revealed – that with this instruction the 'fixed' structure of the system is investigated. From what was stated above it will be clear that my $\gg$ X $>$ Y $\gg$ conceptualisation interprets things differently. My idea is that with this instruction a strategy is implemented in the information processing system – that with this instruction, the 'variable' mode of operation of the system is investigated. In my view, however, with Tsal and Lavie's instruction an ambiguous situation is created. With this instruction the strategy is not completely determined and alternative strategies to perform the 'free-report' part of the task are possible. Two strategies immediately suggest themselves. One consists of reporting as many letters of

Table 5.1 Number of letters reported in addition to the first letter per letter category and per instruction

	Instruction	
	Colour	Location
COLOUR (C)	1.49	0.24
LOCATION (L)	0.05	0.87
C + L	1.54	1.11

Adapted from Van der Heijden et al. (1996, Table 4).

the same colour as the first one as possible. If this strategy is adopted then, according to my conceptualisation, the subjects perform the task with Verbal Intention (1) specified above. Another strategy consists of reporting as many letters adjacent to the first letter as possible. If this strategy is adopted then, according to my conceptualisation, the subjects perform the task with Verbal Intention (2) specified above.

Van der Heijden et al. (1996, Experiment 3) directly investigated this strategy-interpretation of the results. The same stimuli as in the standard paradigm were used. The subjects were presented with two different, straightforward instructions. In one session, the instruction was to name (after naming the digit) all three letters of the same colour; that is, subjects were explicitly told to select all items on the basis of colour. In another session, the instruction was to name (after naming the digit) one single letter of a given colour and then the two letters adjacent to the first one; that is, subjects were explicitly instructed to select the first item on the basis of colour and two further items on the basis of location. Table 5.1 presents the relevant results, which show that subjects are indeed able to perform both tasks: with the colour instruction subjects named more same-colour letters than adjacent letters and with the location instruction subjects named more adjacent letters than same-colour letters. This outcome supports my strategy interpretation.

The results, however, also show that subjects cannot perform the two tasks equally well: with the colour instruction more letters are reported than with the location instruction (1.54 vs 1.11) and more letters are of the required category (1.49 vs 0.87). These results show that the colour-instruction task is much easier to perform than the location-instruction task. In my conceptualisation, this task is easier because it is performed with a 'simpler' Verbal Intention (see above). Van der Heijden et al.'s (1996, Experiment 1) results, in combination with the conceptualisation presented here, then simply suggest that in an ambiguous situation the subjects prefer the easiest strategy.

In a recent study, Tsal returned to the 'position-special' vs 'all-equal' issue (Tsal & Lamy, 2000). In that study, he disputes neither the findings nor the interpretations presented by Van der Heijden et al. (1996). He argues, however, that Tsal and Lavie's (1988) paradigm is flawed, by being not sufficiently sensitive to demonstrate location effects. One of his arguments is that the paradigm is dimensionally asymmetrical. The letters in the colour category were of exactly the same colour as the first reported letter, whereas the letters included in the location category did not occupy precisely the same location as the first letter reported but positions adjacent to it. To remedy this flaw, a different type of stimulus was used. Three of the six letters were enclosed by or superimposed on different-coloured shapes (a square, a circle, and a triangle). The subjects were instructed to name first the shape of a given colour and then as many letters as they could. In all experiments performance was substantially better for the letter that appeared within the to-be-reported shape than for the letter that shared the shape's colour but not its position.

In my view, it is far from clear whether Tsal and Lamy's (2000) paradigm is really capable of discriminating between the 'all-equal' and 'position-special' views. This becomes clear when we look at their results through my 'all-equal' glasses. Three points are of importance here. The first is that a distinction has to be made between (a) what performs the selection and (b) what is selected in Visual Perception.[9] As set out in Chapter 4, in my conceptualisation selection is performed by the 'sending' term, X, of the unit of analysis $\gg X > Y \gg$ of the Verbal Intention, whose content consists of a representation of the defining attribute. What is selected by term X in Visual Perception, however, is not a single attribute but the representation of the complete task-relevant object with all its attributes (see Duncan, 1984, above; see also Section 4.1). So, with colour as the defining attribute, the position (and the colour and the shape) of the relevant object is also selected. Therefore, and in general, in my 'all-equal' conceptualisation position effects like those observed by Tsal and Lamy are not unexpected.

The second point concerns the content of the 'sending' term, X, which performs the selection. That content need not consist of the representation of one single value on a single attribute dimension. That content might be much more complex (see also Section 5.2). In general, in laboratory experiments the content of term X is fixed through task instructions and practice trials. In Tsal and Lamy's (2000) paradigm, instruction and practice might have had as a result that the content of term X consisted of a representation of the coloured shape plus the letter. In other words, term X might effectuate the selection, not of the coloured shape only, but of a complex object that has to be further sorted out by Verbal Intention states Y. (It is worthwhile to know here that in Bundesen's 'all-equal' conceptualisation too, position might be involved when other selection criteria, for instance colour or shape, are used, i.e., in that conceptualisation also more defining attributes can be in effect simultaneously; see Bundesen, 1990, p. 526). However, further research is certainly needed on what exactly an object is.

The third point concerns the involvement and operation of Verbal Intention state Y. Here it is only of importance to note that, at first sight, there is a discrepancy between the results reported by Duncan (1984; see above) and Tsal and Lamy's results (2000). In Duncan's experiments, however, two 'variables' have to be named while in Tsal and Lamy's tasks one 'variable', the shape, has to be named and another 'variable', the letter, has to be read. As stated in Chapter 2, there are reasons to assume that there is a difference between naming and reading. In Chapter 6, Section 6.1, I return to this difference.

Taken together, my 'all-equal' conceptualisation and 'X > Y' approach have no difficulties with the 'stimulus set' tasks, are in line with Duncan's (1984) object selection results, and predict the pattern of results produced by Tsal and Lavie's (1988) ingenious paradigm. Further research concerned with the content of term X would, however, certainly be welcome.

5.2   Rapid serial visual presentation (RSVP) tasks

From what was said in Chapter 4, it will be clear that paradigms can be invented which provide golden opportunities for investigating the adequacy of the Verbal Intention, >> X > Y>> conceptualisation. One basic assumption in this conceptualisation is that the Verbal Intention or intentional sequence develops or unfolds in a number of successive object > attribute steps.[10] Visual information can also be presented in a number of successive steps. The sequence steps of the Verbal Intention and the information steps in Visual Perception can be in phase, and then nothing peculiar is to be expected. The sequence steps of the Verbal Intention and the information steps in Visual Perception can, however, also be out of phase. When the information 'steps faster' than the sequence can step, peculiar but predictable effects are to be expected. These effects have indeed been reported in the literature (see Egeth & Yantis, 1997, for an excellent overview of the relevant research). In this section, I look at a number of experiments that used rapid sequences of information (rapid serial visual presentation, RSVP) and provide the explanations. I end this section with two further explanations.

In the 'simple version' of the RSVP task, a series of letters, digits, or words is rapidly presented (e.g., one item per 100 ms), one after the other, in the same location on a screen. The subjects have to name, or to indicate otherwise, the identity of one (or more) of the items. The relevant items are indicated by one or another cue. Because all items appear on a fixed, known spatial position, the cue indicates the *temporal position*, not the *spatial* position, of the relevant item(s). The spatial position of the relevant item(s) is known far in advance. The cue triggers or has to trigger the initiation of the selection process on that known position.

Weichselgartner and Sperling (1987, procedure 2) used this single-stream paradigm. A stream of numerals, in which a target was embedded, appeared on a screen. There were two cue conditions, an 'outline square' condition (an outline square surrounded one of the numerals) and a 'highlighted numeral' condition (one of the numerals brightened). The subjects had to indicate the identity of the earliest occurring numeral they could remember upon/after cue detection (as well as three subsequent ones; to these three subsequent ones I return later). Weichselgartner and Sperling (pp. 778–779) report:

> For all subjects, the recall probability of the critical numeral (the numeral displayed simultaneously with the target) was well above 0.9. Indeed, all subjects reported that they could achieve high recall of the critical numeral effortlessly; it seemed to "pop out" of the background numerals . . .

Broadbent and associates investigated selection by colour, and selection by other attributes, with the 'simple version' of the RSVP task (see, e.g., Broadbent & Broadbent, 1986, 1987; Gathercole & Broadbent, 1984; McClean, Broadbent, & Broadbent, 1982; see also Keele, Cohen, Ivry, Liotti, & Yee, 1988). In the 'colour cue' condition of McClean et al., subjects were asked to name the (unique) letter (or digit) that possessed a particular, pre-specified, unique colour. In this task the proportion correct was only 0.59. Most errors consisted of report of the letter in the temporal position immediately after the target position. Broadbent and Broadbent (1987, p. 106) comment that

> . . . even when events occur at the same place . . . the letter in a target color . . . tended to be that of an event happening at a time later than the objective target. They [McClean et al., 1982] interpreted this result as due to a delay in the starting of the response-identifying processes until after the target-defining event had been detected.

The general pattern of results obtained in these simple experiments, the correct responses as well as the errors, is easily understood in terms of the >> X > Y >> approach developed here. The >> X > Y >> approach is simply an explicit version of Broadbent and Broadbent's (1987)

> >> initial 'target-defining event' > subsequent 'response-identifying processes' >>,

phrased in Intending Mind, i.e., top-down control terms. Term X defines the target and Y takes care of response identification.

The >> X > Y >> conceptualisation assumes that, given an instruction of the type 'Name the cued character', the Verbal Intention or instruction-derived intentional sequence equals

> >> CUE > SHAPE >>

and that this sequence interacts with Visual Perception, as depicted in Figure 4.2. On arrival of the cued item, the sequence is in the state CUE, the state containing the representation of the defining attribute. The item is bottom-up processed and one of the results of this processing is the activation of the representation of the defining attribute on its position in the attribute's feature module. The interaction between the content of the sequence state CUE and the representation of the defining attribute in that feature module has a result that extra activation is sent downwards to the corresponding position in IN. This position in IN provides extra activation upwards on the corresponding positions in modules C, S, and P and from there enhanced activation progresses to the Intending Mind (see Section 4.1).

In the Intending Mind two situations have to be distinguished. Either the Verbal Intention or intentional sequence is in the meantime in the state SHAPE and receives (the) shape/letter information of the cued item, and the correct response can be produced; or the sequence is still in the state CUE and moves only (much) later into the state SHAPE. Then, however, the character in IN and in S has been replaced by a subsequent character and sequence state SHAPE receives (the) shape/letter information of a (much) later item, and an incorrect response will be produced. It will be clear that in this conceptualisation performance is determined by two factors: the speed of the intentional sequence and the speed of character presentation. If the intentional sequence or Verbal Intention moves fast enough relative to the characters, the correct shape or identity is received. If, however, the sequence moves too slowly and/or if the letters follow each other too fast, the shape of a subsequent item on that position will be received.[11]

Three features of this explanation are worth noting. First, with this explanation correct performance is accounted for (simply the $>> X > Y >>$ explanation). Second, this explanation makes explicit why errors are sometimes made (the errors appear to be the result of a sequence of normal and correct internal 'sending' and 'receiving' operations – the system simply does what it is instructed to do.) Third, this explanation makes immediately clear what type of errors have to be expected – because the intentional sequence is too slow or the letters too fast, errors will mainly consist of the name of an item that (immediately) follows the target item.

Some paragraphs ago we saw that different patterns of results were obtained with Weichselgartner and Sperling's (1987) procedure, with a surrounding square and highlighting as cues (close to perfect performance), and with McClean et al.'s (1982) procedure, with colour as the cue (far from perfect performance). From the foregoing, it will be clear that this difference in results is not difficult to explain in terms of the $>> X > Y >>$ approach. In fact, there are two viable explanations. The first is in terms of speed of initiation of term X. It then has to be assumed that a surrounding square and highlighting are more effective visual cues than a colour cue, i.e., can be 'found' and 'contacted' faster. The second explanation is in terms of the duration of operation of term X. It then has to be assumed that the $X > Y$

transition occurs faster with a surrounding square and with highlighting than with a colour cue. Fortunately, both explanations come down to the same critical explanatory factor. That factor is the moment in time of the initiation of sequence state Y.[12]

Within the field of RSVP research, a highly interesting 'other issue' is that of what happens when subjects are instructed to name, or indicate otherwise, two or more, instead of one, of the items in a single foveal stream of rapidly presented items. Before turning to the experimental results, I first explain what, according to the $>> X > Y >>$ approach, has to be expected in such an experimental situation. From all that has been said up to now it will be clear that when two (or more) items of a single foveal stream have to be named, I have to assume that the task is performed with an instruction-derived intentional sequence of the general form

$$>> X1 > Y1 >> >> X2 > Y2 >> \text{(etc.)}.$$

The first unit of analysis has to ensure the selection of the first item, the second unit of analysis the selection of the second item (etc.). It will be clear that when the items are presented at a sufficiently rapid rate, a 'gap' has to be expected; some items will be missed. When the intentional sequence has arrived in state Y1 and is 'receiving' ('processing') the information required for the first response, the sequence is temporarily 'blind' for the defining attribute of a next item on that position.[13] Only after the Y1 $>>$ X2 transition, does the sequence become sensitive for the defining attribute of a next item again. Of course, the number of items missed depends on the rate of presentation of the items and on the sequence speed.[14] Let us now turn to some experimental results. Two double-response paradigms have to be distinguished, a 'free-report' paradigm and a 'cued-report' paradigm.

Weichselgartner and Sperling (1987, procedure 2) used a 'free-report' paradigm (see also Raymond, Shapiro, & Arnell, 1992). In their paradigm, one item in the stream was cued (surrounded by a square or highlighted). The subjects had to indicate the identity of the first occurring numeral as well as the three subsequent ones. The results were rather unexpected. They '. . . noticed curious bimodal distributions of attention shift times that suggested that [they] were observing not merely a single act of attention but two consecutive, partially overlapping acts' (p. 778).[15] They report:

> The distribution . . . clearly is bimodal. Most numerals were recalled from two separated periods in time, the first mode between 0 and 100 msec after target presentation, the second mode between 300 and 400 msec after target presentation . . . the bimodality did not result from a mixture of early-mode trials and late-mode trials: a single, bimodal distribution characterized all the responses.
>
> (Weichselgartner & Sperling, 1987, pp. 778–779)

So, the free-report procedure produces the expected gap.

Weichselgartner and Sperling (1987) report further that their subjects had no difficulty with distinguishing between 'first-glimpse' judgements (judgements attached to the target) and 'second-glimpse' judgements (judgements of items later in the stream). It will be clear that the X > Y approach has no problems whatsoever with this observation, because each >> X > Y >> unit can be regarded as an independent 'glimpse' or 'act' of attention.[16]

Broadbent and Broadbent (1987) were the first to use a 'cued-report' double-response RSVP paradigm. Later on, this paradigm and variants of this paradigm were used by, e.g., Chun and Potter (1995), Raymond et al. (1992, 1995), Grandison, Ghirardelli, and Egeth (1997) (see also, e.g., Seiffert & DiLollo, 1997; Shapiro, Raymond, & Arnell, 1994). In general, in this type of experiment performance on the second target as a function of the (filled) interval between first target and second target (target onset asynchrony) is approximately U-shaped, with the lowest point between 200 and 300 ms (two and three intervening items). When the second target immediately follows the first target, performance on the second target is relatively good. A performance deficit is observed when there are one, two, or three intervening non-targets With still longer intervals, i.e., more intervening items, between the first and second target, performance on the second target improves (see, e.g., Raymond et al., 1992). So, the 'cued-report' task also produces the expected gap.

The finding that performance on the second target is relatively good when that second target immediately follows the first target deserves a further comment, because, at first sight, this finding seems not to be in accordance with my prediction. Here a trivial case and an interesting case have to be distinguished.

The trivial case can be illustrated with an experiment reported by Broadbent and Broadbent (1987). They asked their subjects to report the two uppercase target words in a stream of otherwise all lowercase words. For the condition in which the second target immediately followed the first target, they report a probability of first word correct of .46, a probability of second word correct of .35, and a probability of both words correct of .075. These data show that in this experiment the subjects often reported the second target but not the first target. I have already described this phenomenon – when the intentional sequence is not fast enough, X1 'selects' the first target but Y1 'receives' the shape information of the second target.

The interesting case can be illustrated with an experiment of Raymond et al. (1992). Here I only mention the critical features of that experiment. In the task, a sequence of letters was presented. One letter, the target, was white and the other letters were black. The subjects had to report the identity of the target. In some of the trials somewhere in the stream of letters following the target was a (black) X (a probe). After reporting the target, subjects had to indicate whether there was an X or not. On the trials with correct target identification, X detection performance steadily declined with 0, 1, and 2 intervening items and then recovered gradually until with 5 intervening items performance was very good. These data show that the subjects often identified the target and detected the probe when it immediately followed the target.

In my view, and according to my conceptualisation, this task is performed with an intentional sequence of approximately the form:

>> WHITE > SHAPE >>
   X

Two points are of importance here. The first is that, in my conceptualisation, 'search for an X' specifies the 'defining attribute' just like the 'white' in 'name the white letter'. I have already mentioned this point in Section 5.1 where I briefly referred to the visual search tasks. The second point is that, in my conceptualisation, a simultaneous search for two different 'defining attributes' or one 'complex' 'defining attribute' is not excluded. I have already mentioned this point in relation to Tsal and Lamy's (2000) experiments in Section 5.1.

With these two points in place, it will be clear how my explanation runs. The intentional sequence or Verbal Intention is first in the object selection states WHITE and X or WHITE X. This sending term 'sends' for an interval of time. It thereby selects either both the white target and the X, when the X immediately follows the target, or the white target only, when the X comes (much) later. Then the sequence moves into the state SHAPE. In the first case, the state SHAPE receives a complex representation consisting of a white letter and a superimposed black X. Both can be reported. In the second case, the state SHAPE only receives the target, not the X (the X is not selected). In the interval of time that the sequence is in state SHAPE, there is no further object or input selection. The Xs appearing in that interval of time are missed. Only when the sequence has left the state SHAPE, can it select again with WHITE X or X. So, in this case, temporally extended object selection explains the relatively good performance when the probe immediately follows the target (see also Raymond et al., 1992, for a closely related explanation).

Raymond et al. (1992) introduced the term *attentional blink* for the phenomena just described, because they saw a likeness between what happens with perceptual processing during an eye blink and what is observed in the 'cued-report' double-response RSVP paradigm with intermediate intervals (or numbers of non-target items). They state that the

> . . . data suggest that the mechanisms involved in target identification are temporally shut down after use. It is as if the perceptual and attentional mechanisms blink.
>
> (Raymond et al., 1992, p. 851)

And they explain:

During the presentation of the RSVP stream of letters, the white color of the target is detected preattentively. This information is then used to initiate an attentional response to facilitate target identification. If attention is allocated episodically, as suggested by Sperling and Weichselgartner (1990), then target identification may involve the opening and closing of a gate to regulate the flow of postreceptoral visual information to recognition centers of the brain . . . According to this model, an attentional episode begins (i.e., the gate opens) when the target-defining feature is detected and continues until target identification is complete . . .

(Raymond et al., 1992, pp. 858–859)

It will be clear that this is almost exactly what is said by the >> X > Y >> approach. In general when, with the Verbal Intention >> X1 > Y1 >> >> X2 > Y2 >>, sequence state Y1 is receiving the information required for responding, i.e., when the gate is open, the mechanism required for second target selection, X2, is 'temporally shut down'. Then, as far as the 'selection' of the second target is concerned, 'the perceptual and attentional mechanisms blink'. (Note that, according to the >> X > Y >> approach, the 'blink' occurs *during*, not *after* the use of 'the mechanisms involved in target identification'. In the >> X > Y >> approach after Y1, X2 can start immediately; there is no non-used, or useless, interval of time.)[17]

As stated, the >> X > Y >> approach predicts that, when in a multiple-response RSVP task the items are presented at a sufficiently rapid rate, a gap will be observed, some items will be missed. The last paragraphs make clear that this prediction is supported by the available data (see also Grandison et al., 1997, for further supporting evidence). In particular, the temporal properties, specified by the >> X > Y >> approach, mean that no further ad hoc assumptions are required. Theories that lack or neglect these temporal specifications require ad hoc assumptions.[18]

Nowadays the RSVP field is a flowering research field producing a wealth of intriguing results (see Egeth & Yantis, 1997, for an overview). In my view, two results still deserve to be briefly considered and explained. The first result is obtained with a simple version of the RSVP task in which two (post-masked) stimuli are sequentially presented in two different locations and subjects have to identify both (see, e.g., Duncan, Ward, & Shapiro, 1994; Moore, Egeth, Berglan, & Luck, 1996; Ward, Duncan, & Shapiro, 1996). The important finding with this task is that imperfect performance with the second of the two stimuli is still found even when the two stimuli are widely separated in time. The assumption in this field of research is that this paradigm measures 'the dwell time of attention'. Dwell times of attention in the order of 500 ms are no exception. Two remarks with regard to this research are in order.

First, it will be clear that in my >> X > Y >> conceptualisation, the global theoretical construct 'dwell time of attention' has no place. In that conceptualisation, these tasks are performed with a detailed intentional sequence of approximately the form

>> POSITION1 > SHAPE >> >> POSITION2 > SHAPE >>.

One assumption is that each of these states takes an interval of time. Another assumption is that the state transitions, > and >>, especially the SHAPE >> POSITION2 transition, also take an interval of time. A further, reasonable, assumption is, of course, that the more difficulties a state encounters in performing its job, e.g., receiving/processing a post-masked stimulus, the more time it needs (see, e.g., Moore et al., 1996; see also Raymond et al., 1992, Exp. 3). So, in my conceptualisation something like 'dwell times of attention' as such come as no surprise. Second, what is measured in these studies is not the average 'dwell time of attention' but the maximum 'dwell time of attention'. Also in my conceptualisation, with an unfortunate combination of long > and >> transitions, a long POSITION1, a long first SHAPE, and a long POSITION2 duration, problems in the second SHAPE are to be expected, and long 'dwell times of attention' therefore come as no surprise.

The RSVP task also allows me to provide the beginning of an explanation of a finding or phenomenon that has up to now been largely neglected and left completely unexplained. The phenomenon is that subjects have no problems whatsoever with their erroneous performance (they neither hesitate nor apologise). They appear to 'see' no problems in responding with the name of a lowercase letter when the name of an uppercase letter is required or with the name of a blue letter when the name of a red letter is required. Lawrence (1971, p. 87) remarks that in this situation subjects are even quite confident that they performed the task correctly. A similar result is obtained with variants of the partial-report paradigm. When, for instance, subjects are instructed to name only the red letters from a display with a mixture of red and blue letters, they quite often respond with the name of the simultaneously presented (adjacent) blue letters (see, e.g., Butler, Mewhort, & Tramer, 1987; Fryklund, 1975; Snyder, 1972).

The analysis in terms of an interaction between a Verbal Intention and Visual Perception immediately explains this indifference on the part of the subjects with regard to these errors. After initiating the selection chain, the sequence moves from a state X to a state Y. In the latter 'receiving state' the system is not concerned with the 'defining attribute'. That state is only concerned with the 'to-be-reported attribute' (letter features or digit features) and is functionally 'blind' for the 'defining attribute' (case or colour).

5.3 Position-cueing tasks

An important selection paradigm, that has led to a great number of productive related selection paradigms, is the partial-report bar-probe task of Averbach and Coriell (1961) which I introduced in Section 2.3.[19] Figure 2.1

in that section presents examples of the stimuli used. In that section, I stated that the fixed instruction used in that paradigm – name the one letter indicated by the bar marker – cannot contribute to the explanation of the interesting detailed pattern of results (see Figure 2.2 for these results). Nevertheless, without that instruction, that interesting pattern of results would never have been produced in the first place. So, it is worthwhile to have a brief look at the instruction-derived Verbal Intention.

In my conceptualisation, in all trials in the partial-report bar-probe task the Intending Mind of the information processing system works with a Verbal Intention of the form:

Y >> >> BAR > SHAPE >>.

First, the system deals with, 'looks at', the fixation point (Y). Upon or before stimulus presentation, the sequence moves into the state BAR and, upon bar appearance, selects the spatial region of the bar marker. Then the sequence moves into the state SHAPE and 'receives' ('processes') the letter aspect in that region, not the colour aspect, the size aspect, or whatever else aspect that can be 'processed' there. After that 'processing' the system goes on and reports the result. This sequence makes clear 'what is done' in this type of task. For the detailed pattern of results, however, additional explanatory ingredients are required (see Section 2.3 and Section 7.2 for these ingredients).

Averbach and Coriell (1961) saw their task mainly as a task for investigating the spatial and temporal properties of an early visual memory, coined 'iconic memory' by Neisser (1967). It was C. W. Eriksen, who saw the importance of this type of task for investigating properties of selective attention in vision. He was sharply aware of the fact that

> This perseverating image, or as Neisser (1967) termed it, icon, has generated considerable interest, but an equally if not more interesting characteristic of this experimental technique is the means by which attention can be selectively directed in a matter of milliseconds to the relevant stimulus item.
>
> (Eriksen & Collins, 1969, p. 254)

And, while at that time nearly all information processing psychologists were mesmerised by that 'iconic memory', Eriksen and associates started a line of research that tried 'to account for the selective capacity of humans ... to respond to certain stimuli and effectively ignore others that appear equally potent on physical and time dimensions' (Eriksen & Lappin, 1967, p. 468).

The research of Eriksen and associates produced important technical innovations and delivered important new results (see Van der Heijden, 1992, for an overview).[20] The linear arrays were replaced by circular arrays with all elements in positions with equal retinal acuity, allowing a better look at the operation of selective attention (see, e.g., Eriksen & Rohrbaugh, 1970;

Eriksen & Steffy, 1964). The task was modified in such a way that, instead of accuracy, latency (RT) could also be used as the dependent variable (see, e.g., Eriksen & Eriksen, 1974; Eriksen & Hoffman, 1972a, 1972b). And instead of simultaneous cueing (and post-stimulus cueing to investigate properties of 'iconic' memory), advance position cueing was introduced to investigate the time course of selective attention (see, e.g., Eriksen & Collins, 1969; Eriksen & Rohrbaugh, 1970). This advance cueing research showed substantial 'precueing effects'; accuracy of report increased and latency of report decreased with increasing temporal interval between the position cue and the display with the target item (i.e., with stimulus onset asynchrony, SOA). Most of the improvement occurred in the first 50 ms and performance reached a maximum at an SOA of about 200 ms.

Further research, and especially the seminal empirical and theoretical work of Jonides (1980, 1981, 1983) and of Posner and associates (see, e.g., Posner, 1980; Posner, Snyder, & Davidson, 1980), has made clear, however, that at least two types of position-cueing tasks have to be distinguished. Figure 5.1 serves to give an impression of these two types of tasks. The panel on the left illustrates the use of a 'location' cue. With location cues (often termed peripheral cues), the position of the target is specified by one or another visual event, e.g., the appearance of a bar or a dot or the brightening of a peripheral box or dot, on or close to the position of the target. The subjects are instructed to name, or otherwise indicate, an aspect or attribute of the target (e.g., name the letter). The panel on the right illustrates the case of a symbolic cue. With symbolic cues (often termed central cues), the position of the target is specified by one or another symbol, e.g., an arrow pointing to the left or to the right in the centre of the display or the auditory word 'left' or 'right'. The subjects are instructed to name, or otherwise indicate, an aspect or attribute of the target (e.g., name the letter). With both types of tasks 'precueing effects' are found. The main difference between the two types of tasks shows up in the experimental data as better, more accurate and faster, performance with location cues than with symbolic cues (for direct comparisons between the two types of tasks see, e.g., Cheal & Lyon, 1991; Jonides, 1981, 1983; Kroese & Julesz, 1989; Müller & Rabbitt, 1989; Nakayama & Mackeben, 1989).

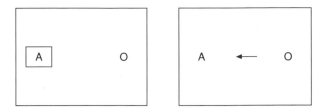

Figure 5.1 Examples of stimuli for position-cueing tasks. The panel on the left gives an example of a 'location' cue (the square around the target letter) and the panel on the right an example of a 'symbolic' cue (the arrow pointing at the target letter). (See text for further explanation.)

In the standard explanations of the 'precueing effects' and the difference between the 'precueing effects', a basic assumption is that one is studying the bottom-up processing of visual information; attention is conceived as a limited commodity or resource, in charge of identifying the selected information.

> Precuing effects are usually discussed in connection with capacity models of attention . . . These models assume that there is a limited pool of resources, capacity, or attention, which can be distributed across a spatial region that varies in size. Perceptual processing is done in parallel within the region, with the quality of processing dependent on the amount of capacity devoted. The rate of processing is assumed to be faster with more capacity . . . When a target location is unknown, resources are evenly distributed across all the spatial regions . . . when the target is indicated by a valid location precue, more of the limited resources can be allocated to this region in advance, thus speeding up the processing.
>
> (Shiu & Pashler, 1994, p. 1038)

In my view, however, the information processing approach is not studying the perceptual processing of visual information but the use of visual information for task performance (see Section 1.4). In particular, for all experimental tasks, so also for position-cueing tasks, my position is that the results observed are produced by an interaction between two representations. One representation is derived from the instruction. This Verbal Intention or intentional sequence, specifies the sequence of required internal operations. The other representation is produced by vision. This Visual Perception contains information about 'what is out there' in the outer world. So the questions I have to answer now are: (1) how to account in these terms for the 'precueing' effects obtained in position-cueing tasks, and (2) how to account for the main difference in results obtained with location cueing tasks and symbolic cueing tasks.

To answer these questions, it is worthwhile to start with the more detailed standard explanations proposed by Müller and Rabbitt (1989). Their explanation of performance in spatial cueing tasks is in terms of two mechanisms, an '*orienting*' mechanism and an '*attention*' mechanism. The 'orienting' mechanism is in charge of guiding attention and the 'attention' mechanism is in charge of processing the information. Their explanation runs as follows:

> Spatial orienting means allocation of a limited-capacity attention system to selected spatial locations. Thus, determining the locations to which spatial cues refer must occur prior to selection and orienting itself . . . Allocation of limited-capacity attention is accomplished through an orienting mechanism that is initiated by the output of the anteceding cue processing.
>
> (Müller & Rabbitt, 1989, p. 315, footnote 1)

Mueller and Rabbitt explain the difference in findings obtained with location cues and symbolic cues in terms of two kinds of 'orienting' mechanisms; a fast acting, reflexive orienting mechanism with location cues (exogeneous orienting) and a slower acting, voluntary orienting mechanism with symbolic cues (endogeneous orienting). Let us now return to the two questions.

With regard to the first question – how to account for the precueing effects – it is worthwhile to see that my X > Y theorising, without anything further, already contains something like an 'orienting' mechanism and something like an 'attention' mechanism. In my conceptualisation, term X performs the job of the 'orienting' mechanism ('selection' or 'sending') and term Y performs the job of the 'attention' mechanism ('processing' or 'receiving'). So the 'precueing' effects pose no problem for my position. These effects are explained by simply replacing the 'orienting' and 'attention' mechanisms of the capacity theories by the 'X' and the 'Y' of my >> X > Y >> approach.

With regard to the second question – how to account for the difference in results obtained with location cueing tasks and symbolic cueing tasks – the situation is different. Of course, it is not difficult to rephrase the essence of Müller and Rabbitt's (1989) explanation, presented above, in my >> X > Y >> terminology. Paralleling the two different 'orientation' mechanisms of their explanation, two different X terms can be postulated, a fast acting, reflexive X*loc*, operative in location cue tasks, and a slower acting, voluntary X*sym*, operative in symbolic cue tasks. With these two Xs, the difference is immediately explained. In my view, however, simply 'postulating' different orienting mechanisms with different properties, for explanatory purposes, is not the way to go. The next paragraph makes clear why, in my conceptualisation, that tactic is not the appropriate one and is not needed.

Consider a position-cueing experiment with two conditions, one with location cues and one with symbolic cues. Assume further that in both conditions the cues are presented 50 ms before the display containing the item information (i.e., stimulus onset asynchrony, SOA, is 50 ms).

- In the location cue condition, the instruction-derived Verbal Intention or intentional sequence has to take care of a series of internal information processing operations that can be represented with:

  Yf >> >> Xl > Yi >>.

The sequence first 'deals' with the fixation point (Yf). Upon or before position cue appearance the sequence moves into state Xl and upon cue appearance selects the spatial region of the position cue (the cue appears as a sudden event/object in an empty field).[21] After cue region selection the sequence moves into state Yi and 'receives' ('processes') the instruction-defined required shape in that selected region.

- In the symbolic cue condition, the instruction-derived Verbal Intention or intentional sequence has to take care of a sequence of internal select-ive operations that can be represented with:

$$Yf \gg \gg Xs > Yc \gg \gg Xt > Yi \gg.$$

The sequence first 'deals' with the fixation point (Yf). Upon or before symbolic cue appearance the sequence moves into state Xs and upon cue appearance selects the region of the symbolic cue (the symbolic cue appears as a sudden event/object in an empty field, so there is no reason to assume that it is treated differently than the location cue).[22] After cue region selection, the sequence moves into state Yc, 'receives' ('pro-cesses') the shape of the cue, and interprets that shape as a position symbol.[23] Then the sequence moves into state Xt. State Xt takes the content of Yc, i.e., Xt = Yc, and selects the position of the target as signified by the symbolic cue. Then the sequence moves into state Yi and 'receives' ('processes') the instruction-defined required shape in that selected region.[24]

In my conceptualisation the difference between the two types of tasks does not need to be explained in terms of two kinds of 'orienting' mechanisms, an X*loc* and an X*sym*. Completely consistent with my theoretical approach, the difference between the two types of tasks is explained in terms of number of units of analysis required for internal task performance. For the internal performance of the simple, easy, location cue tasks only one unit of analysis is required and for the internal performance of the complicated, difficult, symbolic cue tasks, a series of two units of analysis is required.

It is worthwhile here to emphasise two aspects of the proposal just pre-sented. The first is that the sequences do in essence what the standard approach postulates; they take care of the required 'orienting' and 'process-ing'. The only difference is that issues about 'orienting' and 'processing', which remain largely implicit or are not elaborated in the standard approach, are made explicit in the present proposal. The second aspect worth emphas-ising is that the two intentional sequences indeed account for (a) successful performance in the tasks and (b) the better, more accurate as well as faster, performance with location cues than with symbolic cues. The first point is obvious. The second point follows, because the intentional sequence for symbolic cue tasks is longer and more difficult to execute than the inten-tional sequence for location cue tasks (two units of analysis vs one unit of analysis). According to my intuition, especially the Yc >> Xt transition in the Verbal Intention operative with symbolic cue tasks; that is, the internal generation of a to-be-selected position, is a difficult and time-consuming operation about which at present not very much is known.[25]

So, my theoretical position does not have problems with either 'precue' effects or the differences between 'precue' effects observed with location

Table 5.2 Results from Jonides (1983) and Müller and Rabbitt (1989) (I)

		RT	*Prop.*
Valid	Location	529	.87
	Symbolic	569	.76
Invalid	Location	683	.54
	Symbolic	644	.66

Mean RTs in milliseconds (from Jonides, 1983) and proportions correct (from Müller & Rabbitt, 1989; estimated from the 100 ms SOA condition in their Fig. 2) for valid and invalid trials with location cues and symbolic cues.

cues and with symbolic cues. There is, however, one further piece of evidence that, at first sight, appears to be damaging for my >> X > Y >> approach. That piece of evidence is obtained in experiments in which, after Posner and Snyder (1975) and Posner, Nissen, and Ogden (1978), cues are used that are not 100% informative, but give correct position information on only a fraction, e.g., 80%, of the trials (valid trials; the cued position contains the required information) and incorrect or misleading information on the remaining fraction, e.g., 20%, of the trials (invalid trials; the cued position contains no usable information). The same critical evidence was produced in an experiment with latency (RT) as the dependent variable (Jonides, 1983) and in an experiment with accuracy (proportions correct) as the dependent variable (Müller & Rabbitt, 1989). Here I consider both experiments.

In Table 5.2, the relevant results of the two experiments are presented. Both experiments compared location cues and symbolic cues and contained valid and invalid trials. The first column presents the mean RTs observed by Jonides (1983) and the second column presents the proportions correct observed by Müller and Rabbitt (1989; I estimated these proportions from the 100 ms SOA condition in their Fig. 2). This table shows that the valid trials pose no problems. There is better, i.e., faster (529 ms vs 569 ms) and more accurate (.87 vs .76), performance with location cues than with symbolic cues. The problem for my >> X > Y >> conceptualisation arises with the invalid trials.

On the invalid trials, the location indicated by the cue provides no information for responding. After 'noting' this, for correct performance on these trials a kind of 'emergency' measure is required; other positions than the one indicated by the cue have to be 'inspected' in one way or another (for the moment, forgive me the terms 'noting' and 'inspecting', etc.; these terms are used here for explanatory purposes only). That the cued location contains no usable information will be 'noted' relatively early in the location cue condition with the 'simple' intentional sequence consisting of one unit of analysis. That an 'emergency' measure is required will be 'noted' relatively late in the symbolic cue condition with the 'complex' intentional sequence consisting of two units of analysis. So, in my conceptualisation, in the location cue condition more time is still available for 'seeing what can still be done' than in the symbolic cue condition, and therefore better, i.e., faster and more accurate, performance is to be expected on invalid trials with location cues than with symbolic cues. The results, however, show exactly the opposite; worse, i.e., slower (683 ms vs 644 ms) and less accurate (.54 vs .66), performance with location cues than with symbolic cues! Here further assumptions are certainly required.

Müller and Rabbitt (1989) provide a set of additional assumptions. They explain the inferior performance on invalid trials with location cues by (a) assuming that the subjects do what they are instructed to do (i.e., use the cue on all trials) and (b) postulating that the '. . . reflexive mechanism triggered by peripheral cues is more resistant to interruption by a target at an uncued location calling for a competing orienting response' (p. 320). In their view:

> . . . the claim for a fast-acting, reflexive orienting mechanism that is more resistant to interruption (by stimuli at unattended locations) than the slower-acting, voluntary mechanism explains both the greater facil-itation (on valid trials) and the greater inhibition (on invalid trials) from peripheral cueing . . .
>
> (Müller & Rabbitt, 1989, p. 320)

For at least two reasons I cannot accept these assumptions. The first reason I have already made clear earlier in this section. In my conceptualisation, the assumption of two different 'orienting' mechanisms is not appropriate and not required. The two different 'orienting' mechanisms are replaced by two different Verbal Intentions or sequences of internal operations. It will be clear that a further elaboration of the two 'orienting' mechanisms assumption in terms of a greater or lesser 'resistance to interruption' from targets from uncued locations 'calling for a competing orienting response', cannot be a theoretical route I can prefer. In my X > Y approach, and not only in that approach, this kind of theorising is clearly ad hoc.[26] It amounts to postulating an X*loc* with all the properties required for explaining the location cue data and an X*sym* with all the properties required for explain-ing the symbolic cue data. That, however, is post hoc postulation, not theory-based explanation.

The second reason is that Jonides (1980) has already reported data that convincingly refute this two 'orienting' mechanisms explanation. In Jonides' task, the subjects had to search through eight-letter circular arrays, to deter-mine and to report as fast as possible whether either the target letter *L* or *R* was present (the other seven positions were filled with irrelevant 'noise' letters). Just before array presentation, a location cue appeared that sig-nalled the target location with some probability. There were three validity conditions, one with 70% valid and 30% invalid trials, one with 50% valid and 50% invalid trials, and one with 30% valid and 70% invalid trials (each

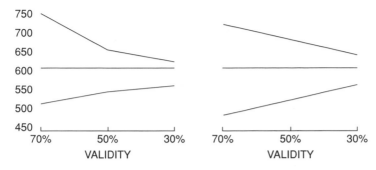

Figure 5.2 Left panel: observed RTs for invalid (upper line), neutral (middle line), and valid (lower line) trials in the 70%, 50%, and 30% validity conditions reported by Jonides (1980, Exp. 2; data estimated from his Fig. 1). Right panel: corresponding predicted RTs (see text and Note 27).

condition also contained trials with uninformative, neutral cues). The two 'orienting' mechanisms explanation predicts no effect of validity condition (see the two assumptions above). The 'fast-acting, reflexive' orienting mechanism, triggered by the location cue, simply exerts its positive effects on valid trials and its negative effects on invalid trials, independent of validity condition (the validity conditions differ only in the *number* of valid and invalid trials; not in *what happens* in these trials). There are, however, huge and systematic effects of validity condition. The data obtained are presented in Figure 5.2. in the panel on the left. Without substantial additional ad hoc assumptions, the two 'orienting' mechanisms explanation cannot cope with this result.

Jonides (1980; see also 1981, 1983) explains this pattern of results by (a) assuming that subjects do not always do what they are instructed to do (i.e., do not use the cue on all trials) and (b) postulating that (with location cues) subjects go through a probability-matching procedure. It is assumed that subjects somehow match the probability of examining the cued position first with the probability that the cue indicates the target correctly; that is, with the probability of cue validity – on 70%, 50%, and 30% in the three validity conditions respectively. On the remaining trials the subjects do not use the cue but search the display in parallel.

At first sight this explanation seems far-fetched and weird. Inspired by disbelief and astonishment, I further investigated this explanation and could not find any serious fault in it.[27] On the contrary, the investigation led to a number of intriguing results (see Van der Heijden, 1989, and Van der Heijden, 1992, sec. 6.7, for details).[28] Eriksen and Yeh (1985) also used the probability-matching hypothesis quite successfully. Now, at second sight and after some further thought, it appears to me that a liberal version of the probability-matching hypothesis is not as weird and far-fetched as it initially seemed to others and to me. That liberal version can account for the pattern of results depicted in Figure 5.2 and the pattern of results presented in Table 5.2. One fact and one simple set of assumptions can make that clear.

The fact is that in cueing tasks using one or more validity conditions, the cue information is not really required for correct task performance. In these tasks, the target is a unique element (e.g., an L or an R among other 'noise' letters in Jonides', 1980, 1983, experiments and an oriented T among 'noise' plusses, +s, in Müller & Rabbitt's, 1989, task). So, subjects can also find the target when they perform the task as a 'search' task, the type of task briefly described in Section 5.1. In fact, without a cue, Jonides' task is the two-choice detection task introduced by Estes and Taylor (1964) and used with great success by Estes and associates at the start of the information processing approach. Moreover, in most experiments using a less than 100% validity condition, neutral, no-cue trials are also used in which a 'search' strategy has to be used anyway. These neutral trials produce RTs and proportions correct in between those for valid trials and invalid trials (see, e.g., Jonides, 1980, and Figure 5.2, and Müller & Rabbitt, 1989, Fig. 2).

The set of assumptions of my liberal version of the probability-matching hypothesis is: (a) subjects do not always do what they are instructed to do (i.e., do not use the cue on all trials), (b) subjects either use the cue (select the item indicated) or do not use the cue (search the display for the target), and (c) the proportion of 'select' trials and 'search' trials is determined by the 'benefits' and 'costs' that the use of the cue brings.[29] It is not difficult to see that this set of assumptions immediately explains the pattern of results depicted in Figure 5.2. In the 70% valid condition, the cue brings benefits on 70% of the trials and costs on only 30% of the trials. This situation encourages the use of the cue and discourages the use of the search strategy. Consequently, performance deviates substantially from the no-cue, neutral, 'search' condition with intermediate RTs. In the 30% valid condition, the cue brings benefits on only 30% of the trials and costs on 70% of the trials. This situation discourages the use of the cue and encourages the use of the search strategy. Consequently, performance approaches the no-cue, neutral, 'search' condition with intermediate RTs. In the 50% validity condition a result in between the 70% and 30% validity conditions has to be expected.

The pattern of results presented in Table 5.2, the critical evidence against my X > Y approach, can be explained along exactly the same lines. The only reasonable additional assumption that is required is the assumption that the types of cue, the location cue and the symbolic cue, co-determine on what proportion of the trials the cue is used. In particular, the required assumption is that the 'easy' location cue encourages the use of that cue and discourages the use of the search strategy (as in the high validity condition in Figure 5.2). Consequently, strong validity effects are to be expected. And the required assumption is that the 'difficult' symbolic cue condition discourages the use of the cue and encourages the use of the search strategy (as

Table 5.3 Results from Jonides (1983) and Müller and Rabbitt (1989) (II)

		RT	*Prop.*
Location	Valid	529	.87
	Invalid	683	.54
Symbolic	Valid	569	.76
	Invalid	644	.66

Mean RTs in milliseconds (from Jonides, 1983) and proportions correct (from Müller & Rabbitt, 1989; estimated from the 100 ms condition in their Fig. 2) for valid and invalid trials with location cues and symbolic cues.

in the low validity condition in Figure 5.2). Consequently, a much weaker validity effect is to be expected. Table 5.2 shows exactly these expected validity effects in RTs and proportions correct. This is shown in Table 5.3 where the same data are presented in a different form.

All this brings me to the following two conclusions. The first is that the critical evidence, presented in Tables 5.2 and 5.3 is not damaging for my $X > Y$ approach when the possibility is admitted that subjects do not always perform according to the instruction, but sometimes invent 'information processing' strategies, or mixtures of strategies, that provide the required outcome in cheaper, less 'effortful' ways. For position-cueing tasks with less than 100% validity conditions, the possibility has to be admitted that subjects perform the tasks with a varying Verbal Intention or intentional sequence of approximately the form

(P) Select
(1-P) Search.

In this 'composite' intentional sequence or Verbal Intention, (P) stands for the probability that the subject uses the cue and (1-P) for the probability that the subject searches [with (P) and (1-P) determined by the type of cue and the effects that the cues produce]. The term Select stands for the Verbal Intentions or intentional sequences specified at the beginning of this section (a short, one unit of analysis sequence for the location cue condition and a long, two units of analysis sequence for the symbolic cue condition) and Search stands for the Verbal Intention or intentional sequence operating in search and detection tasks (see Section 5.1).

The second conclusion is, of course, that position-cueing experiments with less than 100% validity conditions reveal to only a limited extent the effects of the position cues used. Two types of trial contribute to the average proportions correct (and RTs) produced with these experiments, the proper 'select' trials and the 'search' trials. This mixture of trials has as a result that in the average percentages correct (and RTs) the effects of the cues on the 'select' trials are diluted by the results produced by the 'search' trials. To really assess the power and the effects of position cues, a 100% validity condition should be used.[30]

Cheal and Lyon (1991, Exp. 2) compared the effects of location cues and symbolic cues in an experiment with only a 100% validity condition and accuracy as the dependent variable. On each trial, four Ts in four different orientations (one up, one down, one left, one right), were presented, one in each of the four corners of an imaginary square. Because each of the four Ts could be the target, a search strategy was impossible. A location cue or a symbolic cue indicated the position of the target. The cue–target intervals, SOAs, used were 0, 17, 33, 50, 67, 83, 100, 167, 233, 300, 367, 433, and 500 ms. For the relevant single-fixation range of SOAs, i.e., SOAs up to about 300 ms, the following three important results were reported.

- With location cues and with symbolic cues, accuracy of report increased with increasing SOA between cue and target display (the 'precue' effect). In my >> X > Y >> conceptualisation, this outcome reflects the fact that the 'sending' term, X, can start its selective work on the 'defining attribute' (spatial position) in the absence of the to-be-'reported attribute' (the letter or shape information on that spatial position).
- The location cue produced its largest effect within 100 ms, whereas the symbolic cue required approximately 300 ms to achieve maximum effects. In my >> X > Y >> conceptualisation, this finding reflects the fact that in the location cue condition a short and 'easy', one unit of analysis Verbal Intention and in the symbolic cue condition a long and 'difficult', two unit of analysis Verbal Intention is involved.
- The two types of cues produced equal facilitation if enough time was allowed for 'attention' to arrive at the target location prior to target onset. In my >> X > Y >> conceptualisation, this finding reflects the fact that, whatever the amount and duration of the required preliminary and preparatory work, ultimately with both Verbal Intentions the same last term, Yi, has to perform the critical work. With both Verbal Intentions that term has to 'receive' or to 'process' the shape of the target indicated by the cue. In my conceptualisation, term Yi is the 'attention' that has to be allowed enough time 'to arrive at the target location prior to target onset'.

Cheal and Lyon (1991, Exp. 1) also observed that with location cues there was only a slight improvement in performance after a first 6000 trials. With symbolic cues performance continued to improve after 22,000 trials. This observation also suits me well. The long and 'difficult' intentional sequence with symbolic cues provides many more opportunities for learning than the short and 'easy' intentional sequence with location cues. (For me it is far from clear how reflexive and voluntary 'orienting' *mechanisms* can still learn.)

5.4 Limited capacity

A readily observable empirical fact is that people show performance limitations, i.e., cannot do everything at the same time. That fact was intensively investigated and firmly established by what can be called *early* information processing psychology with, e.g., 'shadowing' tasks and 'split-span' tasks in which the subject had to select one of two (auditory) information streams (see, e.g., Broadbent, 1952; Cherry, 1953). That basic fact needs an appropriate explanation. In the last chapter of *Perception and Communication*, Broadbent (1958) presented an explanation in terms of an information processing theory as looked for by the information processing approach (see also Section 3.3 and Figure 3.1).

Broadbent (1958) explained his view with regard to the processing and selection of (auditory) information in a summary of principles. The first principle in Broadbent's list reads: 'A nervous system acts to some extent as a single communication channel, so that it is meaningful to regard it as having a limited capacity' (Broadbent, 1958, p. 297). This 'limited-capacity channel' is, as shown in Figure 3.1, the core of Broadbent's information processing model. Its function is to categorise, recognise, or identify the information. Here the empirical fact that people show performance limitations is translated into the theoretical principle that people suffer from internal capacity limitations. And, since then, the assumption of central limited capacity has figured prominently in a variety of forms in nearly all stories told by information processing psychologists.[31]

At this point it is worthwhile to look back briefly at Broadbent's (1958) model in Figure 3.1. The figure shows that a 'selective filter' protects the limited-capacity channel. This filter has the ability to select a 'sensory channel' on the basis of simple 'physical' properties – e.g., information from the left or from the right, or with a certain pitch or loudness – and to allow all information with this property access to the limited-capacity channel. And now possibly comes a surprise. A comparison of Broadbent's (1958) filter view on information selection and my content view on information selection readily shows that the two views are highly similar. For 'report' tasks, i.e., 'name' and 'read' tasks, my view is captured in the expression

$$\gg X > Y \gg.$$

And, from what has just been said and from inspection of the flow diagram in Figure 3.1, it is easy to see that Broadbent's view can be summarised with

$$\gg \text{Filter} > \text{Channel} \gg.$$

This similarity is not just a similarity of the format of the expressions. From the description of Broadbent's model and from what has been said in the foregoing chapters it is easy to see that my 'X' has by and large the function of Broadbent's 'Filter' and that my 'Y' has by and large the function of Broadbent's 'Channel'.[32] So at first sight the surprising outcome is that my theoretical endeavours have brought me back to where the limited-capacity theorising already was in 1958.[33] This outcome has the positive consequence that my theoretical view can at least explain what Broadbent's theoretical view was capable of explaining.[34]

Of course, it is of importance to make explicit where exactly the relevant theoretical difference is between Broadbent's view and the view defended in this work. The following two quotations serve to make the traditional point of view clear. For auditory information processing, Broadbent (1971, p. 147) remarked:

> If there were really sufficient machinery available in the brain to perform ... an analysis for every stimulus, and then to use the results to decide which should be selected, it is difficult to see why any selection at all should occur. The obvious utility of a selection system is to produce an economy in mechanism. *If a complete analysis were performed even of the neglected message, there seems no reason for selection at all.* (Italics mine.)

For visual information processing, Eriksen and Hoffman (1972a, p. 169) remarked:

> If a large number of letters or digits are simultaneously exposed for a brief duration, the human O is typically able to report only a small number, approximately four. Under the same conditions, if the O is told to report only the stimulus designated by a black bar or similar indicator, he can by some process, select this particular stimulus and report it with perfect accuracy. A necessary condition for this demonstration is the overload of information provided the O. The existence of a limited channel capacity is implied by the concept itself. *Without such a limit, there would be no necessity for selective attention, as all stimuli would then be processed with equal accuracy at all times.* (Italics mine. See also Green, 1991, p. 400, for the same argument.)

These views start with two basic assumptions. The first assumption is that in the relevant information processing experiments the analysis/processing of auditory or visual information, i.e., auditory perception or visual perception, is investigated. The second assumption is that there is insufficient machinery in the auditory and visual part of the brain, a limited channel capacity, for analysing/processing the auditory or visual information. Just because of this limited central capacity, selection of information is necessary – selection is an unavoidable consequence of the limited central information analysing/processing capacity. In these views the observed performance limitations directly reflect and demonstrate the limited central capacity for auditory or visual perception.

My view also starts with two basic assumptions. The first assumption is that in the relevant information processing experiments the use of auditory or visual information, i.e., of auditory perception or visual perception, for task performance is investigated. The second assumption is that there is sufficient machinery in the auditory and visual part of the brain for analysing/processing auditory or visual information. Because a task has to be performed, selection of information is necessary – selection is an unavoidable consequence of task acceptation and task implementation. In my view the observed performance limitations have nothing to do with and therefore say nothing about the capacity for auditory or visual perception.

It will by now be clear where exactly the relevant theoretical difference between the traditional approaches and the approach introduced and defended in the present work lies. For me, it is easiest to characterise that difference in terms of the major information processing structures distinguished in Chapter 4 – the Intending Mind and Visual Perception. The traditional approaches assume that the observed capacity limitations are caused by capacity limitations in Visual Perception. My approach maintains that the observed capacity limitations are the result of task performance by the Intending Mind using Visual Perception. And the question to be considered is: Are the observed capacity limitations caused by capacity limitations in Visual Perception or are they the result of the operations of the Intending Mind?

With regard to the question of capacity limitations in Visual Perception, it is first of importance to remember that Broadbent's (1958) theorising was based on data obtained in auditory information processing tasks. Kahneman (1973, p. 135) surmised that with regard to the capacity issue, there might be a difference between audition and vision.

> It is tempting to speculate that the modern study of attention could have taken a different course if Broadbent (1958) had been concerned with how one sees dancers rather than with how one hears messages. Since it is surely possible to see many dancers while attending to one, the concept of a filter that allows inputs into perception in single file might not have been proposed.

Neumann, Van der Heijden, and Allport (1986) stressed possible differences in capacity between audition and vision. Because I am not sufficiently familiar with work on auditory information processing, I cannot exclude the possibility of limited central capacity in audition. In the context of the present work – the use of visual perception for task performance – a position with regard to this issue is, however, not required. Here the only relevant question is: What about limited central capacity in Visual Perception?

In the recent past a great number of arguments against the assumption of limited central capacity and in favour of the assumption of sufficient central capacity in Visual Perception have been raised. One important argument is that the limited-capacity-in-vision assumption is at variance with a number of well-known neuroanatomical and neurophysiological givens. Neuroanatomy and neurophysiology have shown that the human visual system is not a converging information processing system as suggested in Broadbent's (1958) model, but a highly diverging information processing system. Only about one million ($10**6$) retinal ganglion cells per eye inform the brain about what happens in the outer world, but at the cortical level hundreds of billions ($10**11$) of neurons are involved in visual information processing; some 100,000 cortical cells for each peripheral ganglion cell! So, the best bet seems to be that the brain has no capacity problems in dealing with the information provided by the eyes (see also Allport, 1980a, 1980b, 1987, 1989; Neumann, 1987, 1990a; Van der Heijden, 1992, 1996a, 1996b).

Another important argument is that in nearly all defences of the assumption of limited central capacity in Visual Perception, it is simply neglected that the visual system has severe peripheral limitations and requires saccadic eye movements for complete vision (see, e.g., Tsotsos, 1990). Neuroanatomy and neurophysiology have shown that in the daylight eye the highest visual acuity is found in a very small, central, region off the retina, the fovea. Towards the periphery, acuity falls off progressively and dramatically (see, e.g., Anstis, 1974). A viable alternative for the limited central capacity assumption for Visual Perception is therefore the assumption that the eyes, as movable peripheral filters, prevent the brain from reaching its limits, by passing on per eye fixation only a limited amount of information about the world. In treatments of the capacity issue, however, one looks in vain for words indicating peripheral factors, like 'cones', 'daylight vision', 'retinal acuity', and 'saccadic eye movements'.

Still another important argument is that in the last 50 years, information processing psychology has not really been successful in providing detailed and convincing evidence for the hypothesis that the human information processing system has insufficient capacity for processing the information provided by the eyes (for critical overviews see, e.g., Allport, 1987, 1989; Van der Heijden, 1992, 1995, 1996a, 1996b). Evidence in support of the hypothesis of limited capacity in Visual Perception often only consisted of global, suggestive arguments that were simply borrowed from neighbouring fields of research, e.g., from brain science or from computer science.[35] With adequate exposure conditions, and when the effects of obscuring peripheral limiting factors, such as saccadic eye movements, retinal acuity, and lateral masking, are eliminated or adequately accounted for, not many indications of a central limited capacity for Visual Perception remain. And, when looked for, clear indications of (unlimited capacity) parallel processing are easily obtained in a diversity of tasks (see, e.g., Van der Heijden, 1996a, 1996b). In this context it is worthwhile to note that in the explanations I have presented in this chapter, and in the explanations that I am going to present in the following chapters, the assumption of limited central capacity in Visual Perception was not used and will not be used.

Up to now, however, none of the arguments against limited capacity in Visual Perception has convinced one single limited-capacity theorist. Some information processing psychologists vehemently adhered to the limited-capacity assumption because they were afraid that, without this 'basic given', there is nothing more to be investigated and nothing more to be explained (see Broadbent, 1971, p. 147, and Eriksen & Hoffman, 1972a, p. 169, quoted above). Most information processing theorists, however, maintain the assumption of limited capacity in Visual Perception because it captures something real that has to find its place in the information processing theories. After all, performance limitations are observed and have therefore to be explained in one way or another. Possibly the information processing theorists, with their emphasis on the bottom-up processing of visual information for Visual Perception, see no other way of accounting for the observed performance limitations than in terms of capacity limitations in the visual system.

Of course, my answer to the question of where the observed capacity limitations originate is: in the Intending Mind. This answer is attractive, because it is not faced with the perception/processing problems mentioned some paragraphs ago; the central limitation is not in Visual Perception, but in the use of Visual Perception by the Intending Mind for task performance. Here, however, I have to be careful. This is because at first sight it might seem that my analysis – the analysis in terms of the top-down use of Visual Perception by the Intending Mind for the performance of tasks – directly suggests a way in which the observed performance limitations can be accounted for without postulating capacity limitations for Visual Perception. A prominent assumption of my analysis is that there is an Intending Mind with a Verbal Intention or an intentional sequence that develops step after step in real time. Therefore, the obvious explanation that suggests itself is that exactly the limited rate of development in time of a Verbal Intention or intentional sequence is at the basis of the observed capacity limitations.

It must be clear, however, that such a 'limited-rate-of-temporal-development-of-an-intentional-sequence' explanation is, just as the 'limited-central-capacity' explanation, very close to a *virtus dormitiva* explanation.[36] The outer state of affairs or order of things, e.g., an orderly series of overt responses, is accounted for by about the same inner state of affairs or order of things, an orderly series of states of the intentional sequence in the Intending Mind. Fortunately, within my conceptualisation it is not difficult to show in a non-circular way that, and in what way, the Verbal Intention introduces observed capacity limitations in a system with sufficient capacity for Visual Perception. The crucial point is that the assumption that the Verbal Intention in the Intending Mind develops over time is not an arbitrary ad hoc assumption. My Verbal Intention has to develop over time for performing the proper selections. The following example makes that clear.

Assume that, with the stimulus of Figure 4.1 – a large, red square on the right and a small, blue disk on the left – the subject is instructed: Name the colour of the object on the right and the shape of the object on the left. And assume further that the subject has the 'intention' to perform according to the instruction. Then, that instruction with right, left, colour, and shape as critical and indispensable terms, has to be implemented or stored somewhere, in one form or another, in the subject as an information processing system. Let us now try a number of possibilities. And let us first see what happens when in the subject the 'intention' is somewhere implemented or stored as the set of simultaneous states

>> RIGHT >>
>> LEFT >>
>> COLOUR >>
>> SHAPE >>

without anything further. It is clear that this internal situation cannot lead to adequate, i.e., correct, task performance. Even if it is assumed that this format leads to colour and shape responses, and not to position responses, it is not specified what colour or shape has to be selected and reported. So, some structure, some grammar in the internal representation of the instruction, is required.

Let us now see what happens when the subject tries to perform the task according to the instruction with two subtasks simultaneously. In other words, let us assume that, in order to maintain what aspect of what object has to be reported, the information processing system operates with two sequences that develop simultaneously, i.e., the two sequences

>> RIGHT > COLOUR >>
>> LEFT   > SHAPE >>.

The system is first simultaneously in the sequence states RIGHT and LEFT.[37] These sequence states select all attributes of the object on the right (right, large, red, square) and all attributes of the object on the left (left, small, blue, disk). When the system then moves into the sequence states COLOUR and SHAPE, the state COLOUR is contacted by, i.e., 'receives', 'red' and 'blue', and the state SHAPE is contacted by, i.e., 'receives', 'square' and 'disk'. So, cross-talk causes that in this way the task also cannot be performed correctly.[38] More grammar is required.

Now assume that the system is first simultaneously in the sequence states RIGHT and LEFT (see above) but enters the states COLOUR and SHAPE successively, i.e., assume that the sequences develop as follows:

>> RIGHT > COLOUR >>
>> LEFT   > SHAPE >>

It will be clear that this trick does not solve the problem. Again, the state COLOUR contacts, i.e., 'receives', 'red' and 'blue', and the state SHAPE contacts, i.e., 'receives', 'square' and 'disk'.

From this example it appears that, because of cross-talk, the system can possibly in some circumstances perform the task correctly with two partially overlapping units of analysis

>> RIGHT > COLOUR >>
>> LEFT   > SHAPE >>

(I return to this possibility in Section 8.3) and can certainly perform the task with two non-overlapping units of analysis

>> RIGHT > COLOUR >> >> LEFT > SHAPE >>

(see also Section 9.4 for these two possibilities). In other words: for preventing cross-talk, at least serial selection of objects appears to be required. It is further reasonable to assume that, for proper selection, the Verbal Intention in the Intending Mind has to be in each of its different states for a non-negligible amount of time (see Section 5.2 for evidence supporting this assumption). If that is the case, the temporal properties of the intentional sequences can produce the observed capacity limitations. (See Allport, 1980b; Neisser, 1976; Neumann, 1987, for similar, non-temporal, cross-talk arguments; see Pashler, 1998, for substantial evidence for a bottleneck in a 'response selection stage', the stages COLOUR and SHAPE in the example.)

Of course, this is only an example and many other selection situations have to be considered in further detail.[39] Nevertheless, this example makes sufficiently clear when and how, in my view, observed capacity limitations arise. In my view, there is no need for selection for Visual Perception, as postulated in the traditional perception-for-perception theories. Visual Perception is for selection, and in order to prevent cross-talk and ensure the required task performance, selection is sequential selection of objects/ regions by a Verbal Intention, consisting of a sequence of 'states of mind' in the Intending Mind (see also Turing's machine in Section 3.4).[40] And that Verbal Intention, not Visual Perception, is at the basis of the observed performance limitations.[41]

Notes

1 See also Logan and Zbrodoff (1999, pp. 62–63) who emphasise that in these tasks '. . . the person's response – key press or vocalization – should be interpreted as a "speech act". . . that communicates a proposition to the experimenter . . .'

2 As stated in Chapter 4, in each unit of analysis, >> X > Y >>, the first term, X, is the 'sending' term. The content of term X – the instruction- and task-derived representation of the 'defining attribute' (Duncan, 1985) – has to pick out or

select the required stimulus from among all available stimuli. This 'sending' term initiates and takes care of the 'filtering', 'stimulus set', or 'object set' ('sending' or 'selection'). The second term, Y, is the 'receiving' term. The content of term Y – the instruction- and task-derived representation of the to-be-'reported attribute' (Duncan, 1985) – has to pick out or select the required attribute from among all available attributes. This 'receiving' term initiates and takes care of the 'pigeonholing', 'response set', or 'attribute set' ('receiving' or 'processing').

3 To the best of my knowledge, Sperling (1960) was the first to report the results of a stimulus set task and a response set task. The results were about the same as those reported later on by Broadbent (1970). Sperling used stimuli with three rows of letters in the stimulus set task and letters/digits in the response set task and what can be called a partially coded instruction. For the stimulus set task the instruction was: 'With a high tone name the upper row of letters, with a middle tone the middle row, and with a low tone the lower row'. In my conceptualisation, the instruction-derived Verbal Intention with this stimulus set task was approximately:

$$Y \gg \gg Xa > Ya \gg \gg POSa1 > SHAPE \gg \gg POSa2 > SHAPE \gg \text{ etc.}$$

Initially the sequence 'deals with' the fixation point (Y). Upon tone presentation, the tone is 'selected' (Xa) and the pitch of the tone is assessed (Ya). The pitch is translated into a visual position that is subsequently selected (POSa1) and the letter in that position is 'processed' (SHAPE), etc. For the response set task a similar Verbal Intention is easily constructed.

4 In the stimulus set task, the state RED has to contact the red items, not the black ones. Because RED and visual red are strongly associated, but RED and visual black are not, it is not difficult for RED to perform its selection job (efficient selection). In the response set task there is no state SHAPE that can efficiently contact only the digits, not the letters. An 'appropriate' and 'efficient' state SHAPE is strongly associated with visual digits as well as with visual letters (0 O, 1 I, 2 Z, etc.). Therefore, one or another inefficient state OBJECT or POSITION is used as the 'sending' term in the response set task (inefficient selection).

5 Often the same information, and often even better information, can be obtained with experimental tasks involving only one unit of analysis $\gg X > Y \gg$. Why this is so, is not difficult to see. In experiments involving only one unit of analysis, a more analytical look at what happens within the information processing system becomes possible. An investigator, interested in properties of X, can emphasise, vary, and investigate the function of X with Y constant, and an investigator interested in properties of Y can emphasise, vary, and investigate the function of Y with X constant. So, under appropriately chosen conditions one can either mainly investigate the operation of term X or mainly investigate the operation of term Y. Over the last 40 years a consistent trend in this direction can be discerned in the experiments in the information processing approach.

6 In particular, the outcome of research using varieties of visual search tasks has provided evidence for the view

> ... that the deployment of attention may sometimes depend on the properties of the image almost exclusively (e.g. sudden movement in the periphery); other times it may be under strict supervision according to the observer's goals. Mounting evidence has revealed that these two domains of attentional control almost invariably interact. With a few possible exceptions, both the properties of the image and the expectations and goals of the observer determine the attentional consequences of a given perceptual episode.
>
> (Egeth & Yantis, 1997, p. 270)

So, within the field of visual search, the importance of 'the expectations and goals of the observer' (my Intending Mind), of the visual world (my Visual Perception), and of the interaction between the two, is clearly recognised.

7 The interaction between top-down factors and bottom-up factors in visual search was explicitly modelled by Wolfe and associates (see, e.g., Cave & Wolfe, 1990; Wolfe, 1994, 1996; Wolfe, Cave, & Franzel, 1989). Central in Wolfe's (1994) Guided Search model is a 'priority map' or 'attention map' that determines the serial order in which objects are selected. Two factors determine in combination, by summation of activation, the priority order in this map. One, the top-down factor, functions exactly like my 'sending' term, X. The closer an object matches the current intention or attentional set, the more top-down activation and the higher the priority. The other, the bottom-up factor, is not yet included in my conceptualisation. The more an object differs from neighbouring objects the more bottom-up activation and the higher the priority. The top-down effects were modelled in a similar way by Treisman and associates (see, e.g., Treisman, 1988; Treisman & Sato, 1990). In this way of modelling, priority maps determine the order of the selective operations. In my conceptualisation a chain of $\gg X > Y \gg$ units introduces the order of selective operations. For me it is not clear how the priority-map-theorising can be generalised in such a way that it can also account for performance in report tasks like 'Name first the colour of the square and then the size of the circle' without introducing explicit temporal control.

8 In my conceptualisation, in search tasks as well as in other tasks, term X either operates over the entire visual field (object specification but no position specification in X) or over a sub-region of the visual field (object specification and position specification in X). In general, the efficiency and ease with which X can perform its job depends on (1) the content of X (the appropriateness/adequacy of the content of the sending term for finding the required information), (2) the content of the visual field (the appropriateness/adequacy of the content of the visual field in displaying the required information), and (3) the ease of establishing a relation or association between the two contents. (Of course, here again we have Verbal Intention, Visual Perception, and their interaction, elaborated in Chapter 4.)

9 Please note that this is the distinction between Intending Mind and Visual Perception again.

10 At the end of this chapter and in Chapter 9 I return to this 'succession'. To anticipate: in some tasks some overlap of units of analysis in the intentional sequences is possible.

11 When the sequence is too slow, in IN and in S a next item receives the enhanced activation.

12 When sequence state Y is instantiated fast enough, either because X is fast, the X > Y transition is fast, or both, the required, i.e., cued, visual information will still be available in Visual Perception and can be 'received'. When sequence state Y is instantiated too late, either because X is slow, the X > Y transition is slow, or both, the required cued information has disappeared and is already replaced in Visual Perception and therefore can no longer be 'received'. Then the sequence state Y will 'receive' the later, replacing information (then the report will be of 'an event happening at a time later than the objective target'; Broadbent & Broadbent, 1987).

13 It is possibly worthwhile to note that the intentional sequence also provides an adequate starting point for explaining the phenomenon that nowadays goes under the name 'change blindness'.

14 The sequence speed also depends, of course, on the quality of the visual information, i.e., on the time needed to 'send' and to 'receive'. With the same rate of item

presentation, with high-quality visual information less evidence of a gap is to be expected than with low-quality visual information. One way of improving the quality of the visual information is by removing backward masking. Raymond, Shapiro, and Arnell (1992, Experiment 3) provide the relevant evidence.

15 For me it is not clear how they arrive at that 'partially overlapping'. See, however, Sections 5.4 and 9.4 for the possibility of some overlap.

16 For me, from the data reported by Weichselgartner and Sperling (1987), it is not completely clear whether per 'glimpse' only one or more than one numeral is 'selected' and 'received'. Of course, *a priori* the parallel 'selection' and 'receiving' of two successive items cannot be excluded (e.g., 73 as one unit, instead of 7 as a first unit and 3 as a second). This raises the question of the possibility of parallel 'selection' and 'processing'. At the end of this chapter and in Chapter 9, I return to this issue. To anticipate: parallel 'selection' and 'processing' is possible when there is no danger of 'cross-talk' or 'confusion'.

17 In the $\gg X > Y \gg$ conceptualisation, the duration of $\gg X1 > Y1 \gg$ is the relevant parameter that determines the blink period.

18 It often seems as if theorists try to get rid of temporal aspects of visual information processing as fast as possible and feel safe with only a non-temporal, stimulus-driven, bottom-up approach. One example will suffice to make this clear. I have indicated already that McClean et al. (1982) and Broadbent and Broadbent (1987) explained the observation that in a simple RSVP task, instead of the target, a following item was often named as '. . . due to a delay in the starting of the response-identifying processes until after the target-defining event had been detected.' That is clearly the temporal $\gg X > Y \gg$ explanation. Of course, the same explanation applies to the observation that in a 'cued-report' double-response RSVP task, with the two targets in immediate succession, often the second target and not the first target is reported. That is exactly the same observation (see the text for explanation). Broadbent and Broadbent (1987, p. 108), however, neglect their initial $\gg X > Y \gg$ explanation and state:

> The most plausible way of explaining these results is that whichever of the two targets is encoded first gains an advantage over the other. As Intraub (1985) has shown, the relative time of arrival of different RSVP stimuli is hard to assess; the second of two adjacent stimuli may be encoded first, and thus exclude the other.

In their otherwise excellent treatment of the literature, Egeth and Yantis (1997, p. 289) repeat:

> Roughly speaking, poor performance on the second target may be viewed as reflecting the duration of processing of the first target. However, this is a simplification. When items follow one another rapidly, subjects often process them in the "wrong" order.

The 'wrong order of processing hypothesis' is clearly an ad hoc hypothesis, simply invented on the spot to explain a pattern of results (which was already earlier observed and adequately explained but, in the target–target form, not recognised as such).

19 A closely related paradigm is the partial-report paradigm introduced by Sperling (1960). See also Section 5.1 and Note 3.

20 Some of the work of Eriksen and associates we have already met in Section 2.3, Note 18. See also Sections 6.3 and 7.2).

21 It is often stated that a location cue attracts 'attention' automatically and reflexively. It cannot be excluded that two factors contribute. The first is that

a location cue appears on the position that has to be selected. This makes fast and errorless selection possible. The second factor is that bottom-up visual processing possibly 'assists' in selection of the position. The location pre-cue appears in an empty field and therefore possibly selects itself (see Van der Heijden, 1992, Ch. 8). This makes 'effortless' selection possible.

22 The symbolic pre-cue also attracts 'attention' automatically and reflexively (see Note 21).

23 See Logan (1995) and Logan and Zbrodoff (1999) for a detailed analysis of these interpretation processes.

24 The content of state Yi is specified in most experiments in the verbal instruction. There are, however alternatives. Müller and Rabbit (1989), for instance, first presented a T in one of four orientations, for 1500 ms on the point of fixation. The subjects had to judge whether the later presented target was the same as or different from this T. Here subjects have to select that first T (with $Yf \gg X > Yi \gg$) and have to use the information obtained (the value of Yi) in the intentional sequence.

25 Sperling and Reeves (1980; see also Weichselgartner & Sperling, 1987, procedure 1) provided further evidence supporting this analysis. In their tasks, the subject had to monitor a stream of alphabetic letters for a target letter. The letters were flashed one on top of the other to the left of fixation. Upon detection of the target letter, the subject had immediately to 'shift attention' to a stream of numerals presented one on top of the other at fixation. So, on target detection the subject had to generate internally the fixation position. The subject had to report the earliest occurring number in that number stream. The subjects reported a number that occurred about 300 to 400 ms after the detection target (the number simultaneous with the target and the number following it were almost never reported). In my $\gg X > Y \gg$ conceptualisation, the time measured here equals $\gg Xd > Yd \gg \gg Xn$ (with d for detection target and n for numeral). With one single stream at fixation, the numeral simultaneous with the target was almost always reported (Weichselgartner & Sperling, 1987, procedure 2). In my $X > Y$ conceptualisation the intentional sequence operating with this procedure is $\gg Xd > Yn \gg$ (with d for detection target and n for numeral). See also Section 5.2.

26 Most information processing psychologists have no difficulties whatsoever with Müller and Rabbitt's (1989) 'two orienting mechanisms' explanation (see, e.g., Egeth & Yantis, 1997).

27 It even appeared possible to 'predict' or 'construct' the complete pattern of results (9 data points), presented in the left panel of Figure 5.2, using an incomplete set of data (4 data points) reported by Jonides (1983) and the probability matching hypothesis (see the right panel of Figure 5.2). For details see Van der Heijden (1989).

28 One important outcome of this investigation was that there is the possibility of probability matching with location cues but then certainly not with symbolic cues.

29 As stated, in most experiments using a less than 100% validity condition neutral, no-cue trials are also used in which a 'search' strategy has to be used anyway. These trials are randomly mixed among the valid and invalid trials. Of course, this state of affairs facilitates, and possibly induces, the use of a 'mixed' information processing strategy as described in the assumptions.

30 It is worthwhile to note here that the idea is not that the less than 100% validity experiments are 'wrong' or 'biased' experiments. In my view, these are beautiful and very informative experiments that reveal what is really happening after some quite highly satisfying detective work. The point is simply that these experiments do not show directly the effects of the position cues.

31 One variety we have just met in Section 5.3. As stated there, in the standard explanations of 'precueing effects' attention is conceived as a limited commodity or resource, in charge of identifying the selected information. The quality and rate of information processing are assumed to be dependent on the amount of resources devoted. When the target location is unknown, the resources are equally distributed over all possible target positions. When the target is indicated by a valid cue, more of the limited resources can be allocated to the region containing the target, speeding up and enhancing the information processing in that region.

32 The argument that Broadbent (1958) was concerned with the processing of auditory information, not visual information, is irrelevant. Broadbent (1971) extended and generalised the theory in such a way that the results obtained in visual information processing tasks could also be accounted for. The argument that Broadbent's model is concerned with continuous information streams (listening to speech), not with discrete bits of information, is also irrelevant. In Section 9.4, I show that the discrete $>> X > Y >>$ theorising is easily extended in such a way that continuous task performance can also be accounted for.

33 This first impression is, of course, false. To anticipate, the important point to see is that the functions of the two major structural information processing components in Broadbent's model, the selective 'filter' and the 'limited-capacity channel', reappear in the present approach as functions of the Intending Mind with its Verbal Intention or intentional sequence; sequence term X takes care of Broadbent's filtering and sequence term Y takes care of the processing. In Broadbent's theorising it remains unclear who or what 'sets' the filter and who or what 'determines' the processing that is required. Therefore the $>> X > Y >>$ approach improves on Broadbent's theorising by replacing the 'rigid', hardware structures by 'flexible', task-dependent functions.

34 A second positive consequence is that I need not be concerned with all subsequent versions of the capacity theorising (i.e., with 'mental energy', 'limited resources', varieties of 'attention'; see Neumann, 1987, for an excellent overview of the twists and turns in this limited-capacity theorising).

35 In general, with regard to the defence of the relevance and adequacy of the assumption of limited central capacity in Visual Perception, two groups of theorists can be distinguished. One group of theorists emphasises the amount of information in the world:

> The human organism exists in an environment containing many different sources of information. It is patently impossible for the organism to process all these sources, since it has a limited information capacity . . .
>
> (Garner, 1974, pp. 23–24)

Another group of theorists emphasises the size of the brain:

> To deal with the whole visual input at once, and make discriminations based on any combination of features in the field, would require too large a brain, or too much "previous experience," to be plausible.
>
> (Neisser, 1967, p. 87; see also Broadbent, 1971, p. 9)

For the capacity issue, however, neither the amount of information in the environment as such nor the size of the brain as such is of any relevance. Only the amount of information picked up by the receptors in the senses *relative* to the information processing capacity of the brain is of relevance. (For 'stomach capacity' neither 'the amount of food in the world' nor 'the absolute size of the stomach' is of relevance. What matters is the amount of food that enters the mouth in relation to the size of the stomach.)

36 According to Neumann (1991), the explanation of the outer limitations in terms of internal limitations is not a real explanation but an explanatory fiction. The result is a *virtus dormitiva* theory (after Molière, who put a candidate doctor on the stage who explained the soporific working of opium with: it has a *virtus dormitiva*, a power that puts you to sleep). In such a pseudo explanation, a single aspect of the observed behavioural phenomena is selected, that aspect receives an intriguing and suggestive scientific name, and that name with its denotations and connotations is then used as the very explanation of the total set of observed phenomena. According to Neumann, that was exactly what happened when Broadbent (1958) translated the empirical observation that people cannot do everything at the same time into the theoretical construct of "a single communication channel . . . having a limited capacity."

37 There is some evidence that more positions can be selected simultaneously; see, e.g., Kramer and Hahn (1995). This observation is not at variance with my theoretical position. My theoretical position is that at each moment in time only one state X can be implemented. Such a state can, however, specify more than one spatial position. It is of importance to distinguish between the number of codes (one X at a time) and the content of the codes (e.g., two objects/positions, one object/position, etc.).

38 This cross-talk is to be expected when both objects are in the same modality, not when in different modalities (an auditory word has no colour and a visual object has no pitch). Duncan, Martens, and Ward (1997) indeed reported the expected type of interference within but not between sensory modalities.

39 To relate the example to the relevant literature and appreciate its importance, the following information is possibly of value. In general, there is substantial evidence indicating interference and severe capacity limitations when features that belong to different objects have to be reported. Features that belong to the same object can, however, be simultaneously processed without apparent capacity limitation and interference (for relevant research see, e.g., Allport, 1971; Biederman & Checkosky, 1970; Duncan, 1980, 1984, 1993a, 1993b; Saraga & Shallice, 1973; Treisman et al., 1983; see also Neumann, 1987, pp. 366 and 385, and Pashler 1998, pp. 124–134). After reviewing the relevant empirical evidence Pashler (1998, p. 132) concludes:

> If the task requires reporting more than one attribute from a display . . . interference is usually found if the reported attributes reside in different objects. This interference seems to be avoided when the attributes are part of a single object.

Why there is interference 'if the reported attributes reside in different objects' is explained with the example presented in the text. The absence of interference 'when the attributes are part of a single object' is also easily understood. With a Verbal Intention or intentional sequence of, for instance, the form

$$\text{>> LEFT > COLOUR >>,}\quad\begin{matrix}\text{SHAPE}\\ \\\text{SIZE}\end{matrix}$$

no cross-talk is to be expected (e.g., the state COLOUR cannot select, and therefore cannot be hindered by, the attributes shape and size).

40 The cross-talk demonstration also makes explicit the explanatory tactics of past and current information processing psychology. The instruction, with its causal central selective effects, is neglected and *in its place* limited central capacity in the visual system is invoked to do the explanatory work.

41 There are, of course, other factors that cause observable performance limitations, for instance, the limited number of effectors and, in experiments, the length and complexity of the intentional sequence and the short-term memory capacity for storing instructions (the problem of '. . . maintaining goals appropriate to several different tasks independently active', Allport, 1980b, p. 146.) Because these factors are generally recognised, they are in the present context not of theoretical importance.

6 Paradigms with latency as the dependent variable

6.0 Introduction

This chapter is concerned with evidence produced by paradigms with latency or response time as the dependent variable. In these paradigms, the subjects are instructed to report as fast as possible one or another attribute of one or more selected items. The research question of interest is what determines the speed of initiating the expression of a proposition – for instance, the speed of initiating 'red' of 'this square is red' or the speed of initiating 'horse' of 'that word is HORSE'. Response time is determined by and dependent on several perceptual and post-perceptual factors. Therefore, response time can reflect and reveal a range of properties and strategies of the information processing system that accuracy cannot.

In Section 6.1, the empirical and theoretical distinction between 'name' tasks and 'read' tasks is first elaborated. The empirical finding that reading is faster than naming is explained in terms of two 'input–output' or 'attribute–response' routes – a strong intentional route and a strong automatic route for reading and a strong intentional route and a weak automatic route for naming. These routes are not simply postulated. The conceptualisation in terms of number of routes simply follows from the theoretical proposals presented earlier together with the concept of 'association'. An experiment investigating the effect of extended practice is used to clarify the conceptualisation.

In Section 6.2, the difference between 'name' tasks and 'read' tasks, introduced in Section 6.1, is used to explain one of the most spectacular, still unexplained, empirical phenomena from the experimental literature: the Stroop effect. It is shown that the major empirical phenomena that have to be explained simply follow directly from the two-routes view for reading and for naming. It is also shown that the $>> X > Y >>$ approach is more complete than the prevalent alternatives – the 'relative speed of processing account' and the 'automaticity account' – because it is explicit about how the correct response is selected. In this section we also look at a highly intriguing 'nuisance' factor, the sudden appearance of visual displays, as used in most experiments in information processing psychology.

It is argued and demonstrated that this factor can introduce peculiar phenomena that are not often observed in normal life. For investigating the use of visual information for task performance better previewed displays can be used.

In Section 6.3, experiments that purportedly demonstrated 'perceptual inertia', an initial period of time without detailed information processing, are discussed. It is argued that these experiments only demonstrate that there is an initial period of time in which detailed information is not used. We also have a closer look at an ingenious variant of the position-cueing task with peripheral location cues which produces effects that pose explanatory problems for all current theories. In that variant, there is either a preview of the visual information or no preview and the visual information is either degraded or not degraded. It is shown that the $>> X > Y >>$ approach has no difficulties with the effects reported. It is argued that preview experiments can form an important source of information about information processing and selection.

In Section 6.4, the generally accepted theoretical point of view that in the processing of visual information two stages have to be recognised is discussed. It will appear that my conceptualisation is in accord with most of what is said in the traditional theories. A theoretical controversy concerns the issue of where the major divide has to be, within Visual Perception or between Visual Perception and an Intending Mind. It is argued that my approach with the major divide between Visual Perception and Intending Mind does not run into the theoretical difficulties faced by the current two-stage views.

6.1   Naming and reading[1]

In Section 2.2, I argued that it is highly likely that a distinction has to be made between three types of tasks, 'report' tasks and 'act' tasks, and within 'report' tasks 'name' tasks and 'read' tasks. Up to now I have simply neglected the distinction between 'name' tasks and 'read' tasks. For instance, I have nowhere emphasised that Averbach and Coriell (1961) and Broadbent (1970) used 'read' tasks and that Cheal and Lyon (1991) employed a 'name' task. The reason for this deliberate neglect is simple. In the paradigms with accuracy as the dependent variable, responses are given at leisure. And, just because there is no time pressure, a possible difference between 'read' tasks and 'name' tasks is not apparent. However, this changes when time pressure is introduced, i.e., when subjects are asked to name a colour or a shape or to read a word or a letter as fast as possible. Response time is determined by and dependent on several perceptual and post-perceptual factors. Therefore, response time can reflect and reveal a range of properties and strategies of the information processing system that accuracy cannot. And response time immediately shows an important difference between reading and naming that still needs to be explained.

Wundt was already concerned with aspects of the production of symbolic, verbal responses (see James, 1890/1950, pp. 557–561, for an overview). One of his students, Cattell (1886), reported that naming objects and attributes of objects took longer than reading the corresponding names. For instance, he observed that it took appreciably longer to name colours than to read the corresponding colour names. This colour naming – colour word reading difference was replicated later on many occasions. Stroop (1935), for instance, presented one group of subjects with a stimulus card containing 100 (10 × 10) colour patches and another group of subjects a card with 100 (10 × 10) corresponding colour words (the colours and colour words were red, blue, green, brown, and purple). The mean naming time per colour was 633 ms and the mean reading time per colour word was 410 ms (see also Table 6.1). Similar results were later reported by, e.g., Fraisse (1969), Gholson and Hohle (1968), and MacLeod (1991).[2]

A highly interesting point is that over more than a century exactly the same explanation for this time difference has repeatedly shown up in the literature. Please consider the following series of quotations. As stated, Cattell (1886) found that reading is faster than naming. He stated:

> Other experiments I have made show that we can recognize a single color or picture in a slightly shorter time than a word or letter, but take longer to name it. This is because, in the case of words and letters, the association between the idea and name has taken place so often that the process has become automatic, whereas in the case of colors and pictures we must by a voluntary effort choose the name.
>
> (Cattell, 1886, p. 65)

Some 50 years later, Stroop (1935) observed that colour-word reading was faster than colour-patch naming (see above). He concluded that:

> The associations that have been formed between the word stimuli and the reading response are evidently more effective than those that have been formed between the color stimuli and the naming response. Since these associations are products of training, and since the difference in their strength corresponds roughly to the difference in training in reading words and naming colors, it seems reasonable to conclude that the difference in speed in reading names of colors and in naming colors may be satisfactorily accounted for by the difference in training in the two activities.
>
> (Stroop, 1935, pp. 659–660)[3]

Again some 50 years later, MacLeod (1991), in an excellent review of the relevant literature, rephrases this explanation by leaving out the ancient term 'association' and introducing modern terms like 'automaticity' and 'attention'. He describes the 'automaticity' account, derived from the work of LaBerge and Samuels (1974), Posner and Snyder (1975), Shiffrin and Schneider (1977), and Logan (1978), as follows:

> Here the basic idea is that processing of one dimension requires much more attention than does processing of the other dimension. Thus, naming the ink color draws more heavily on attentional resources than does reading the . . . word. Moreover, reading the word is seen as obligatory, whereas naming the ink color is not. Presumably, this imbalance derives from our extensive history of reading words as opposed to naming ink colors . . . Words are read very automatically; colors require considerable more attention to be named.
>
> (MacLeod, 1991, p. 188)

So, for more than a century the difference between reading and naming has been sought in a difference in 'strength of association', nowadays often called a difference in 'degree of automaticity'.

Of course, an explanation that has already survived more than 100 years, albeit in different forms, cannot lightheartedly be dismissed. And, as I am now going to show, the conceptualisation presented and defended in this work has no problems whatsoever in dealing with the reading–naming results or with the traditional explanation in terms of automatic obligatory association and voluntary attentional effort. In fact, as I will show below, the explanation of the reading–naming difference in terms of association and attention simply follows from the theoretical proposals presented and elaborated in the foregoing chapters. Moreover, that explanation is fully consistent with what is nowadays suggested in the literature about the processes of reading and of naming. For ease of exposition, I start with that literature.

Inspection of the literature reveals a major difference between models for reading (of words) and models for naming (of pictures, colours, etc.). In this field of modelling it is nearly generally assumed that reading is (also) possible without semantic mediation but that naming always requires semantic mediation. Nearly all models for reading recognise one or another direct, non-semantic, conversion of orthographic input into phonological output (see, e.g., Besner, 1999; Coltheart, 1978; Coltheart, Curtis, Atkins, & Haller, 1993; Coltheart, Rastle, Perry, Langdon, & Ziegler, 2001; Plaut, McClelland, Seidenberg, & Patterson, 1996; Seidenberg & McClelland, 1989). Picture and colour naming models generally assume that in naming an indirect object–sound path, which runs via the semantic system, is always involved (see, e.g., Glaser, 1992; Humphreys, Price, & Riddoch, 1999; Snodgrass, 1984; Theios & Amrhein, 1989).

In the past, I tried to capture this reading–naming difference with the figure in the left panel of Figure 6.1 (Van der Heijden, 1981, p. 184, Fig. 6.3; see also Phaf et al., 1990, p. 311, Fig. 11). In this 'anatomy of a logogen', V stands for visual code, S for semantic code, and A for articulatory code.[4] In

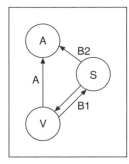 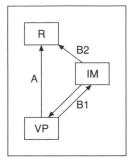

Figure 6.1 Left: The 'anatomy of a logogen' according to Van der Heijden (1981); V is Visual code, S is Semantic code, and A is articulatory code (A, B1, and B2 are connections between codes). Right: The model for reading and naming; VP is Visual Perception, IM is Intending Mind, and R is set of responses (A, B1, and B2 are connections between components). (See text for further explanation.)

this conceptualization, the visual code can 'contact' the articulatory code in three ways:

1 the visual code, or a subset of its features, directly 'triggers' the articulatory code via connection A;
2 the visual code, or a subset of its features, 'triggers' a semantic code via B1, and this semantic code 'triggers' the articulatory code via connection B2;
3 the visual code directly 'triggers' the articulatory code as in (1) and indirectly 'triggers' the articulatory code via the semantic code as in (2). In this case it is assumed that activation from the two routes adds in the articulatory code.

My assumption was that in (word, letter, digit) reading both routes, the direct route and the indirect route, are simultaneously involved ('dual route' processing; (3) above) while in (picture, colour, shape) naming only the indirect route is involved ('single route' processing; (2) above). A related position was and is defended by Coltheart (1978), Coltheart et al. (1993), and Coltheart et al. (2001).

In the right panel of Figure 6.1, the main components of the theoretical position I now adopt are sketched. The important point to note is that my current theoretical position also recognises three different, but interacting, representations or code domains, Visual Perception (VP), Intending Mind (IM), and a set of available/allowable responses (R) (see Chapter 4, Section 4.1). So, my current top-down theoretical position only invites me to re-interpret my former bottom-up position.

A first reinterpretation concerns the semantic code, S. That code has to be replaced by a Verbal Intention or intentional sequence(s) $>> X > Y >>$ in the Intending Mind.[5] A second reinterpretation concerns, of course, the visual code, V. That code has to be replaced by Visual Perception. The articulatory codes in A can simply be equated with the set of available/allowable responses, R. The outcome is a 'three-stage' model as suggested by Duncan (1980) with a 'selection schedule' between input and output. With these components and interpretations of components, neither the 'dual route' for reading nor the 'single route' for naming has to be postulated. A difference between reading and naming in terms of number of relevant routes simply follows from the reinterpreted model.

To see that the number-of-routes difference between reading and naming need not be postulated but simply follows from this reinterpreted model, it is first of importance to note that the to-be-reported attribute of a selected object is represented twice in the information processing system, both times in a 'privileged' way.

- The to-be-reported attribute is represented in Visual Perception. It is represented there in a privileged way because it is selected, with all other object properties, by 'sending' term X through enhanced activation.
- The to-be-reported attribute is represented in the Intending Mind. It is represented there in a privileged way, because it is the only attribute, from among all object attributes enhanced by 'sending' term X, that is picked out by 'receiving' term Y.

In this system, with the to-be-reported attribute represented in a privileged way twice, the 'double route' for reading and the 'single route' for naming now arise in the following way.

- With reading, 'sending' term X selects a word with all its properties and 'receiving' term Y 'receives' the shape of that word. What is learned in learning to read, is the associative connection between this received shape in the Intending Mind and the corresponding response in the set of available/allowable responses. After sufficient learning, the content of term Y, the received shape, selects the response via associative connection B2. Because nearly without exception words are 'selected' (and 'processed') for reading purposes, just before and likely also for some period of time during the process of response selection, the shape of the word is also in a privileged, enhanced, status in Visual Perception. Therefore, the shape of the word in Visual Perception and the corresponding response are nearly always simultaneously 'active' and become strongly associated (the law of contiguity; see Section 2.4). So, a second, direct, route from Visual Perception to the set of responses, associative connection A in the figure, is automatically firmly established.[6]

- With naming, 'sending' term X selects an object with all its properties and 'receiving' term Y 'receives' the to-be-named attribute, say the colour, of that object. What is learned in learning to name the colours of objects, is the associative connection between the received colour attribute in the Intending Mind and the corresponding response in the set of available/allowable responses. After sufficient learning, the content of term Y, the received colour, selects the response via associative connection B2. Objects are, however, selected for many purposes, e.g., for grasping, reaching, scrutinising, inspecting, etc., not only for attribute naming purposes. And, when selected for attribute naming purposes, they are not always selected for colour naming but also for shape naming, size naming, position naming, and many more naming purposes. So, while the colour of the object is in a privileged, enhanced, status in Visual Perception after object selection, only in a very few cases is the corresponding colour name simultaneously selected by state Y. Consequently, a second direct route from the colour in Visual Perception to the corresponding response in the set of available/allowable responses can possibly be established but will never become firmly established.[7]

So, after learning to name and to read, in terms of my conceptualisation the difference between naming and reading can be formulated as follows:

- In intentional naming, i.e., in naming controlled by a Verbal Intention in the Intending Mind, the intentional sequence

    $\gg$ X > Yn/report $\gg$

    is in control. Term X selects the relevant object, term Yn selects the attribute to be named, and the selected attribute controls the response (selects the required response from the set of available/allowable responses). There is cognitive mediation for response selection (voluntary, attentional selection). With naming, only a minor positive contribution from a direct Visual Perception to response set route is to be expected (see above, and Note 7). In summary: Naming is mainly a Yn task.
- In intentional reading, i.e., in reading controlled by a Verbal Intention in the Intending Mind, the intentional sequence

    $\gg$ X > Yr/report $\gg$

    is in control. Term X selects the relevant object in Visual Perception, term Yr selects the attribute required for reading, and the selected attribute controls the response (selects the required response from among the set of available/allowable responses). There is cognitive mediation (voluntary, attentional selection). The shape of the selected object in Visual Perception, however, also directly selects the required response from the set of available/allowable responses (involuntary, automatic selection; see Note 6). So, in intentional reading, besides cognitive mediation by term Yr, there is in addition strong learned 'direct parameter specification' for response selection. In summary: Reading is a Yr plus X task.

It will be clear that this 'dual-route' conceptualisation – a strong and a weak route for naming and two strong routes for reading – can directly account for the naming–reading difference reported in the literature and described above. Two strong routes can come up with a response faster than a strong route plus a weak route through adding activation. With reading, term Yr even does not need to be involved, because a 'bypass' from selected object to required response is available. Then, however, reading is not intentional reading but merely consists of 'barking' at selected words.[8]

As stated, the conceptualisation presented here is consistent with proposals in the literature about reading and naming. It is completely consistent with the current 'dual-route' views on reading. It deviates only in a minor way from the current 'single-route' views on naming; my analysis in terms of association suggests that in naming a minor contribution from a direct route also has to be recognised. As stated and shown, the conceptualisation presented simply follows from the views on selection and processing set out in earlier chapters; no additional assumptions were introduced, only consequences were taken. Moreover, the conceptualisation is in terms of 'association', as was insisted upon earlier (Section 4.2). Finally, a re-reading of the quotations at the beginning of this section will show that the conceptualisation is fully in line with the association proposals of the past.[9] Only some elaboration was required.

I end this section with a set of experiments that allow me to clarify my position a bit further. MacLeod and Dunbar (1988) reported a series of three colour–shape experiments that are of fundamental importance here because they show the effect of training and of the resulting associations. In these experiments subjects had to learn and to practise arbitrary, but systematic one–one relations between shapes (four highly discriminable random polygons) and colour names (green, pink, orange, and blue). In the first experiment the (maximum) number of [(visual) shape] – [(colour) word] training trials was 576, in the second experiment 2304, and in the third experiment 10,656. In each experiment, after this training, subjects received a series of trials with the shapes in incongruent colours, e.g., the shape named 'green' presented in red, the shape named 'pink' in blue, etc. There were two tasks; in one task subjects had to name the shapes (green, pink, etc.) and in the other task subjects had to name the colours (green, pink, etc.).[10] Of interest with these tasks is, of course, the shape naming and colour naming performance, i.e., the latencies, observed with these incongruent combinations of forms and colours, as a function of amount of practice.

Over the three experiments, MacLeod and Dunbar (1988) observed a pattern of interference that clearly developed with practice:

- Initially, after 576 training trials, an asymmetric pattern of interference was found; incongruent colours considerably interfered with shape naming but incongruent shapes had no effects on colour naming.
- Later in training, after 2304 training trials, interference became symmetrical; incongruent colours still considerably interfered with shape naming but now incongruent shapes equally affected colour naming.
- Finally, with extended shape naming practice, after 10,656 trials, the original asymmetrical pattern of interference was reversed; now incongruent shapes interfered with colour naming but incongruent colours had no effects on shape naming.

MacLeod and Dunbar (1988) explain this pattern of results in terms of a 'continuum of automaticity'. They refer to Logan (1985, p. 371) who remarked that '... there is clear evidence that practice is important in producing automaticity, which suggests that automaticity may be learned ...' It will be clear that, in principle, this account in terms of practice and resulting automaticity is compatible with and supports my view.

There is, however, one problematic issue in MacLeod and Dunbar's (1988) explanation that has to be made explicit and dealt with. It is easy to agree with them and with Logan (1985) that 'automaticity may be learned'. At first sight, however, it is difficult to agree with them that, even after 10,656 shape naming practice trials (2664 trials per shape), shape naming (green, pink, orange, and blue) has to be judged as more automatic than colour patch naming (green, pink, orange, and blue). Their subjects had a (student's) lifetime of practice with active and passive colour naming but practised shape naming intensively only during 20 days (even the experiments reported contained substantial colour naming parts). Total amount of practice and recency (again, all three experiments contained colour naming parts) cannot completely explain the results.

My conceptualisation easily provides an indication of how MacLeod and Dunbar's (1988) explanation might be made complete (see also Woodworth, 1938, in Note 3 for some suggestions). In my conceptualisation, the subjects performed their task during shape naming practice with an intentional sequence or Verbal Intention of, about, the following general form (I return to the exact format in Chapter 9):

>> OBJECT > SHAPE >> >> shape/colour name > ... >>.

Here the first unit of analysis of the Verbal Intention specifies what has to be done with the stimulus and the second unit of analysis consists of one of the arbitrary shape–colour name relations specified in the instruction and stored in the Intending Mind.

With this task, there are no reasons to assume that the subjects faced any difficulty in the first, the >> OBJECT > SHAPE >> part of the task. Shape selection is an over-learned internal activity. There are, however, reasons to expect that the subjects initially faced great difficulties with the SHAPE >> >> shape/ transition, and possibly with the second, the >> shape/colour name > . . . >> part; the relation between the four shapes and the four colour names was fully arbitrary, was specified in the instruction, and had to be learned.

With this analysis of the task, the results obtained are not difficult to understand. That initially the incongruent colours considerably interfered with shape naming but incongruent shapes had no effects on colour naming does not come as a surprise. With shape naming, the complete object is selected by 'sending' state OBJECT. Three factors play a role:

1   The shape content of the 'receiving' state SHAPE faces severe difficulties in picking out the required >> shape/colour name > . . . >> unit from among the set of available units.
2   The enhanced colour in Visual Perception automatically selects, through its weak but direct connection with the set of responses, its corresponding response.
3   Direct connections between the enhanced shape attribute in Visual Perception and the set of allowable/available responses do not exist.

With these three factors, interference from colour words selected by the colour in Visual Perception on the selection of colour words by the shape content of state SHAPE is to be expected.

That initially with colour naming no interference caused by the shapes is observed also does not come as a surprise. With colour naming the Verbal Intention is

>> OBJECT > COLOUR/report >>.

First, the complete object is selected by 'sending' state OBJECT. Again, three factors play a role:

1   The colour content of the 'receiving' state COLOUR faces no problems whatsoever in picking out the required response from among the set of allowable/available responses.
2   The enhanced colour in Visual Perception automatically assists, through its weak but direct connection with the set of responses, this response selection process.
3   Direct connections between the enhanced shape attribute in Visual Perception and the set of allowable/available responses do not exist.

With these three factors, no interference from (colour words selected by) the shape in Visual Perception on the selection of colour words by the colour content of state COLOUR is to be expected.

That with increasing practice in shape naming (green, pink, etc.) the pattern of interference changes, and that with extensive practice the pattern ultimately reverses, also does not come as a surprise. To see this, it is worthwhile to consider in detail what is learned during shape naming practice. Two different learning processes have to be distinguished:

- The intentional learning of the . . . SHAPE >> >> shape/colour name . . . transition, i.e., the learning of the arbitrary, instruction-derived, relation between the shape content of state SHAPE and the corresponding response in the set of allowable/available responses.
- The incidental learning of the relation between the enhanced shape in Visual Perception and the corresponding response in the set of allowable/available responses. Because, after some training, on each further training trial this relation is consistently reinforced, this, initially absent, direct relation can become very strong.[11]

Because, as a result of the consistent incidental learning, the connection between an enhanced shape in Visual Perception and the corresponding response in the set of available/allowable responses gradually improves and strengthens with practice, a changing pattern of interference, and ultimately a reversal of interference, is to be expected. After sufficient practice, activation running along the direct connection will strongly assist intentional shape naming and hinder intentional colour naming. This completely explains why

> Degree of practice in processing each of the dimensions of a multi-dimensional stimulus is very influential in determining the extent of interference from one dimension on another. The greater the practice in processing a dimension, the more capable that dimension seems of influencing the processing of another dimension.
>
> (MacLeod, 1991, p. 203)

6.2 The Stroop task

As shown in Section 6.1, from my Verbal Intention – Visual Perception – Association approach a 'dual-route' – 'single-route' explanation for the difference between reading and naming simply follows. In the reading of words, two strong routes are involved – a strong 'intentional' route (B2 in Figure 6.1) and a strong 'automatic' route (A in Figure 6.1). In the naming of attributes, e.g., the attribute colour, two routes are also involved – a strong 'intentional' route (B2 in Figure 6.1) and a weak 'automatic' route (A in Figure 6.1). Of course, it is highly satisfying to find that this conceptualisation simply follows from the line of interpretation introduced and defended in this work. This result shows that my approach is certainly defendable. The result, however, does not prove that the approach is indeed correct. As everybody knows, no result can prove a theory.

The only tactic available for demonstrating the viability of a theory, is to show that the proposed account is capable of handling many more results reported in the literature than rival theories can. And here the 'Stroop effect', first reported by Stroop (1935; however, see also Jaensch, 1929), comes in very handy. The Stroop effect is not only one of the most intensively investigated 'spectacular' phenomena in the experimental literature (MacLeod, 1992; see MacLeod, 1991, for an extensive review of the literature), it is also still a theoretical problem. As MacLeod (1992, p. 12) remarks '. . . in the 57 years of its existence, the Stroop effect has never been adequately explained, making it a source of continuing theoretical fascination.' So, the Stroop effect can be used for further demonstrating the viability, adequacy, and versatility of the conceptualisation proposed here.

Earlier in this section I mentioned that Stroop (1935) studied colour naming and word reading with stimulus cards containing 100 (10 × 10) colour patches and 100 (10 × 10) colour words. What I did not say was that Stroop also used a third type of stimulus card with 100 (10 × 10) coloured colour words. The words and ink colours were red, blue, green, brown, and purple. All the words on this card were printed in incongruent colours, e.g., the word red was printed in green ink, the word green was printed in blue ink, the word blue was printed in red ink, etc. One group of subjects had to name as fast as possible the (ink) colours of the words in reading order (and to neglect the words). Another group of subjects had to read as fast as possible the words in reading order (and to neglect the ink colours). The second row in Table 6.1 presents the results (the first row presents the comparable reading and naming times mentioned above). Stroop's research showed two important results:

•   With colour naming as the task, performance with the 'incongruent' colour–word card was appreciably worse than performance with the 'control' card with colour patches; much more time was required for naming (1103 – 633 = 470 ms per item) and many more errors were made.

Table 6.1 Mean word reading and colour naming times (ms) with the control cards and the 'Stroop' card

	Reading	*Naming*
Control	410	633
'Stroop'	433	1103

See text for further explanation.

• With reading as the task, performance with the 'incongruent' card was not really different from performance with the 'control' card; about the same time was required for reading (433 − 410 = 23 ms per item) and not many more errors were made.

The difference in time between naming/reading with the incongruent 'Stroop' card and with the 'control' card is generally referred to as 'interference'. So, what Stroop showed was an asymmetrical pattern of interference; irrelevant colour words interfered with the naming of colours (390 ms interference per item) but irrelevant colours did not interfere with the reading of colour words (23 ms interference per item). Since Stroop (1935), this pattern of results – a 'Stroop' interference effect with colour naming but no 'Stroop' interference effect with colour-word reading – has been replicated innumerable times in a great variety of sometimes highly ingenious experimental paradigms (see MacLeod, 1991, for an extensive overview).

The asymmetrical outcome just described is exactly what has to be expected, given the conceptualisation of reading and of naming presented in Section 6.1. Let us first look at the reading task. With both cards, the 'incongruent' card and the 'control' card, the reading task is performed with an intentional sequence or Verbal Intention

>> POSITION > SHAPE/report >>.

With both cards the term POSITION selects the object with all its attributes. Then, three things happen:

• With both cards, the state SHAPE of the intentional sequence receives the shape attribute and this shape attribute picks out the corresponding response from among the set of allowable/available responses (strong intentional selection of the required word).
• With both cards, the selected and enhanced shape attribute in Visual Perception picks out the same corresponding response from among the set of available/allowable responses through learned direct parameter specification (strong automatic selection of the required word).
• With the incongruent 'Stroop' card, the selected and enhanced colour attribute in Visual Perception possibly picks out a different response in the set of responses (weak automatic selection of a wrong name). With the control card, the selected and enhanced colour in Visual Perception has no matching name in the set of responses and nothing is selected.

So, with both cards and with reading as the task, two strong forces work together in selecting the required word while either no force (with the control card) or only a weak force (with the incongruent card) works against this selection. With this combination of internal forces, no convincing interference and therefore similar performance with the control card and with the incongruent card is to be expected. With both cards relatively small mean reading times and very few errors are to be expected.[12]

Let us now look at the naming task. With both cards, the 'control' card and the 'incongruent' card, the task is performed with an intentional sequence or Verbal Intention

>> POSITION > COLOUR/report >>.

With both cards the term POSITION selects the object with all its attributes. Then three things happen:

• With both cards, the state COLOUR of the intentional sequence receives the colour attribute and this colour attribute picks out the corresponding response from among the set of available/allowable responses (strong intentional selection of the required name).
• With both cards, the selected and enhanced colour attribute in Visual Perception possibly also picks out the required name from among the set of available/allowable responses (weak automatic selection of the required name).
• With the incongruent 'Stroop' card, the selected and enhanced shape attribute in Visual Perception picks out a different response in the set of responses (strong automatic selection of a wrong word). With the control card, the selected and enhanced shape in Visual Perception has no matching word in the set of responses and nothing is selected.

So, with the control card and naming as the task, a strong force and a weak force work together in selecting the required response and no force works against this selection. With this combination of forces no interference is to be expected. With the incongruent card, a strong force and a weak force work together in selecting the required response but a strong force works against this selection. With this combination of forces substantial interference is to be expected. With the incongruent card much larger mean naming times and many more errors are to be expected than with the control card.[13]

Taken all together, my approach does not have problems either with explaining the naming–reading difference (see Section 6.1) or with the asymmetrical pattern of interference presented in Table 6.1 (this section). So, as claimed, my conceptualisation has no difficulties with accounting for the basic phenomena reported by Stroop (1935) and by many others after him. It is possibly worthwhile here to note that the conceptualisation is in terms of old-fashioned association, not in terms of stimulus–response compatibility. In Chapter 9, Section 9.3, I return to this association.

Within the field of Stroop research there is, however, much more to be explained than the basic observations (see MacLeod, 1991). One important fact in need of explanation is that subjects can perform according to the instruction – read words when word reading is the task and name colours when colour naming is the task. In particular, an explanation is required for the highly relevant observation that subjects are capable of performing in the difficult 'incongruent' colour naming condition. In that condition, most colour naming responses are simply correct responses, not errors consisting of reading the irrelevant word.

The observation that subjects can perform the task, i.e., can come up with the correct response, in the difficult, time-consuming incongruent colour naming task, is nearly always neglected in accounts of the Stroop effect. A brief consideration of the two prevalent accounts of the Stroop effect, the 'relative speed of processing account' and the 'automaticity account', can make this clear (see also MacLeod, 1991, p. 187). The 'relative speed of processing account' assumes that:

> The various analyzers [for colour and word] . . . operate in parallel and will each give rise to an appropriate naming response. If multiple responses are available they will compete for entry into the single channel exit . . . the crucial variable is the relative speed of naming the various attributes of the stimuli.
>
> (Morton & Chambers, 1973, p. 388)

The 'automaticity account' assumes that:

> . . . word reading [is] very automatic, and color (or picture) naming [is] much less automatic. More automatic processing [can] . . . interfere with less automatic processing, but not vice versa. The Stroop task is an interesting case expressly because the two dimensions differ so much in how automatically they are processed.
>
> (MacLeod, 1991, p. 189)

These two quotations make clear that both are accounts of how a problem arises, not of how a problem is solved. Both are accounts of interference. They are completely silent about how in the incongruent colour naming condition the required response – in these accounts the latest, the weakest, the less automated response – is selected from among the multiple competing responses. In his otherwise excellent review of research on the Stroop effect, even MacLeod (1991) fails to see this critical issue. (That subjects can perform according to the instruction is not mentioned in his Appendix B that lists 'Eighteen major empirical results that must be explained by any successful account of the Stroop effect'.)

My conceptualisation can easily make clear by what means subjects are capable of coming up with the correct name of the colour in the difficult incongruent colour–word condition. To see this, it is worthwhile to realise that in this conceptualisation in the Verbal Intention or intentional sequence

>>X > Yn/report >>

that is in control in this task, term X is responsible for creating the problem and term Yn is in charge of solving the problem. By selecting the complete object with all its attributes, term X causes a situation in which the word can trigger a (wrong) response through direct parameter specification (automatic selection of a wrong response). By selecting the attribute colour, term Yn can take care that the (correct) response is singled out from among the available/allowable responses (intentional selection of the correct response). So, my conceptualisation has a parameter that can account for the consistently observed correct, albeit often effortful, task performance. Subjects can come up with the required response when, in one way or another, term Yn can perform a proper attribute-receiving and response-selection job.

Two modifications of the standard Stroop task provide support for this conceptualisation of what happens.[14] Both modifications show that subjects can respond much faster when the effect of object selection through term X is diminished or eliminated. In the first modification, introduced in experimental psychology by Dalrymple-Alford and Budayr (1966), instead of cards with rows of items, individual incongruent Stroop items and control items are tachistoscopically presented and timed per item.[15] In a series of experiments, La Heij, Van der Heijden, and Plooy (2001) compared a condition in which the coloured word remained (on a screen) until the subject responded and a condition in which after 120 ms the colour of the word changed to white and the white word stayed on the screen until there was a response. They consistently found a 'paradoxical exposure effect'; the interference was less, i.e., colour naming was easier, when the colour disappeared from the screen than when the colour remained. This outcome is now readily understandable. When the colour information disappears, object selection by term X is of no use any more for intentional selection; it can only deliver a useless white object for colour attribute selection. In this situation, continued object selection is even disadvantageous because the word in Visual Perception automatically selects a wrong response from the set of responses. When object selection stops, the selection power of the incongruent word diminishes. When term Yn has received the colour, that colour can pick out the required response from among the set of allowable/available responses without much competition from the irrelevant colour word.

The second modification was introduced by Dyer (1973). Dyer separated word and colour, placing the colour (a colour patch) on one side of the fixation point and the word (a black word) on the other. Variants of this 'attribute separation' paradigm were subsequently used by, e.g., Gatti and Egeth (1978), Merikle and Gorewich (1979), Kahneman and Henik (1981), Kahneman and Chajczyk (1983), and Van der Heijden, Hagenaar, and Bloem (1984). MacLeod (1991, pp. 176 & 203) studied the literature using this modification and concluded:

> If the to-be-named color and the to-be-ignored word are presented in separate spatial locations, interference will be reduced (but not

eliminated) relative to the standard, integrated version of the task. Locational uncertainty makes an important contribution in nonintegrated situations.

So with this modification less interference, and in some conditions even no interference, is observed (see, e.g., Kahneman & Henik, 1981).[16] This outcome is also readily understandable given the conceptualisation presented here. With integral combinations, object selection by term X inevitably means that the word is selected and strong interference has to be expected. With separate bilateral presentation of word and colour, correct object selection by term X means that the word is not selected and therefore either no or only minor interference is to be expected.[17]

As stated, theories concerned with the Stroop effect have to explain much more than just the Stroop effect. They have also, for instance, to explain the outcome of a large range of intriguing and ingenious modifications (see MacLeod, 1991, for an extensive overview). Space does not allow me to perform this exercise and to show that my conceptualisation, with few additional assumptions, can easily handle the relevant findings. Here I restrict myself to two sets of further important Stroop-related observations and my explanations of these observations (see Note 19 for a third set of findings). And I end this section with a methodological note.

The first set of data is produced by the research concerned with the question of what kinds of 'incongruent' words cause interference. Since Klein (1964), it is well known that not only incongruent colour words, but also other 'incongruent' words, can interfere with colour naming. In his study, Klein used four colours (red, green, yellow, and blue). He manipulated the relation of sets of four words to these ink colours. The sets of words were (a) the colour words (red, green, yellow, and blue), (b) other colour words (tan, purple, grey, and black), (c) colour-related words (fire, grass, lemon, and sky), (d) common words (put, heart, take, and friend), (e) rare words (sol, helot, eft, and abjure), and (f) nonsense syllables (hjh, evgjc, bhdr, and gsxrq). Klein found interference with all sets of words; interference was largest with the colour words and least with the nonsense syllables, and decreased gradually with the sets of words in between.

Similar and closely related results have often been reported later on in the literature. Scheibe, Shaver, and Carrier (1967), for instance, first determined the strength of association between colours and five sets of words: common colour names (e.g., red), uncommon colour names (e.g., violet), the names of uniformly coloured objects or substances (e.g., blood), the names of ambiguously coloured objects or substances (e.g., paint), and unrelated words (e.g., reason). Then these words were used as 'incongruent' words in a colour naming task. The amount of interference produced by these irrelevant words appeared to increase with the strength of the association with colour. In a similar experiment, Proctor (1978) showed that the amount of interference induced by colour words that were not names of the colours to be named, depended on the strength of association to the colour domain in general; red, blue, and green induced more interference than black, white, and grey. In a related experiment, Singer, Lappin, and Moore (1975) used as 'incongruent words' the colour words and the first, middle, and last two letters of the colour words. They observed that first letters interfered more than later letters but less than the full incongruent colour word. (For similar and related results see, e.g., Dalrymple-Alford, 1972, and Fox, Shor, & Steinman, 1971; see MacLeod, 1991, for an overview.)

With my conceptualisation, these and similar outcomes are not difficult to understand. The colour naming task is performed with a Verbal Intention or intentional sequence

$$\gg X > Yn/report \gg.$$

Term X selects the coloured object with all its attributes in Visual Perception, and term Yn receives the colour attribute required for report and picks out the required response from the response set. The operation of term X causes that in Visual Perception the irrelevant word is selected and enhanced. The interfering power of that irrelevant word depends on its associative relation with elements in the set of available/allowable responses. When the irrelevant word is capable of picking out an (incorrect) response, as with the set of incongruent colour words, strong interference is to be expected. If the irrelevant word is not capable of picking out an (incorrect) response, as with the nonsense syllables, no interference is to be expected. With the other sets of words the interference is expected to be in between. In this conceptualisation, the strength of the associative relation or connection between the selected and therefore enhanced irrelevant word in Visual Perception and one (or more) of the incorrect alternatives in the set of available/ allowable responses determines the amount of interference observed.

The second set of important data was produced by the research concerned with the viability of the 'relative speed of processing account' proposed by Dyer (1973), Morton (1969), Morton and Chambers (1973), Posner and Snyder (1975), and many others. Remember that, according to this account

> . . . the direction of interference depends upon the time relations involved. Words are read faster than colors can be named, thus a color naming response receives stronger interference from the word than the reverse . . .
> (Posner & Snyder, 1975, p. 57)

So this account assumes that the word and the colour are both (automatically) processed and that the winner in this 'horse race' interferes with and thereby delays the loser.[18]

From the 'relative speed of processing account' it directly follows that, when in one way or another the colour is given an appropriate head start, a reversed pattern of Stroop interference should be obtained. Then the colour is processed faster than the word and thus the word reading response receives stronger interference from the colour than the reverse. In the literature, several attempts to produce this reverse pattern of results, i.e., this delayed word reading with advance presentation of the colour, have been reported (see, e.g., Glaser & Glaser, 1982; Glaser & Düngelhoff, 1984; Van der Heijden, 1981, Ch. 5). These attempts were not successful: 'Previewing the slower dimension does not lead to the clear reversal of the direction of interference expected . . .' (MacLeod, 1991, p. 188). This outcome is, of course, damaging for the 'relative speed of processing' account.[19]

With my conceptualisation this result – undisturbed word reading with advance presentation of the incongruent colour – is exactly what has to be expected. Let us assume, for the sake of exposition, that first a red colour patch is presented for 500 ms and that then the word BLUE is superimposed upon that patch. The subject is instructed to read the word, so, according to my conceptualisation, the subject performs the task with the intentional sequence

$$\gg X > Yr/report \gg.$$

Let us now consider what happens in the first interval of time, when only the colour patch is available, and in the second interval of time, when both colour patch and word are available.

In the first interval of time, term X has to select a word. There is, however, no word, only a colour patch. There are then two possibilities. Either nothing is selected and then nothing of interest happens (the sequence remains in state X until object selection is possible). Or, the colour patch is erroneously selected by state X but then the intentional selection of the attribute for responding is impossible because state Yr receives no word shape attribute.[20] So, in this first interval of time only the weak, automatic, selection of a wrong response through a selected and enhanced colour attribute in Visual Perception is to be expected (the colour is never intentionally selected by a state Yn). In both cases, in the second interval of time the situation is exactly the same as with the reading of an incongruent-coloured colour word. There is strong intentional selection of the shape attribute by state Yr and strong automatic 'selection' by the enhanced shape in Visual Perception, and only a minor effect of the enhanced colour in Visual Perception. So, in this interval no interference from the colour on word reading is to be expected.[21]

In my conceptualisation, the only way in which something of a reversed Stroop effect can possibly be induced is through extended and consistent colour naming practice, an amount of practice comparable to that in MacLeod and Dunbar's (1988) shape naming task discussed in Section 6.1. After such practice, the initially weak association between the enhanced colour in Visual Perception and the responses in the set of available/allowable responses may become so strong that it can interfere somewhat with the robust 'dual-route' selection of the word to be read. Stroop (1935, Exp. 3) reported exactly this result (see MacLeod, 1991, p. 165).

I end this section with a methodological note. In nearly all experiments performed by investigators concerned with the processing of visual information, rather peculiar exposure conditions are used. The subject first looks at a fixation point. Then suddenly the relevant stimulus is presented with an abrupt onset. In my view, there are important arguments for propagating the use of previewed displays, instead of sudden short displays as currently used.

One argument is based on ecological validity considerations. In real life, it is seldom that a completely new scene suddenly pops up. Most of the time, permanent static scenes are scanned with a series of (saccadic) eye movements. So preview is the normal situation in real life; what is presently fixated, was already peripherally perceived before. Short-duration sudden exposures are rare exceptions.

Another argument is based on theoretical considerations. As stated earlier, information processing psychologists concerned with vision are convinced that they are studying the processing of visual information, i.e., the processes leading to perception. If that is indeed what is investigated in the experiments, the use of sudden abrupt displays is certainly adequate. With such displays, visual information processing has to start from scratch and the whole process leading to visual perception can be probed and studied. I am convinced, however, that with few exceptions the visual information processing approach is not investigating the processes that lead to visual perception, but the use of visual information for task performance (see Section 1.4). But then there is no need to use sudden abrupt displays – under appropriate conditions, previewed displays can be used as well (see Section 6.3 for an example).

Yet another argument is based on the suspicion that the use of sudden abrupt exposures introduces artifacts – phenomena that are highly interesting as such but are not really relevant for the study of visual information processing and the role of attention therein. And this is the topic I am concerned with here. Basically the point I want to emphasise is that

> With multiple simultaneous onsets . . . a situation is created in which attention is attracted by several new events simultaneously . . . this stimulus situation results in an ambiguous system situation . . . But 'something' has to be done, and it is not surprising that the [visual] system has its own solutions for handling such a situation and that as a result unique phenomena are observed.
>
> (Van der Heijden, 1992, p. 264)

When it is true that, with multiple simultaneous onsets, the visual system has its own solutions and when that system 'itself gives temporal priority to

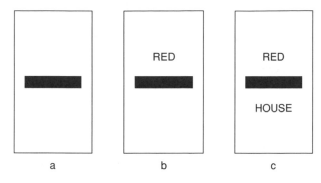

Figure 6.2 Examples of stimuli for a colour naming task. Panel a: stimulus with a (blue) colour patch in the middle. Panel b: the same stimulus with an incongruent colour word. Panel c: the same stimulus with an incongruent colour word and a neutral word. (See text for further explanation.)

one abrupt onset from among a number of simultaneously occurring abrupt onsets' (Van der Heijden, 1992, p. 266), a problematic situation for task performance arises. Then, in terms of the $\gg X > Y \gg$ conceptualisation, it is highly likely that the 'sending' term, X, is severely hindered in performing its proper selective job.

Evidence pointing in this direction – delays as a result of an inadvertent 'attentional capture' by an irrelevant element ('cognitive masking' or 'filtering cost') – was, for instance, reported by Eriksen and Schultz (1978) and by Kahneman, Treisman, and Burkell (1983). Several investigators have pointed to the delaying effects of inadvertent 'capture of attention' by irrelevant items in, for instance, visual search tasks, variants of the Stroop task, and Eriksen's flanker task (see Section 6.3).[22] I will not go into the details of this, now flowering, field of research – I restrict myself to demonstrating what effects 'attentional capture' can bring about in a system in which an intentional sequence, $\gg X > Y \gg$, is in control.

Consider an experiment with the three different types of stimuli depicted in Figure 6.2; stimuli with a single colour patch in the middle (panel a), stimuli with a colour patch in the middle and an incongruent colour word above or below the patch (panel b), and stimuli with a colour patch in the middle, an incongruent colour word above or below that patch, and a neutral word below or above (panel c). The subject is instructed to name the colour of the colour patch in the middle. In my conceptualisation, with all the stimuli the subject performs this task with a Verbal Intention or intentional sequence of the form

$\gg$ MIDDLE > COLOUR/report $\gg$.

With the type of stimulus presented in panel a, nothing peculiar is to be expected. Let us assume that with this type of stimulus the subject needs 500 ms before the response can be initiated. Now assume that in this boring colour naming, colour naming, colour naming task, the selective power of the sending term MIDDLE varies over trials. In particular, let us assume that on some 20% of the trials that power is so weak that an irrelevant item can 'capture attention' in the bottom-up way as just described. (The visual system itself selects.)

With the panel a stimulus, nothing peculiar will happen because there are no irrelevant items. With the type of stimulus of panel b, however, this will mean that the colour patch in the middle is correctly and immediately selected on 80% of the trials. In the other 20% of the trials the incongruent colour word is selected. As elaborated earlier in this section, a selected incongruent colour word will severely interfere through 'direct parameter specification'. Let us assume that the delay, the 'cost', incurred by such an inadvertent and inappropriate selection is 200 ms. Then, with the type of stimulus depicted in panel b, the subject needs on average $(.80 \times 500) + (.20 \times (500 + 200)) = 540$ ms.[23] So, as compared with the type of stimulus of panel a, with these stimuli a Stroop interference of $540 - 500 = 40$ ms is to be expected.[24]

With the type of stimulus of panel c, the sending term MIDDLE will also correctly and immediately select the colour patch on 80% of the trials. In the other 20% of the trials one of the two words is selected. Let us assume that on half of these trials the incongruent word is selected and on the other half of the trials the neutral word is selected. What happens when the incongruent word is selected is given in the preceding paragraph – a delay of 200 ms. What happens when a neutral word is selected we know from the experiments of, for instance, Klein (1964) – not very much delay (say q ms). Then, with the type of stimulus depicted in panel c, the subject needs on average $(.80 \times 500) + (.10 \times (500 + 200)) + (.10 \times (500 + q)) = 520 + .10q$, and is therefore about 520 ms, because q is 'not very much'. So, with this type of stimulus a diminishing, a 'dilution', of the interference as compared with the panel b stimulus has to be expected, a 'dilution' of about 50% (from 40 ms interference with the panel b stimulus to 20 ms interference with the panel c stimulus).

Exactly this pattern of dilution results was reported by Kahneman and Chajczyk (1983; see also Brown, Roos-Gilbert, & Carr, 1995; Mitterer, La Heij, & Van der Heijden, 2003). And, the explanation just presented is very close to the explanation proposed by Kahneman and Chajczyk (1983).[25]

From this example it will be clear that inadvertent selections through 'attentional capture' complicate explanatory issues considerably and easily lead to erroneous interpretations and explanations. Up to now, for instance, I still do not really know whether, with adequate object selection, there is Stroop-like interference in Dyer's bilateral presentation task (see earlier in this section) and in Eriksen's flanker task (see Section 6.3). Moreover, it is far from clear what the dilution paradigm and similar paradigms with multiple simultaneous abrupt onsets teach us about the normal control of human information processing, except that apparently top-down control ultimately wins and prevails. If the information processing approach concerned with vision is interested in the use of visual information for task performance in normal situations, and not in the 'processing' of visual information in adverse situations, previewed displays have to be favoured over sudden, short displays. In the next section I return to previewed displays.

6.3 Preview and a prediction

In the recent past, Stroop interference, or Stroop-like interference, has been demonstrated with a great number of intriguing paradigms (see McLeod, 1991, for an overview). One paradigm still deserves to be briefly mentioned here. Eriksen and Hoffmann (1973) and Eriksen and Eriksen (1974), and many researchers after them, demonstrated identity-specific interference in a 'flanker' task. In the Eriksen and Eriksen experiment, the subjects had to move a lever in one direction when a centrally positioned target letter was a member of a set of two (for instance, an H or an M) and in the opposite direction when it was a member of another set of two (for instance, an A or a U). There was also a set of neutral letters, requiring no response (for instance, an X and a Y). Different combinations of central target and adjacent 'noise' letters (NTN) were used. With response-compatible noise (e.g., MHM) some facilitation was found, and with response-incompatible noise (e.g., AHA) some interference was found, as compared to performance with neutral noise (e.g., XHX). So Eriksen and associates demonstrated identity-specific interference (and facilitation) with equivalent items, with letter–letter combinations. Later on, related results obtained with word–word combinations and colour–colour combinations were reported (see, e.g., Glaser & Glaser, 1982; Hagenaar & Van der Heijden, 1986; Van der Heijden, 1981). However, whether with these 'flanker' tasks *with perfect object selection* interference is still found is presently not clear (see Pashler, 1998, p. 61). Harms and Bundesen (1983) showed that with improved object selection, interference decreases (see also Baylis & Driver, 1992; Driver & Baylis, 1989; La Heij, Helaha, & Van den Hof, 1993).

Eriksen, Webb, and Fournier (1990) used a temporal variant of this 'flanker' paradigm for investigating information processing on a position while another position was initially cued, i.e., information processing in a *non-cued* position. In the experiment and conditions that are relevant here (Eriksen et al., Exp. 1), first an underline pre-cue appeared that 'directed attention' to one of eight locations in the visual field. After 50 ms, a circular array of letters followed. In 50% of the trials the underlined position contained a target, T (an H or an M), and in the other 50% of trials a noise letter, N (another letter). Then a second underline cue appeared in another position 50 ms after the letter array began. Until the second cue appeared, that position contained one of two possible items: a target, T (an H or an M), or a noise letter, N (another letter). Simultaneously with the appearance of the second cue, the letter in that cued position either continued unchanged (T-T condition), changed from a noise letter into one of the targets (N-T condition), or changed from the target to the other target (T2-T condition). The whole display was turned off 50 ms after appearance of the second cue. The subjects had to report as fast as possible the identity of the target in the first or second underlined position. The important finding was that, with the target in the second underlined position, the mean times in the three conditions, N-T, T-T, and T2-T, did not reliably or appreciably differ (there was no facilitation in the T-T condition and no interference in the T2-T condition, compared with the N-T condition). So, preview had no observable effects.

Eriksen et al. (1990) consider a number of explanations for the absence of any identity-specific facilitation and interference in the T-T condition and T2-T condition in this temporal 'flanker' task. They favour an explanation in terms of the absence of detailed information processing during an initial period of 'dead time', due to 'perceptual inertia':

> Clearly, the first 50 msec of stimulation did not result in any processing that was beneficial to the . . . discrimination. The experiments of B. A. Eriksen and C. W. Eriksen (1974) and Hoffman (1975) used different tasks but revealed the same phenomenon: The first 40 to 50 msec of processing following stimulus onset may not be able to make use of information in the stimulus that is critical for discrimination. There is a phenomenon similar to perceptual inertia during which the processing system is being turned on, so to speak, and until the system is revved up, the presence of discriminatory detail cannot be used.
>
> (Eriksen et al., 1990, p. 481)

In their view, this 'perceptual inertia' means that the N of N-T, the first T of T-T, and the T2 of T2-T are simply not processed. Only after this initial period of 'dead time' are the details of the visual information processed. Then the T of N-T, the second T of T-T, and the T of T2-T are processed. And, because T is T is T, nothing special has to be expected.

Related selection experiments, with position as the 'defining attribute' and letter shape as the to-be-'reported attribute', described by Hoffman (1975) and Shiffrin, Diller, and Cohen (1996), produced similar data and led to the same 'dead time' explanation. In the opinion of the investigators their selection experiments showed that

> . . . the visual information processing system does not use the complete target or noise element information for the first 50 msec when confronted with a multicharacter display.
>
> (Hoffman, 1975, p. 352)

or that

> . . . there is a period of time . . . when general information is accumulated that does not distinguish one character from another, followed by accumulation of distinguishing information.
>
> (Shiffrin et al., 1996, pp. 238–239)

Here I will not go into the details of this further 'perceptual inertia' research (see Wienese, La Heij, Van der Heijden, & Shiffrin, 2000, for a detailed description and an empirical evaluation). At this point it is only worthwhile to note that two interpretations of the outcome of the 'inertia' research and of the three quotations are possible:

• The first interpretation is the 'delayed processing' interpretation. The assumption is that there is an initial period of time in which no detailed, distinguishing, information is accumulated and that this delay in information processing is at the basis of the findings. This is the standard interpretation of the information processing approach which squares with the basic assumption that the experiments investigate the *processing* of visual information.

• The second interpretation is the 'delayed selection' interpretation. The assumption is that there is an initial period of time in which the detailed, distinguishing, information is not selected and that this delay in information selection is at the basis of the findings. This is my alternative interpretation which squares with my basic assumption that the experiments investigate the *use* of visual information for task performance (see Section 1.4).

That the 'delayed selection' interpretation is at least consistent with the data is easily illustrated with the data reported by Eriksen et al. (1990) which were presented above (see Wienese et al., 2000, for a more detailed account). In my $>> X > Y >>$ conceptualisation, the subjects performed this task with an intentional sequence of approximately the form

> $>>$ POSITION1 $>$ SHAPE/(report) $>> >>$ POSITION2 $>$
> SHAPE/report $>>$.

The first unit of analysis suffices when the target is in the first underlined position – POSITION1 selects all information from the first underlined position and SHAPE selects the information required for response – but that condition is not of interest here.[26] The whole sequence is required when the target appears not in the first but in the second underlined position. Of course, the second unit of analysis can only start *after* the second underline cue has appeared and after the first SHAPE noted: no target. Then, the POSITION2 term has to select the object marked by the second underline cue. Only *after* that selection can the term SHAPE in the second unit of analysis start to select, i.e., to receive/process, the to-be-'reported attribute'. In all conditions, the information required and selected by that state was already there (long) *before* POSITION2 had finished its selective work (remember, when the letter was changed, that change occurred simultaneously with the onset of the second cue). So, in none of the conditions is something special to be expected. In all three conditions the unit of analysis >> POSITION2 > SHAPE/report >> interacts with a stable, unchanging, visual representation. The experimentally introduced letter changes are simply irrelevant because they occur (long) *before* the relevant selective operations take place (see also Shiffrin et al., 1996, p. 228, for a closely related explanation). This >> X > Y >> >> X > Y >> explanation is supported by the observation that a delayed letter change, in my conceptualisation a letter change *after* the start of the relevant selective operations, produces the predicted interference in time and in errors (see Eriksen et al., 1990, Exp. 2).

In general, according to my >> X > Y >> conceptualisation, in the position-cueing experiments providing evidence for 'perceptual inertia' there is an initial interval of time that detailed information is *not required* and is *not used*. The initial term X of the Verbal Intention or intentional sequence is concerned with (global) position information, not with detailed identity information. The intentional sequence is 'blind' for the to-be-'reported attribute' when it is in state X (and 'blind' for the 'defining attribute' when it is in stage Y). The sequence is blind for shape information, because the initial state X is working on position information – position information is needed but precise shape information is not. Only after that interval of time, when the sequence moves from state X into state Y, is the detailed letter information required. This, however, does not entail that when term X is operating, detailed information is *not accumulated* or is *not available*.

Of course, it can be argued that 'perceptual inertia' experiments, like those of Eriksen et al. (1990), can never decide between the 'delayed processing' hypothesis and the 'delayed selection' hypothesis (see, however, Wienese et al., 2000). In these experiments, on each trial processing has to start from scratch and selection has to start from scratch. So, what is measured can be interpreted as the early stages of the processing operation (the 'perceptual inertia' interpretation). And what is measured can be interpreted as the later stages of the selection operation (the 'X > Y' interpretation). To decide between the two hypotheses, experiments are needed that give either the 'processing' or the 'selection' a sufficiently large head start. Experiments that gave selection such a head start have already been described and interpreted in 'selection' terms in Section 5.3, where I discussed the position-cueing tasks. Let us now look at a paradigm that gives processing such a head start.

Starting with Averbach and Coriell's (1961) partial-report bar-probe task, Pashler (1984) invented an elegant and ingenious paradigm that gave processing a large head start (see Mewhort, Johns & Goble, 1991, and Fera, Jolicoeur, & Besner, 1994, for replications and extensions). At first sight, that paradigm produced a set of facts that is not easily explained in terms of a model which assumes that visual information is processed/identified before it is selected. The fact that in a recent overview of these experiments Pashler (1998, pp. 253–256) uses terms like 'striking' and 'paradoxical', however, can be taken to indicate that these empirical facts are difficult to explain in terms of whatever extant model. Indeed, up to now I have never seen a satisfying explanation of these facts in the literature. Let us look at the paradigm and the results and then see what the >> X > Y >> approach can make of the results.

In Pashler's (1984) paradigm, the subject sees a display with letters, e.g., a row of six letters, and a cue, e.g., a bar-marker, indicating one of the letters. There are two 'display' conditions; either all letters in the display are 'intact' or all letters in the display are 'degraded' in one or another way. Two effective ways of degradation are increasing the confusability between the letters (Pashler, 1984) and superimposing dots on top of the letters (Mewhort et al., 1991). There are two relevant 'timing' conditions; either the bar-marker is presented (150 ms) before the letter array (the early probe condition) or the letter array is presented (400 ms) before the probe, allowing a 'preview' of the letters (the late probe condition). These timing conditions are depicted in Figure 6.3. The subjects are instructed to react to the letter indicated by the probe as fast as possible. Latencies are measured from the first moment at which both array and probe are present.

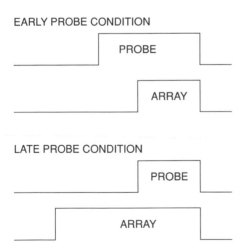

Figure 6.3 The relevant timing conditions in Pashler's (1984) 'preview' design (adapted from Pashler, 1998, Fig. 5.2). Upper panel: Early probe condition without preview of letter array. Lower panel: Late probe condition with preview of letter array. (See text for further explanation.)

One outcome of this experiment is that the observed latencies are smaller in the early probe condition than in the late probe condition. Of course, this is what is to be expected with this type of location cueing task (see Section 5.3). The 'striking' outcome with this paradigm is that not only in the early probe condition, but also in the late probe condition, a substantial delaying effect of stimulus degradation is found. In fact, in the two timing conditions the effect of degradation is about equally as strong.

The latter outcome is damaging for *late* selection theories as proposed by Mewhort and associates (see Mewhort et al., 1981; see also Coltheart, 1984). These theories postulate that in this task all letters are immediately processed in parallel and are stored as abstract identities, along with location information, in a memory for identified information (the 'character buffer'). An 'attentional mechanism', using position information, selects the required item in this memory. Thus, according to these theories, in the late probe condition the degradation can be dealt with during the (400 ms) preview and no effects of degradation should be found in this condition. In Pashler's (1998, p. 253) words: In these models what 'the identification process lengthens is already over and done with by the time the cue appears, so any variation in how long this identification took should be absorbed.'

According to Pashler (1998, p. 253) 'The results argue that even when observers have the opportunity to preview a display and every incentive to process as many items as possible, they still identify the probed item *after* the probe arrives'. And, while he admits that 'visual input can hardly sit waiting at the retina until more central mechanisms call for it' (pp. 253–255) he concludes that with (400 ms) preview 'On balance, then, the evidence favors the view that identification takes place after detection of the cue' (p. 255).

This conclusion is, of course, very difficult to accept. It reminds one strongly of Sperling's (1960, p. 11) naive instruction:

> You will see letters illuminated by a flash that quickly fades out . . . You will hear a tone during the flash or while it is fading which will indicate which letters you are to attempt to read. Do not read the card until you hear the tone, . . .

Averbach and Coriell (1961), however, had already provided substantial evidence for pre-bar-marker reading in partial-report bar-probe tasks as used by Pashler (1984; see also Coltheart, 1972, for this pre-bar-marker identification). And of course, it is highly unlikely that subjects can prevent reading when reading is their task.

My $\gg X > Y \gg$ conceptualisation, a version of the *early* selection views, has no problems with explaining the degradation results just described. Here three points of that conceptualisation are of importance:

- The first point is that, given the conceptualisation of reading presented in Section 6.1, there is nothing to prevent me from assuming that all items presented are automatically processed/identified via the direct Visual Perception – Response set connection – connection A in Figure 6.1 (see also Section 5.4 and Section 6.4).

- The second point is that in my conceptualisation, also when the items are automatically processed/identified, for voluntary intentional selection the indicated/required item still has to be 'selected' by term X and to be 'received' by term Y of the unit of analysis >> X > Y >>.[27]
- The third point is, of course, that in my conceptualisation for this 'selection' by term X and this 'receiving' by term Y, Visual Perception, the visual representation of the stimulus, is required.

As in the partial-report bar-probe task (see Section 5.3), the sequence used in that 'selection' and 'receiving' is

>> BAR > SHAPE/report >>.

Of course, the sequence can only start after appearance of the bar-marker – the X-part, the term BAR, cannot work without the position information provided by the bar-marker. After starting from BAR, and top-down reaching the position of the representation indicated by the bar-marker, the sequence moves into the state SHAPE. Then, in the 'intact' condition a 'channel' with intact information, and in the 'degraded' condition a 'channel' with degraded information, gets involved in the Y-part, the receiving part, of the intentional selection process. In the 'intact' condition, the state SHAPE receives intact shape information and faces no difficulties in picking out the required response from among the set of available/allowable responses – there is a strong, intact, association between intact attribute and response. In the 'degraded' condition, the state SHAPE receives degraded shape information and faces difficulties in picking out the required response from among the set of available/allowable responses – there is a weaker, degraded, association between degraded attribute and response. With and without preview, these weak associations will show up as delayed responding in the degradation condition as compared to the intact condition. So, in this regard, no differences between the two timing conditions are to be expected. In short, the >> X > Y >> approach can easily explain the critical unexpected result without assuming that the information is not processed.[28]

In Pashler's (1984) experiment, during the 400 ms letter preview the visual information can certainly not be used for task performance. The internal operations required for the appropriate use of visual information for task performance can only start after the 400 ms preview, when the bar-marker has indicated the information that has to be used. This, however, does not entail that during preview no information processing is going on. There is no reason to assume that there is a 400 ms interval of time with 'perceptual inertia', during which the system is 'revved up', so to say. It is highly unlikely that during preview, before appearance of the bar-marker, the visual information sits 'waiting on the retina'. And it is highly likely that under appropriate conditions (i.e., when the light is on, the eyes are open and properly adapted, the script is sufficiently clear, etc.) subjects automatically process the visual information in a reading task like Pashler's task.

In Pashler's (1984) task, just as in all other tasks used by the information processing approach, the processing/identification of information is necessary but not sufficient for task performance. In my >> X > Y >> view, the processing/identification is also not the information processing operation that is addressed and measured in the preview task and other types of tasks. In my view, it is the selection of the required objects and the selection of the required attributes that show up in the dependent measures in the information processing approach. When in all textbooks and papers the general term 'processing' is replaced by more specific terms referring to aspects of 'selection', great theoretical progress is made without any loss.

It will be clear that, in my view, Pashler's (1984) paradigm is an important one because it can help to probe and decide what exactly is investigated in the experiments of the information processing approach – the processing of selected information, as suggested in the standard approach, or the selection of processed information, as suggested in the >> X > Y >> approach. The paradigm, and variations of it, deserve much more investigation. Fortunately, modifications and extensions of the preview paradigm are easily invented. On the basis of the >> X > Y >> approach I have, of course, to predict that, e.g., with appropriate modifications of the Stroop task (see Section 6.2) and of the visual search tasks (see Section 5.1), with preview and without preview, the same effects will be found.[29] For search tasks there is already some evidence (see Pashler, 1998, Ch. 5, endnote 8).[30]

6.4   Two stages

Visual perception, the detailed and coloured visual world in which we live, is a wonderful given. It therefore does not come as a surprise that for many information processing psychologists, or cognitive psychologists, the ultimate, ambitious, aim is to explain (visual) perception (see Section 2.1). Neisser (1967, p. 4), for instance, states that 'Visual cognition . . . deals with the processes by which a perceived, remembered, and thought-about world is brought into being from as unpromising a beginning as the retinal patterns.' And, according to Neisser, the topic cognitive psychology has to be concerned with is exactly these processes and transformations that lead to perception. Pashler (1998, p. 13), in comparing early introspective psychology and information processing psychology, states: 'A second change reflected the emergence of new concepts that permitted the events that make up perception to be fractionated.' And, according to Pashler, the main aim of the information processing approach is the fractionation of perception; that is, the characterisation of perception as a 'process of achieving more elaborated and defined internal descriptions of a stimulus.'

For explaining visual perception, it must be clear what problems the visual system encounters and has to solve. At the start of the information processing approach the main problem for vision was not difficult to find. For auditory perception the main problem was introduced and further specified by Broadbent (1958): limited central capacity (see Section 5.4). Not much later, limited central capacity was also regarded as the main problem for visual perception. In their influential works Broadbent (1971), Kahneman (1973), and Neisser (1967) emphasised and elaborated this limited-central-capacity assumption for vision. The main and crucial question thus became, how to explain (visual) perception, given limited central capacity as the starting point. And Broadbent's, Kahneman's and Neisser's answer to this question was: In terms of linear two-stage, limited capacity – limited capacity, models!

Two-stage limited capacity – limited capacity theories square perfectly well with phenomenological intuitions and introspective observations. They are fully consistent with the general observation that 'consciousness' is not an all-or-none phenomenon and that what is in consciousness comes in degrees. Within early introspective psychology not only James (1890/1950), with his 'stream of consciousness', had already emphasised this point.

> The most influential proponent of selection-within-consciousness in 19th century psychology was Wilhelm Wundt. He distinguished between the 'field of consciousness' (Blickfeld des Bewustseins) and the 'focus of consciousness' (Blickpunkt des Bewustseins). The focus of consciousness, which encompassed only part of what was represented in consciousness, was determined by the direction of attention. Thus, a shift of attention was equivalent to bringing some contents from the field of consciousness into its focus, while others, which had been in the focus of consciousness, receded in the field of consciousness.
>
> (Neumann, 1996, p. 429)

The initial two-stage models of the information processing approach postulate an initial pre-attentive stage of information processing that processes all the information available, but only partly, and a subsequent attentive stage of information processing that processes only part of the information, but that part completely. In Neisser (1967, p. 89), for instance, we find: '. . . the processes of focal attention . . . can come into play only *after preliminary* operations have . . . segregated the . . . units involved'; '. . . they produce the objects which *later* mechanisms are to flesh out . . .'; 'Each . . . object must be separated from the others . . . for the *subsequent* and more detailed analysis of attention'; '*Following* the pre-attentive mechanisms comes the *second level* of pattern analysis . . .' (italics mine; see also Neisser, 1967, p. 90). And, since then, the assumption that there are two subsequent stages in visual perception has figured prominently in a variety of forms in nearly all stories told by information processing psychologists about the development in time of visual perception (see Van der Heijden, 1996b, for a critical overview of two-stage models).

In the resulting two-stage models, at the first, pre-attentive stage, there is a global, preliminary form of information processing.[31] After Neisser (1967) and Kahneman (1973), it is quite generally accepted that at this stage, the information processing mechanisms partition the visual field into object regions against a ground on the basis of Gestalt properties such as spatial proximity, continuity of contour, etc.[32] According to main-stream theorising, these pre-attentive processes are:

- 'automatic', i.e., triggered by and under the control of external information,
- 'spatially parallel', i.e., operating simultaneously on all locations of the visual field, and
- ' "unlimited" in capacity', i.e., capable of performing their very limited tasks when and where required (see, e.g., Folk & Egeth, 1989, p. 97).

At the second, attentive stage, attention comes in and finishes the perceptual work. Attention takes care of a more detailed analysis of part of the visual information and causes the selected information to reach awareness. According to main-stream theorising, these attentive processes are:

- 'controlled', i.e., guided and directed by the information processor's goals and intentions,
- 'spatially restricted', i.e., operating on a small region of the visual field, and, of course,
- 'limited in capacity', i.e., only capable of performing their sophisticated task once per unit of time (see, e.g., Folk & Egeth, 1989, p. 97).

From what was said in Section 5.4, it will be clear that in my content view of attention there is no place for the limited-capacity-in-vision assumption. My starting point is that the visual system faces no problems in analysing the information provided by the eyes. Given this alternative starting point, it is of interest to see that something like the distinction between *pre-attentive processing* and *attentive processing* of the traditional theories also shows up in my alternative and well as the distinction between *Visual Perception* and *Intending Mind*. Moreover, my Visual Perception is:

- 'automatic', i.e., triggered by and under the control of external information,
- 'spatially parallel', i.e., dealing simultaneously with all locations of the visual field, and
- ' "unlimited" in capacity' (see Section 5.4).

And my Intending Mind is:

- 'controlling', i.e., guides and directs the 'information processing',
- 'spatially selective', i.e., interacts with objects/regions in visual space, and
- 'limited in capacity' (see Section 5.4).

So there is an almost perfect one-to-one relation between the main processes and characteristics of the processes recognised in the traditional two-stage theorising and the main processes and properties of the processes postulated in the alternative I have introduced and used in the preceding chapters.

This one–one mapping shows a number of important points, two of which are worth noting briefly here. First, when the traditional theorising is approximately correct then my proposal also cannot be far from the mark (and vice versa). Second, when the traditional theorising can explain most of the experimental results then my alternative can also explain the bulk of the experimental results (and vice versa). It is generally agreed that the two-stage theories provide appropriate explanations for the bulk of the relevant experimental results in selective-attention-in-vision tasks. Therefore my alternative can also explain most of the pertinent results obtained in selective-attention-in-vision tasks. This point has already been partially demonstrated in Chapters 5 and 6. The present conclusion saves me a lot of work by completing that demonstration.

It will, however, be clear that there is an essential theoretical difference between the traditional approach and the approach introduced and defended in this work. For me, it is easiest to phrase that difference in terms of the major information processing structures distinguished in Chapter 4, Visual Perception and Intending Mind. The traditional approach assumes that in the information processing system the theoretically relevant main divide is within Visual Perception. This assumption is consistent with the assumption that the experiments probe the process of visual perception. My approach maintains that in the information processing system the theoretically relevant main divide is between Visual Perception and Intending Mind. This assumption is consistent with the assumption that the experiments probe the use of visual information for task performance. Let us end this chapter by considering the question of where the theoretically relevant main divide is, within Visual Perception or between Visual Perception and Intending Mind.

My position is, of course, that the traditional theories start with an assumption that is difficult to defend – the assumption of limited central capacity in Visual Perception (see Section 5.4). When the traditional two-stage theorising is indeed derived from and built around a fictitious assumption of limited central capacity in Visual Perception, that theorising must be extremely vulnerable. And indeed, traditional two-stage theories face a great number of difficulties in nearly all steps and components (see, e.g., Van der Heijden, 1996b, for a detailed evaluation). Here, only two groups of difficulties in the traditional two-stage theories will be considered – one group connected with selection from the first stage in Visual Perception, and one group connected with the processing of the information in the second stage of Visual Perception.

A first group of problems is encountered with the postulated first-stage, pre-attentive representation in Visual Perception from which, according to the traditional theories, information for further processing is selected.[33] With regard to this pre-attentive representation, theorists are confronted with an unsolvable dilemma. When the first stage of Visual Perception contains only a little bit of information, how is adequate selection possible? When the first stage of Visual Perception contains much more information, why is selection and a second stage with further processing required? Exactly the solution of this dilemma has led to inconsistencies and contradictions in all prevailing two-stage perception theories (see Van der Heijden, 1996b).

Just to illustrate this problem, we briefly look at the once influential theory of Kahneman (1973) and the nowadays influential theory of Bundesen (1990). As 'observed behaviour' or 'data' I use the well-established fact that subjects are capable of selecting an element from among a number of elements when target and distractors differ in obvious 'physical' character-istics. In particular, I use the fact that subjects can name the shape of the red object that is presented together with a number of differently coloured – green, blue, pink, brown, etc. – objects.[34] The question we are going to look at is how the two versions of the limited-capacity two-stage theory deal with this basic result.

Kahneman's (1973) theory postulates that in the first stage of processing pre-attentive analysers segregate the visual field into objects against a ground (Kahneman, 1973, p. 68; see also Neisser, 1967, p. 89). These objects can be regarded as visible conjunctions of position, colour, and form, albeit that these visible objects '... have only a marginal claim to being called "conscious" at all' (Neisser, 1967, p. 301; see also Kahneman, 1973, p. 68). In the second stage of processing, attention takes care of a more detailed analysis. This attentional processing is a necessary operation, because 'Parallel processing of different units is possible, but perception draws on a common pool of capacity, and the ability to carry out detailed analyses of several units is limited' (Kahneman, 1973, p. 129). In this view attention only affects the *degree* of perceptual processing. 'Attended events are more likely to be perceived consciously, and more likely to be perceived in detail. They have a higher probability of eliciting and controlling responses, and they are more likely to be stored in permanent memory in a manner that permits intentional retrieval' (Kahneman, 1973, p. 68).

At first sight, this 'classical' limited-capacity perception proposal seems perfectly capable of accounting in a very natural way for observed selective behaviour in general and for observed selective performance in our 'name the shape of the red object' task in particular. The difficulty faced by this theory is, however, that an *explicit formulation* shows a contradiction. Kahneman (1973) is well aware that in '... tachistoscopic presentations of complex arrays ... the subject can be set to select ... items of a particular color . . . and he performs almost as well as if the irrelevant material had not been present' (p. 114). This illustrates '. . . that it is easy . . . to control visual attention by the attribute of color . . .' (p. 72). So, from the selection facts we have to conclude that for colour perception the second stage of processing is *not needed*; the first stage of processing is perfectly *capable* of providing unambiguous colour information. In Kahneman's 'schematic model for perception and attention' (p. 67, Fig. 5-1), however, there is a 'selection of interpretations' stage *after* a 'figural emphasis' stage in which 'attention is allocated to objects'. This interpretation stage '. . . guarantees that no more than one interpretation is assigned to each object in each set or dimension. Thus a homogeneous patch of color is not seen as both red and yellow . . .' (p. 68).[35] So, the theory also states that for colour perception the second stage of processing is *needed*; the first stage of processing is also *not capable* of providing unambiguous colour information.

Bundesen's (1990) theory is a modern variant of Kahneman's (1973) theory containing a milder variant of Kahneman's contradiction problem. According to the theory, in the first stage of processing, the visual field is segregated into 'elements', i.e., into perceptual units in the sense of Kahneman (1973, p. 68). In the second stage, each element receives an 'attentional weight' that determines its speed of processing. Selection of an element in the visual field, e.g., of our red object from among differently coloured ones, is accomplished by increasing the attentional weight of that object rather than of the other objects. The processing of all attributes of the red object is then sped up at the expense of the processing of the attributes of the other objects. In the theory '. . . the recognition problem is resolved for no elements except those that are selected' (Bundesen, 1990, p. 527).

Again, at first sight it seems that this theory can account for selective behaviour in general and for selective performance in our 'shape of the red element' task in particular. The problem in Bundesen's (1990) theory, however, becomes apparent when we look at two different selective instructions. Under the instruction 'Name the shape of the red object', the sensory evidence, produced by the first stage of processing, is of sufficient strength to enable the system to select that red object so that its shape – 'It is a square' – can be determined. Under the instruction 'Name the colour of the square', the sensory evidence produced by the first stage of processing is of sufficient strength to enable the system to select that square so that its colour – 'It is red' – can be determined. But, if there is sufficient sensory information for the *selection* of 'the red one' and 'the square-shaped one', why then is there not sufficient sensory information for the *recognition* 'it is red' and 'it is a square'? In short, there is an arbitrary 'quantitative' distinction between 'the evidence needed for proper selection' and 'the evidence needed for proper recognition'. The assumption that less evidence is needed for appropriate, errorless, selection than for appropriate, errorless, recognition is an arbitrary assumption without any supporting evidence.

A second group of problems for the limited-capacity perception theories which assume that the theoretically relevant main divide is within Visual Perception, is encountered with the transition from the postulated first stage of Visual Perception to the hypothetical second stage of Visual Perception, i.e., with regard to the 'attentive processing' of the information. As already shown in Section 4.2, it appears that, with regard to the processing operations performed during attentive processing and which are assumed to result in complete Visual Perception and categorisation/identification, theory has not very much of relevance to say. Remember, for instance, Cave and Wolfe (1990), who remark with regard to their computer simulation of visual search:

> The simulation says little about how the serial stage operates, except that it is capable of deciding conclusively whether or not an element is the target. The serial stage is undoubtedly a large collection of complex processing mechanisms. For present purposes, the important aspect of these mechanisms is that they operate over a limited part of the field at any one time, and that they use the quickly-prepared evidence from the parallel stage to decide what to process next.
>
> (Cave & Wolfe, 1990, p. 237)

The main reason for this state of affairs is not too difficult to find. In the traditional theories, the processing of the information delivered by the first stage of perception in the second stage of perception has to result in categorisation/identification. The relation between digits and digit names, between letters and letter names, between shape and shape names, between objects and object names, between colours and colour names, etc., is, however, fully arbitrary. For instance, for the colour of the sky on a dark night the word black is as good as noir, nero, zwart, and schwartz, and for the colour of a dandelion in sunlight the word yellow is as good as jaune, giallo, geel, and gelb. These arbitrary relations or associations are learned early in life and practised further through applications and encounters later on (see Section 9.3 for this learning). Because these relations are fully arbitrary, neither 'processing', nor 'more processing', nor 'still more processing' of the information provided by a first stage with 'pre-attentive analysis' (Neisser, 1976, p. 17) can come up with these relations; the association is not in that information.[36] Non-existent implications cannot be computed, existent relations can be used. Most information processing experiments concerned with the selection of information within a single eye-fixation capitalise on already existing, over-learned associations; when subjects enter the laboratory they already know how to apply letter names, digit names, colour names, etc.

When the alternative approach introduced in this work, with the theoretically relevant main divide between Visual Perception and Intending Mind and with overt capacity limitations resulting from internal task performance, is on the right track, then these difficulties should not be encountered. And, fortunately, in my conceptualisation the selection and processing problems faced by the traditional two-stage theories indeed do not arise.

The contradiction in Kahneman's (1973) theory and the arbitrariness in Bundesen's (1990) theory arise from the assumption that both a first stage of processing, the pre-attentive analysers, and a second stage of processing, attention in one form or another, contribute to Visual Perception. In my analysis, this divide is neither what is studied nor what is revealed in the information processing experiments. What is studied in selective attention experiments is not the 'processing of information', as supposed in the traditional theories, but the use of already fully processed information for the required task performance. The two-stage assumption that there is a theoretically relevant main divide within Visual Perception is rejected and is replaced by the assumption that the theoretically relevant main divide is between Visual Perception and the Intending Mind concerned with task performance.[37]

The solution for the processing problem has already been introduced in Section 4.2 and further elaborated in Section 6.1. Two points are of importance here. The first concerns our knowledge of the processing of visual information in the absence of a Verbal Intention. Because in all experiments in the information processing approach there is always an instruction and therefore a Verbal Intention, not much of relevance can be said about this processing for Visual Perception, except that this processing suffices for a Verbal Intention to perform its job. The second point concerns our knowledge of the 'processing' of visual information for task performance in the presence of a Verbal Intention. In Section 4.2, where I discussed the interaction between Visual Perception and Intending Mind, I suggested that three types of 'processing' have to be distinguished – concatenation, propagation, and association. The analyses of experiments, presented in Chapter 5 and in this chapter, provide me with no reasons to alter that suggestion.

Recently, Logan and Zbrodoff (1999, p. 64) advanced a theoretical position with regard to the processing of information with which I cannot disagree and that summarises my point of view with regard to the 'inner happenings' in report tasks:

> Many researchers believe that simple basic-level concepts (Rosch, 1978) can be identified without attention . . . Our disagreement may stem from a different interpretation of identification. Other researchers may interpret identification as the activation of knowledge structures in memory (. . .); we interpret identification as the formation of an explicit propositional representation that asserts "object x is a member of category i." In our view, knowledge structures . . . may become active without attention, but they do not become propositions unless some attentional routine is executed . . .

Indeed, in my view with Visual Perception '. . . knowledge structures . . . may become active without attention'. And indeed, for 'the formation of an explicit propositional representation', as required in report tasks, in my conceptualisation an Intending Mind, with a Verbal Intention consisting of $>> X > Y >>$ units, which interacts with Visual Perception, is required.

Notes

1 The writing of this section and the next section was considerably facilitated by Colin M. MacLeod's (1991) excellent study 'Half a century of research on the Stroop effect: An integrative review'.

2 With both types of tasks, naming and reading, a limited set of responses is repeatedly used. Therefore, 'priming' of the allowable responses cannot explain the difference between reading and naming.

3 At about the same time, in considering why colour-word reading is faster than colour naming, Woodworth (1938, pp. 355–356) remarks:

> The colors are easier to see than the names . . . ; and the motor process of naming is the same in both cases. The difference must lie in the intervening central process. The association between a seen word and the saying of the word must be closer than between a seen color and saying the color name. The difference may be due to practice: every time we notice a printed word we read it, silently at least; but we often see a color without naming it. As a result, not only is the association between printed and spoken word more practiced, but also it has no strong competitors. About the only response to a seen word is to read it, whereas there are many possible responses to a seen color, form or object.

4 This conceptualisation was derived from Morton's (1969) logogen model (*logos* means word, *genus* means birth).

5 This reinterpretation is not too difficult to defend. The semantic system can be regarded as part of LTM (long-term memory; see, e.g., Tulving, 1985). STM (short-term memory) can be regarded as that part of semantic memory in LTM that is presently activated (see, e.g., Cowan, 1999). The Verbal Intention or intentional sequence can be regarded as that aspect or part of the activated information in STM that 'interfaces' with Visual Perception.

6 It is worthwhile to note the symmetry in this reading case. With word reading it is nearly always the case that, when the word shape is enhanced in Visual Perception the corresponding word response is selected by sequence state Y, and that, when the word response is selected by sequence state Y, the corresponding word shape is enhanced in Visual Perception.

7 It is worthwhile to note the asymmetry in this naming case. With colour naming (and other kinds of attribute naming) it is almost never the case that, when the colour is enhanced in Visual Perception the corresponding colour response is selected by sequence state Y, but it is almost always the case that, when the colour response is selected by sequence state Y, the corresponding colour in Visual Perception is enhanced.

8 In intentional reading there is a term, Yr, for the voluntary control of the response and for 'receiving' word information for further cognitive operations in the semantic system. It is possible, however, that Yr is not, or only minimally, involved in picking out the correct response from among the available responses in speeded response tasks as used in the laboratory.

9 It is worthwhile to note that the proposed conceptualisation can account for Cattell's (1886) and Woodworth's (1938) observation that colours are recognised faster than words; the colour is recognised when term Yn has 'received' the colour (a 'simple' attribute) and the word is recognised when term Yr has 'received' the word (a 'complex' attribute). The observation that there is a stimulus set size effect with colour naming but not with word reading (see, e.g., Fraisse, 1969; Gholson & Hohle, 1968; see also MacLeod, 1991, p. 177) can be accounted for in terms of 'intentional' selection by term Y with colour naming vs automatic direct parameter specification with word reading.

10 It is of importance to note that in this experiment the set of stimuli and the set of responses were the same in both tasks. So, only the representation of the instruction can account for task performance, naming the shapes (green, pink, etc.) vs naming the colours (green, pink, etc.).

11 It is worthwhile to note the symmetry here that we already met with reading but not with naming (see Notes 6 and 7). With the shape naming training trials it is *always* the case that, when the shape is enhanced in Visual Perception, the corresponding colour name is selected by sequence state SHAPE, and that, when the colour name is selected by state SHAPE, the corresponding shape is enhanced in Visual Perception. So, in a sense, MacLeod and Dunbar (1988) taught their subjects to 'read' shapes.

12 Taking the automatic forces together, it can be said that with both cards, intentional selection of the required response is more helped than hindered by automatic selection.

13 Taking the automatic forces together, it can be said that with the control card intentional selection of the response required is helped by automatic selection and that with the incongruent card intentional selection of the response is hindered by automatic selection.

14 It is worthwhile to note that the long reaction times observed with incongruent combinations also support this conceptualisation. For correct responding, the system has to wait until the adverse automatic effects of object selection are over, i.e., in terms of my $\gg X > Y \gg$ conceptualization, has to be in state Y and wait until the effects of state X are over.

15 In this field of research 'congruent' combinations of colours and words are often also used, e.g., the word RED in red ink, GREEN in green ink, etc. With these combinations some *facilitation* of colour naming is often found. This result is not easy to interpret, however, because it is not known whether subjects named the colour or read the word.

16 Theoretically, these observations are of great importance. Once, there was a lively dispute about the processing, i.e., identification or categorisation, of unattended, non-selected, (visual) information (see, e.g., Broadbent, 1958; Deutsch & Deutsch, 1963). One group of theorists, the 'early selection' theorists, maintained: 'only attended, selected, information is processed'. Another group of theorists, the 'late selection' theorists, assumed: 'all information is processed'. Then some researchers, for instance Dyer (1973) and Eriksen (B. A.) and Eriksen (1974), demonstrated clear identity effects of unattended, non-selected, information; the 'breakthrough of the unattended', in Broadbent's (1982, p. 257) words. This outcome definitively showed that the 'only' group was wrong; the experiments showed that not only selected and attended information is processed. This outcome does not, of course, demonstrate that the 'all' group was right; the experiments do not show that *all* unattended visual information is *always* processed. But that demonstration was not required because the 'all' group had other reasons and arguments in support of their assumption (see, for instance, Deutsch & Deutsch, 1963, for a careful listing and elaboration of these arguments.)

The remarkable point is now that in the limited-capacity literature this history nearly always appears in a reverse or inverse form (see, e.g., Pashler, 1998, pp. 60–70). It is suggested that the 'all information is processed' assumption predicts severe effects of unattended information and that the absence of interference therefore demonstrates limited capacity. Clearly, a logical error is made here, the error of 'confirming the consequence'. Interference clearly indicates processing, but the absence of interference simply indicates nothing. The 'all information is processed' group does not require interference effects. There is simply no *a priori* theoretical reason to assume that processed unattended information should show identity effects. (The historical fact is that, even for proponents of the 'all information is processed' assumption, interference came as a surprise; Deutsch & Deutsch, 1963, nowhere mention Stroop interference.) Because of a lack of theoretical arguments, the issue of whether, and if so how strongly, unattended information will reveal its presence as unwanted identity effects, has up to now been largely an empirical matter that requires careful investigation (see, e.g., Kahneman & Chajczyk, 1983, for an impressive demonstration; see also Section 6.4).

17 In Section 6.1, I used the assumption that associations are formed between selected and enhanced attributes in Visual Perception and available/allowable responses. Here I use the assumption that selected and enhanced attributes in Visual Perception can cause response interference, but non-selected, non-enhanced attributes cannot. While, in my view, both assumptions are reasonable, they are certainly not identical. Some interference from non-enhanced attributes of non-selected objects in Visual Perception cannot be excluded (see MacLeod, 1991, quoted in the text). According to my conceptualisation, it has then to be expected that non-selected words and letters cause more interference (strong associations with items in the response set) than non-selected colours, shapes, or sizes (weak associations with items in the response set).

18 It is worthwhile to note that this account has still to explain (a) why words are read faster than colours are named, and (b) how in the Stroop situation the correct response is selected. The latter problem is not a trivial one because the distributions of 'arrival times' for colours and for words will certainly overlap (see MacLeod, 1991, Fig. 1). My solution for both problems was presented earlier in this chapter.

19 There is another intriguing refutation of the 'relative speed of processing' account. The account states that under 'normal conditions' words are read faster than colours can be named. Schweickert (1983) used 'normal conditions' and showed, by means of a careful and sophisticated analysis, that the order of processing was task-dependent. Ironically, what he literally showed was that in a task that required the subject to name the colour, first the word was processed and then the colour, while in a task that required the subject to read the word, first the colour was processed and then the word! Here is how MacLeod (1991, p. 182) describes how Schweickert accomplished this feat and what the resulting theoretical problem is:

> Schweickert's (1983) experiment used a colored rectangle above a color word. There were 2 subjects. One was to press a key indicating the color of the rectangle before reading the word aloud; her data suggested that she decided about the ink color first. The other subject was to press a key for the word and then name the ink color aloud; her data suggested that she decided about the word first. This outcome is difficult to handle under a differential speed-of-processing account, which explains the usual asymmetry as being due to the decision about the word preceding the decision about the ink color. This appears to be true when the subject names the ink color.

However, the decision order is reversed when the word must be read, so why is there an asymmetry in the standard Stroop task?

My conceptualisation has no theoretical problems with Schweickert's results. The first subject performed the task with an instruction-derived intentional sequence of approximately the form

>> RECTANGLE > COLOUR/ (key) >> >> WORD > SHAPE/ (name) >>,

and the second subject performed the task with an instruction-derived intentional sequence of approximately the form

>> WORD > SHAPE/ (key) >> >> RECTANGLE > COLOUR/ (name) >>.

The intentional sequence, >> X > Y >>, approach is compatible with a great number of 'processing' strategies (see also Section 5.1).

20 It cannot be excluded that state X only stops when state Y can perform its task, i.e., that there is partial temporal overlap of states X and Y. To this possibility I return in Section 9.4. One intriguing possible assumption is that an increase in activation of state Y inhibits, and ultimately removes, activation of state X.

21 It is worthwhile to see that the results obtained in naming tasks with preview and post-view of the word can be explained in the same way.

22 Presently, within the field of visual search, there is a fierce debate about the strength or power of the top-down control. Some investigators maintain that singletons – objects that strongly differ in one or more attributes from their neighbours – escape from top-down control and 'capture' attention (see, e.g., Theeuwes, 1991, 1992; Theeuwes, Atchley, & Kramer, 2000). Others maintain that even such singletons can be held in check by top-down task-determined control (see, e.g., Bacon & Egeth, 1994; Folk, Remington, & Johnston, 1992; Yantis & Egeth, 1999). Yantis and Egeth (1999) present a thoughtful overview of this field of research. The interested reader can easily work out that the excellent experiments reported by Folk et al. fit in precisely with my >> X > Y >>, top-down and bottom-up approach. Theeuwes et al. (2000), however, showed that the issue is still open. Because it cannot be excluded that some of the critical phenomena are just the result of the peculiar stimulus exposure conditions used in the experiments (no peripheral preview, abrupt onsets, short exposures), I do not address this issue in more detail here.

23 Here I use the assumption that a non-selected, i.e., not enhanced, incongruent word produces no perceptible interference (see Note 17: see also later on).

24 This example also shows that 'capture' is capable of explaining the reduced, but not eliminated, interference when the to-be-named colour and to-be-ignored word are presented in separate spatial locations as reported by Dyer (1973) and many others after him (see MacLeod, 1991, pp. 176 & 203).

25 In Van der Heijden (1992), I presented a bottom-up explanation of 'dilution'. The present explanation is a top-down explanation. On a proportion of trials top-down selection is too weak or too late, leaving room for bottom-up influences.

26 When the first position is selected, all and only information in that position is enhanced, and not much effect of congruent or incongruent information from the second target position is to be expected (see Section 6.2).

27 Eriksen et al. (1990, p. 486) advance a closely related theoretical position:

We propose that the human has two separate processing systems: one that is automatic and the other that corresponds to focal attention and the conscious noting of stimuli and responses . . . these two processing systems operate concurrently. The automatic system is not a precursor or an initial stage in the attentive system. The two systems are separate . . . If the attentive system is directed to stimuli . . . the attentive system controls the responses, but the automatic system also processes the stimuli even though the product of its processing is overridden by the attentive system . . . The implication of such a conception of two separate systems is that, when the attentive system is directed to a stimulus, its processing of that stimulus is largely independent of the processing that is occurring or has already occurred in the automatic system. In other words, with attentional processing, it is as though that stimulus had just occurred.

When in this proposal the 'automatic system' is equated with my 'Visual Perception' and the 'attentive system' with my 'Intending Mind' (and when the relation between the two systems is further elaborated as in Figure 6.1), the similarity between Eriksen et al.'s proposal and my proposal immediately becomes clear.

28 For ease of exposition, in this analysis I have neglected the contribution of the automatic selection of the required response by the enhanced shape attribute in Visual Perception. It is easy to see that for this contribution the same explanation holds.

29 Imagine an experiment in which a subject looks at a screen that continuously displays one Stroop word, for instance the word BLUE, written in red. Tell the subject that he or she has to name the colour on hearing a high tone and that he or she has to read the word on hearing a low tone. Present a random series of high and low tones, say one tone per 5 seconds. My prediction is that at least with the first, say, 10 trials, the regular Stroop effects will be found.

30 Egeth and Dagenbach's (1991) ingenious search task with a within-trial quality manipulation diagnostic for serial and parallel 'processing' is an excellent task to start with.

31 It is interesting to note that the two-stage theories simply postulate that the first stage of processing results in a preliminary form of perception. For instance, the problem of how to get from wavelengths or photons to perceived colour is simply neglected. The assumption is that subjects are presented with coloured stimuli and that they process the colours.

32 It is worthwhile to note that this is a very liberal interpretation of the findings reported by the Gestalt psychologists. The Gestalt psychologists described complete visual perception, not a first preliminary stage in visual perception (see also Van der Heijden, 1996b).

33 From the literature it appears that there are theorists who start from the point of view that no representation for selection is required. In their views, 'subjects' can select and attend to information in the outer world (see, e.g., Posner, 1978, p. 191; Treisman, 1990, p. 461; Treisman & Schmidt, 1982, pp. 110–112). These naïve realist errors reflect the intuitive phenomenological position that selection is selection from a complete visual world, not from a pre-attentive representation. This error, therefore, supports the point of view defended in this work: selection is selection from full-blown Visual Perception, not from a vague precursor of full-blown Visual Perception.

34 For evidence see, e.g., Von Wright, 1968, 1970; Snyder, 1972; Fryklund, 1975; Bundesen, Pedersen, and Larsen, 1984; Bundesen, Shibuya, and Larsen, 1985; Nissen, 1985; Tsal and Lavie, 1988; Van der Heijden et al., 1996.

35 It is worthwhile to note the word 'seen' in this quotation. The theory is attempting to explain 'to see', i.e., visual perception, not responding.

36 Of course, letters can be processed into words, words can be processed into sentences, and with digits computations can be made. These operations can very

well be named 'information processing operations'. However, at the basis of these operations are always the arbitrary relations just specified.

37 In the context of a theory concerned with the use of visual perception for the performance of tasks, the assumption that visual information is fully processed makes sense, because

> ... if an organism's choice of action at any instant is to be efficient, that choice must be based on as rich as possible a description of its surroundings, in which multiple objects are already described in terms of "semantic" properties as well as of their locations and other sensory attributes.
>
> (Allport, Tipper, & Chmiel, 1985, p. 109)

Part III
Act tasks

7 Towards an effective visual position[1]

7.0 Introduction

In Chapter 4, I modelled Visual Perception in a highly simplified way as 'fixed' activations (codes) in a system consisting of an input map (IN) and three feature maps: a colour map, (C), where colour information is made explicit, a form map, (F), where the shapes are made explicit, and a position map, (P), where the positions are made explicit. That simple model, with unchanging projections and with activations firmly in place, sufficed for my explanatory purposes – the explanation of the results obtained in single-fixation experiments in Chapters 5 and 6. In real life, however, single-fixation situations with unchanging projections and with activations firmly in place never occur. Perceivers continuously make body movements, head movements, and eye movements and, as a result, the projections in the retina and in the higher centres of the visual system continuously change.

In this chapter, Visual Perception is further elaborated in such a way that the given – that the activations (codes) in the modules continuously move – is taken into account. Because the activations (codes) change position, in particular the problem of how to conceive the perception of spatial position is dealt with. An appropriate view on the perception of spatial position is required for discussing the cognitive control of act tasks, e.g., pointing, reaching, grasping, walking – tasks in which the performance critically depends on the perception of spatial position.

In Section 7.1, the traditional and still dominant view on the perception of spatial position, the view that position in one or another anatomical map serves as the code for position, is discussed. This view is neither consistent with what I have said up to now about Visual Perception nor compatible with my >> X >Y >> view with regard to the selection of visual information. So, already, to *maintain* my position, an alternative is required. Some of the theoretical problems the dominant view introduces are listed. An alternative two-factor view suggested by Husserl (1907) is introduced.

In Section 7.2, this two-factor view is tested. The two-factor view states that in the visual perception of spatial position two sources of information contribute, a visual source for 'filling in' a topological space and a kinaesthetic source for 'structuring' the metrical space. Some recent data, obtained with the partial-report bar-probe task and with a relative position judgement task, are presented. These data indeed strongly suggest that in the perception of spatial position, besides the visual system, the (saccadic) eye movement system is also involved.

In Section 7.3, the two-factor view is elaborated in further detail. The perception of spatial position is modelled with two densely connected maps, one with codes for the visual information and another with codes for actual and possible eye positions. It is shown that this model solves the problems encountered by the now dominant view on position perception and some problems besides.

In Section 7.4, it is shown that the two-factor view on the perception of spatial position, as expressed in the two-maps model, is consistent with and fits in with my view on Visual Perception and the selection of visual information by an Intending Mind, as presented in the preceding chapters. With this two-factor model for Visual Perception I am also in the position to approach and analyse act tasks.

7.1   Position as a code for position?

It is often assumed that for the visual perception of spatial position no operations or calculations are required. That assumption is based on the knowledge that in the visual system a number of topographic maps are encountered. The retina in the eye is a topographic map, and there are topographic maps in the pathway to the brain and in a number of visual regions higher up in the visual system as well. The assumption states that the location of an object, X, in the outer stimulus field is represented geometrically by the location of a set of neurons firing in one, or possibly more, of these topographic maps (see Smythies, 1994a, 1994b). Thus, anatomical location in one or another map, or in a number of maps, is taken to be the code for location of an object in the outer world – anatomical position is taken as the code for position.

Quotations that express the point of view that anatomical position serves as the code for position are not difficult to find.[2] Here are two from well-known celebrities:

> Recall what happens to optical images in your eyes. Patterns of light and shadow must flash rapidly across your field of vision every time you shift your eyes . . . You see the world as fixed because this is your tacit theory of space – if "theory" can be used so loosely. In order to believe in your theory, you have to learn a very precise and delicate relation between the movements of your eyes and the changes in your visual experience.
>
> (G. A. Miller, 1964, p. 116)

The classical problem of space perception in psychology concerns *visual depth*. It seems easy to understand the visual perception of direction; the light reflected by objects in different directions from the eye strikes different parts of the retina . . . which means that cues to direction are available. But the retina functions optically as a two-dimensional surface, like a photographic plate at the back of a camera: why therefore is the perceived visual world not flat like a photograph?

(D. O. Hebb, 1966, p. 277)

The assumption that position (in a position map P) is the code for position is an attractive assumption for standard views on visual attention that conceive attention as a 'spotlight' or a 'zoom lens' dealing with a limited region of visual space (see Section 1.3 for these views).[3] The assumption is, however, neither consistent with what I have said up to now about Visual Perception nor compatible with my >> X >Y >> view on selection of visual information.

- The assumption is inconsistent with my view on Visual Perception, because I explicitly assumed that features of the outer world are internally represented in feature maps as patterns of activation or 'codes'. Consequently, the assumption is that positions in the outer world are represented as patterns of activation or 'codes' on positions in a position map; not by the positions in the position map themselves.
- The assumption is incompatible with my >> X >Y >> view on selection of visual information because that view presupposes the possibility of interactions via associative connections between states of a Verbal Intention or intentional sequence in the Intending Mind and features of objects in visual perception. Associations between two patterns of activation or 'codes' are possible – associations between patterns of activation or 'codes' and bare, inert, spatial positions in one or another anatomic map, however, are not.

Fortunately, it is not difficult to show that the assumption that anatomical position in one or another map serves as the code for external position can hardly be maintained.[4] That there is something weird with the view that position serves as the code for perceived position already becomes apparent when we look at how other object attributes are coded in the brain. Assume, for example, that the visual system is presented with a patch of light that we perceive as bright and red and to our right. A neurosurgeon or a neurophysiologist, looking for the representation of that patch in the brain, is *a priori* convinced that he or she will never find something bright or something red there. What she/he will look for are stimulation-dependent patterns of activation in smaller or larger groups of neurons; that is, for the outcomes of the stimulus-induced calculations or operations. The assumption that anatomical location in one or more anatomical maps serves as the code for location entails that the brain deals with position in an essentially different way. No operations or transformations are assumed to be required because an inert anatomical position is assumed to suffice.

Moreover, the assumption that anatomical position serves as, and is sufficient as, the code for position has repeatedly led and still often leads to theoretical problems, most of which are not unambiguously solved even today.[5] The problems can be classified into two groups – problems for visual perception that arise when the eyes are stationary and problems for visual perception that arise when the eyes move. Because most readers are familiar with these problems I introduce and list them only briefly.

The stationary eye

The lens system in the eye inverts (top > < down) and reverses (left > < right) the image on the retina. From the retina the information is transported to the brain. The major pathway is through the lateral geniculate nucleus (LGN) to the visual cortex, striate cortex, area 17 or V1. All the axons stemming from the left half of each retina go via the left LGN to the left hemisphere of the brain and all the axons originating in the right half of each retina travel via the right LGN to the right hemisphere of the brain. So, information from the left side of the point of view and information from the right side of the point of view is processed in different, spatially separated, maps. In the two hemispheres the visual information is further processed in a great number of distinguishable modules. Most modules in the brain involved in visual perception are organised as kinds of spatial maps, albeit maps with several and severe distortions (e.g., the cortical magnification factor; see Cowey, 1981).[6]

Among the problems for visual perception that arise when the eyes are stationary are:[7]

- the inverted and reversed image on the retina and upstream in the visual system while we nevertheless perceive a correctly oriented world (the inverted image problem);
- the distorted and split topographic map in V1 and the even worse topography upstream in the visual brain while we nevertheless see a topographically correct visual world (the topography problem);
- the representation of different object features in different anatomical maps while we nevertheless see integrated colour-form objects on their appropriate places (the feature integration problem).

The moving eye

The human daylight eye is markedly inhomogeneous with regard to its capacity for resolving detail. Sensitivity, acuity, is highest in the central part of the retina, the fovea, and declines progressively and dramatically from there to the periphery of the retina (see, e.g., Haber & Hershenson, 1974, p. 51; see Anstis, 1974, for an impressive demonstration). So the visual apparatus is built in such a way that most of its computing power is devoted to a small portion of the visual field.

For a detailed inspection of a part of the visual field that part has to be brought into or close to central vision, i.e., in the fovea. The visual system has means to bring this about. The direction in which the eyes are pointing can be changed. Six eye muscles, which act as antagonistic pairs, control these changes of direction. A great number of eye movements are distinguished in the literature. For most visual information processing tasks the saccadic eye movements are of prime importance.[8] For instance, in an information processing task like reading, saccadic eye movements occur at a rate of about four or five per second (one saccade takes between about 30 and 40 ms). Saccadic eye movements are 'ballistic' movements – their duration is too short for new visual information to be used during their trajectory. In the fixational pauses or fixations between two saccades the eyes are relatively still (one fixation takes between about 150 and 350 ms).

A saccadic eye movement has two effects with regard to the retinal projections within the fixations. First, the part of the visual world that was projected in the fovea in fixation N is projected on a region of lesser acuity in fixation N+1. Second, a part of the visual world that was projected on a region of lesser acuity in fixation N is projected on the high acuity region of the fovea in fixation N+1.[9] Of course, with each (saccadic) eye movement the positions of the projections (activations, codes) in the different specialised modules in the visual brain also change.[10] It is interesting to note that we are hardly aware of all these drastic changes on the retina and in the higher visual centres in the brain (see Woodworth, 1938, p. 577).

Among the problems for visual perception that arise when the eyes are moving are, for instance:

- the moving image in retina and brain when the eyes saccade (or move otherwise) while we nevertheless see a stable visual world (the stable perceptual world problem);
- the fixed afterimage in retina and brain when the eyes saccade that we nevertheless see as moving in visual space (the moving afterimage problem);
- the fixed image in retina and brain of an object followed with pursuit movements and the moving background image while we nevertheless see the object moving and the background as standing still (the moving object – stable background problem).

There are a number of related problems with pursuit movements that one can easily observe when sitting in a train and looking at different distances in the landscape (what is apparently moving and what is apparently standing still?). These psychological problems, for which several principled and ad hoc solutions can be found in the literature (see, e.g., Bridgeman et al., 1994), make it abundantly clear, in my view, that a search for alternatives for 'position as a code for position' is in order.

As stated, the view that anatomical position serves as the code for position is neither consistent nor compatible with my theoretical points of view. My view requires codes for perceived position, conceived as patterns of activation, because only position codes conceived as patterns of activation can be associated with Verbal Intention or intentional sequence states, conceived as patterns of activation. So I have to find position codes conceived as patterns of activation.

Of course, an adequate solution of my position perception and association problem must simultaneously solve the longstanding, classical, position perception problems listed above; if I solve my perception/association problem but have no idea whatsoever about how the classical position perception problems have to be solved, I have not very much reason to assume that my 'local' solution is on the right track. So, the task I am now faced with is to solve the perception/association problem given the set of classical problems as a constraint. Let us now first turn briefly to early introspective psychology and to phenomenological philosophy to find intuitions about how to proceed.

An alternative to the 'position as a code for position' assumption was proposed by Lotze (1846, 1852). In Lotze's time, most psychologists were Kantians who assumed that space was simply given in perception. In Lotze's view, however, a true theory of space perception had to go behind space and show how space is derived from what is non-spatial (see Boring, 1950, p. 267). The theory Lotze came up with became the most influential 'motor theory of space perception' in the second half of the 19th century and was subsequently subscribed to and elaborated by Von Helmholtz and Wundt. In the theory it is assumed that each retinal position, which only exists as a sensation, becomes associated with a unique pattern of activity in the eye muscles. These patterns, the 'local signs', uniquely determine the position of the sensations (see Scheerer, 1984, p. 81). So, in this theory a pattern of eye muscle activity forms the code for position.

In my view, the most important next step was made by the originator of phenomenological philosophy, Edmund Husserl, in his *Ding und Raum* (1907/ 1957; see Scheerer, 1986, for a brief description in English).[11] According to Husserl's 'constitutional analysis', the general scheme of space constitution requires two contributions: vision (for 'filling in' space) and kinaesthesis (for 'structuring' space). The visual sensations constitute, fill in, the 'visual field'. That visual field is not a mosaic of sensations as in Lotze's theory; every unit in the visual field corresponds to some object and in the visual field the objects are spread out in front of the observer. The order in the visual field is, however, topological, not metrical. For providing the metric in the visual field, the kinaesthetic information accompanying (saccadic) eye movements is required. Saccadic eye movements transform or 'augment' the visual field into the 'oculomotor field'. The oculomotor field is the visual field with two metrical dimensions, one horizontal and one vertical (see Scheerer, 1986, for a further detailed description).

For the set of problems I am concerned with here, Husserl's 'two-factor' view of space perception is very attractive as a starting point for two reasons. The first has to do with Husserl's 'visual field'. Whatever theory of space perception one endorses, there simply *is* the neuroanatomical and neuro-physiological given of massively parallel processing of nervous messages in a great number of anatomically separate maps or space structures. This given invites one or another version of the 'position as a code for position' assumption. The version that the maps provide a visual field or a *topological space* is an attractive and not a dangerous version. With Smythies (1994a, p. 276) we can, therefore, be relatively mild with respect to this version of the 'position as code for position' assumption:

> Is topographic representation in the brain really a code? That is, does the fact that . . . neurons project in an orderly map-like manner . . . carry any information, or is it just a convenient way of running cables around the brain's computers? That does not seem very likely, as the topographic location of a representative event in a brain map can carry information about the position of the external stimulus in the stimulus field on its own without having to use up valuable computing space to record the same information.

With this 'space filling' topological space we have a visual world, but of course, with this 'space filling' topological space only, the theoretical problems mentioned before in this section are not solved.

The second reason why Husserl's two-factor view is attractive as a starting point has to do with his 'oculomotor field'. For solving the position perception problems, Husserl's oculomotor field comes in very handy and provides a promising perspective. As stated, (saccadic) eye movement information transforms the topological space into a *metrical space*. It cannot be excluded that exactly the eye movement information in this oculomotor field, when characterised in the appropriate way, can solve my perception/association problem as well as all the classical position perception problems mentioned before in this section.

It will by now be clear how I have to proceed. Three jobs are still waiting for me in the remainder of this chapter. First, to conform to the way of working in the information processing approach, I have to provide evidence in support of Husserl's two-factor view on space and position perception. Second, if supporting evidence can be provided, I have to present a characterisation of the eye movement information in the oculomotor field that solves all the position perception problems listed earlier in this section and preferably some problems besides. And third I have to show that this characterisation also solves the problem of finding codes for position, conceived as patterns of activation, which can be associated or become associated with other system states, conceived as patterns of activation – the perception/association problem.

7.2   Partial-report and position-judgement tasks

A task that gives important information about the coding of position is the partial-report bar-probe task, introduced by Averbach and Coriell (1961) and modified by Eriksen and associates, which I have already introduced in Section 2.3 (see also Sections 5.3 and 6.3). As stated in Section 2.3, there are two variants of the task, a linear variant and a circular variant, that produce a different pattern of results. The two types of stimuli are depicted in Figure 7.1 (for the moment, ignore the thin arrows). With both variants a bar marker or an arrow indicates one of the letters. That visual position indicator appears either before, simultaneously with, or after the array. The exposure conditions are such that observers cannot make useful (saccadic) eye movements (the experiments are single-fixation experiments). The observers are instructed to name the letter indicated by the bar or arrow.

The most important difference, in the present context, between the main results obtained with the two variants of the bar-probe task is approximately sketched in Figure 7.2 (the figure is based on Fig. 1 in Eriksen & Collins, 1969, and Fig. 2a in Hagenaar & Van der Heijden, 1997). The figure presents the proportions of letters correctly reported with pre-exposure, simultaneous exposure, and post-exposure of the indicator for the circular variant (solid line) and the linear variant (broken line). The figure shows that with the circular variant performance decreases monotonically as a function of moment of presentation of the indicator relative to the display (see Eriksen & Collins, 1969; Eriksen & Rohrbaugh, 1970). With the linear variant, however, performance first increases and then decreases, yielding an inverted U-function (see Hagenaar & Van der Heijden, 1997). So the main difference in performance between the two variants of the task is found with pre-exposure of the indicator.

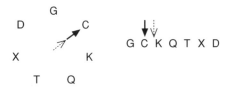

Figure 7.1 An example of a stimulus with a circular array and with a linear array in partial-report bar-probe tasks (see text for further explanation).

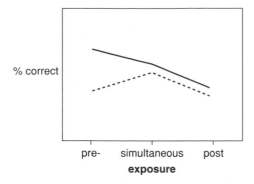

Figure 7.2 Percentage correct letter reports with pre-exposure, simultaneous exposure, and post-exposure of the indicator with the circular (solid line) and linear (broken line) variants of the bar-probe task.

A careful further analysis of the *errors* observed with the linear variant by Mewhort et al. (1981) revealed that the bulk of the errors consisted of *localisation* errors, not of identification errors. In addition they noted that the bulk of these localisation errors consisted of *near* localisation errors; that is, of the report of the name of a letter in a position adjacent to the target letter. Further experiments and analyses by Hagenaar and Van der Heijden (1997) confirmed these results. In addition their research revealed that the majority of the near localisation errors consisted of *central* near localisation errors; that is, of the report of the name of the letter adjacent to and at the foveal side of the target letter. Moreover, their analyses revealed that central near location errors occurred about equally frequently with pre-exposure as with post-exposure of the visual indicator and appreciably less with simultaneous presentation of indicator and linear array. A further analysis of the errors observed with the circular variant never revealed anything really spectacular. The bulk of the errors consisted of letter identification errors, not of localisation errors as observed with the linear arrays. Virtually no position errors were reported (Eriksen & Collins, 1969) and only a very modest increase in the number of these errors with delay of the indicator (Eriksen & Rohrbaugh, 1970).

The pattern of results described in the preceding paragraph and the one depicted in Figure 7.2 is easily understood when we use one, seemingly terribly ad hoc, assumption. That assumption is that a short-duration visual indicator, an arrow or a bar, when presented in relative isolation, is seen closer to the point of fixation than it really is or than inspection at leisure would reveal. Stated otherwise, the assumption is that, without visual 'anchors', a short-duration arrow or bar appears as shifted or displaced in the direction of the fixation point. Let us see how this assumption works out with circular arrays and with linear arrays.

With circular arrays and with an indicator shifted in the direction of the fixation point, nothing of relevance happens (see the thin arrow in Figure 7.1). With and without such a shift, with pre-exposure, simultaneous exposure and post-exposure, the indicator points in the same correct direction and neither an abundance of localisation errors nor a dependence of proportion of localisation errors on moment of presentation of the indicator is to be expected. Only ease of letter identification determines the results depicted in Figure 7.2.

With linear arrays, however, the situation is different (see the thin arrow in Figure 7.1). With pre- and post-exposure of the indicator, the indicator is presented in relative isolation, and, by ad hoc assumption, is shifted in the direction of the point of fixation. So, under these conditions, an abundance of central near localisation errors is to be expected. With simultaneous presentation of array and indicator, the indicator is not presented in relative isolation but in the company of the array. By the ad hoc assumption, in this condition appreciably fewer central near localisation errors are expected. So, not ease of letter identification but localisation problems with pre- and post-exposure of the indicator determine the results depicted in Figure 7.2.

So, the ad hoc assumption that a short-duration visual indicator, an arrow or a bar, when presented in relative isolation, is seen closer to the point of fixation than it really is, is perfectly capable of explaining the total pattern of results described. Fortunately, that assumption is not as ad hoc as it seems at first sight. In fact, a great number of investigators have reported position judgement studies that revealed such an effect (see, e.g., O'Regan, 1984; Osaka, 1977; Rauk & Luuk, 1980; Rose & Halpern, 1992; Skavenski, 1990; see Van der Heijden, Van der Geest, De Leeuw, Krikke, & Müsseler, 1999, for further references). In none of these studies, however, were the exposure conditions exactly the same as those that are generally used in the linear partial-report bar-probe tasks. Therefore, we investigated the perception of position of a short-duration small bar, presented on an otherwise empty screen, in a situation mimicking the situation with pre- and post-exposure of the visual indicator in the linear partial-report bar-probe task. These experiments allowed us to conclude that, under the exposure conditions used, observers underestimate the eccentricity of the bar by about 10% (see Van der Heijden et al., 1999).

For the search for the codes for position, this finding – that observers underestimate the position of the bar by about 10% – is of great theoretical importance because the literature concerned with the precision of saccadic eye movements often reports a comparable 'undershoot' of about 10% obtained in a comparable situation.

> Most experiments with visually elicited saccades use the following paradigm: A subject fixates a stimulus, usually a small light dot in a dark field, that suddenly jumps to a new location. The subject is instructed to follow the target and does that by making one or more saccades. Under

these conditions, and if the size and direction of the target jump is randomized, the saccade usually undershoots the target, and a correction saccade or smooth movement is necessary in the same direction. The amount of undershoot found in the literature varies considerably, but most authors agree now at an average value of about 10%.
(De Bie, Van den Brink, & Van Sonderen, 1987, p. 85)

For neither the saccadic undershoot nor the perceptual undershoot are good explanations presently available.[12] For the saccadic undershoot one might speculate that this is an optimal strategy because for any motor system it is easier to correct a movement in the same direction than in the opposite direction. It is also true that with undershoot the representation of the target remains in the same cortical hemisphere (see Section 7.1) and possibly a switch of hemisphere, for one or another reason, is disadvantageous (see, e.g., Becker, 1972, and Henson, 1978, for this point of view). In the present context, however, these explanations are not important.[13]

Of importance here is the finding that in similar experimental situations highly similar outcomes are obtained in position judgement tasks and in saccadic eye movement tasks – with both tasks 10% undershoot is observed. Of course, this similarity forces one to assume that position perception and saccadic eye movements are tightly linked. Moreover, this similarity is fully compatible with, and therefore strongly supports, Husserl's two-factor view of space perception which postulates that the (saccadic) eye movement information (the kinaesthetic information) contributes to the creation of the experienced visual space by providing the metric in the visual field.[14] To the best of my knowledge, Husserl's two-factor view is the first and only theory that *predicts* that in comparable situations with saccadic eye movement tasks and with position judgement tasks similar patterns of (correct or deviating) results have to be found.

For further clues about the codes for position in visual perception and for further evidence supporting Husserl's two-factor view, it is worthwhile to look at the results of a relative position judgement task that corroborates and summarises what was said above and adds important information. The task is a variant of the relative position judgement tasks used by Müsseler, Van der Heijden, Mahmud, Deubel, and Ertsey (1999). Figure 7.3 shows the types of stimuli used and the two main conditions.

In the unilateral condition (see upper panel) a row of five squares and one single square appear either to the left or to the right of a central fixation cross. In the bilateral condition (see lower panel) a row of five squares appears to one side of the fixation cross and a single square to the other side. In both main conditions the single square can precede the row of squares (pre-exposure, SOA −112 ms), appear simultaneously with the row (simultaneous exposure, SOA 0 ms), or follow it (post-exposure, SOA +112 ms). In both main conditions the single square is, averaged over trials, equally as distant from the fixation cross as the square in the middle of the row. The position

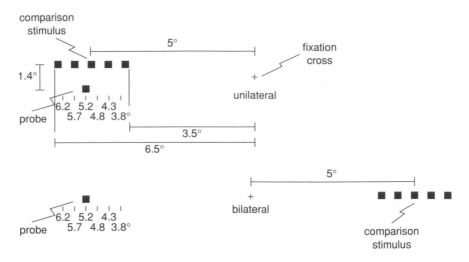

Figure 7.3 Examples of stimuli in the relative position judgement tasks. In both presentation modes the subjects first fixated a cross in the middle. In the unilateral mode the task was to judge the position of the probe (the lower single square) relative to the mid-position of the comparison stimulus (the upper row of squares). In the bilateral mode the task was to judge which of the two was more peripheral.

of the single square is, however, varied randomly over trials in small steps around its mean position. The task for the observer is to report the position of the small square relative to the position of the square in the middle of the row, in terms of more peripheral (outer) or more central (inner).

Figure 7.4 presents the results obtained. The complete interpretation of the figure is, in the present context, not of importance. What is of importance is that with unbiased performance the number of 'outer' responses should approximately equal the number of 'inner' responses. This level of performance is indicated in the figure with the dashed line. The figure shows that this level of performance is found only with unilateral and simultaneous presentation of the square and the row of squares. Clear 'undershoot' is found with unilateral presentation and pre- and post-exposure of the single square (see Müsseler et al., 1999, for replications and extensions). This pattern of results mimics the pattern obtained with the partial-report bar-probe task with linear arrays: good performance with simultaneous presentation of bar and array and 'undershoot' with pre- and post-exposure of the indicator. With bilateral presentations 'undershoot' is found with all three SOAs. For this part of the relative position judgement task no equivalent bar-probe task exists. The data obtained in this condition therefore add to the existing knowledge of the perception of position.

In my view, these data and the data obtained in the linear partial-report bar-probe task are consistent with, and provide important further supportive

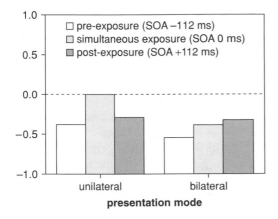

Figure 7.4 Deviations from perfect performance in the relative position judgement tasks with pre-exposure, simultaneous exposure, and post-exposure for the unilateral and bilateral presentation mode. Veridical performance is indicated with the dashed horizontal line.

Table 7.1 Good or optimal performance (+) and systematic deviations (–) for four different spatio-temporal exposure conditions

	Adjacent	*Separate*
Simultaneous	+	–
Successive	–	–

evidence for, Husserl's two-factor view of space perception with vision (for 'filling in' space) and kinaesthesis (for 'structuring' space) as contributors. The data are summarised in Table 7.1. The table shows when good or optimal performance and when 'undershoot' was found.

- Good or optimal performance was only found when the assessment of position could be based on pieces of information that were close together in space and in time – adjacent and simultaneous. (This was the case in the linear partial-report bar-probe task with simultaneous presentation of bar and array, and in the unilateral relative position judgement task with simultaneous presentation of row of squares and single square.) This outcome indicates that in this condition a 'local' operation in vision is involved and suffices for task performance.
- A systematic deviation, 'undershoot', was found in all other conditions, i.e., in all conditions in which the relevant pieces of information for the assessment of position were separated in time or/and in space. (This was the case in the linear partial-report bar-probe task with pre- and post-exposure of the bar, in the unilateral relative position judgement task with

pre- and post-exposure of the single square, and in all exposure conditions in the bilateral relative position judgement task and also in the absolute position judgement tasks in which only a single piece of information
was presented in an otherwise empty field.) This outcome indicates that in
these conditions a 'global' operation that produces 'undershoot', hinting
at the involvement of the (saccadic) eye movement system, was involved.

So, the results strongly suggest two contributions to the perception of visual
space – vision allowing local operations in visual space (Husserl's vision for
'filling in' space), and the (saccadic) eye movement system permitting global
operations in visual space (Husserl's kinaesthesis for 'structuring' space).

In this context, the results obtained in the bilateral relative judgement
task with simultaneous but spatially separated presentation of the single
square and the row of squares are of special importance. These data indicate
that not only do pre- or post-exposure, that is, temporal separation, invite
the workings of the 'global' operation, but also distance in the visual field,
that is, spatial separation. This outcome therefore strongly suggests that the
'local' and 'global' operations, the 'visual field' and the 'oculomotor field' in
Husserl's terminology, work simultaneously in providing the layout and
spatial structure of the visual field.

In line with Husserl, in the recent past a number of theorists have argued
that in the visual perception of spatial position two different 'sources', 'mechanisms', or 'codes' are involved, a 'local' (visual) code and a 'global' (motor)
code (see, e.g., Koenderink, 1990, and Wolff, 1987, 1999a; for earlier versions of this view see, e.g., Poincaré, 1902, 1905; Taylor, 1975). Koenderink
(1990, p. 126), for instance, distinguishes between a local 'simultaneous correlation structure or local receptive field structure' and a multi-local operation that 'requires a lot of additional structure'. He assumes that (saccadic) eye
movements are at the basis of the global or multi-local code. The evidence
presented in this section is fully consistent with this and Husserl's (1907/
1957) proposal.

This state of affairs makes it worthwhile to further elaborate the two-
factor proposal. That elaborated version has to 'solve', i.e., to evade, the
classical position perception problems (see Section 7.3), to be consistent
with the views on perception and selection presented in the preceding chapters (see Section 7.4) and to provide an adequate starting point for handling
act tasks (see Chapters 8 and 9).

7.3   The perception of position

In this section an elaborated version of Husserl's two-factor view on space
perception is presented. This tentative model makes explicit what, in my
view, can be at the basis of the visual perception of position (the model
neglects head and body movements and also excludes the third dimension
[z-axis] and vergence movements; for my purposes only the basic principle is
of importance). The basic assumption of the model is that in the visual

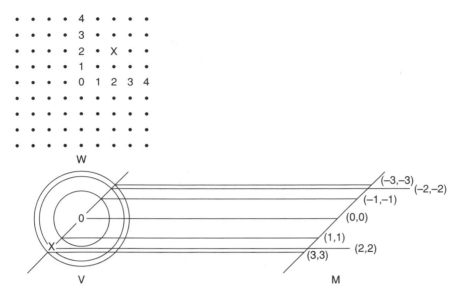

Figure 7.5 World (W), visual sensory map (V), and motor map (M). Eyes straight
ahead fixating 0 in W. (See text for further explanation.)

perception of spatial position – that is, in the construction of the full, complete, visual field – two densely connected maps with different codes or
representations are involved.

The static eye

In Figure 7.5, the situation in the two maps is depicted for the situation
when the eyes are straight ahead. In this figure, a simple outer world, W, is
depicted. The map on the left, the visual map (V), can be regarded as 'space
filling' (Husserl in Scheerer, 1986) and as a 'simultaneous correlation structure or local receptive field structure' (Koenderink, 1990). In the origin of
this map the information coming from the middle of the fovea is represented. This map is not conceived as an orderly topographic map. All kinds
of deformations in terms of squeezing and stretching are allowed as long as
neighbourhood relations are preserved (I return to properties of this map
later). The map can possibly be identified with V1 with all its deformations
(e.g., the cortical magnification factor).

The map on the right, the motor map (M), has to be regarded as an eye
position map; that is, a map that codes (eye) positions on (map) positions.[15]
In the origin of this map the current eye position is coded [(0, 0) equals
'straight ahead']. For the moment, and for explanatory purposes only, this
map can be regarded as an exact replica of map V (I return to this issue
later). Consequently, in the other positions in this map are coded the eye
positions that are required, or are to be realised, for bringing the spatially

corresponding points of W into the middle of the fovea and in the origin of map V [e.g., for bringing the point marked X in W into the middle of the fovea and in the origin of V, the eye has to move to eye position (2, 2)].[16]

As stated, map M and map V are densely connected. Both maps determine what is seen. This can be taken to mean that the perceived positions result from map V 'enriched' by map M about the spatial positions in the visual field in terms of realised and required eye positions. Or this can be taken to mean that what is perceived results from map M 'enriched' by map V with modality-specific visual information and local neighbourhood relations. It will be clear that this conceptualisation of space perception maintains the essence of Husserl's two-factor view; map V plays the role of the 'space filling' factor and map W the role of the 'space structuring' factor.

This conception of the visual perception of position evades the classical static-eye problems that result from the assumption that anatomical position serves as, and is sufficient as, the code for position.

- The inverted (and left–right reversed) image problem does not arise because the codes in map M tell, in terms of how the eye has to be positioned for foveating, what is up and down and left and right.
- The topography problem, the problem of the distorted and split topographic map in V1 and the even worse topographies upstream in the visual system, appears to be a pseudo-problem in the present conceptualisation; the map positions in one or another weird topographic map, for example in V1, are not the codes underlying perceived metrical position but the eye position codes in map M.
- The feature integration problem, which is supposed to arise because different object features are represented in different anatomical maps, can be solved in exactly the same way as the position perception problem. Other maps, for example a colour map that codes colours in its map positions, when densely and appropriately connected with map V, can inform that map about other object features than position, for example about colour (see Zeki, 1992, 1993; see also later).

There are further phenomena that can be understood given this framework for position perception. For instance, there is the observation, made by Purkinje and replicated by Von Helmholtz (1866), that with a light tap on the canthus of the eye an illusory displacement of the whole visual field (against the direction of the passive eye movement) is obtained. (It is easy to replicate this observation.) The tapping displaces the whole retinal image, comparable to the displacement due to a saccadic eye movement. So, in V (and in other maps) the positions of the projections change. Because no real (saccadic) eye movement was intended and/or made, however, there is no reason to assume that the eye position codes in M also change (see later). So, the projections change but the position codes stay the same and an illusory displacement is observed.[17]

The conceptualisation of position perception presented here can also easily be extended in such a way that position-related phenomena can be explained. There is, for instance, the problem of the different sizes of the retinal projections of an object with different object distances while we nevertheless see the object as approximately the same size – the 'size constancy' problem. This problem is solved when the reasonable additional assumption is introduced that what the values of the codes in map M stand for is co-determined by cues for distance, vergence and accommodation, for instance.[18]

The moving eye

Figure 7.6 shows how, in the functional two-factor model, the codes in map V and M (have to) change when a (saccadic) eye movement is or has been made. The figure shows the codes after an eye movement resulting in a new eye position (2, 2); that is, after a saccade of size and direction (2, 2) – (0, 0) = (2, 2) (i.e., intended position minus actual position) is made. Now, in the origin of map V the visual information corresponding with eye position (2, 2), the X in W that is now projected in the middle of the fovea, is represented. The neighbouring and further surrounding information is represented in neighbouring and further surrounding regions in map V, subject to the fixed, inherent distortions in the map. In the origin of map M the current eye position (2, 2) is coded. All other eye position codes are incremented in the same way; that is, by (2, 2).

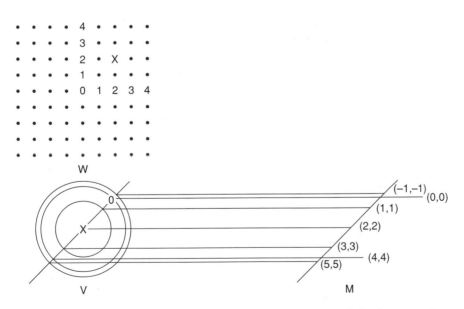

Figure 7.6 World (W), visual sensory map (V), and motor map (M). Eyes up and to the right fixating X in W. (See text for further explanation.)

With regard to the problem of when and how the eye position codes in map M are changed, there are more possible answers:

• One possibility is that after the eye movement has been executed the new eye position (x, y) is assessed and that this 'inflow' parameter is entered into the origin of map M and is used to update the other eye position values in the map. This solution is close to Bridgeman et al.'s (1994) proposal: assessment of spatial position anew within each fixation.

• Another attractive possibility is that before (or during) the eye movement, information about the size and direction of the intended movement, for example, (x, y) – (a, b), with (a, b) the actual eye position and (x, y) the intended eye position, is used to increment all eye position values in map M. This solution comes close to Von Helmholtz's (1866) and Von Holst and Mittelstaedt's (1950, 1971) 'neural command' or 'efference copy' solution.

In my view, it is reasonable to assume, especially in view of the opportunities for perceptual learning (see Wolff, 1987), that both solutions, during the movement the 'neural command' and after the movement the 'inflow', are used.[19] In Note 4 in Section 8.1, I turn to the question of where the required signals, the eye position signal and the 'efference copy', can come from.

This conception of the visual perception of position when the eyes move evades the classical moving-eye problems that result from the assumption that anatomical position serves as, and is sufficient as, the code for position.[20]

• Problems with the perception of a stable visual field with (saccadic) eye movements do not arise because the 'neural command' ensures that during or before a (saccadic) eye movement the position codes in map M are adapted in correspondence with the displacement of the representation of the visual world in map V. After the movement 'inflow' is available to correct any errors in this adaptation process.

• The moving afterimage problem – that is, the problem that an afterimage on a fixed retinal position is seen as moving with the eye during (saccadic) eye movements – is accounted for because, while the position of the afterimage in map V is fixed, the corresponding eye position codes in map M change with each eye movement in proportion to the size and direction of the eye movement.

• The moving object–stable background problem – that is, the problem that a moving object that is followed with pursuit movements (and that therefore is projected on a fixed position on the retina) is seen as moving and the background, whose projection is continuously moving on the retina, is seen as standing still – can be accounted for in a similar way. In map V the representation of the moving object is fixed and the representation of the background moves, but in map M the position code corresponding to the object changes in exact correspondence with the position of the eyes while the position codes corresponding to the objects in the background remain unchanged. The problems originating when looking out of a moving train can be accounted for in exactly the same way. I leave these problems for the interested reader.

There are further phenomena, observed with the moving eye, that can easily be understood in terms of the conceptualisation of position perception presented here. There is, for instance, the phenomenon observed in experiments in which attempts are made to move a partly paralysed eye. Under these conditions, subjects perceive apparent motion (in the direction of the intended eye movement) of the entire visual field (Mach, 1885; Stevens et al., 1976). This situation is the opposite of the situation with the eye tap (see above).[21] Now, due to the paralysis, there is little or no change in the retinal projections and therefore also not in V (and in other maps). Internally, however, a saccade is planned and executed (but somewhere, externally, frustrated). The assumption that the internal preparation and/or execution of the saccadic eye movement 'updates' the eye position codes in M, suffices for explaining the illusory displacement (in the direction of the intended saccade). (See Bridgeman et al., 1994, pp. 250–251 for further interpretations of these experiments.)[22]

The conceptualisation presented here can also easily be extended in such a way that further position-related phenomena can be understood. Wolff (1999b, pp. 41–42) offered the following generalisation:

> The model . . . can be generalized to the perception of motion. According to [the] account, motion will be perceived as soon as the code of the eye position corresponding to the relevant object changes. Consider an object that changes its retinal position smoothly while the eye is at rest. By changing its retinal position, the object passes different eye position codes that define the path of the eye movement necessary to pursue the object. From this point of view, it takes only one small step to arrive at the assumption that the perceived motion is coded by the eye movement required to track the object. Thus, just as perceived location is conceived as being coded by the required eye position, perceived motion can be conceived as being coded by the required pursuit eye movement.

Other generalisations I leave as an exercise for the reader.

As set out in Section 7.2, Husserl (1907/1957) introduced and defended a two-stage view on space perception with a 'space filling' component and a 'space structuring' component. In this section, a further elaboration and specification of that view has been presented. It appears that the version of Husserl's two-factor view presented here is capable of 'solving', i.e., evading, the classical position perception problems plus some other and related problems besides. Moreover, this two-factor model can be generalised in such a way that other phenomena can also be explained. My conclusion is, therefore, that the model presented here is a viable and promising space perception model.[23]

At this point it is appropriate to move from the tentative functional model, depicted in Figures 7.5 and 7.6, towards neuroanatomy to answer the question: What spatial properties are required of the possible neuroanatomical equivalents of map V and map M to perform the functions specified in the functional model?

The 'space-structuring' eye position map, M, was introduced as separate from map V and it was stated that, for explanatory purposes only, map M could best be regarded as an exact replica of map V.[24] With regard to the spatial properties of the neuroanatomical equivalent of map M it is important to realise that it need not be an exact replica of map V, but can have any shape and internal order whatsoever. Map M codes positions on positions that are themselves meaningless (in the sense that the coordinates where the information is coded are arbitrary and have no meaning in themselves).[25] What matters is only the dense connectivity that allows elements in map M and in map V that deal with the same regions in the external world to communicate.

The 'space filling' visual map, V, was introduced as a spatial map in which all kinds of deformations in terms of squeezing and stretching were allowed as long as, in one way or another, neighbourhood relations were preserved. With regard to the neuroanatomical equivalent of map V it is of importance to see that for performing its postulated function – creating a spatio-temporal extension – that map does not need to have either a particular orientation or a particular intrinsic metric. The neuroanatomical equivalent of map M 'injects' orientation and distance.

At the start of this section, I also suggested that V1, the first and 'lowest' visual map in the brain, is possibly the neuroanatomical equivalent of the 'space filling' map, V. It is worthwhile to know here that this suggestion is consistent with Zeki's (1992, 1993) views about how the brain 'produces' visual perception. Zeki, knowing that V1 is the cortical map with the strongest topography, assumes that V1 is the highest visual area of the cortex, not the lowest, as is normally assumed. The observation that there are as many axons going 'down' from the visual centres in the temporal and parietal lobes to V1 as there are going the other way brings him to this assumption. In Zeki's hypothesis, information is fed by V1 to the specialised computational areas 'higher up' in the brain, is further processed there, and then all this further elaborated information is fed back to V1 and there put together to construct the visual field.

Figures 7.5 and 7.6 can be taken to depict Zeki's (1992, 1993) conceptualisation as far as the perception of spatial position is concerned. The neuroanatomical equivalent of map M, which codes eye positions on otherwise meaningless positions, informs the neuroanatomical equivalent of map V, V1, about its results; a 'higher' map, which codes positions on meaningless anatomical positions, informs, and thereby structures a 'lower' map in the desired way.[26] Taken in this way, it appears that the version of Husserl's (1907/1957) two-stage view presented here extends and elaborates Zeki's (1992, 1993) proposal in the required way.

7.4 An effective position

As stated in Section 7.0, the exposure situation used in single-fixation tasks is never encountered in real life. In normal situations, the eye continuously moves with respect to the outer world and, as a result, the projections in the retina and in the maps in the higher centres of the visual system continuously change position. In a model like the one depicted in Figure 4.2, this fact is not made explicit. To approach the real-life situation, it has at least to be assumed that in all modules distinguished the activations (codes) continuously change position, i.e., move.

I am now in the position that I can present an elaborated functional model for visual information processing, an elaborated Visual Perception, that is immune to, and therefore compatible with, the continuous movements of the activations (codes) in the modules. That Visual Perception is presented in Figure 7.7. Of course, it is the model already presented in Figure 4.2 in Chapter 4, and which I used in Chapters 5 and 6 to explain the results observed in single-fixation experiments. The considerations in the present chapter are simply used to fill in that model in further detail.

Inspection of Figure 7.7 readily shows that it is simply the combination and integration of the information processing and selection model of Figure 4.2 and the model for position perception elaborated in this chapter and depicted in Figures 7.5 and 7.6. The input module, IN in Figure 4.2, is identified with the visual map, V in Figures 7.5 and 7.6, and the position map, P in Figure 4.2, is identified with the motor map, M, in Figures 7.5 and 7.6. So, the resulting model of Figure 7.7 is simply the model we have already worked with, enhanced with the (eye) position information introduced and elaborated in the present chapter.

It follows that Visual Perception, as depicted in Figure 7.7, is immune to, and therefore compatible with, the continuous movement of the activations (codes) in the modules distinguished, because in the model a clear distinction is made between the positions of the codes and the codes (for position, colour, and shape) themselves. The figure illustrates this important point by showing what happens in the model in all visual modules, i.e., in the input module (IN/V) and in the feature modules (C, S, and P/M), when the eye moves (saccades) from 'straight ahead' (see Figure 7.5) to the X in W (see Figure 7.6). In all modules, the codes for (i.e., the representations of features of) the X move from a peripheral position into the centre of the map (see the arrows); in IN/V the composite representation (X), in C the representation of the colour (C), in S the representation of the shape (X), and in P/M the representation of the position (2,2). The positions of the codes change, but that is irrelevant because positions do not serve as a code. What is relevant

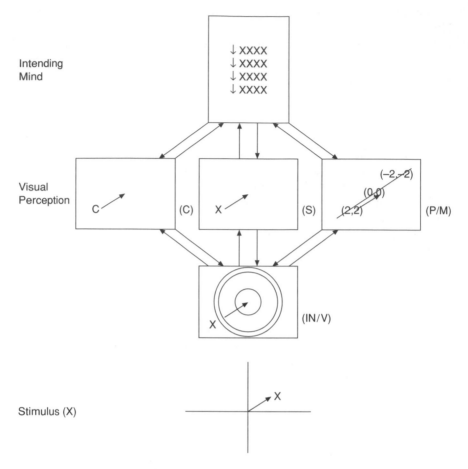

Figure 7.7 The visual information processing and selection model of Figure 4.2, combined with the conceptualisation of position perception elaborated in this chapter and depicted in Figures 7.5 and 7.6. (See text for further explanation.)

is that, while the positions of all the representations change, all the representations themselves remain the same.[27] Because the positions of the representations change in exactly the same way, the information in the different maps remains 'in register'. So, the codes remain the same, and the linked pattern of codes remains the same, and therefore in the model in Figure 7.7 nothing of relevance for perception is occurring with a (saccadic) eye movement.

This conceptualisation is consistent and compatible with my views on perception and selection, introduced in the preceding chapters. Remember that my theoretical view on perception presupposes that positions (and colours, shapes, etc.) are represented as patterns of activation (or codes) on positions in the position map (colour map, shape map, etc.); not by the positions (colours, shapes, etc.) in the position map (colour map, shape map, etc.) themselves. Remember also that my theoretical view requires the possibility of interactions via associative connections between states of an intentional sequence or Verbal Intention (see the box Intending Mind in Figure 7.7) and features of objects in Visual Perception (see the boxes C, S, and P/M in Figure 7.7). A bare, inert, anatomical position in one or another anatomic map cannot play the required role. Associations between intentional sequence states as patterns of activation and visual features as patterns of activation are clearly possible because intentional sequence states and features are in the same 'pattern of activation' language; patterns of activation and bare positions do not share 'language' because a bare position cannot talk.

In the model of Figure 7.7, actual and intended eye positions provide the metric in visual space, i.e., are the basis of visual position perception. These actual and intended eye positions are represented or coded in P/M as patterns of activation on positions in a map, just as colours and shapes are represented as patterns of activation on positions in a map. Because these representations are immune to and remain the same with (saccadic) eye movements, an association between an intentional sequence state in the Intending Mind and a feature of the visual information – e.g., between POSITION in the Intending Mind and (2,2) in position map P/M or between RED in the Intending Mind and (Red) in colour map C – is the same before and after a (saccadic) eye movement. This makes it possible for the states of the intentional sequences in the Intending Mind to keep track of the relevant visual information despite intervening (saccadic eye) movements. A target selected before the (saccadic eye) movement is the target selected after the (saccadic eye) movement when the intentional sequence or Verbal Intention remains in the same state.

So, the position perception proposal presented here is, in principle, compatible and consistent with my view with regard to properties and functions of Visual Perception and the use of Visual Perception for task performance presented in the preceding chapters. With this elaborated proposal, that view can be *maintained*. Let us now turn to the question of whether this view can also be *extended*. Let us investigate whether this proposal also provides an appropriate and fruitful starting point for discussing the cognitive control in act tasks – tasks in which the performance critically depends on the perception of spatial position. And let us start with the control of saccadic eye movements.

Notes

1 Adapted from Van der Heijden, A. H. C., Müsseler, J., & Bridgeman, B. (1999). On the perception of position. In G. Aschersleben, T. Bachmann, & J. Müsseler (Eds.), *Cognitive Contributions to the Perception of Spatial and Temporal Events*. Amsterdam: Elsevier. Copyright © (1999), with permission from Elsevier Science.

2 For evidence for the general acceptance of this point of view or assumption, see the next two quotations and ask yourself whether you agree. See also the 'problems' further on and ask yourself whether you see these problems as real problems.

3 These views implicitly presuppose that position serves as the code for position.

4 Basically the issue is that maps are only maps when viewed by an external observer, i.e., from the outside. For her/him the maps are perceivable 'objects'. For the 'internal' perceiver, however, the maps are not perceivable 'objects'. There is no internal homunculus looking at maps.

5 It is interesting to note that for auditory perception no comparable problems are specified in the literature. The basic reason probably is that in the ear no map is found. So for auditory perception it is simply taken for granted that position has to be calculated.

6 '. . . we are faced with the difficulty that the topographic code in V1 is geometrically and topologically incongruent with the topographic code in the visual field – as Lord Brain (1951) put this: "When we perceive a two-dimensional circle we do so by means of an activity in the brain which is halved, reduplicated, transposed, inverted, distorted and three-dimensional"' (Smythies, 1994b, p. 326).

7 A first problem is that the eyes are never really stationary. Even during steady fixation small eye movements, micro-saccades, drifts, and tremors, occur (see, e.g., Bridgeman, Van der Heijden, & Velichkovsky, 1994).

8 In the total field of eye movements:

> The most important single fact, it is true, was discovered by Javal (1878) without any more special technique than simply watching the eye of a school child who was reading. His very eminent predecessors had assumed the truth of common belief in "sweeping the eyes over a scene or along a line of print." He found, not a steady sweep, but a series of little jumps with intervening fixation pauses. The eye moved, as he said, "per saccades," from which expression comes the name *saccadic* now applied to this class of quick eye movements.
>
> (Woodworth, 1938, p. 577)

9 While generally only the last effect is emphasised, it is likely that both effects are important.

10 One of these changes is really spectacular – the change from one hemisphere to the other. When the eye is moved to the right, some of the information that was transported to the left hemisphere before the movement will become projected in the right hemisphere after the movement, and when the eye is moved to the left, some of the information that was projected right will become projected left. So, with each (saccadic) eye movement there is not only a change in position of codes within maps, there is also a deletion in the maps in one hemisphere and a corresponding accretion in the complementary maps in the other hemisphere (see, e.g., Kandel, 1985, p. 370).

11 Husserl was a philosopher, not a psychologist. He relies on 'phenomenological reduction', not on introspection. His aim is an epistemological explication of space perception, not an empirical description.

12 At present even the exact conditions under which undershoot will be found are far from clear (see, e.g., De Bie et al., 1987, and Carpenter, 1988). It cannot be excluded that, given some further conditions, undershoot will be mainly found with isolated targets in an otherwise empty field. In other words, it cannot be excluded that undershoot will be mainly found when nearly all cues for depth are eliminated. (In structured fields the undershoot may not be important, as retinal information is available to calibrate visual direction.) Further research with regard

to saccadic undershoot and with regard to the relation between saccadic under-shoot and underestimation in position judgement tasks is certainly in order.

13 It is worthwhile to realise that an uncertain, peripheral, intended eye position attracts the fovea (see Chapter 8). Because this intended position is uncertain, and because there is possibly also some uncertainty about the actual eye position, undershoot and underestimation are possibly the result.

14 I am well aware that the reasoning here can go in two directions: 'saccadic eye movements go to perceived positions' and 'perceived positions result from saccadic eye movements'. Problems with the first alternative arise because one then has to define 'perceived position' in such a way that an adequate saccadic eye move-ment can indeed be made. 'The subject knows the position' is clearly not suffi-cient for this purpose. In one way or another, the goal coordinates for the movement have to be available within the system. But, when one indeed assumes that these goal coordinates are available, one can as well assume that exactly these goal coordinates are the essence of the subject's 'knowledge of position', i.e., that the targets for the saccadic eye movements form the metric in visual space. The viability of this position is demonstrated in further sections of this chapter.

15 The assumption that in map M eye positions are coded (and that eye position codes are 'corrected' or 'adjusted' using 'extra-retinal information'; see later) possibly deserves a short comment. The objection that can be raised against this assumption is that introspection easily shows us that we are hardly aware, and if so then only very roughly and approximately, of the position of the eyes in their orbits. So, how can eye positions of which we are hardly aware be coded in map M (and be used for correcting codes in map M; see later)? The important issue is, of course, whether this argument based on 'direct' introspection is of any value. It is far from clear whether the information that the system uses for one or another purpose in creating the visual field, needs also to be available to us in introspection in 'raw' or 'unprocessed', that is, non-visual, form. With auditory stimulation, for instance, there are tiny inter-aural arrival time differences that the system uses for working out the position of the sound source. These time differences, which are used for creating the auditory field, are not available to us in 'raw' form in introspection. It is further worthwhile to note that it is generally assumed that the 'neural command' or the 'efference copy' is used for maintain-ing a stable visual field despite eye movements, while it is far from clear whether, and if so to what extent, this information is available to introspection.

16 For evidence for the existence of this kind of maps see, for example, Andersen, Snyder, Li, and Stricanne (1993).

17 With the model of Figure 7.5 it is not difficult to see why an illusory movement in the *opposite direction* to the passive movement is observed. Assume that the before-tap situation is the situation depicted in Figure 7.5. Now consider a tap that has as a result that the X in W becomes projected in the fovea, i.e., a tap that has as a result that the eye changes from pointing at world coordinates (0,0) to pointing at world coordinates (2,2). In the eye position map, M, nothing changes (see above; see also later). Therefore, the X that first had eye coordinates (2,2) in M now has, because it is projected in the fovea, eye coordinates (0,0) in M. So, while the eye changes from (0,0) to (2,2) in world coordinates in W, the X moves from (2,2) to (0,0) in eye position codes in M. The illusory displacement is in the direction opposite to the passive eye movement.

18 Wolff (1999b, p. 42) comments:

> Presumably, this additional assumption differs fundamentally from the traditional idea of determination by cues. According to the basic idea of the . . . account, the co-determining cues should have the same status as the

eye position codes, that is, they are codes for additional movements (vergence, head movements, locomotion, etc.). Accordingly, size constancy can be explained in principle by exactly the same line of arguing as visual stability during eye movement.

19 It is worthwhile to note that there are no space-constant maps in the present proposal; that is, maps with neurons with receptive fields with constant locations in the world rather than constant locations on the retina (see Bridgeman, 1999b, for evidence supporting this position).

20 In general, it is worthwhile to see that all 'moving-eye' problems are 'secondary' problems. When correct position perception is accounted for, all 'moving-eye' problems are accounted for. This does not apply the other way around. When, for instance, the stable visual world problem is solved (see, e.g., Bridgeman et al., 1994), the correct position perception problem is not necessarily also solved.

21 The phenomena observed with eye taps and the paralysed eye are possibly of great theoretical importance. Wolff (1999a, pp. 56–57) remarks:

> There is ample empirical evidence that the visual system is not informed about the actual motor characteristics of saccades: First, if the subject's eye is moved passively when a subject intends to fixate an object, he or she perceives a motion in the opposite direction to the passive movement (Brindley & Merton, 1960, Von Helmholtz, 1866, Skavenski, Haddad, & Steinman, 1972). Second, if the subject's eye is held forcibly when he or she intends a saccade, the subject perceives a motion in the same direction as the intended saccade (e.g., Brindley & Merton, 1960).
>
> According to these findings, the visual system processes visual information as if the saccade had been executed as intended, that is, the saccade as a motor event seems not to exist. Therefore, from the viewpoint of the visual system, we have to deal with the intended saccades instead of the actual ones; in other words, we have to substitute the dimension of the actual movement with the dimension of the intended movement.

22 With the model depicted in Figures 7.5 and 7.6 it is not difficult to see why an illusory displacement in the *same direction* as the intended saccadic eye movement is observed. Assume that the before-intended-saccade situation is the situation depicted in Figure 7.5. Now consider an intended saccadic eye movement that has to bring the X in W into the middle of the fovea and in the origin of map V, i.e., a saccadic eye movement from (0,0) to (2,2) in world coordinates in W and of size (2,2) − (0,0) = (2,2). Because the eye is paralysed, the eye does not move and the projections in V remain the same. Because of the intended and internally executed eye movement, all eye position codes in M are incremented with the size of the intended saccade, i.e., with (2,2). Therefore, the eye position code for X in M changes from (2,2) to (4,4). So, the intended saccade is from (0,0) to (2,2) in world coordinates and the perceived position of X moves from (2,2) to (4,4) in eye position codes in M. The illusory displacement is in the same direction as the intended saccadic eye movement.

23 It is worthwhile to note that a subset of the information presented in this section plus common everyday experience also provides strong support for the two-factor model. In fact, what we can now construct is a complete 2 × 2 factorial combination of the factor visual-information-derived 'topological space' with the levels 'still' and 'moving' and the factor motor-command-derived 'metrical space' with the levels 'still' and 'moving'. In the following table, Situation specifies the 'experimental' situation, Topological Space and Metrical Space specify what happens in these spaces in these experimental situations, and Visual World specifies

whether the visual world is perceived as stable or as moving. From this table it readily appears that a stable visual world is only perceived with a proper *combination* of levels of the two factors topological space and metrical space.

Situation	Topological Space	Metrical Space	Visual World
Steady fixation	still	still	stable
Normal saccade	moving	moving	stable
Eye tap	moving	still	moving
Paralysed eye	still	moving	moving

24 It is worth noting that map M need not be anatomically separated from, and can just as well be fully integrated with, map V to perform its required functions. What matters are only the appropriate dense connections between elements of map M and map V that deal with the same regions of the external world. There is, however, abundant evidence that nature wanted them to be separated.

25 In his comment, Wolff (1999b, p. 39) explicates and elaborates this point:

> The spatial structure of the retinal stimulation that corresponds to the spatial structure of the visual map in the model is "meaningless" in the sense that it does not code position or anything else; in other words, it does not have any representational function. [It fills in space] The same applies to the spatial structure of the motor map (which has to be distinguished carefully from the coded spatial structure) and of other anatomical maps such as a color map to code colors. But "meaningless" does not mean functionless. The anatomical positions separate and distinguish the pieces or elements of information, making it possible to trace them, and, therefore, connect them with the relevant pieces of other maps. Thus, the "meaningless" spatial structures of the anatomical maps, like interfaces, serve the function of communication between these maps. This communication ensures the integration of features that are represented in different maps. It is obvious why the spatial structure of the maps does not need to be ordered topographically. The only condition needed to integrate the features correctly is for the maps to be connected appropriately.

26 That V1 is cut into two halves (see Section 8.2) seems to me to be of minor importance because the vertical meridian is represented in both hemispheres (seeing at exactly the same time, at exactly the same place, in exactly the same way cannot cause much confusion in visual perception).

27 Because of the inhomogeneity of the retina, some changes are to be expected (see Section 7.1).

8 The cognitive control of saccadic eye movements

8.0 Introduction

For two reasons it is worthwhile to devote a chapter to the cognitive control of 'ballistic' saccadic eye movements. One is that for most visual information processing tasks, e.g., for inspecting an object or a scene and for reading a text, the 'ballistic' saccadic eye movements are of prime importance (see Section 7.1). The other is that saccadic eye movements, unaccompanied by other behaviours, are the vast majority of behavioural acts (see Section 8.1). Therefore, when I can adequately handle the cognitive control of saccadic eye movements, I have not only dealt with the vast majority of behavioural acts but also with the acts that are of prime importance in real-life visual information processing tasks.

Functional models concerned with the generation and control of saccadic eye movements are dealing with sequences of the form . . . F M F M F M . . . , with F standing for 'fixate' and M standing for 'move'. After a short stay (F), the eye jumps to a new position (M) and stays there a while (F), jumps to a next position (M) and stays there a while (F), etc. What the models have to explain is *where* the eyes move and *when* the eyes move (and/ or *where* the eye fixates and *how long* the eye fixates). Because the eyes move in order to fixate, and not fixate in order to move, the sequence just specified can be written as

$$. . . F \gg \gg M > F \gg \gg M > F \gg \gg M . . . ,$$

i.e., as a sequence with $\gg M > F \gg$ as the unit of analysis.

In Chapter 4, I introduced an Intending Mind with a Verbal Intention or intentional sequence of the form

$$. . . Y \gg \gg X > Y \gg \gg X > Y \gg \gg X . . . ,$$

i.e., a sequence with $\gg X > Y \gg$ as the unit of analysis and with X as the 'sending' term, in charge of 'selection', and Y as the 'receiving' term, in charge of 'reception'. In Chapters 5 and 6 these intentional sequences were used to explain observed behaviour in single-fixation report tasks with accuracy and latency as the dependent variable.

It is not difficult to see that the intentional sequence, with $\gg X > Y \gg$ as the unit of analysis, offers great opportunities for explaining the cognitive control of saccadic eye movements, with $\gg M > F \gg$ as the unit of analysis. Because two different eye movement parameters have to be accounted for, the where and the when, and because the intentional sequence recognises two different functional states, state X and state Y, an unambiguous relation between intentional sequence states and eye movement parameters directly suggests itself. The 'sending' term, X, that is already concerned with the spatial selection of the information required for task performance, can be assigned the dominant role in the selection of the *where* of the saccadic eye movement. The 'receiving' term, Y, that is already in charge of the reception of the selected information, can be assigned a dominant role in the determination of the *when* of a saccadic eye movement.

In Section 8.1, the role of state X in the generation of saccadic eye movements is considered. The emphasis is on 'double tasks' in which subjects are instructed to make a saccadic eye movement while performing another, related or unrelated, visual information processing task. These tasks are used in the information processing approach for investigating the relation between 'attention' and saccadic eye movements. The conclusion in this section is that the entering of state X is the start of the programming of a saccadic eye movement.

In Sections 8.2 and 8.3, models for the control of saccadic eye movements that can account for a broad range of results are introduced and discussed.[1] Section 8.2 introduces Findlay and Walker's (1999) functional model for the generation and control of a single saccadic eye movement. It is argued that a modification of this model is in order. It is shown that the intentional sequence, $\gg X > Y \gg$, can simply be inserted as a 'cognitive top' in this model. The result is a model for the generation of saccadic eye movements.

Section 8.3 introduces Morrison's (1984) functional model for the control of saccadic eye movements in reading and Reichle, Pollatsek, Fisher, and Rayner's (1998) elaborated version of that model. These models are mainly concerned with information processing tasks that require a sequence of saccadic eye movements. It is argued that a reinterpretation of Reichle et al.'s model is in order. It will appear that, when properly interpreted, the intentional sequence $\gg X > Y \gg$ is already part of these models. The outcome is a model for the control of saccadic eye movements during reading.

In Section 8.4, the interaction of bottom-up and top-down control of saccadic eye movements and the power of top-down control is briefly considered.

8.1   X and the where

Bridgeman (1992, p. 76) correctly notices that

The vast majority of behavioral acts are saccadic jumps of the eyes, unaccompanied by any other behaviors. Saccades occur several times per second throughout waking life; even during what we think of as steady fixation, microsaccades continue at the same rate. These movements are miniature versions of the larger exploratory saccades . . . The fact that we are blissfully unaware of them, so much so that they were discovered only relatively recently, speaks to the minor role that consciousness plays in governing and monitoring behavior.

And indeed, with some 15,000 jumps per hour, the 'ballistic' saccade is the clear winner in our repertoire of behavioural acts.

With regard to our awareness of the vast majority of behavioural acts, however, the situation is even more striking than Bridgeman (1992) suggests. Not only the microsaccades, but also the large exploratory saccades had to be explicitly discovered before they were recognised as such (see Javal, 1878, in Section 7.1, Note 8). In fact,

> [The] O[bserver] cannot count his own saccadic eye movements and . . . he usually has an entirely false impression of the behavior of his eyes in reading or surveying a scene. He imagines himself to be sweeping his eyes by a continuous gradual movement along the line or about the room, whereas all the objective methods show that he is really moving his eyes by jumps separated by fixation pauses.
>
> (Woodworth, 1938, p. 584)

Of course, my answer to the question of how it is possible that observers are generally unaware of the vast majority of their behavioural acts is that in normal situations observers are simply not interested in, occupied by, or concerned with these acts. What, in my conceptualisation, observers are interested in, occupied by, or concerned with, is captured and summarised in the Verbal Intention or intentional sequence . . . Y >> >> X > Y >> >> X . . . , etc. Observers are interested in regions or objects and features or characteristics of the visual world, not in their saccadic eye movements.

My theoretical position further forces me to assume that the Intending Mind, with the Verbal Intention or intentional sequence as its instrument for guiding the system in the visual world and for making sure that tasks are appropriately performed, can dispose of the eyes as its means and slaves for reaching its ends. This entails that the Intending Mind, via the Verbal Intention or intentional sequence, has to control the saccadic eye movement system in such a way that it can avail itself of the required visual information at the proper moment in time. For this control, neither an awareness of the control nor of the execution of the saccadic eye movements is required and therefore to be expected.

In my conceptualisation, with proper control and execution of saccadic eye movements, what is to be expected is appropriate selection of visual information by sequence state X and reception of adequate visual information by sequence state Y. What is to be expected is that the states X and Y of an intentional sequence

$$\ldots . \, Y \gg \gg X > Y \gg \gg X \ldots$$

can control the movements and fixations in a saccadic eye movement sequence

$$\ldots . \, F \gg \gg M > F \gg \gg M \ldots$$

in such a way that the eye provides the visual information required for task performance at the right moment in time. And the problem we have to be concerned with is: How to conceive that control of F and M by sequence state X and by sequence state Y.

In the literature, this topic is generally designated as that of the relation between attention and saccadic eye movements. In treatments of this issue, it is generally assumed that attention moves from position to position and that the eye moves from position to position, and the question elaborated and investigated is that of the relation between the two kinds of movements.

Logically, a number of relations between attention and saccadic eye movements can be specified (see, e.g., Posner, 1980; Shepherd, Findlay, & Hockey, 1986). In my view, and using for the moment the term attention instead of terms of the intentional sequence X > Y, the three main categories of relations are: (1) the two types of movements are independently controlled, (2) the control of the eyes entails the control of attention, and (3) the control of attention entails the control of the eyes. A highly interesting point in this field of research is that there is evidence pro (and contra) all three possibilities.[2]

In my conceptualisation, defended in the preceding chapters, the term 'attention' has to be replaced. The 'control of attention' consists of the development in time of intentional sequences consisting of units of analysis $\gg X > Y \gg$. And, if the intentional sequence is indeed regarded as the instrument of the Intending Mind of the human information processor for dealing with the visual world, then there is no place for an independent eye (the independence assumption is unacceptable) let alone for a leading eye (the 'premotor hypothesis' is unacceptable). So, my theoretical position forces me to endorse the third theoretical position mentioned above: the theoretical position that, in one way or another, the 'control of attention' entails the 'control of the eyes' (the 'pre-attention hypothesis').

This then, in combination with what was said in previous chapters, leads to the following general theoretical position with regard to the roles of state X and state Y in the cognitive generation and control of saccadic eye movements:

- State X is already responsible for the selection of objects/regions in the visual world. It is therefore obvious that I have to assume that this state is involved in and concerned with the determination of the *where* of the saccadic eye movement. In particular, I assume that the entering of state X is simultaneously (1) the start of the selection of all the information from the object or region specified by the content of X, and (2) the start of the programming of a saccadic eye movement to the position specified by the content of state X (the saccade target). This assumption is consistent with the outcome of Hoffman's (1998) evaluation of the available evidence.

• State Y is already responsible for the reception of the task-relevant visual information. It is therefore obvious that I have to assume that this state is involved in and concerned with the determination of the *when* of the saccadic eye movement. For the moment, in particular, I assume that the duration of state Y is simultaneously (1) the interval of time required by state Y for finishing the 'processing' of the information required for task performance and (2) the interval of time that the eye, on average, remains at rest (the fixation duration). This assumption is consistent with the outcome of Rayner's (1995) evaluation of the available evidence.[3]

I return to the role of state Y in Section 8.3. In this section, the role of state X is made explicit and some objections against my theoretical position with regard to the role of state X are considered.

With regard to the operation of state X, it is important to remember and to recognise that in the augmented Visual Perception model, presented in Figure 7.7,

> Spatial positions are defined in terms of eye positions required to foveate the related visual elements. It is this information about the required eye position that constitutes . . . the *perceptual* position of the visual information. To the extent that the coded eye positions can be used to control eye movements directly, the perceptual positions "afford" (Gibson, 1979) eye movements. Accordingly, perceptual positions "mean" information about how to use position for movement. This is a genuinely ecological point of view: The only purpose in perceiving position is to use it for movement control, including triggering and controlling actions by visual selective attention.
>
> (Wolff, 1999b, p. 40)

Figure 8.1 shows *how*, in my view, the coded eye positions in P/M can be used to control saccadic eye movements (because my main concern is with the cognitive control of saccadic eye movements, I restrict myself to a 'broad functional sketch'; see, e.g., Deubel, 1996, and Findlay and Walker, 1999, for detailed expositions).[4] In Figure 7.7, an eye movement control unit (EMC) is inserted. This EMC is just like P/M a retinotopic map (because the unit is not part of the cognitive system but has only an executive function, a circle instead of a square is used). Each map position in the EMC specifies one and only one unique and fixed saccadic eye movement.[5] The positions in the

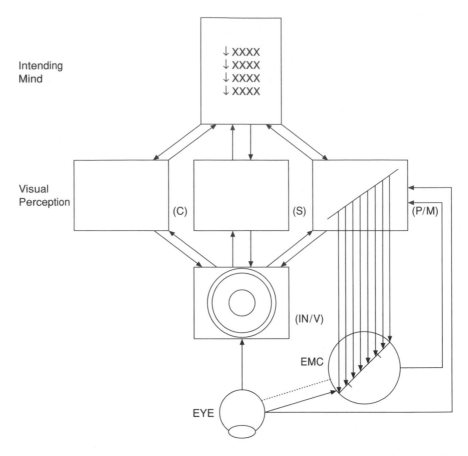

Figure 8.1 Model for the generation of (saccadic) eye movements, consisting of the perception and selection model of Figure 7.7 with an eye movement control unit (EMC) controlling the eye (dotted line). (See text for further explanation.)

position map P/M are one–one hardware connected with the corresponding positions in the EMC (I turn to the connections received from the eye in Section 8.4). Enhanced activation in a region in P/M results in enhanced activation on the corresponding position in the EMC, and that position in the EMC, when sufficiently activated, triggers its saccadic eye movement by attracting the eye. (For a similar conceptualisation, see the 'move centre' or 'salience map' in Findlay & Walker's, 1999, model.)

It is of importance to note that in this conceptualisation it is not the subject who moves the eyes to the target. It is the selected target that, via an activation peak in the EMC, attracts the fovea of the eye to its position. In this view, the direct or indirect selection of an object's position by state X in P/M *is* the selection of the eye movement parameters required for foveating that object in the EMC.[6] No further subject is required.

Posner (1980), however, has already argued that a theoretical position like mine – the start of state X is the start of the programming of a saccadic eye movement – is understandable but possibly wrong.

> ... no one would dispute the close connection between movements of our eyes and shifts of attention. Nonetheless, there has always been speculation that one can shift attention independent of eye movements. For example Wundt (1912, p. 20) commented on the ability to separate the line of fixation from the line of attention. Natural language refers to the ability to look out of the corner of our eyes, and athletic coaches instruct their players to do so in order to confuse their opposition.
>
> (Posner, 1980, pp. 5–6)

So, anecdotal introspective evidence seems already fatal for my point of view.

Fortunately for me, introspective psychologists never agreed. James (1890/1950, p. 438) quotes Hering, who remarked:

> Whilst attending to the marginal object we must always *attend at the same time* to the object directly fixated. If even for a single instant we let the latter slip out of our mind, our eyes move towards the former.... The case is then less properly to be called one of translocation, than one of unusually wide *dispersion*, of the attention, in which dispersion the largest share still falls upon the thing directly looked at.

So, the introspective givens need not be really damaging for the point of view that the start of state X entails the start of the programming of a saccadic eye movement.

It can, however, be argued that the data obtained in single fixation experiments – experiments of the type discussed in Chapters 5 and 6 – show that state X does not entail the programming of a saccadic eye movement. In these experiments, for instance in the partial-report bar-probe tasks (see Sections 2.3 and 5.3), exposure durations were used that were short enough to prevent the target from being foveated. So at first sight it seems that in these experiments there was adequate selection by state X but no programming of a saccadic eye movement.

With regard to these experiments, however, three different issues have to be clearly distinguished. First, it is certainly true that in these experiments, for instance in the partial-report bar-probe experiments, exposure durations were used that did not allow useful saccadic eye movements *during* stimulus presentation. Second, however, this does not entail that no eye movements were programmed. And, third, it has often been reported that, for instance in the partial-report bar-probe task, saccadic eye movements were made in the direction of the target *after* stimulus presentation (see, e.g., Bryden,

1961; Crovitz & Daves, 1962; Hall, 1974; Henderson, Pollatsek, & Rayner, 1989; Rayner, McConkie, & Erlich, 1978; see also Teichner, LeMaster, & Kinney, 1978). So, the results of these experiments are also not damaging for the point of view that the start of state X entails the start of the programming of a saccadic eye movement.

It can, however, be argued that the results reported by Posner and associates (see, e.g., Posner, 1980; Posner et al., 1978; Posner & Snyder, 1975) are really fatal for my point of view with regard to X and the programming of saccadic eye movements. These investigators were clearly aware that the use of brief displays does not guarantee that no overt eye movements are programmed (and executed after stimulus exposure). To ensure that in a single-target position (pre)cueing task (see Section 5.3) the results obtained did not depend on the shifting of the eyes, they monitored eye movements by use of EOG and used only those trials in which the eyes remained fixated. In the appropriate subsets of trials, clear and substantial effects of valid, neutral, and invalid position cueing were found for simple RTs (to luminance increments) and for choice RTs (above versus below and letter versus digit). Because in these experiments positions were cued, it seems that here we have proof that the start of state X need not entail the start of the programming of a saccadic eye movement. State X was involved but no saccade was executed.

With regard to these experiments, however, it is of importance to realise that the *start* of the programming of a saccadic eye movement need not entail the actual subsequent *execution* of that saccadic eye movement. Morrison's (1984) reading model can serve to make that clear. A key assumption of that model is that an eye movement program to fixate a target t1 can be cancelled by a subsequent eye movement program to fixate a target t2 (see also Reichle et al., 1998, p. 129). In this model this will happen when target t1 has finished processing and the processing of target t2 has already begun some (small) interval before the eye movement program of the saccade to target t1 is executed. The saccade program to target t2 then cancels the saccade program to target t1.

Using a variant of Morrison's (1984) assumption and the $\gg X > Y \gg$ conceptualisation, what can have happened in the experiments of Posner and associates can be represented with

$$\ldots Yf \gg \gg Xt > Yt \gg \gg Xf \ldots$$

The sequence is first 'dealing with' the fixation point (Yf). Upon presentation of the cue, the location indicated by the cue is selected (Xt) and the target at that location is processed (Yt). After target processing, the sequence returns to the fixation point (Xf).[7] Morrison's assumption says that the program to fixate target t, initiated by state Xt, is cancelled (and the eye remains at the fixation point) if state Xf follows soon after Xt. Because in the tasks of Posner and associates not very much processing was required, i.e., Yt was short, it is reasonable to assume that this was indeed what happened.

The foregoing general considerations show that there is not very much *a priori* evidence to convincingly show that the assumption that the control of attention entails the control of the eyes – in my terminology: that the start of state X entails the start of the programming of a saccadic eye movement to the content specified by X – is inappropriate. There is, however, some further evidence suggesting otherwise that we have to consider; evidence obtained in 'double tasks'.

Within information processing psychology, double tasks are the main tasks used to investigate the relation between attention and saccadic eye movements (see Hoffman, 1998, for an overview). Within this field of research, a great diversity of experiments is found and an equally great number of critical remarks with regard to methods and interpretation of results.[8] (See, e.g., Hodgson & Müller, 1995; Klein et al., 1992; Posner, 1980; Shepherd et al., 1986; Stelmach et al., 1997; Walker, Kentridge, & Findlay, 1995, footnote 2.)[9] We will first have a closer look at these tasks and then see what conclusions can be arrived at in this complex and heterogeneous field of research.

With double tasks, two targets or target positions are specified – (a) a target for a saccadic eye movement, and (b) a target for one or another second task (e.g., for flash detection, letter recognition, button pressing, etc.). With regard to the specification of the target for the saccadic eye movement, a distinction must be made between two types of tasks – those using location cues (peripheral or exogeneous cueing) and those using symbolic cues (central or endogeneous cueing). (These two types of cueing have already been introduced in Section 5.3.) With both types of tasks, the target for the second task (e.g., the button press or the flash detection) is specified by another central or peripheral event. Let us call the position of the target for the saccadic eye movement Pe and the position of the target for the second task Ps. The positions of the two targets either coincide (Pe is Ps) or differ (Pe is not Ps). The interval between moment of cue appearance and of appearance of the target for the second task, the SOA, is varied.

As already stated, in this field of research a great variety of different paradigms is used. Nevertheless, from my theoretical analysis one general prediction, applicable to all these experiments, can be derived. This becomes clear when we look first at condition Pe is Ps and then at condition Pe is not Ps.

When Pe is Ps, there is only one single position that contains the parameters for both the eye movement task and the second task. In this situation no problems are to be expected. The selection of the position delivers the parameters for the second task and *is* the start of the programming of a saccadic eye movement to that position. As already argued and shown in Section 5.4, in this situation there is no danger of interference or cross-talk. The parameters can be extracted in parallel (see Section 5.4).

When Pe is not Ps, the parameters for the eye movement task and for the second task are in two different positions. Because of the assumption that the selection of an object/region *is* the start of the programming of a saccadic eye movement, problems are to be expected. In this situation interference or cross-talk is invited and has to be prevented (see Section 5.4); the eye has to move to Pe and not to Ps and the second task has to be 'triggered' or 'informed' by Ps and not by Pe. The only way to prevent this cross-talk is by performing the two tasks in series, i.e., by first performing the eye movement task and then the second task, or by first performing the second task and then the eye movement task (see Section 5.4).

The parallel processing with Pe is Ps and the serial processing with Pe is not Ps leads to the following prediction. The possibility of parallel performance of the two tasks with Pe is Ps will mean that nothing of importance with varying SOA is to be expected ('no problems'). The serial performance of the two tasks with Pe is not Ps is, however, expected to show up as a delay or a deterioration of the performance in one of the tasks or in both tasks for that range of SOAs where the performance of one of the two tasks has to be postponed ('problems'). Let us now turn to the literature.

Experiments using location cues (or peripheral cues or exogenous cueing) for the saccadic eye movement were reported by, e.g., Hodgson and Müller (1995), Posner (1980), Remington (1980), Schneider and Deubel (1995), and Stelmach et al. (1997). To the best of my knowledge, with these tasks the performance pattern specified above is always found. All investigators report 'no problems' with Pe is Ps and 'problems' with Pe is not Ps when the two targets appear close together in time. These results are generally taken to indicate that attention moves to the target position prior to the eye (Posner, 1980), that attention precedes the eye to the cued location (Stelmach et al., 1997), or that the direction of attention is constrained to be compatible with the direction of the eye movement (Hodgson & Müller, 1995). In short, these results are in accord with my prediction.

Experiments using symbolic cues (or central cues or endogenous cueing) were reported by, e.g., Deubel and Schneider (1996), Hodgson and Müller (1995), Hoffman and Subramaniam (1995), Kowler et al. (1995), Remington (1980), Shepherd et al. (1986), and Stelmach et al. (1997). To the best of my knowledge with these tasks generally the performance pattern specified above and found with location cues has also been found. There are, however, two notable exceptions.[10] Remington (1980) and Stelmach et al. (1997) reported 'no problems' with Pe is not Ps; they failed to find any convincing effect of the eye movement task on the second task with Pe is not Ps with the critical SOAs. Remington (1980, p. 738) concludes that his '. . . results show that shifts of attention prior to the onset of an eye movement do not occur for all types of saccades. In particular, they do not seem to accompany saccades that are initiated by a central cue.' And Stelmach et al. (1997, p. 823) summarise the results they obtained with the conclusion that '. . . participants were able to hold attention at one location while executing an eye movement to another location.' Both exceptions deserve a closer examination.

Remington (1980, Exp. 3) used a central arrow to indicate the direction (left or right) of the saccadic eye movement. On 50% of the trials either prior to (SOA = −200 ms), simultaneously with (SOA = 0 ms), or after (SOA = 150, 250, 400, and 600 ms) that arrow, a 3 ms probe stimulus was presented either on the left, on the right, or in the middle of the display. Subjects were instructed to saccade in the direction indicated by the arrow as quickly as possible and to report subsequently whether a probe was present/absent.

As stated, Remington (1980) concluded: 'no problems'. There are, however, two important and related findings that indicate otherwise. First, for the relevant range of SOAs (0, 150, and 250 ms)[11] and for the comparable positions (left and right) a significant advantage in probe detection performance was observed in the trials with Pe is Ps over trials with Pe is not Ps (see Remington, 1980, p. 737). Second, for the same range of SOAs and positions, appreciably smaller saccadic latencies were observed with Pe is Ps (311 ms) than with Pe is not Ps (332 ms). Both observations, i.e., the better detection performance and the smaller saccadic latencies with Pe is Ps, have to be considered simultaneously, and together point to a substantial differential effect.[12] The results are simply fully in line with my prediction.

Stelmach et al. (1997) used a verbal cueing procedure (the words *left* or *right*) for indicating the target of the saccadic eye movement, and a temporal order judgement task as the second task to assess the allocation of attention. The stimuli for the temporal order judgement task were either presented simultaneously with the onset of the verbal cue (SOA = 0) or at an interval after the onset of the verbal cue (SOA > 0). The subjects were instructed to saccade in the direction specified by the verbal cue as fast as possible and to report the temporal order of the stimuli at the end of the trial.

For an understanding of the main outcome of the experiments, detailed knowledge of the procedures and outcomes is not required. It is of importance to know that in this experiment an SOA of 300 ms is a critical SOA. The main outcome of the experiment was: For none of the SOAs was there any effect whatsoever of the performance of the eye movement task on the performance of the order judgement task (see Figs. 2, 5, and 6 in Stelmach et al., 1997). But then, of course, the important question is: Was there an effect of the judgement task on the eye movement task? Table 8.1 presents the relevant subset of eye movement results.

Table 8.1 Mean saccadic latencies, percentage too fast reactions, and percentage too slow reactions in Stelmach et al.'s (1997) experiments 1, 3, and 4. (See text for further explanation.)

Experiment	1		3		4	
SOA	0	300	0	300	0	300
Saccadic lat. (ms)	300.0	417.0	301.0	428.0	306.0	423.0
Too fast (%)	1.2	17.3	0.8	19.1	1.5	10.9
Larger than 500 (%)	0.3	25.2	0.7	20.0	0.5	23.1

The row labelled 'Saccadic lat. (ms)' shows that the mean saccadic latencies are appreciably smaller when the judgement task can be performed before the saccadic eye movement can be initiated (i.e., with SOA = 0) than when it has to be performed at about the same time that the saccadic eye movement can be initiated (i.e., with SOA = 300). This could, of course, indicate that the subjects delay the saccade to perform first the second task, and only subsequently the eye movement task. Stelmach et al. (1997), however, have another explanation for this increase in saccadic latencies with SOA. In their treatment of the data, they reject saccadic latencies that are too fast, i.e., saccadic latencies smaller than 90 ms with SOA = 0 and smaller than 300 ms with SOA = 300. These percentages of rejected saccades are presented in the row labelled 'Too fast (%)'. Stelmach et al. (1997, p. 834) comment:

> ... mean saccadic latency increased systematically with ... SOA in all the experiments reported here. We argue, however, that these changes in saccadic latency reflect the rejection criteria adopted in the experiments namely that as the duration of the ... SOA increased, more fast saccades were rejected, thereby artificially inflating the mean latency.

This *reasoning* is understandable but one important *fact* remains. The row labelled 'Larger than 500 (%)' in Table 8.1 shows that substantially more saccadic latencies larger than 500 ms were found with SOA = 300 than with SOA = 0. This outcome simply *directly* indicates that the latencies in the two SOA conditions come from different distributions – as compared to the SOA = 0 condition, the distribution of latencies in the critical SOA = 300 condition is shifted towards the larger latencies.[13] This fact on its own allows the conclusion that with an SOA where interference is to be expected, the mean saccadic latencies do indeed dramatically increase.[14] And this outcome is fully in line with my prediction.[15]

Taken all together, it appears that also the results obtained with double tasks provide no reasons to doubt my theoretical position that the start of state X *is* the start of the programming of the saccadic eye movement. With location cues the expected pattern of results is always found. With symbolic cues the expected pattern is also generally found and the exceptions are not difficult to understand; they simply are not exceptions.[16]

8.2   Findlay and Walker's (1999) model

In this section we have a look at Findlay and Walker's (1999) 'A model of saccade generation based on parallel processing and competitive inhibition'. The functional model these authors present in this paper is not only attractive because of its explanatory power or because it is recent and has been intensively studied and commented upon (see the comments in Findlay and Walker, 1999). It is especially attractive because this model, while mainly concerned with lower-level factors, nevertheless makes clear how higher-level,

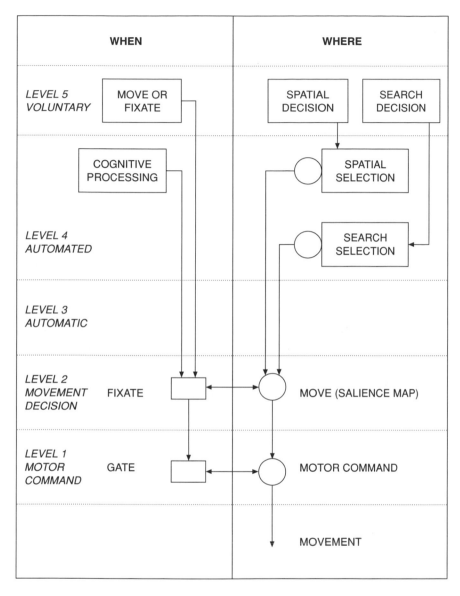

Figure 8.2 Diagram indicating pathways and information flow in Findlay and Walker's (1999) model of saccade generation. (Adapted from Findlay & Walker, 1999, Fig. 1.) (See text for further explanation.)

cognitive, processes can be integrated with and made compatible with, i.e., can be 'interfaced' with, lower-level control functions. Moreover, as will appear further on, the model contains the explanatory ingredients I am trying to introduce and to defend, albeit in different form.

Figure 8.2 presents the core of Findlay and Walker's (1999) model in a simplified form (I have deleted some components that are not important in the present cognitive context). The figure shows the information flows and competitive pathways thought to be involved in saccade generation. The model recognises two separate, parallel, pathways, one concerned with the spatial programming (the where) and the other with the temporal programming (the when) of the saccadic eye movement. Information in the where stream is transmitted in spatial (retinotopic) maps (circle symbols), information in the when stream consists of a single non-spatial signal (rectangle symbols). A hierarchy of five levels is postulated. Let us first have a brief look at the lower levels 1, 2, and 3, and then turn to the higher levels 4 and 5.

The processes in the lower '. . . levels 1, 2 and 3 operate in a stereotyped way which is not modifiable by cognitive influences other than through descending pathways . . .' (Findlay & Walker, 1999, p. 662) originating in levels 4 and 5. At level 1 the motor command to the eye muscles is produced (coding is in terms of muscle activation). At level 2 the various competing signals are integrated. At this level a reciprocal competitive push–pull interaction between a fixate centre and a move centre determines whether and where a saccade should be made. When the activity level in the fixate centre falls below a certain threshold, i.e., when the fixate centre 'disengages', a saccade is generated (the when). The salience map in the move centre is construed in such a way that it makes sure that one single 'salience peak' determines the metrics of the saccade (the where). Level 3 makes sure that some important visual factors, e.g., changes, onsets, and offsets, can directly affect and turn the level 2 fixate–move balance. Because I am mainly concerned with cognitive control, I have summarised all these functions in Figure 8.1 in the EMC.

At the – in the present context most important – cognitive levels 4 and 5, voluntary and automated influences are modelled. Let us first look at the 'where' stream and then at the 'when' stream.

In the where stream, at level 5, we find 'spatial decision' and 'search decision', which interact, at level 4, with a spatial map for 'spatial selection' and a search map for 'search selection'. In the model the 'spatial decision' works via a sensory map representing visual space and the 'search decision' works via sensory maps representing features in the visual field such as colour. These maps in their turn modify the pattern of activation in the salience map at level 2.

It will be clear that, if we neglect the details of this proposal,[17] levels 4 and 5 in the where pathway can be directly mapped onto functions and components in my conceptualisation. The 'spatial decision' and the 'search decision' perform exactly the same function as the 'sending' term X in my $\gg X > Y \gg$ conceptualisation. The map for spatial selection can be equated with the eye position map, P/M, elaborated in Chapter 7 and depicted in Figures 7.7 and 8.1, and the maps for search selection can be equated with the colour map, C, and the form map, F, in Figures 7.7 and 8.1. And, in my conceptualisation, state X determines the where of the saccadic eye movement.

In the when stream at level 5 we find 'voluntary' and 'move or fixate' and at level 4 'automated' and 'cognitive processing'. Both levels deserve a short comment. First, the 'voluntary', 'move or fixate', at level 5 is better deleted. The goal of any serious modelling effort must be to replace such intangible concepts as 'voluntary' by something less ghostly and more real. I return to this issue in Section 8.4. Second, the 'cognitive processing' at level 4 can better be placed at level 5. In earlier chapters we saw that what is exactly dealt with in 'cognitive processing' is completely dependent on the task to be performed. For instance, when 'search selection', after a saccade, presents 'the red one', it has still to be determined in a 'processing decision' whether the red one's shape, position, size, texture, brightness, etc. will be 'cognitively processed'. So, when the 'spatial decision' and the 'search decision' are placed at level 5, the required 'processing decision' should also be placed at level 5.

If these modifications of Findlay and Walker's model are accepted and when the details of the proposals are neglected, the when pathway at level 5 (now containing a 'processing decision') can be directly mapped onto functions (not components) in my conceptualisation. The when channel performs exactly the function that the 'receiving' term Y in my $\gg X > Y \gg$ conceptualisation performs; the 'receiving' term Y is in charge of what is traditionally called 'the processing of the information' (see Sections 4.1 and 4.2). And, as stated in Section 8.1, in my conceptualisation state Y plays a dominant role in the determination of the when of a saccadic eye movement.

So, what we find here is a close functional correspondence between my $\gg X > Y \gg$ conceptualisation and Findlay and Walker's two-channel conceptualisation of the cognitive control of saccadic eye movements. Just as in my conceptualisation, depicted in Figure 8.1, in Findlay and Walker's model the pertinent cognitive operations originate and occur in a 'top level' and have their effects by influencing the information processing operations in visual structures 'downstream'. Moreover, in Findlay and Walker's model, either the 'processing decision' – my state Y – dominates and takes care of maintaining fixation, or the 'spatial/search decision' – my state X – dominates and takes care of initiating the programming of a saccade. So, when looking at this model from bottom to top, in terms of dominance in information processing (send/select or receive/process) and in terms of control of the eye (move/saccade or stay/fixate), the system goes through a sequence of states . . . $Y \gg \gg X > Y \gg \gg X$ . . . This shows that, when details are neglected, the Verbal Intention or intentional sequence, $\gg X > Y \gg$, can simply be inserted as a cognitive top in this model for the generation and control of saccadic eye movements. The core of my conceptualisation, a concatenation of sequences $\gg X > Y \gg$, with X as the 'sending' term in charge of 'selection' and Y as the 'receiving' term in charge of 'reception', is clearly compatible with the essential functional explanatory components in Findlay and Walker's eye movement model.

At this point it is first of all worthwhile to see how Findlay and Walker's (1999) theorising and my theoretical approach differ from the traditional approaches. To make this clear, it is worth starting with Posner, Walker, Friedrich, and Rafal's (1984) theoretical view on the dynamics of attention (see also Section 4.4). In that view – in fact in nearly all current views on attention – attention is seen as a single, unitary, 'spotlight' or a single, unitary, 'zoom lens', which deals successively with different regions of the visual world (see Section 1.3).[18] In Posner et al.'s view, attention is first 'engaged' somewhere, then 'disengages' and 'moves' away, and then 'engages' again somewhere else.

Findlay and Walker evaluate Posner et al.'s (1984) theory and state:

> An influential attention theory, which has relevance to oculomotor control, has been developed by Posner and colleagues ... As described by Posner et al. (1984, p. 1864), "One can consider the act of orienting attention toward the target in terms of three mental operations: disengaging from the current focus of attention, moving attention to the location of the target and engaging the target." ... We argue that, at least as applied to saccadic eye movements, the concept is flawed. In our model, processes equivalent to disengagement and attentional allocation both occur but we entirely reject the idea that the same process is involved in each case, in other words, the idea that whatever is disengaged is the same as what is moved. In our view, disengagement occurs in the channel, which is not spatially specific and so is not connected with the spatial aspect of attentional allocation.
>
> (Findlay & Walker, 1999, p. 673)

So, Findlay and Walker (1999) reject the 'unitary attention' view; they replace that concept by a 'two-channel' view (see above).

With Findlay and Walker (1999), I also reject the 'unitary attention' view and replace it by a 'two-state' view (the states X and Y). Nevertheless, in my >> X > Y >> conceptualisation, processes equivalent to Posner et al.'s (1984) 'disengagement', 'movement', and 'engagement' also all occur; the 'receiving' term, Y, takes care of the 'engagement' as long as it has to receive and of the 'disengagement' when it has received enough, and the 'sending' term, X, takes care of the task-dependent 'moving' after disengagement of Y and before a next 'engagement'. So, contrary to Posner et al.'s (1984) suggestion and in correspondence with Findlay and Walker's proposal, my >> X > Y >> view entails that what is 'engaged' and 'disengaged' (state Y, 'receiving' and concerned with the when of the saccadic eye movement) is not the same as what takes care of the 'moving' (state X, 'sending' and concerned with the where of the saccadic eye movement).

While all this shows that Findlay and Walker's model and my theoretical view are highly similar and merge surprisingly easily together, there is nevertheless a major point of disagreement between the two positions. Findlay and Walker's model is a 'two-channel' model and my >> X > Y >> conceptualisation is a 'two-state' conceptualisation. Findlay and Walker (p. 673) '. . . question whether covert attention plays any role in normal visual scanning' and are

> . . . unclear what is gained by using attentional terminology since the properties assigned to attention mimic closely those of the eye itself (unique pointing direction; rapid movement from one location to the next).

In Findlay and Walker's model, *foveal* vision and *peripheral* vision are assigned different roles. In their model it is assumed that the when channel is concerned with the 'cognitive processing' of (all and only) the *foveal* information, and that the where channel searches and handles (all and only) the *peripheral* information. In what they call a functional model, the distinction between the when stream and the where stream is basically a structural distinction (between fovea and periphery), not a functional distinction (between 'selection' and 'processing'). In their view, the struggle (the competitive inhibition) between the two separate but simultaneously operating processing streams – the foveal stream engaged in 'processing' and the peripheral stream engaged in 'searching' – can account for all phenomena that have to be accounted for.

In my view, Findlay and Walker's assumption that 'attentional terminology' is superfluous and that two separate but interacting information processing streams, a foveal stream and a peripheral stream, can account for all results, is very difficult to defend, i.e., is simply wrong. Findlay and Walker's theorising confuses functions and structures.[19] The (two) different functions the information processing system has to perform (selection, connected with the where, and reception, connected with the when) do not coincide with, or are not matched by, the (two) different structural streams that can (possibly) be distinguished (a foveal stream and a peripheral stream). The following three points serve to substantiate this position (see also Pollatsek & Rayner, 1999).

The first point regards, of course, the single fixation experiments discussed in Chapters 5 and 6 (for instance, the partial-report bar-probe task). In all these experiments exposure durations were used that did not allow useful (saccadic) eye movements and useful re-fixations; information presented in the fovea stayed in the fovea and information presented in the periphery stayed in the periphery. In all these experiments a target had to be selected and that selected target had to be 'processed'. So, in these experiments either both selection and 'processing' occurred in the 'foveal channel' or both selection and 'processing' occurred in a 'peripheral channel'. The main outcome of these experiments was: successful selection and 'processing'. This outcome already sufficiently shows that the structural distinction (between fovea and periphery) is irrelevant and that only the functional distinction (between selection and reception) is relevant. Let us nevertheless consider two further points.

The second, related, point regards selection. Spatial selection and search selection are not confined to the periphery. There is abundant evidence from reading research concerned with saccadic eye movements clearly indicating that the system is not simply and indiscriminately working on all the foveal information, but on a task-dependent, precisely spatially selected, subset of the foveal information. By systematically mutilating parts of the text, eye movement research has provided a detailed insight into exactly what information is used within in an eye fixation during reading (see Henderson & Ferreira, 1990, for an overview). This research has shown that the 'perceptual span' extends from about four characters to the left of the character at the precise fixation point to about nine letters to the right of the fixation point for precise letter information, and to about 15 letters right of the fixation point for word-length information (McConkie & Rayner, 1975, 1976; Rayner, Well, & Pollatsek, 1980; Underwood & McConkie, 1985). The asymmetry is reversed for readers fluent in both English and Hebrew when reading a Hebrew text that runs from right to left. Both the task-dependent asymmetry and the task-dependent spatial selectivity indicate that 'cognitive processing' of foveal information, as postulated in Findlay and Walker's model, can in no way account for what is really going on.

The third point regards the relation between selection and 'processing' (between X and Y in my conceptualisation). Figure 8.2 makes clear that in Findlay and Walker's model the when stream and the where stream only start talking (or better, fighting; competitive inhibition) at the movement decision level, level 2. At levels 4 and 5, the two processing streams are operating simultaneously. There is no cognitive coordination whatsoever between the postulated search functions and the postulated processing function. For the cognitive control of saccadic eye movements, such a blind, chaotic battle between two largely independent, simultaneously operating streams, a foveal stream and a peripheral stream, certainly cannot be recommended.

These three points make clear that the primary and relevant distinction is not the structural two-channel distinction between fovea (for the when) and periphery (for the where) as supposed by Findlay and Walker. The primary and relevant distinction is the functional distinction between the task-dependent (input) selection (for the where) and the task-dependent (attribute) processing (for the when), i.e., the distinction captured with $\gg X > Y \gg$. Because intentional sequences consist of a concatenation of these two-state control structures or units of analysis, the Intending Mind can perform the required selections and take care that the appropriate functions are executed at the appropriate places at the appropriate times. And the eyes can do nothing but comply (see also Section 8.1).

As far as I can see, the replacement of the structural fovea–periphery distinction by the functional when–where distinction neither reduces the explanatory power nor changes the explanatory range of Findlay and Walker's model. If I see this correctly, then my modification of the model (with >> X > Y >> at level 5) can explain what that model can explain.[20] Findlay and Walker provide intriguing explanations of the results obtained and phenomena observed in standard eye movement tasks (the 'gap effect', 'express saccades', the 'remote distractor effect', the 'global effect') and tasks involving high-level control (search and reading tasks). Findlay and Walker deserve all the credit for these explanations. The interested readers are referred to their important work.

8.3 Morrison's (1984) and Reichl et al.'s (1998) models

For a number of reasons, Morrison's (1984) functional model for reading deserves a central position. The first reason is that this model is indeed concerned with the cognitive control of, or the cognitive processes influencing, move–fixate sequences (in reading) as specified in Section 8.0. A second reason is that even the core of the model alone is capable of explaining quite a lot of data in the field of reading research. A third reason is that the model is highly influential in reading research. In that field it is often taken as a starting point inviting further elaboration, modification, and refinement (see, e.g., Henderson & Ferreira, 1990; Pollatsek & Rayner, 1990; Rayner & Pollatsek, 1989; Reichle et al., 1998). Another reason is that the model is easily generalised to the field of visual search and scene perception (see Henderson, 1992; Henderson, Weeks, & Hollingworth, 1999). And a final reason is that the model provides a good starting point for a look at the control of the *when* of a saccadic eye movement, a topic that I have largely neglected up to now.

The – in the present context important – core of Morrison's model states that in reading, at the beginning of an eye fixation, attention is focused on the word centred on the fovea (word n). When lexical access of that word is complete, or when a preset criterion of processing of that word is reached, attention shifts or moves to the next word (word n+1). This shift of attention automatically initiates, i.e., entails, the programming of an eye movement to fixate the new attended location (word n+1). So, in this model completion of processing provides the signal for shifting attention and the shift of attention initiates the programming of the saccadic eye movement.[21] The model can be summarised with

Time: →

Attention: . . . > Focuses n >> >> Shifts to n+1 > Focuses n+1 >>
            >> Shifts to n+2 > . . .

Eye: . . . > Fixates n >> >> Moves to n+1 > Fixates n+1 >>
            >> Moves to n+2 > . . .

Of course, in this summary the exact timing relations are not presented; the timescale can only be regarded as an ordinal scale.

From this brief exposition and from what was said in Section 8.1, it will be clear already that Morrison's model is nearly exactly the model I am proposing, albeit in a different terminology. In the proposal I am defending, the terms 'attention' and 'the movement of attention' are regarded as inadequate. The unitary concept 'attention' is replaced by an intentional sequence consisting of a concatenation of 'units of analysis' of the form

$$ \gg X > Y \gg, $$

with X the 'sending' term concerned with the 'selection' of the new, relevant, information, and Y the 'receiving' term, in charge of the 'reception' of the selected information.

Because in my conceptualisation the completion of 'processing' or 'receiving' is the end of state Y and the beginning of a next state X, the core of Morrison's (1984) model can be rephrased as follows in my terminology. At the beginning of an eye fixation, a term Y of the intentional sequence is working on the word centred on the fovea (word n). When that 'receiving' state Y has completed its job, i.e., when a preset criterion is reached or when lexical access is completed, the sequence moves into the next 'sending' state X and starts selecting the next word (n+1). This entering of state X automatically initiates, i.e., entails, the programming of an eye movement to fixate the new selected location (word n+1). So, to rephrase Morrison's model in terms of my conceptualisation, nothing else has to happen except to replace the attention sequence states that have the terms 'Focuses' and 'Shifts to', with the intentional sequence states that have the content terms 'Y' and 'X'.

With regard to this replacement of one 'thing' (attention that moves and fixates) by two 'things' (an X that selects and a Y that receives), it is of interest to know that in the field of reading research there are the beginnings of attempts to move in exactly this theoretical direction. In an impressive study, Reichle et al. (1998) present several versions of a (computational) model of eye movement control in reading. Their major goal is to relate cognitive processes, in particular aspects of lexical access, to eye movements. Their starting point is Morrison's (1984) model. Reichle et al., however, want to decouple eye movements from attention. When discussing the link between attention and eye movements, they express their dissatisfaction with the global construct 'attention' which does not allow such a decoupling. They state:

> . . . most of the evidence showing a close link between attention and eye movements has implicated *input selection* . . . or those processes related to spatial selection, rather than *analyzer selection*, or those processes related to target identification. This distinction is important because the

decoupling of eye movements from attention in our model naturally lends itself to such an interpretation: Although saccadic programming includes covert shifts of spatial attention to the upcoming target location (i.e., input selection), "shifting of attention" refers to the processes of disengaging the mechanisms responsible for word identification so that they can be used elsewhere (i.e., analyzer selection).

(Reichle et al., 1998, p. 132)

So, a clear distinction is made between 'input selection ... or those processes related to spatial selection', in my conceptualisation the job of term X, and 'analyzer selection, or those processes related to target identification', in my conceptualisation the duty of term Y.

Reichle et al., however, do not use the 'input selection' – 'analyzer selection' distinction later on in their work. They present a modification of Morrison's (1984) model because:

One feature of Morrison's (1984) model is that it predicts that the amount of information extracted from the parafovea is independent of the difficulty of processing the word in the fovea. This prediction follows from the tight locking of the shift of covert attention with the programming of the eye movement. That is (according to Morrison's model), when the reader accesses the fixated word, covert attention moves immediately to the next word ($n+1$) and the saccade follows with a latency determined by properties of the eye movement system. Thus, the time spent attending to the parafoveal word will merely be equal to the mean latency of executing the eye movement program and will be unaffected by the time it took to access word n.

(Reichle et al., 1998, p. 131)

And that prediction is incorrect – 'preview benefit' decreases as the difficulty of foveal processing increases (see Reichle et al. for the evidence). So, a modification of Morrison's (1984) model and of my conceptualisation of the role of Y, specified in Section 8.1, is in order.[22]

In Reichle et al.'s view, 'The way that Morrison's model needs to be modified to account for these [preview] data seems clear: shifts of covert attention need to be decoupled from eye movement programming' (p. 131). Therefore a key assumption is added to Morrison's model. That assumption is 'that the signal for an eye movement program is different from the one that shifts covert attention' (p. 150), i.e., 'that there are separate signals for the eye movement program and the shift of covert attention' (p. 151). Clearly, this proposal is completely at variance with my proposal, presented in Section 8.1 and further tested in Section 8.2., with its tight coupling between the initiation of state X and the start of the programming of the saccadic eye movement. It is therefore worthwhile to consider how this key assumption is implemented.

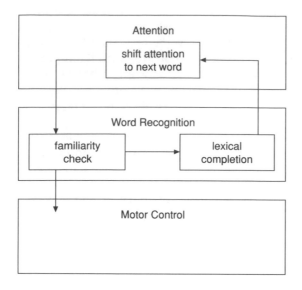

Figure 8.3 Schematic diagram of the component processes in Reichle et al.'s (1998) reading models. (Adapted from Reichle et al., 1998, Fig. 3a.) (See text for further explanation.)

Figure 8.3 gives in schematic form the component processes in Reichle et al.'s hypothetical readers. Inspection of what happens in the upper two levels, Attention and Word Recognition, shows that the sub-processes run in a circuit, e.g., from 'shift attention to next word' (S) to 'familiarity check' (F) to 'lexical completion' (L) to 'shift attention to the next word', etc. This circuit can be represented with

$$\ldots L >> >> S > F > L >> >> S > F > L >> >> S > \ldots$$

Because the 'familiarity check' (F) and the 'lexical completion' (L) are both stages of the 'word recognition' process (W),[23] this circuit can also be written as

$$\ldots W >> >> S > W >> >> S > W >> >> S > \ldots$$

and therefore also as

$$\ldots L >> >> S > F;L >> >> S > F;L >> >> S > \ldots$$

The crucial difference between Morrison's (1984) model and Reichle et al.'s (1998) model is in how the (initiation of an) eye (movement program) is hooked up with this internal information processing sequence.

- In Morrison's model, the end of lexical access, L, is the start of the shift of attention, S, and simultaneously the start of the initiation of an eye movement program (see above).
- In Reichle et al.'s model, the end of the familiarity check, F, is the signal for the eye, and the end of lexical access, L, is the signal for attention, S.

Indeed, in Reichl et al.'s model shifts of covert attention (the end of L) are decoupled from shifts of the eye (the end of F). The shift of attention *follows* the initiation of an eye movement program, or, the eye precedes attention.

In my view, eyes that precede attention perform a highly desirable job. They ensure that detailed visual information is available at the moment in time this information is asked for. Moreover, Reichle et al. convincingly show that, with the introduction of two different signals in Morrison's (1984) model, an impressive amount of data can be explained in an impressive way (see later). So, also in this respect, their modification of the model is certainly warranted/justified. Nevertheless, there are reasons that argue against the decoupling of eye movement signals and attention movement signals as proposed by Reichle et al., and that invite the search for an alternative.

The most important reason is that there are no (other) data that convincingly indicate that attention shifts and eye movement programming are not as tightly coupled as Morrison's (1984) model and my conceptualisation, presented in Section 8.1, assume. In this context of other, supporting, data, Reichle et al. (1998, p. 132; see also their p. 151) refer to some results obtained with 'double tasks' which suggest that attention can be drawn to a different location than the target of a saccadic eye movement. In Section 8.1 I discussed these tasks. There I showed that this evidence is highly debatable and that all evidence points to a close coupling of shifts of attention and initiation of eye movements. So, the only real and non-debatable evidence in favour of the decoupling hypothesis consists of the successful simulations presented by Reichle et al. But then, if the same simulation results can be obtained without using the decoupling hypothesis, all evidence in favour of that hypothcsis is gone.[24]

To find an alternative for the decoupling hypothesis, it is also worthwhile to note that there is something weird in Reichle et al.'s theoretical approach to the concept of attention. As I have already said, they present an insightful analysis of that concept in terms of 'input selection' and 'analyzer selection'. In their main simulation work, however, they simply forget this analysis, this 'fractionation of attention', and return to Posner et al.'s (1984) and Morrison's (1984) unitary attention concept. To arrive at what they want to arrive at, they introduce a distinction between an initial 'familiarity check' (F) and a subsequent 'lexical completion', (L), in the process of word recognition. Given the theoretical analysis of attention resulting in separate 'input selection' and 'analyzer selection' processes, it comes as a surprise that a 'familiarity check' (F) and 'lexical access' (L) are invoked to do the 'job', together with 'attention', when it comes to simulations.

As just stated, when the same simulation results as presented by Reichle et al. can be obtained without using the decoupling hypothesis, all evidence in favour of that hypothesis has gone. Fortunately, it is not too difficult to show that this hypothesis is not required and that exactly the same simulation results can be obtained with a model which assumes that 'a shift of attention' (Morrison, 1984), or the start of term X (my conceptualisation) initiates the programming of a saccadic eye movement. Consider again the intentional sequence >> X > Y >>. When the unitary concept 'attention' is abandoned, and when the distinction between 'input selection' (the job of term X) and 'analyzer selection' (performed by term Y) is taken seriously, it is not difficult to see that in normal reading 'input selection' can proceed to word n+1 while 'analyzer selection' continues working – for some short period of time – on word n. In other words, when a distinction is made between a 'sending state', X, and a 'receiving state', Y, *partially overlapping* sequences are possible (see Section 5.4 for this possibility).

In normal reading, as well as in other ecologically valid visual information processing situations, state Y nearly always receives high acuity foveal information while state X is nearly always concerned with less detailed, more peripheral, parafoveal information (see also Findlay & Walker's, 1999, model in Section 8.2). So, the structure of the peripheral (and central) visual information processing system, with its high acuity centre and less sensitive surround (see Section 7.1) already introduces a severe information processing bias in favour of the proper operation of sequence state Y.[25] In this situation, with proper timing and given reasonable processing delays, no problems are to be expected with partially overlapping sequences. With a unitary concept of attention as used by Reichle et al., however, partially overlapping sequences are not possible. This is for the simple reason that one and the same 'thing', attention, cannot move ('shift to') and stay ('focus') at one and the same time. One 'thing' cannot engage, disengage, and move at the same time.

So, the unnecessary adherence to the unitary concept of attention forced Reichle et al. to invent their 'two-signal' familiarity check – lexical access trick. That trick is not required. Sub-sequences with two different states can partially overlap:

>> X > Y >>
   >> X > Y >>
      >> X > Y >>

(see Section 5.4). In words: after entering a state Y, a subsequent state X can be instantiated; that X starts the process of selecting a parafoveal or peripheral word n+1 and of initiating the programming of a saccade to word n+1 while state Y is still 'receiving' the detailed foveal information about word n. In my view, it is reasonable to assume that in ecologically valid situations, especially after extended practice as is the case with normal reading, this efficient way of information selection and processing develops (see also Section 9.4).[26]

Of course, when required, further refinements are possible here. If, after Reichle et al. (1998), in state Y, the word recognition state, two subsequent sub-stages are distinguished, familiarity check, F, and lexical access, L, the following set of semi-parallel subsequences can be constructed:

$$\gg X > F > L \gg$$
$$\gg X > F > L \gg$$
$$\gg X > F > L \gg$$

In words: after finishing the familiarity check part of state Y, F, a subsequent state X can be instantiated; X starts the process of selecting word n+1 and of initiating the programming of a saccade to word n+1 while the lexical access part of state Y, L, continues the 'receiving' of high-acuity word n information.

It is not difficult to defend the latter set of partly overlapping subsequences (the set with X, F, and L) as a model for eye movement behaviour in skilled reading (and in extended, continuous, search). Here I simply list four arguments:

- The model, summarised with these expressions, performs exactly the same functions as Reichle et al.'s successful reading model. Of course, when implemented in the same way, the model produces exactly the same results.
- The model embodies the view that a shift of attention (in my terms, the entering of state X) precedes the movement of the eye. All evidence obtained with 'double tasks' points at this relation between attention and eye movements (see Section 8.1).
- In this model the eye behaves as a perfect servant for the central information processor. It delivers the high-acuity visual information at about the time the information is asked for by a next state Y; not after it is asked for, as is the case in Morrison's (1984) model. While still in state Yn, the saccade that has to provide the high-acuity information for a subsequent state Yn+1 is already programmed.
- The model is explicit about how state Y is involved in the determination of the when of a saccadic eye movement. Not the full completion of state Y, but the completion of some sub-stage of state Y appears to be the start of a next state X. This point, however, deserves much further investigation.[27]

As already stated, the latter set of sequences (with X, F, and L) performs exactly the same functions and, when implemented for simulations, produces exactly the same results as Reichle et al.'s (1998) model for reading. Reichle et al. provide intriguing explanations for a broad range of results obtained and phenomena observed in reading tasks (total time spent on a word, the probability of fixating and skipping a word, the durations of individual fixations on individual words, the number of fixations on individual words, preview benefit, word frequency effect, etc.). For these explanations, the reader is referred to their important work.

8.4   Top-down control

It is nowadays well known that in the generation and control of saccadic eye movements a number of parallel loops or circuits at different levels of the visual information processing system are involved.[28] In the functional model of Figure 8.1, I only broadly sketched this multiplicity of parallel loops with different inputs to the EMC (i.e., inputs from the eye and from P/M). In that model, an Intending Mind with a Verbal Intention or intentional sequence with >> X > Y >> as its basic unit exerts top-down cognitive control directly or indirectly by influencing the pattern of activation in the position module P/M. In fact, in the model the Intending Mind is a unit in the highest control loop that runs from the eye via IN/V, feature modules, Intending Mind, (feature modules, IN/V), and P/M to EMC. In a sense, the Intending Mind with its intentional sequence is the 'rider' that 'sits on' and 'leads' a complicated, highly sensitive 'horse' (see also Section 6.2).

In basic saccadic eye movement research highly simple experimental situations are often used.

> Indeed, the majority of studies on saccade control in the past 35 years have been done in the typical, visually heavily impoverished laboratory environment. Typically, the subject is sitting, with head fixed, in darkness and is asked to direct the gaze to a single, tiny spot of light. After a delay, the fixation target disappears and is simultaneously replaced by the onset of an eccentric target. The subject is normally instructed to follow this 'target step'.
>
> (Deubel, 1996, p. 153)

Of course, the ecological validity of this type of experimental situation with abrupt, transient onsets is highly questionable (see Deubel, 1996, p. 173; see also Section 6.4). Nevertheless, the conviction is that with this type of experiments the essential properties of the saccadic eye movement system, of 'the horse', can be discovered (see, e.g., Deubel, 1996, and Findlay & Walker, 1999, for overviews of this research; see also Section 8.2).

With regard to this basic saccadic eye movement research, two concluding remarks are in order. The first is that in this field of research the effects of top-down control, e.g., of tasks and instructions, pop up everywhere. Deubel (1996) presents an excellent overview of these effects. Here one example has to suffice. Let us have a brief look at the anti-saccade task, introduced by Hallett (1978), because that task clearly shows the importance and strength of top-down control. In that task, a sudden single target is presented at an unpredictable position and

[the observers are instructed] to make a saccade of the target's eccentricity, but in the opposite direction of the target . . . Interestingly, subjects manage to overcome this competition between foveation reflex and instruction after little training, producing saccades of low variability and relatively short latencies. This seems to suggest that the mapping from the sensory input onto the motor response can be 'rescaled' quickly at a volitional level, depending on instruction and situation.

(Deubel, 1996, p. 156)

So, even in this situation with a single sudden onset, the instruction-induced top-down effects prevail – even in this situation the 'rider' controls the 'horse'.

The second remark is that the theorists in this field of research do not avail themselves of an adequate theoretical apparatus to explain these top-down effects. Deubel (1996) talks about the involvement of 'a volitional level' and Findlay and Walker (1999, p. 669) explain:

Antisaccades involve the voluntary inhibition of a reflexive saccade and the cognitive manipulation of the spatial parameters to produce a saccade in the opposite direction. In our model, the ability to voluntarily suppress a saccade can be performed by the level 5 voluntary decision process connected to the central fixation system. This route enables reflexive saccades to be cancelled. The cognitive control over saccade metrics . . . must also depend upon level 5 processes. These might work through controlling spatial selection but could also use search selection processes, the search target being a region of absence of stimulation.

So, they invoke a 'voluntary decision process' with 'the ability to voluntarily suppress a saccade' through 'voluntary inhibition' (see also Section 8.2 for this 'voluntary'). Of course, with a 'volitional level' or a 'voluntary decision' in one's model, one can explain everything and nothing. Moreover, Von Helmholtz convincingly argued that it is not 'volition', not the will as such, but *what* is willed that exerts the control (see Section 3.1). An adequate model has to contain 'control by content', not control by the 'will'.

In my conceptualisation, the contents of the subsequent states of the intentional sequence, the Xs and the Ys, are intended to replace these 'voluntary decisions' at a 'volitional level' (and, at the same time the 'persons', 'agents', 'subjects', and 'she/hes' that will). And, in terms of content, what happens in Hallett's (1978) anti-saccade task can be summarised with the instruction-derived intentional sequence:

$$\ldots \text{Yf} \gg \gg \text{Xp} > \text{Yo} \gg \gg \text{Xo/act} > \ldots$$

(I return to this format in Chapter 9). The system is first 'dealing with' the fixation point (Yf). Upon or before peripheral target presentation, the sequence moves into state Xp and selects the target with all its attributes. Then the sequence moves into state Yo, and receives/processes the required position information. Because the instruction, which is stored in the Intending Mind, said 'opposite', the outcome of that processing is 'the position opposite to the target position'. The sequence then moves into state Xo. That state takes the outcome of the 'processing' operation by Yo, the instruction-and-target derived position, as its content; Xo *is* the outcome of the processing of state Yo. From what was said in Section 8.1, it follows that both the entering of state Xp and the entering of state Xo entail the initiation of the programming of a saccadic eye movement (to the target position and to the position opposite to the target, respectively). The program initiated by state Xo, however, cancels the program initiated by state Xp when state Xo is entered fast enough (see Section 8.1 for the same sequence and program cancellation, i.e., for Morrison's, 1984, cancellation assumption).[29]

Of course, this explanation requires further specification and experimentation. Because it is an explanation in terms of content and not in terms of a 'volitional level' producing a 'voluntary decision', however, it deserves further specification and experimentation. Logan and Zbrodoff (1999), and especially Logan (1995), provide many intriguing suggestions about the 'cognitive manipulation of spatial parameters' thereby indicating how to proceed here.

Notes

1 Because I have never worked in the field of eye movement control, in these sections I rely upon authorities in this field of research who propose models based on a broad range of data. The models discussed in these sections were chosen in such a way that the whole range from high-level cognitive control to low-level visual control is spanned. In this way I hope to make sure that my cognitive views are compatible with what is known about the control of saccadic eye movements.

2 Evidence supporting the independence assumption was provided by the research of, e.g., Klein (1980), Remington (1980), and more recently of Stelmach, Campsall, and Herdman (1997). Posner (1980) and Shepherd et al. (1986), however, rejected this assumption. Evidence supporting the assumption that the control of the eyes entails the control of attention (i.e., evidence in favour of a 'premotor hypothesis') was provided by, e.g., Rizolatti, Riggio, Dascola, and Umilta (1987) and Wurtz and Mohler (1976). Klein (1980) and Klein, Kingstone, and Pontefract (1992), however, rejected this assumption. And evidence that the control of

attention entails the control of the eyes (i.e., evidence in favour of a 'pre-attention hypothesis') was provided by, e.g., Deubel and Schneider (1996), Hoffman and Subramaniam (1995), Kowler, Anderson, Dosher, and Blaser (1995), Posner (1980), Schneider and Deubel (1995), and Shepherd et al. (1986). Remington (1980) and Stelmach et al. (1997), however, doubted the general applicability of this assumption (see Stelmach et al., 1997, for an overview and an attempt to reconcile the conflicting findings).

3 Gould (1973) provided substantial evidence for this set of assumptions with regard to state Y with a memory search task. The subjects had to scan an array of letters and to decide whether or not the letters were a member of a previously memorised set of letters. Memory set size was varied. A substantial effect of size of memory set on fixation duration was found. So, the amount of 'processing' required had a clear effect on fixation duration.

4 This figure makes clear where the 'efference copy' and the eye position information, required for position perception, can come from (see Section 7.3). The EMC can deliver the 'efference copy' and the eye can deliver the eye position information.

5 If the EMC codes the corresponding retinal positions on its positions, each position contains the information necessary for its saccadic eye movement.

6 In this conceptualisation, only a selected position in map P/M can cognitively control a saccadic eye movement. That position in P/M can be selected in a number of ways, for instance, directly by an intentional sequence state X and indirectly by an intentional sequence state X via feature maps C and S and via IN/V. Direct connections between feature maps C and S and map P/M also cannot be excluded. For clarity of exposition I did not enter all these possibilities in Figure 8.1.

7 The example given here is for valid trials only. It is, however, not difficult to elaborate this explanation in such a way that it is also applicable to neutral and invalid trials.

8 This state of affairs reflects the fact that with double tasks severe problems of interpretation arise (see, e.g., Pashler, 1998, for an excellent treatment of this issue). For the analysis and interpretation of the results presented in this section, the details of this issue are not of importance.

9 Walker et al. (1995, p. 307, footnote 2) remark that there is

> ... a possible problem with the use of dual task paradigms ... [saccade] latencies are much slower than observed in simple saccade experiments ... This suggests that the dual task situation is adding extra demands on the subject which are drastically slowing saccadic latency. This extra interference effect could well be masking subtle attentional effects that are normally observed in simple covert attentional orienting experiments. We feel that more attention should be paid to the absolute values of saccade latencies and manual RTs as well as to the differential values in attentional orienting experiments.

10 There is a third exception. Klein (1980) used a very peculiar type of double task and failed to find evidence for the movement of attention prior to the eye movement. See Hodgson and Müller (1995) for an insightful evaluation of this task.

11 The mean eye movement latency in the conditions with probe was 320 ms. So, with SOA −200 the probe appears about 500 ms before the initiation of the saccadic eye movement and no effect is to be expected. With the SOAs of 400 and 600 ms the probe appears after the saccadic eye movement and no effect is to be expected.

12 The results suggest that, in case of conflict between Pe and Ps, subjects tend to give priority to the detection task (only a minor, but significant, performance decrease as compared to the situation where Pe is Ps) at the cost of the saccadic eye movement task (an increase in latency of the saccadic eye movement as compared with the condition where Pe is Ps). Remington, however, only really considers the (significant) probe detection performance (and talks that effect away).

13 A second important point is that Stelmach et al.'s (1997) rejection criteria treated these 'too large' latencies in exactly the same way as the 'too small' latencies, thereby, of course, 'artificially deflating the mean latency'; Table 8.1 shows that the percentage of 'too large' latencies is at least as large as the percentage of 'too small latencies'.

14 This result suggests that, just as in Remington's (1980) task, in Stelmach et al.'s (1997) task subjects tended to give priority to the second task and postponed the saccade.

15 In their second experiment Stelmach et al. (1997) used location cues and obtained the standard result. In their experiment 5 they do not vary SOA. In their experiment 6 another secondary task was used.

16 It is interesting to note that both Remington (1980) and Stelmach et al. (1997) used relatively easy second tasks – flash detection and temporal order judgement. This state of affairs might have caused the subjects preferred to perform this task first and only then the eye movement task.

17 One important detail to note is that in the Findlay and Walker (1999) model there is no visual input into level(s) 4 (and 5). Although it complicates matters considerably, I nevertheless prefer a model in which a spatial map receives spatial information and the feature maps receive feature information (see Figure 7.7).

18 See Logan and Zbrodoff (1999) for a courageous alternative (see Section 4.3).

19 It is interesting to note that a similar problem has already appeared with Broadbent's (1958) information processing model. Broadbent distinguished two functions, 'filtering' and 'processing', and modelled this insight with two structures, a peripheral 'filter' and a central 'channel' (see Section 3.3.). Findlay and Walker also distinguish two functions, a 'when' function and a 'where' function, and also model this with two structures, a foveal stream and a peripheral stream.

20 Because I do not recognise two different structural information processing streams, my modification of Findlay and Walker's model entails a single 'salience map' with a 'fixate centre' and a 'move surround' (in competition) at level 2. The EMC in Figure 8.1 performs this function.

21 A second important core assumption of the model, the possibility of cancelling a program by a subsequent program, has already been described in Section 8.1.

22 There is another, related, reason for modifying Morrison's (1984) model and for elaborating my view with regard to the operation of Y, presented in Section 8.1, for reading and related automated tasks. Here I first discuss that reason in terms of Morrison's model. In that model, and in my proposal, because the eye always *follows* attention after a fixed non-negligible interval of time, *the high acuity foveal data are always delivered too late* ('attention moves immediately . . . and the eye follows with a latency determined by the properties of the eye movement system'; see the quotation).

There is abundant evidence showing that 'the eye' is not that stupid and often anticipates. This evidence comes from visual search tasks in which subjects are instructed to find one, specified, object among a number of different objects (for this task see also Section 5.1). With this task, it is often observed that subjects fixate the target, make an eye movement away from the target, and subsequently return to the target, i.e., make a 'return saccade' (see, e.g., Engel, 1977; Gould, 1973; Hooge & Erkelens, 1996a). Hooge and Erkelens (1996a), for instance, used displays with a circle as the object to be found and a number of Cs as irrelevant objects. The displays were constructed in such a way that in each fixation only one object could clearly be seen. They report that on 5–55% of the trials that the target was found, the subjects fixated the target, continued search and made a saccade to a next element, and then went back to the target.

Hooge and Erkelens (1996b) further investigated this phenomenon with a modified search paradigm. Subjects again searched for a circle target among non-targets. Now the non-targets provided unambiguous information about the direction in which the target had to be found; the gaps in all the Cs pointed in the direction of the target. On 65–80% of the trials the saccade went in the direction of the target. This result shows that subjects were able to make saccades in the direction indicated by the information in the fovea, but that they were not able to make all saccades in that direction. This result, in combination with the results of further research with the same paradigm, strongly suggested to Hooge and Erkelens that subjects cannot voluntarily extend their fixation durations during a cognitive task like visual search.

The important implication of this research is that it shows that, when generalised to search tasks, Morrison's (1984) model and my view with regard to Y are inadequate when the assumption is that the *end* of 'processing' or the *end* of state Y determines the when of a saccadic eye movement. Using the $\gg X > Y \gg$ terminology, Morrison's model says that the Hooge and Erkelens (1996b) search task is performed with an intentional sequence of the form:

$$Y \gg \gg Xt > Y \gg \gg Xt > \text{etc.}$$

The intentional sequence 'receives' information about one of the objects and derives the direction of the target (Y). The next object is selected and a saccadic eye movement in the direction of the target is initiated (Xt). Information about that object is received (Y), etc., until the target is found. The direction errors (and also the 'return saccades' observed in the standard task), however, show that the content received by state Y does not always function as the content of a subsequent state Xt. This outcome strongly suggests that in these tasks an eye movement is already planned when the foveal information is still not completely analysed.

23 'The familiarity and lexical identity of a word are computed in a module responsible for word recognition' (Reichle et al., 1998, p. 133; see also their pp. 151–152).

24 There are other reasons for doubting the decoupling hypothesis. A second reason is that a familiarity check (F) in a word recognition module can provide a 'when' signal but not a 'where' signal. This means that in Reichle et al.'s (1998) model the Motor Control level has to determine the position where the eye has to go next (see their model in Figure 8.3). Reichle et al. are clearly aware of this problem: '. . . we have ignored how the eye movement system selects a spatial target for an eye movement and how the movement is planned and executed' (p. 149; see also their discussion on p. 150). A third reason is that Reichle et al. do not completely discard the connection between attention and the 'where' of saccadic eye movements. In what they regard as the important simulations they use the 'more reasonable assumption' that 'The target for a "refixation" saccade is the attended word (word *n*) even when the attended word is not the fixated word and is to the left of fixation' (p. 141). So, there is a remarkable difference between the control of refixations (attention determines the 'where') and of regular fixations (attention is not involved).

25 It is worthwhile to note here that there is a difference between the normal reading situation (and other ecologically valid visual information processing situations),

and the experimental situations generally used in the information processing approach. In the normal reading situation and in other ecologically valid situations, state Y is concerned with high acuity foveal information while state X is working with less detailed more peripheral information. In the relevant experiments in the information processing approach, state X and state Y work with information that is identical in this respect, either because all information is foveal, i.e., is presented on the fixation point (see the RSVP tasks in Section 5.2) or because all information is 'peripheral', i.e., is presented on non-foveal retinal positions of equal acuity (see the 'limited-capacity' example in Section 5.4). In my view, it is this factor that makes partially overlapping sequences possible in ecologically valid situations and prevents partially overlapping sequences in most of the experimental situations.

26 With reading, the content of state X, the 'criterion attribute', remains the same from fixation to fixation. Crudely stated, each time 'the next word' has to be selected (see McConkie, Kerr, Reddix, & Zola, 1988, for a detailed specification of the content of state X in reading). It cannot be excluded that this property of state X also makes the partial temporal overlap of states X and Y possible. Moreover, this property of state X shows that the system is only cognitively concerned with the subsequent Ys; i.e., reads for or attends to content.

27 An important implication of the results reported by Hooge and Erkelens (1996a, 1996b; see Note 22) is that they show that other information than the result of a 'familiarity check' in a word recognition module can also function as an early trigger for the shift of attention and the start of the initiation of the programming of a saccadic eye movement (i.e., for the initiation of a new state X). They observed 'anticipations' in a visual search task. It is highly unlikely that in their search task a word recognition module, with a 'familiarity check' stage and a 'lexical access' stage, was involved. At least two different theoretical directions are possible here:

•   The first starts from the assumption that different tasks involve unique, devoted modules, all with something like a 'preliminary access' stage and a 'full access' stage.
•   The second theoretical direction starts from the assumption that also in reading it is not really something 'lexical' but something 'visual' that determines the start of the shift of attention and the initiation of the programming of a saccadic eye movement (one possible candidate is 'success of selection'; For Reichle et al.'s, 1998, simulations the assumption 'the longer a word the more difficult to select and the more difficult to process' suffices).

It will be clear that this issue deserves a lot of further investigation.

28 'Visual information can reach the brainstem oculomotor centers by at least four different possible routes, namely: (1) directly from the retina via the superior colliculus (SC); (2) via the lateral geniculate nucleus (LGN), the primary visual cortex (V1), and the superior colliculus; (3) via the LGN, visual cortex, and the frontal eye fields (FEF); and (4) via LGN, striate, prestriate and parietal cortices and the FEF' (Deubel, 1996, p. 150).

29 Findlay and Walker (1999, p. 669) point out that there is a relation between the functioning of the frontal cortex and the performance in the anti-saccade task. They mention the observation that damage to the human frontal cortex greatly increases the number of (reflexive) pro-saccade errors, saccades to the position of the target (see Guitton, Buchtel, & Douglas, 1985). They also mention the observation that in normal subjects the number of pro-saccade errors increases with increasing working memory load (see Roberts, Hager, & Heron, 1994) and working memory is generally thought to be located in the frontal cortex. And they

also mention the case of a patient with frontal lobe damage who was unable to suppress his reflexive saccades in the anti-saccade task and was also found to be impaired on tests of working memory (see Walker, Husain, Hodgson, & Kennard, 1998). It will be clear that these observations are of great value for my line of theorising. In Section 4.4, I surmised with Posner and Badgaiyan (1998) and LaBerge (1995) that the intentional sequences, the strings of units of analysis >> X > Y >>, are localised in and develop in time in the frontal cortex (are content sequences in working memory).

9 Act tasks and report tasks

9.0 Introduction

In Chapter 2, I argued that a disciplined distinction between tasks is required because without such a distinction it is not possible to know what one is talking about, and theorising ends up in a mess. For such a distinction, a theory of internal task performance is required – a theory that provides the theoretical means and concepts for expressing similarities and differences between tasks. Because in Chapter 2 neither an appropriate characterisation of the mind nor a decent unit of analysis was available, I had to rely on what authorities said about differences in tasks. With the help of Bridgeman, Gibson, and Neumann, I arrived at a preliminary classification of laboratory tasks in 'report' tasks and 'act' tasks, with within the 'report' tasks a further distinction between 'name' tasks and 'read' tasks.

Now, seven chapters further on, the theoretical scene has changed. I have now introduced the kernel of a theory of internal task performance and a unit of analysis for name and read tasks (see Chapter 4). I showed that this theoretical apparatus was consistent with and could account for a broad variety of data (see Chapters 5 and 6). I also indicated where, in terms of my conceptualisation, the difference between name tasks and read tasks is. Moreover, in the meantime we also had a brief look at one important type of act task – the saccadic eye movement task (see Chapter 8). All this now provides me with sufficient background for formulating and defending a disciplined distinction between the tasks in terms of units of analyses, and for elaborating act tasks.

Section 9.1 is concerned with the units of analysis. I introduce a distinction between report tasks and act tasks in terms of two different units of analysis. It is a distinction between '>> X > Y/report >>' tasks (or 'report' tasks) and '>> X/act > . . . >>' tasks (or 'act' tasks). The report tasks and the act tasks have object or region selection, performed by term X, in common. In report tasks, attribute selection by term Y selects the required parameters. In act tasks, devoted action modules take care of the selection of the parameters – there is 'direct parameter specification'.

In Sections 9.2 and 9.3, two current views on the generation and control of acts (and reports) are introduced and discussed.[1] In Section 9.2, the proposed distinction between report tasks and act tasks is related to Bridgeman's (1992, 1999a) distinction between 'communicatory' acts and 'instrumental' acts and further interpreted in terms of his two-visual-systems analysis. The cognitive control of pointing movements of the hand is further elaborated. In this interpretation and elaboration the distinction between 'code for position' and 'position of code', introduced in Chapter 7, appears to be essential. This distinction allows me to explain how the mind uses the brain for controlling the body in act tasks; that is, to solve the mind–body problem for act tasks.

In Section 9.3, I introduce an alternative, competing, unit of analysis, proposed by Prinz (1997a, 1997b) in his 'common coding' approach to perception and action. This unit of analysis allows me to elaborate my view on short-term goals and to connect my views with the theorising and research in an important action-oriented tradition. The analysis presented allows me to clarify how 'reports' are learned, thereby clarifying how the mind uses the brain for controlling the body in report tasks; that is, to solve the mind–body problem for report tasks.

In Section 9.4, the views presented are generalised. It is shown that with the two units of analysis distinguished, it is possible to account for observed task performance in a broad variety of experimental situations and ecologically valid real-life situations.

9.1   Two units of analysis

In *Plans and the Structure of Behavior*, Miller et al. (1960) make two important successive steps. First, in the chapter 'Images and Plans' (Ch. 1), a distinction is introduced between 'the image' and 'the plans'; the image is all the accumulated, organised knowledge that the organism has about itself and its world (p. 17) and a plan is any hierarchical process in the organism that can control the order in which a sequence of operations is to be performed (p. 16). Then, in the chapter 'The Unit of Analysis' (Ch. 2), the Test-Operate-Test . . . Exit, i.e., TOTE, unit is introduced as a general description of the control processes; that is, as the basic building block of the plans (see also Section 3.2). So, Miller et al. were convinced that the

>> Test > Operate >>

unit, given an appropriate exit, was a unit of analysis that could capture the control aspects of all important and/or interesting internal and external (human) behaviour (hammering, grasping, remembering, searching, planning, speaking, driving, walking, etc.).

From what was said in the preceding chapters, it will be clear that my line of theorising is in some respects very close to Miller et al.'s (1960) line of thought. First, just like Miller et al., who distinguish between 'the image' and 'the plans', I introduced and elaborated a comparable distinction between Visual Perception and Intending Mind with a Verbal Intention or intentional sequence. Because I am concerned with the use of visual information for task performance and not, as Miller et al., with task performance in general, my restricted Visual Perception plays the role of their general 'image' and my restricted Verbal Intention or intentional sequence plays the role of their general 'plans'. Second, just like Miller et al., who regard the >> Test > Operate >> unit as the basic building block of their plans, I introduced and elaborated the >> X > Y >> unit as the basic building block of the intentional sequence or Verbal Intention for report tasks, i.e., name and read tasks.

As is well known, Miller et al.'s (1960) >> Test > Operate >> unit has never really flowered in subsequent theoretical work and has not survived on the theoretical battlefield. Reasons for the rather cool reception and relatively fast disappearance of the >> Test > Operate >> unit are not too difficult to find. One important reason must, of course, have been that Miller and colleagues had no real place for 'attention' and 'the effects of attention' in their theorising, while that topic subsequently, especially after Broadbent (1958), became the core of the research endeavour and the theorising in visual information processing psychology.[2] Another important reason might, of course, have been that their broad-stroke theorising was incomplete and, because it missed an essential part, was not compatible with the detailed empirical findings produced by the experimental research of the information processing approach. Other reasons can certainly be found but, because I do not need additional reasons, I restrict myself to the 'attention' reason and the 'completeness' reason, the two reasons just mentioned. I start by elaborating the completeness reason.

As just stated, it cannot be excluded that Miller et al.'s (1960) broad-stroke theorising never really flowered and did not survive the theoretical battlefield because it was incomplete and, because it missed an essential part, was not compatible with the detailed empirical findings of the information processing approach. That Miller et al.'s analysis was indeed incomplete and that at least two different units of analysis have to be recognised – one like Miller et al.'s >> Test > Operate >> unit for the performance of act tasks and one like my >> X > Y >> unit for the performance in name and read tasks – can be made clear with a simple example. Let us look again at the partial-report bar-probe task, the task from which we now know about all there is to know (see Sections 2.3, 5.3, 7.2, and 8.1).

- In Section 5.3 I was concerned with this task as a read task. There I described how, in my conceptualisation, the correct answer is arrived at. Intentional sequence state X first selects the object indicated by the bar marker and intentional sequence state Y then selects the required shape information for subsequent report.

- In Section 8.1 I was concerned with this task as an act task. There I described how, in my conceptualisation, a saccadic eye movement to the object indicated by the bar marker is made. Intentional sequence state X selects the object indicated by the bar marker and the start of this object selection stage is the initiation of the program for a saccadic eye movement to the position of the selected object.

So, what we then have in this partial-report bar-probe task, where subjects report the letter and make a saccadic eye movement to its position, is an intentional sequence of the form

>> X/eye movement > Y/verbal report >>.

Term X selects all properties of the relevant object. Thereby term X determines the goal (the parameters) of the saccadic eye movement. For that saccadic eye movement no term Y is required. To receive the shape information required for verbal report, a term Y, determining the content (the parameters) of that verbal report, is required in addition.

Most eye movement researchers are not interested in the verbal report aspect of this task. When we, with them, now look at this task as a pure eye movement task or act task, and simply neglect the fact that the subject has also to read the letter, we see that for the control of the eye an

>> X/eye movement > . . . . >>   (1)

unit (or >> Test > Operate >> unit) suffices.[3] The object is selected and 'direct parameter specification' takes care of the further execution of the saccadic eye movement (see Chapter 8).[4]

Most information processing psychologists are not interested in the eye movement aspect of this task. When we, with them, now alternatively look at this task as a pure letter report task or read task, and simply neglect the fact that the subjects also make a saccadic eye movement, we see that for the control of the report an

>> X > Y/verbal report >>   (2)

unit is required. The object is selected and a subsequent attribute selection takes care that the letter aspect of that object is going to control the report (see Chapters 4, 5, and 6).

This example shows that in this task two different units of analysis can be distinguished:

- An >> X/saccadic eye movement > . . . . >> unit for the saccadic eye movement.[5] This unit of analysis is close to the one emphasised by Miller et al. (1960) for actions in general. So, their >> Test > Operate >>

unit (or >> Test/operate > . . . . >> unit) is possibly adequate to account for task performance in what I called act tasks in Chapter 2 (e.g., hitting a nail or grasping an object). I turn later to that adequacy.

• An >> X > Y/verbal report >> unit for the verbal report of the letter. This is the unit of analysis for report tasks, i.e., name and read tasks, that I introduced and emphasised in this work and used in Chapters 5 and 6 to explain observed performance in a variety of experimental tasks such as the rapid serial visual presentation task and the Stroop task. I do not return to the adequacy of this unit.

The report tasks, in which the subjects have to express a proposition, e.g., 'that square is red' or 'the letter indicated is a Z', are the tasks that are most often used in the research of the information processing approach. So, if my diagnosis is correct, Miller et al. (1960) simply missed the unit of analysis for the tasks with which, after the publication of their work, mainstream experimental psychology became mainly concerned. The act tasks, in which subjects just have to do something in or to the world, e.g., to hit a ball with the head or to hammer a nail into a piece of wood, were never in the focus of interest of the information processing approach. So, Miller et al. emphasised the unit of analysis that was of minor importance for the mainstream information processing approach.

Of course, a complete theory of task performance using vision has to deal with tasks in which subjects are expressing a proposition and tasks in which subjects are not expressing a proposition but are changing something in the world. And my final position with regard to the units of analysis required for task performance using vision will by now be clear. In my view, to account for the use of visual information for task performance, two different units of analysis are required – an >> X > Y/report >> unit in control in report tasks and an >> X/act > . . . >> unit in control in act tasks.[6]

The functions of X and Y in these units of analysis have been specified in the preceding chapters. For the report part of >> X > Y/report >> tasks and for the act part of >> X/act > . . . >> tasks, devoted action modules are required. What devoted action module(s) get(s) involved in task performance is determined by the task that has to be performed, i.e., is instruction- or task-dependent. In one way or another, the acceptation of and commitment to an (instruction-derived) task must be capable of invoking and assembling the appropriate and required devoted executive modules in the sensorimotor system. When that has happened, a further cognitive control of the *execution* of the overt report or overt act is not required. In fact, in my conceptualisation, with acts and reports controlled by a single unit of analysis, that cognitive control of the overt act or report is simply impossible; in my conceptualisation acts and reports controlled by a single unit of analysis are best regarded as 'ballistic' acts and reports (see later).

As stated, it also cannot be excluded that Miller et al.'s (1960) theoretical views never really flowered and did not survive the theoretical battlefield because the theory had no real place for 'attention' and 'the effects of attention'.[7] The replacement of term Test in Miller et al's (1960) >> Test > Operate >> unit by term X in the >> X/act > . . . >> unit, 'updates' Miller et al.'s unit of analysis in this respect and brings it on speaking terms with the findings and insights of contemporary information processing psychology. The following two points make this 'updating' more clear:

- Miller et al.'s term Test assesses the *difference* between a desired state and an actual state, a difference essential in control and automaton theory. In line with the interests of and the results provided by the current information processing approach, term X performs *object/ region* selection.
- Miller et al.'s term Test determines *whether* an action is appropriate, an issue closely related with a psychology of values and motivations. In line with the interests of and the results provided by the current information processing approach, term X determines *what* object/region in space the action has to be directed at.

So, in my information processing point of view, besides the >> X > Y/report >> unit for reports, we need the >> X/act > . . . >> unit, not the >> Test > Operate >> unit, for acts.[8]

That this change from 'Test' to 'X' really updates Miller et al's (1960) theorising and brings it in line with the current theorising in the information processing approach can also be demonstrated and defended in the following way. The, in my view, highly interesting point is that the >> X/act > . . . >> unit of analysis is completely consistent with, and only formalises and summarises, the important theoretical work of the theorists in the perception for action camp in the current information processing approach, the work that we have already met in Chapter 2. In that chapter, I mentioned that Allport (1987, 1989) and Neumann (1987, 1990a) emphasised that perception is for action and showed that in this use of perception for action two selection mechanisms are involved:

- A selection mechanism in charge of determining which action is given priority at a certain moment in time. In the unit of analysis for act tasks, >> X/act > . . . >>, the term '/act' captures this action selection aspect.
- A selection mechanism determining which object is acted upon at a certain moment in time. In the unit of analysis for act tasks, >> X/act > . . . >>, the term 'X' captures this object selection aspect.

So, by replacing Miller et al.'s (1960) 'Test' by my 'X', Allport and Neumann's important theoretical work on perception and selection for action finds a proper and disciplined place in my complete and final information processing theory.

That in general a principled distinction between report (name and read) tasks and act tasks along the lines just indicated – >> X > Y/report >> and >> X/act > . . . >> – can and has to be made, can be demonstrated in a great number of ways. Of course, Miller et al.'s (1960), Allport's (1987, 1989), and Neumann's (1987, 1990a) theoretical work, emphasising the necessity of some kind of X/act unit for action, and my theoretical work in Part II of this book, emphasising the necessity of an X > Y/report unit for report, already sufficiently supports this position. In the remainder of this chapter, in Sections 9.2 and 9.3, some further demonstrations based on objective behavioural evidence are presented. I end this section with some demonstrations based on subjective evidence, obtained with introspection.

For seeing that a distinction between >> X > Y/report >> tasks and >> X/ act > . . . >> tasks is also welcome for clearing and cleaning up our introspection, consider, as an example, the following two quotations.[9]

> It is surely true that speech and language convey information of a certain sort from person to person . . . The human observer can verbalize his awareness, and the result is to make it communicable. But my hypothesis is that there has to be an awareness of the world before it can be put into words. You have to see it before you can say it. Perceiving precedes predicating.
>
> (Gibson, 1979, p. 260)

> When we apperceive the stimulus, we have as a rule already started responding to it. Our motor apparatus does not wait for our conscious awareness, but does restlessly its duty, and our consciousness watches it and has no right to give it orders.
>
> (Münsterberg, 1889, p. 173; Neumann, 1990b, trans.)

So, in Gibson's view, before 'a task' can be performed, 'awareness' of the world is required, while in Münsterberg's view, in the performance of 'a task' the motor apparatus does not wait for 'conscious awareness'.

Of course, it is highly likely that Gibson and Münsterberg are talking about different types of tasks; verbal report tasks in Gibson's case and motor act tasks in Münsterberg's case. According to Gibson (1979), 'perceiving precedes predicating', and the unit of analysis >> X > Y/report >> was especially designed for the internal construction of propositions and therefore accounts for that 'perceiving' that precedes the 'predicating' (see Section 4.3). And, according to Münsterberg (1889), 'our consciousness watches our motor apparatus', and the unit of analysis >> X/act > . . . >> has indeed an 'empty' interval of time, > . . . >>, in which 'consciousness' gets the opportunity to watch what the 'motor apparatus' is doing.

However, when it is agreed that Gibson (1979) and Münsterberg (1889) are indeed talking about different types of tasks, report tasks and act tasks, it is not just the problem of how to formulate the distinction between the two types of tasks in terms of internal operations and units of analysis that deserves an answer. Then the problem also arises of how to formulate that distinction in terms of corresponding 'awarenesses' or 'consciousneness'. That 'awareness' or 'consciousness' problem is a complicated one, because the available 'awareness' or 'consciousness' theories allow only a crude presence –absence dichotomy. What can be expressed in terms of these theories is not much more than: there are tasks that for their performance require awareness (before something can be put into words, i.e., a report can be given) and there are tasks that for their performance do not need conscious awareness (before the motor apparatus does its duty, i.e., an act can be performed).[10]

The theoretical position, that (a) two different units of analysis (b) of the type just specified, have to be postulated, does not force me into the counter-intuitive and therefore unattractive theoretical position that with report tasks (conscious) awareness is involved, but not with act tasks. Term X and term Y can be related to a different aspect of the contents of conscious awareness – X to awareness of a region or an object and Y to awareness of a property or an attribute of that region or object. The difference between the two units of analysis is then not in terms of whether or not (conscious) awareness is involved, but in terms of how conscious awareness is involved.

* With the $>> X > Y$/report $>>$ unit, both the content of X and of Y are accessible to cognition before the overt report (perception is used twice). This control unit is used in reporting or describing some of the contents and/or the properties of the mental representation. Examples are the unit for reporting that in this trial of a selective attention study 'the *square* is *red*' or the unit for reporting that in this trial of a position judgement task 'the *spot* is on the *left*'.
* With the $>> X$/act $> ... >>$ unit, only the content of X is accessible to cognition before the overt act; the overt act is controlled through 'direct parameter specification' (perception is used once). This unit is used in instrumental acts that change the world. Examples are the unit for selecting the *light* to be pointed at, or the unit for selecting the *object* to be grasped.[11] I turn to what happens in the 'empty' interval of time, $> .... >>$ at the end of this section.

So, with the assumption that there are two different types of units with the structure specified here, the crude dichotomy between aware and not aware is not required. At variance with most current proposals, I can assume that in the internal control of report (name and read) tasks, perceptual awareness is involved twice (X and Y), not once. And, at variance with most current proposals, I can assume that in the internal control of act tasks perceptual awareness is also involved once (X), not only automatic 'direct parameter specification'. So, here it appears that a two-units-of-analysis view, as proposed in this section, directly leads to a more adequate and more detailed understanding of the involvement of 'awareness' or 'conscious awareness' in the control of task performance.[12]

In this context, it is worthwhile to return briefly to Lange's (1888) sensorial and muscular reaction times – the different reaction times obtained after extended practice in experiments with identical stimuli (a single light) and identical responses (a simple button push) but with different instructions (see also Sections 2.2 and 3.1). In the past, these results were explained in terms of perception and apperception (Lange and Wundt) and in terms of habit and attention (Angell and Moore). Given the distinction between report tasks and act tasks that we now have arrived at, the difference between the sensorial task and the muscular task as well as one longstanding theoretical issue can be further clarified.[13]

In the conceptualisation presented here, the 'sensorial' task is a report task that requires an intentional sequence of the form >> X > Y/report >>. In Wundt's terminology 'apperception' is required. The 'muscular' task is an act task that only requires an 'aborted' intentional sequence of the form >> X/act > . . . >>. In Wundt's terminology only 'perception' is required. Of course, given this interpretation it is not unexpected that shorter RTs are obtained under the 'simple' X/act instruction than under the 'more complicated' X > Y/report instruction.[14] And of course, it is highly satisfying to find that, after more than a hundred years of guesses and discussions, it now becomes clear what exactly the difference between Wundt's apperception and perception is. In terms of experienced internal control operations: (Apperception) minus (Perception) = (X > Y) minus (X) = Y, i.e., attribute selection and the corresponding awareness of that attribute![15]

One last introspective remark is in order here. It concerns what happens, or can happen, in the empty interval of time indicated with > . . . >> in the >> X/act > . . . >> unit of analysis. In my view, in this interval of time three things can happen and often do happen (however, see also Section 9.4). First, in this interval of time an expectation can arise and/or exist about the effects the selected act is going to produce in the outer world, for instance the expectation that the red object there is now going to be grasped. Second, in this interval of time the performance of the selected act and the results of that performance in the outer world can be perceived, for instance the movement of the hand and the actual grasping of the red object. Third, just because there is an anticipating expectation and an actual perception, in this interval of time it can be assessed whether things go as wished. The information, the feedback, obtained in this interval of time can be at the basis of the learning and/or the improvement of the performance of acts.[16]

9.2 The cognitive control of acts

In Chapter 2, Section 2.2, I introduced Bridgeman's (1992, 1999a) intriguing empirical and theoretical work concerned with the perception of spatial position. I described how his theoretical work started with a paradox or dissociation. Evidence indicated that '. . . perception can suffer spatial illusions that are not shared in spatial behavior, and visually guided behavioral orientation can be modified without affecting perception' (Bridgeman, 1992, p. 79). The evidence led him to a distinction between 'perceptual tasks' with a 'symbolic output' (a cognitive measure) and 'behavioral tasks' with 'isomorphic motor responses' (a motor measure). In terms of acts, instead of tasks, the distinction is between 'communicatory' acts through which subjects are 'offering their opinion about target position to the experimenter' and 'instrumental' acts in which subjects 'do something to the world rather than simply indicate a position to another person.'

From this brief exposition it will be clear that what we meet here is exactly my 'report' – 'act' distinction.[17] The 'perceptual tasks with a symbolic output' in which subjects are 'offering their opinion about target position to the experimenter' are the '>> X > Y/report >>' tasks and the 'behavioral tasks with isomorphic output' in which subjects 'do something to the world rather than simply indicate a position to another person' are the '>> X/act > . . . >>' tasks. And, it will also be clear that in my conceptualisation the fact that different results are obtained with the two types of tasks is not completely unexpected. When 'output' is neglected, it is easy to see that, as far as cognition is involved, there is an important difference between the two types of tasks – a difference consisting in $(X > Y) - (X) = (Y)$, i.e., in attribute selection (see also Section 9.1).

Given this analysis, the remaining problem is, of course, that of how to conceive this difference in attribute selection in such a way that the paradoxes or dissociations can be understood. It is not too difficult to see in general terms in what direction a solution has to be sought. In one way or another, the presence of a cognitive state concerned with attribute selection in the report task with its Y/report transition and the absence of such a cognitive state in the act task with its X/act transition, must be at the basis of the dissociation. Let us first look at Bridgeman's (1992, 1999a) explanations for some more detail.

Bridgeman (1992, 1999a) finds the core of his explanation for the dissociations in the given that 'two visual systems' with different properties can be distinguished – a 'cognitive' or 'what' system and a 'sensorimotor' or 'how' system (see Chapter 2 for a brief description):

> An interpretation of the [behavioural evidence] that is consistent with cortical neurophysiology, as well as with the literature . . . , is that the cognitive and motor measures access information from different maps of visual space. The motor map is accessed by a pointing measure that requires a 1:1 relationship between stimulus position and behavior . . . The cognitive map, in contrast, requires a categorization in which the relationship between target position and behavior is arbitrary. Thus the normal human possesses two maps of visual space.
>
> (Bridgeman, 1992, p. 83; see also Bridgeman, 1999a, pp. 10–11)

For one or another reason, and in my view for a good reason, Bridgeman (1999a) is not fully satisfied with this explanation.[18] He adds a second explanation to this core explanation where he discusses the relation between the 'cognitive or "what" system' and the 'sensorimotor or "how" system'. Bridgeman (1999a, p. 3) is well aware that:

> In some circumstances the two systems must communicate with one another. For example, motor activities are usually initiated when the cognitive system informs the sensorimotor system about what to do – to grasp one of several available objects, to poke a particular button, etc.

With regard to this communication, Bridgeman (1992, p. 85) only remarks: 'It is likely that the two modes are not independent, but that limited information exchange occurs even at the most central levels. This is an area that needs further investigation.' Bridgeman (1999a, pp. 10–11) is much more explicit in this regard. He remarks:

> It is not clear how the communication is accomplished, because the codes of the cognitive and the sensorimotor systems should be incompatible. The cognitive system's code for visual information is object-centered, with spatial relations represented as relations among visual objects. Location is not coded relative to the body, at least not with an accuracy comparable to the egocentric calibration in the motor system. The ubiquity of . . . context-based illusions in perception . . . is evidence for this . . . The sensorimotor system, in contrast, possesses an egocentric calibration that is insensitive to visual context and is inaccessible to perception, but can be used to control visually guided behavior . . .

And he then suggests:

> Oculomotor position, driven by visual attention, might link the two incompatible codes. If selective attention makes the fixation position the only relevant location for the sensorimotor system, visual space would collapse around that single point, and context would become irrelevant . . .
> This theory would require either oculomotor fixation on the intended target or a planned saccade to the target, however . . .
>   (Bridgeman, 1999a, pp. 11–12)

I am well aware that this suggestion is not all too clear. Fortunately, here it is only of importance to notice that we have already met an explanation like Bridgeman's additional explanation. That explanation was presented in Section 8.1 where we were concerned with the problem of how positions in a cognitive map, P/M, could control (saccadic) eye movements (see Figure 8.1). Let us briefly return to that explanation.

The solution to the problem of the cognitive control of saccadic eye movements, proposed in Section 8.1, involved two maps – a cognitive map, P/M, concerned with the perception of spatial position, and a motor map, the eye movement control unit, EMC, with only an executive function, not a cognitive function (see also Findlay & Walker, 1999). Map P/M is one of the maps in Bridgeman's 'cognitive system' and the control unit EMC is one of the maps in Bridgeman's 'sensorimotor system'. In the cognitive map P/M, external positions are coded in terms of eye positions. In the executive control unit EMC, each spatial position specifies one and only one eye movement. The positions in P/M are one–one hardware-connected with the corresponding map positions in the EMC (see Figure 8.1). This complete construction effectuates that enhanced activation in a region in P/M, i.e., 'selective attention' in the cognitive system, results in enhanced activation on the corresponding position in the EMC, i.e., 'collapses space around a single point' in the 'sensorimotor system'. That 'single point' or position in the EMC triggers its saccadic eye movement. The selection of the position of the target in map P/M is simultaneously (after a small P/M – EMC transition delay) the selection of the parameters of the saccadic eye movement to the target position.

It will by now be clear that Bridgeman's (1999a) story about the cognitive and executive control of pointing is very close to the story I have already told about the cognitive and executive control of saccadic eye movements. Figure 9.1 serves to make this more clear. In that figure we meet again the cognitive map, P/M. Now another motor map – a hand movement control unit, HMC, with executive, not cognitive, functions – is inserted. The HMC is one of the maps in Bridgeman's 'sensorimotor system'. It receives its information directly from the eye. In the HMC, the actual hand position, H1, is represented in fovea-centred retinal coordinates. Each other spatial position in the HMC specifies one and only one unique and fixed hand position in fovea-centred retinal coordinates. The positions in P/M are one–one hardware-connected with the corresponding positions in the HMC (see the figure). Enhanced activation in a region in P/M results in enhanced activation on the corresponding retinotopic position in the HMC. The selection of a target, T, in P/M is simultaneously (after some small transition delay) the selection of the required position of the hand at target position T, H2, in the HMC. The required hand movement, M, equals H2 – H1.[19] So, if the HMC codes the actual and possible retinal positions of the hand on its positions, after the cognitive selection of the target, T, in P/M, the HMC contains the necessary information for the execution of the hand movement towards Target T.[20]

The theoretically interesting point is now that, given this conceptualisation of the cognitive control of pointing, no further explanatory ingredients are required for the explanation of the behavioural dissociation data. Moreover, in this conceptualisation there is no problem of incompatible codes that

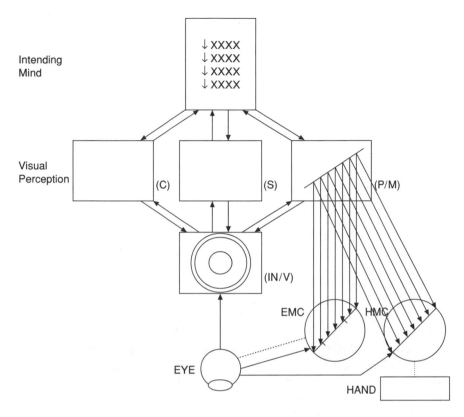

Figure 9.1 Tentative model for the generation of a hand movement consisting of the perception, selection, and saccadic eye movement model of Figure 8.1 with a hand movement control unit (HMC) controlling the hand (dotted line). (See text for further explanation.)

have to 'communicate', as Bridgeman (1999a) suggests. To see this, we first need to have a closer look at the exact nature of the dissociations.

A closer look at the dissociation data readily indicates that in all findings reported by Bridgeman and associates, perception faces problems (is context-sensitive and susceptible to various illusions) but motor action (virtually) does not (see Bridgeman, 1992, 1999a, for overviews). So, the double dissociations are always dissociations heading in one direction: correct performance when a motor measure (e.g., pointing or jabbing) is used and erroneous perform-ance when a perceptual measure (e.g., reporting or indicating) is used. There are no reported cases that – as the term 'double dissociations' might pos-sibly suggest – head in the opposite direction, i.e., double dissociations in which perception appears veridical (e.g., as indicated by verbal report) but something goes wrong with the motor action (e.g., as revealed by pointing). Indeed,

In the end the brain benefits from the dual representation, because it can use both pattern recognition based on context information and unbiased spatial action in the control of visually guided behavior.

(Bridgeman, 1999a, p. 12)

As a next step, it is of importance to consider what effects the visual stimulation, used in the double dissociation experiments, brings about or causes in map HMC, which is at the basis of Bridgeman's 'motor measure', and in map P/M, which is accessed by Bridgeman's 'cognitive measure'.

For the HMC the situation is simple. As stated, the HMC is one of the maps in Bridgeman's 'sensorimotor system' that directly receives its information from the eye (see Figure 9.1). In the HMC the actual hand position is coded in retinotopic coordinates and each further spatial position in that map specifies one and only one possible hand position.

To understand the effect of visual stimulation in P/M, let us look at one case or condition in detail, the condition with a fixed target in front of the subject and a background that is displaced left right left right etc. (see also Section 2.2). To describe the effects this stimulus brings about in P/M, we need the distinction that I have already introduced and used in Chapter 7; the distinction between 'the code for position' and 'the position of a code'. With this distinction it is easy to see that in the fixed target and shifting background condition *the code for position of the target* changes under the influence of the background (the subject's reports indicate the illusion; so something influenced the code for position of the target). In this condition, however, *the position of the code for position of the target* remains the same despite the movement of the background (map P/M, as all other maps, is simply hardware-connected with the retina, so the moving background does not alter or influence the position of the code for position of the target).

With the two maps, the HMC and P/M, and with this analysis in terms of code for position and position of code, it is not difficult to explain what happened in Bridgeman's 'communication' tasks (the '>> X > Y/report >>' tasks) and 'instrumental' tasks (the '>> X/act > . . . >>' tasks) and to explain the dissociation(s).

In the >> X > Y/report >> tasks or communication tasks, an intentional sequence state, X, selects one of the available objects (the target; not the moving frame or an object in the background) with all its properties. After that selection, a subsequent intentional sequence state, Y, receives or 'processes' the to-be-reported attribute. That state Y receives the code for position from a 'cognitive map', i.e., from map P/M in Figure 9.1. This code for position suffers from the illusion induced by the frame (see the evidence above). So, the verbal expression of this code for position, the report of the position, will reveal the effect of the moving frame, i.e., of the illusion.

In the >> X/act > . . . >> tasks or instrumental tasks, again an intentional sequence state, X, selects one of the available objects (the target) with all its properties. Because all properties are selected, the property position is also selected. The property position is coded on a position in a 'cognitive map', i.e., in map P/M in Figure 9.1. That position does not suffer from the illusion induced by the frame (see above). The positions in P/M and the corresponding positions in HMC are hardware-connected. So, if a code for position in P/M is selected, the position of that code for position can 'trace' and 'select', i.e., 'address' and 'arouse', the corresponding position in HMC and thereby the parameters required for the action (see above). Because in this 'hardware' selection not position codes but code positions and their hardware connections are involved, there is simply no problem of incompatible codes. Moreover, because in this hardware selection not illusion-prone position codes but illusion-immune code positions are involved, no effect of the illusion in map P/M will show up in the execution of the overt action. And, with its lifetime of feedback about its performance in the outer world, in the system as conceptualised errorless performance is to be expected (see Section 9.1 for this feedback).

As explained at the start of this section, my conceptualisation forces me to assume that there is an essential difference between communication tasks and instrumental tasks. That difference will now be clear. In communication tasks a sequence state Y, concerned with attribute selection, selects the *code* required for report. In instrumental tasks, however, no state Y is involved. Because no state Y is involved, there is no need to assume that a code is involved in the communication between maps. Because state X selects codes *on positions*, one can also assume that it is the *position* of the selected code that is involved in the selection of the parameter(s) required for action. Activation on that position triggers via appropriate hardware position–position connections the required motor code. In this way Bridgeman's (1992, 1999a) dissociations as well as Bridgeman's theoretical view on these dissociations are easily understood in terms of the conceptualisation here presented.[21]

In general, my position is that in all communication tasks or 'report' tasks, cognitive states, i.e., codes, are involved in the selection of the object and of the attribute required for report. And, in general, my position is that in all instrumental tasks or 'act' tasks, the 'cognitive' selection of an object suffices for the 'hardware' selection of the parameters required for the overt action (direct parameter specification in visual maps devoted to action, for instance, to reaching, grasping, and pointing).[22]

About the 'hardware' selection in act tasks one further remark is in order here. The important point is that the assumption that in act tasks the position of the selected code selects the parameters required for action in a devoted action module or set of devoted action modules is not simply another trivial assumption devoid of theoretical interest. This assumption is of crucial importance, because it points to the way to solve the mind–body problem, i.e., the problem of how an experienced visual object can be effective in such a way that it can put the body to work in the outer world. That problem is not solved with theorising in terms of (incompatible) codes that have to communicate. With 'codes' that interact and with 'communication between codes', the theorising remains on one and the same level. For solving the mind–body problem, a real boundary has to be crossed.

The solution for the mind–body problem, captured by the assumption, is that there are two incompatible levels that do not communicate but are simply hardware-connected. What is experienced are patterns of activation, the visual codes, on positions in the cognitive part of the brain, in Bridgeman's 'cognitive' system. Actions are controlled by cognitively inaccessible patterns of activation, the motor 'codes', on positions in the executive part of the brain, in Bridgeman's 'sensorimotor' system. The 'cognitive' system does not communicate with the 'sensorimotor' system by sending codes, propagating patterns of activation, or transmitting information. The cognitive system only arouses or triggers the executive system via position–position connections. Not the pattern of activation, but only the activation of the pattern, is involved in this 'communication'.

So, the solution for the mind–body problem captured by the assumption is:

Code on Position/Position of code > Position of 'Code'/'Code' for action,

or, in abbreviated form,

Mind/Brain > Brain/Body,

with position–position connections between anatomical maps in the 'cognitive' and 'sensorimotor' parts of the brain as the bridge between Mind and Body.

What act the executive system has performed in the outer world, and whether it has executed that act as intended, the cognitive system only experiences after the act, in the 'empty' > . . . >> part of the unit of analysis >> X/act > . . . >> (see Section 9.1).

9.3 Control by short-term goals

Over the years, Prinz has consistently worked on a theory of the relation between perception and action (see, e.g., Prinz, 1987, 1990, 1997a, 1997b; see also Hommel, 1997). For a number of reasons it is worthwhile to consider the theoretical views at which he ultimately arrived. One reason is that in several works Prinz explicitly recognises that instructions (in experiments) and tasks (in real-life situations) have to be incorporated in the theorising, and indicates the lines along which that can be done. Another reason is that Prinz proposes a single unit of analysis that, at first sight, is not unlike the units of analysis I am proposing and defending in this work. Still another reason is that, with his theoretical help, I can introduce and further elaborate my ambitions and views with regard to goals. And a last reason is that in this theoretical context I can clarify my view on the cognitive control of reports. In this section I restrict myself to the theoretical work in Prinz (1997b) and to the closely related views in Hommel (1997). I start with goals.

The topic of 'goals' is a difficult one for a cognitive psychologist to cope with. The reason is that in the concept 'goal' not only cognitive factors but also motivational factors have to be recognised. In my view, the reasons *why* an organism selects a goal and tries to attain that selected goal do not belong to the province of cognitive psychology proper. That is a topic for the psychology of motivation. What remains then for the cognitive psychologist is to elucidate *how* a goal is reached, given that a goal is selected. Remember that in the previous chapters nothing was said about *why* a subject was willing to perform in a partial-report bar-probe task and about why a subject was willing to perform according to the instruction. That she/ he was willing to perform and to perform according to the instruction was simply taken for granted. What was explained was how the subject was capable of performing the task, given the fact that she/he was willing to perform the task and of doing that according to the instruction (see Miller et al., 1960, Ch. 4, for an intriguing discussion of this motivation–cognition distinction).

Even when we restrict ourselves to the cognitive aspects of goals, however, the theoretical scene is still very complicated. These complications arise because, especially for real-life tasks, the goals are difficult to specify. To see where these complications come from, it is worthwhile to have a brief look at a remark Prinz (1997b) makes with regard to goals. Prinz correctly notices a fundamental distinction:

> Goals vary along several dimensions: For instance, they can be quite concrete (e.g., catching a rolling ball with a particular grip) or rather abstract (e.g., winning a game of chess).
>
> (Prinz, 1997b, p. 253)

It can be argued, however, that this analysis is incomplete and is in need of further elaboration. A simple rephrasing of the quotation might make the relevant issue already clear:

> Goals vary along several dimensions: For instance, they can be quite concrete (e.g., catching a rolling ball with a particular grip or picking a bishop with the right hand) or rather abstract (e.g., winning a ball game or winning a game of chess).

The relevant point here is that in all interesting human behaviour, at each moment of time, more goals are simultaneously involved; ranging from long-term, abstract goals (e.g., having a nice and productive day), via a diversity of intermediate goals (e.g., winning this game of chess), to short-term, concrete goals (e.g., picking the bishop with the right hand). And the issue that must first be agreed upon is, of course, the issue of what types of goals we are talking about.[23]

My conviction is that the complicated issue of the control of actions by goals is best approached by a divide and conquer technique. In this section, therefore, I only look at short-term goals – those that can be reached with tasks controlled by a single unit of analysis, i.e., by one $>> X > Y$/report $>>$ or one $>> X$/act $> \ldots >>$ unit (or by a simple concatenation of units; see later). So, I restrict my analysis to what I called 'ballistic' acts and reports (see Section 9.1). To some aspects of the issue of how intermediate goals can be reached, i.e., to stretches of behaviour controlled by a series or chain of units of analysis, I turn in the next section. Let us now look at the kernel of Prinz's (1997b) theoretical views with regard to goals.

The theory of the cognitive control of behaviour Prinz (1997b) works with, contains three theoretical entities; a 'stimulus code' (SC), a 'goal code' (GC), and a 'movement code' (MC). With these three theoretical entities, for all (experimental and real-life) tasks, the relation between perception and action can be summarised with:

[SC][GC][MC].

This is Prinz's unit of analysis. This unit of analysis is derived from an important consideration and two essential assumptions.

In the context of this work, the important consideration is that a stimulus just gives rise to a stimulus code [SC] and to nothing more and that this is clearly insufficient for task performance. For goal-directed task performance there has to be in addition an appropriate instruction (or task) derived intention. Within the information processing system, that intention is implemented as an 'action code' consisting of a goal code [GC] and a movement or motor code [MC], i.e., of [GC][MC].

The first assumption is that the stimulus code [SC] and the goal code [GC] are in the same representational domain; both the stimulus code and the goal code represent events in the world and are therefore 'made of the same stuff'. This is the 'common coding' assumption. In Prinz's theory there is a representational gap between the goal code and the motor code but not between the stimulus code and the goal code.[24]

The second assumption is that the goal code [GC] represents events to be realised in the outer world. It represents instruction (or task) derived intended and anticipated events in the outer world that are continuous with the presently perceived events. These instruction (or task) derived intended and anticipated events as kinds of interfaces, play the critical causal role in the control of the (laboratory or real-life) action. This is the 'action effect' principle.[25]

From this brief exposition it will already be clear that there are a number of differences between Prinz's (1997b) unit of analysis and my units of analysis. In the present context, the most important difference concerns the first terms in the units of analysis, Prinz's term SC and my term X. With regard to this term the views agree and disagree. The views agree in the assumption that in the units of analysis the first term has always to refer in one or another way to a 'stimulus' or an 'object'. The views disagree, however, in what that first term has to express. In Prinz's view the first term, SC, stands for a 'stimulus code' that is simply given. In my view, the first term, X, stands for an internal operation that has to result in the availability of the 'stimulus code'. Because (a) in each experimental and real-life situation more potential stimuli are available, and (b) the now relevant stimulus is specified in the instruction or by the task to be performed, in my view X has to be preferred over SC.[26]

That in the units of analysis X has to be preferred over SC as an initial term becomes more clear when we have a closer look at the goal code, GC, in Prinz's (1997b) theorising and at the closely related 'action concepts' in Hommel's (1997) theoretical work. As stated, in Prinz's (1997b) theory, in the control of actions a goal code, GC, representing intended and anticipated events in the outer world, is involved and in control.[27] In this context it is worthwhile to know that Prinz faces serious difficulties in explaining where these goal codes come from and how they can exert their effect. Prinz (1997b, p. 254) notes that it is

> . . . puzzling . . . how goal codes could play a causal role in the *control* of movements. As movements must always be performed before their goals are attained, it is natural that the system can learn to 'expect', or anticipate, certain goal states when it performs certain movements, but less natural that goal codes can contribute to the activation of movement codes. Thus, in order to account for control, one has to find a way to act against the temporal order of events.[28]

In his 'action concept' model, Hommel (1997) expresses a point of view that is rather close to Prinz's (1997b) view. Hommel starts with and elaborates the view, advocated by Lotze and James in the 19th century, that associations between movements and effects are learned and that, after learning, (intended) effects can control (voluntary) movements. After the learning of the movement–effect correlations,

> . . . the *actor* is prepared to act voluntarily, that is, to produce intended effects by performing planned movements. Thus, the *actor* is not only able to anticipate movement effects before executing the movement, but *he* or *she* can also select among possible movements by choosing among codes of the effects they would produce. In other words, the cognitive control of voluntary action can be understood as choosing between and selectively activating codes of intended action effects.
>
> (Hommel, 1997, p. 286, italics mine)

Of course, with this model one is left with the nasty question of what that 'actor', that 'he or she', who chooses between and selectively activates codes, consists of.[29]

These unsolved 'backward association' problems arise, in my view, because the *outer appearance* of things is confused with the *inner order* of things. Of course, when we see somebody – an 'actor', a 'subject', a 'he', or a 'she' – acting, e.g., picking an apple, we see the arm and hand moving before the goal of the hand, the apple, is reached. This, however, does not entail that in the information processing system the movement is first and the goal of the hand is second. The information processing system works with codes, e.g., codes for apples on positions and codes for hands on positions. Within that information processing system there is no need to start with (codes for) hands that 'move' and subsequently arrive at (codes for) apples on positions. In that system it is equally possible to start with the (code for an) apple on a position that subsequently attracts, calls, or invites the (code for a) hand in another position; to start with 'attractors' that pull instead of with 'effectors' that have to be pushed.[30]

If we abandon the view that the outer appearance of things reflects the inner order of things, what happens in the performance of tasks with short-term goals can be phrased without any 'backward association' problems. What we have to assume then, is that goal-directed task performance does not start with a given stimulus or given stimulus code, SC, but with a stimulus that is selected by the system just because a goal has to be reached. That assumption makes stimulus selection the first step in goal-directed behaviour.

To show that, with the assumption that goal-directed task performance starts with goal-directed stimulus selection, 'backward associations' are not needed, I am going to confront the elements in my two units of analysis with the elements of Prinz's (1997b) unit of analysis. That confrontation can also make clear whether, and if so how, something like a 'goal code' is involved in my units of analysis that start with stimulus selection by state X and thereby clarify my view on short-term goals and on how these goals are attained. Let us first look at report tasks and then at act tasks.

For the report tasks consider, for illustration, a colour naming task. On each trial, the subject sees a single colour patch and has to name as fast as possible the colour of that patch (as in the control condition in the Stroop tasks in Section 6.2). In my view, in this task the subject's instruction-induced goal is to report, i.e., to communicate, as fast as possible the perceived colour to the experimenter. The question is: In the internal performance of this report-of-colour task, is something like a 'goal code' involved?

In my conceptualisation, because the goal is specified in the instruction, goal-directed task performance starts with an instruction or goal-derived intentional sequence of the form '>> X > Y/report >>' in place and waiting. Upon stimulus presentation, the internal operation starts with the selection of the relevant target by sequence state X. This selective operation results in the availability of the stimulus code, SC, in Prinz's unit of analysis. Then,

internal task performance continues with the selection of the instruction/
task-derived attribute of interest by the subsequent sequence state Y. This
selective operation results in the availability of something like the goal code,
GC, in Prinz's unit of analysis. In the last step the content of state Y is
overtly expressed in a report. This corresponds to the operation of Prinz's
motor code, MC. So, my expression '>> X > Y/report >>' is simply another
way of writing of Prinz's expression [SC] [GC] [MC].[31]

For the act tasks, consider, for illustration, the task of picking an apple.
There are many apples in the tree and one of these apples, a red and ripe
one, has to be picked. In my view, in this task the subject's (hunger-
induced?) goal is to have (and eat?) that apple. And the question to be
answered is: In the internal performance of the picking-the-apple task, is
something like a 'goal code' involved?

In my conceptualisation, because the system has learned and 'knows'
how to reach the goal, in such an act task goal-directed task performance
starts with a goal-derived intentional sequence >> X/act > . . . >> in place
and waiting. State X selects the relevant object or region resulting in the
availability of the stimulus code, SC. This stimulus code, however, not only
represents an object or a region. Because it is the selected task-relevant
object or region, it is *simultaneously* the target of the intended act; the target
for the act is simply given with the selected stimulus code.[32] And, because it
is the selected object, a devoted action module for picking, i.e., for the act,
can extract the required motor codes and execute the act ('direct parameter
specification'). This corresponds to Prinz's operation of the motor code,
MC. In this case, the expression '>> X/act > . . . >>' appears to be another
way of writing Prinz's [SC] [GC] [MC] expression, when it is seen that
in these act tasks in cognition the goal code, GC, and the stimulus code,
SC, coincide.[33]

So, in my conceptualisation, in act tasks there is not something like a
separate goal code, or, stated otherwise, the goal code, GC, coincides with
the stimulus code, SC.[34] It is worthwhile to note that we have already met a
similar situation twice. In Section 8.1 we saw that for a saccadic eye movement as an act, a selected/perceived object is not just a selected/perceived
object. The selected object is simultaneously the target of the saccadic
eye movement. The, implicit, representation of the position of the selected
object attracts the eye.[35] In Section 9.2 we saw that for a pointing movement
as an act, the selected/perceived object is not just a selected/perceived object.
The selected object is also the target of the pointing movement. The,
implicit, representation of the position of the selected object attracts the
hand.[36] In a similar vein, the selected/perceived apple is not just the selected/
perceived apple. It is simultaneously the target of the picking movement.
The, implicit, representation of the position of that selected apple attracts
the arm and the hand.[37]

In Prinz's (1997b) and Hommel's (1997) theorising, the 'goal codes' and
'action concepts' are rather mysterious theoretical concepts from which it is

far from clear how they can exert their effects (see above). In my view, the prime reason that Prinz and Hommel nevertheless insist on the involvement of these 'goal codes' or 'action concepts' has to be found in the type of experimental tasks with which they are mainly concerned in their theoretical work. The task that is central in both Prinz's and Hommel's theoretical work is the choice-reaction task. Prinz introduces this task as follows:

> Consider, for illustration, a choice-reaction task in which the subject has to press one of two keys (with, say, the left vs. right hand) in response to one of two lights (say, red vs. green). A task like this requires a mapping device that *translates*, as it were, colors into hands (or, more precisely, sensory codes representing colors into motor codes controlling muscles).
>
> (Prinz, 1997b, p. 251)

And the problem with this task is that, at first sight, it is difficult to decide what type of task we have here – an act task or a report task.

The interesting point here is that we have already met a similar or closely related experimental situation three times. To emphasise the correspondences between the paradigms, I characterise them using the same, uniform terminology.

- The first time we met a closely related experimental situation was in Section 5.3, where I discussed the use of a symbolic cue in position-cueing tasks. In this experimental situation, the subject is told that she/he has to select the stimulus element indicated by an arrow positioned in a neutral, non-informative position. The subject has to store the what-to-do-with-the-arrow part of the instruction as a set of condition–action rules in the Intending Mind. In this paradigm, upon appearance of the arrow, the arrow has to be selected and the appropriate rule has to be retrieved and applied in such a way that the required stimulus element is selected.
- The second time we were confronted with a similar situation was in Section 6.1, where I discussed MacLeod and Dunbar's (1988) shape naming task. In that shape naming task the subject was instructed to call the square 'red', the triangle 'blue', etc. The subject has to store the how-to-name-the-shapes part of the instruction as a set of condition–action rules in the Intending Mind. In this paradigm, upon appearance of a shape, the shape has to be selected and the appropriate condition–action rule has to be retrieved and used in such a way that the correct colour name is produced.
- The third time we met a similar situation was in Section 8.4, where I discussed Hallet's (1978) anti-saccade task. In this saccadic eye movement task, the subject is instructed that upon appearance of a peripheral target he/she should make a saccade in the opposite direction

from that target, i.e., further away from the target. The subject has to store the where-to-move-the-eye part of the instruction as a set of condition–action rules in the Intending Mind. In this paradigm, upon appearance of the target, the target has to be selected and the appropriate condition–action rule has to be retrieved and used in such a way that the correct eye movement is made.

Because I have already discussed this experimental situation three times, for the choice-reaction tasks I do not need to invoke any additional explanatory concepts. In line with what I said in Sections 5.3, 6.1, and 8.4, I have to assume that this task is performed with an intentional sequence of the form

$$>> Xv > Yv >> >> \{colour - Key\} >> >> Key/act > \ldots >>.$$

Upon stimulus presentation, sequence state Xv in the Intending Mind selects the visual stimulus with all its attributes. Then the sequence moves into state Yv and receives the colour attribute. In the Intending Mind is the instruction derived set of condition–action rules {'red – left key', 'green – right key'}. Because Yv is a state in the Intending Mind and because Yv receives the required information about the colour attribute, Yv is a state that can select the appropriate colour–key rule. The sequence then moves into state Key/act. That state takes the outcome of the 'processing' operation by Yv, the instruction and colour derived key, as its content (i.e., Key/act is the outcome of the interaction of the content of state Yv with the set of condition–action rules). Finally the, implicit, representation of the position of the key in Key/act attracts the hand, i.e., triggers the act.

This analysis shows that the choice-reaction task is basically a 'report' task – the system selects the colour for subsequent report with $>> Xv > Yv >>$. In this task, however, an arbitrary over-learned Yv/report transition is not used. The report is accomplished with an 'act' – the system reports the perceived colour, with the unit of analysis $>> Key/act > \ldots >>$, by hitting a key. In this task the set of {colour–key} rules in the Intending Mind forms a 'bridge' between the report part and the act part, and therefore the isomorphic Key/act transition can be used for report.[38]

This analysis also shows that in this choice-reaction task something like Prinz's (1997b) 'goal codes' or Hommel's (1997) 'action concepts' are indeed involved. In fact, the intentional sequence for this task presented above is Prinz's (1997b) unit of analysis [SC] [GC] [MC], with

[SC] = $>> Xv > Yv >>$,
[GC] = $>> \{colour - Key\}>>$, and
[MC] = $>> Key/act > \ldots >>$.

So, the 'bridge' between the report part, $>> Xv > Yv >>$, and the act part, $>> Key/act > \ldots >>$, that is, the set of {colour–key} rules, can thus indeed be regarded as a set of 'goal codes' or 'action concepts' that are separate from and follow the 'stimulus code'. That 'bridge' indeed represents instruction-derived intended and anticipated events in the world and plays, as a kind of interface, the critical causal role in the control of the act. So, Prinz and Hommel are right in insisting that in this type of choice-reaction task something like a 'goal code' or an 'action concept' is involved. But the choice-reaction task is a complicated, peculiar type of task. It is not a one-unit-of-analysis task but a three-units-of-analysis task. It is an >> X > Y/ report >> task in which an independent and unrelated >> X/act > .... >> task is made responsible for the overt report and a {colour–key} bridge is required to connect the two.

One further remark about choice-reaction tasks is in order. As set out in Section 6.1 in relation to MacLeod and Dunbar's (1988) experiments, with this task and experimental situation there are ample opportunities for learning. Here, one step in this learning process is worth consideration. This step becomes clear when I write what happens internally in this task not in terms of functions (see above), but in terms of contents. After receiving the instruction and after stimulus presentation, the system works with a sequence of contents that can be written as

>> STIMULUS > COLOUR >> >> {COLOUR – KEY} >> >> KEY/ act > .... >>.

It will be clear that, after sufficient practice, through association/assimilation this sequence can reduce to

>> STIMULUS > COLOUR – KEY/act >>

and, after extended practice to

>> STIMULUS > COLOUR/act >>

(see Hebb in Chapter 4). But then the choice-reaction task has become a regular 'report' task. The system has learned to report the colour of the stimulus with hand and key. This analysis underscores the point of view that the choice-reaction task is basically a report task, not an act task, albeit a peculiar type of report task.

This analysis also shows how a great variety of reports can be learned, i.e., how the cognitive control of reports is acquired (see also Section 6.1). In my conceptualisation, simply repeating a heard word, as a child often does, is an act, not a report. Selecting the colour of an object is constructing an internal proposition. Now assume that a child selects the colour of an object, then selects the corresponding colour word spoken by somebody else, and then repeats that word. In terms of contents, this internal sequence of events in the child can be summarised with:

>> STIMULUS > COLOUR >> >> WORD/act > . . . >>.

After sufficient practice this sequence will reduce to

>> STIMULUS > COLOUR/act >>

(see Hebb in Chapter 4). And this is the unit of analysis for report tasks. The child has learned the cognitive control of this report.

In general, in my preferred conceptualisation the basic units of analysis for cognition, i.e., of the mind, that everybody starts with are internal object selection units (>> X > . . . >>) and internal proposition selection units (>> X > Y >>). Overt acts can be learned through imitation and by trial and error with the help of the feedback received in the 'empty' part, > . . . >>, of the object selection unit of analysis, leading to the unit of analysis for act tasks, the >> X/act > . . . >> unit (see Section 9.1). Through association/assimilation, already learned acts can become connected with the Y part of the proposition selection unit, thereby leading to the unit of analysis for report tasks (>> X > Y/report >>), which allow the internal propositions to be expressed in overt reports (this section). In this conceptualisation, the cognitive control of 'isomorphic' acts, described in Section 9.2, comes first. The cognitive control of 'arbitrary' reports, elaborated in this section, comes later, and is based and built on the cognitive control of acts. Because learning to report is based on knowing how to act, the solution of the mind–body problem for 'ballistic' reports thus reduces to the solution of the mind–body problem for 'ballistic' acts.

Prinz's (1997b) and Hommel's (1997) theorising is of great importance because of the explicit recognition of goals and intentions. In my view, however, two types of tasks have to be distinguished. The first type of task is the >> X > Y/report >> task, in which the cognitive system makes a goal code explicit ('attribute selection' in order 'to know' what has to be reported). The second type of task is the >> X/act > . . . >> task, in which a goal code remains implicit and devoted action modules are in charge of attaining the goal ('direct parameter specification' in order 'to do' what is required). And with both tasks a term X, in charge of object/region selection, is required for attaining a short-term goal.[39]

9.4 The structure of behaviour

The emphasis on two simple units of analysis, one for act tasks and one for report tasks, can easily give the impression that the view on the control of overt (and covert; see later) action at which we have now arrived, is only applicable to the behaviour observed in simple laboratory tasks. This impression is wrong, however. What we have mainly looked at up to now have been the 'proper elements'. Now we can turn to 'the laws of their combination' (see Miller, 1964, in the Prologue). And it will appear that it is quite easy to generalise and extend the view we have now arrived at in such a way that much more complicated laboratory and real-life actions can also be accounted for, from reading textbooks to driving cars.

What follows is a brief look at the basic molecular structure, the skeleton, of stretches of behaviour. I refrain here from asking the question where the Xs, the Ys, the acts and the reports, come from, i.e., from asking whether their equivalents are 'built in' (as is possibly the case in instincts), are 'learned' in one way or another (through trial and error, operant conditioning, supervised training, or imitation), or are simply 'known' (for instance, through explicit verbal instruction, or memorisation of procedures). In my view, this is not a question to be answered by an experimental psychology concerned with the use of visual information for task performance. Moreover, in *Plans and the Structure of Behavior*, Miller et al. (1960) present an excellent discussion of these issues to which I have nothing of importance to add.

In the work just mentioned, Miller et al. (1960) convincingly argue and show that extended stretches of behaviour can be analysed with Test–Operate elements as the unit of analysis (see also Section 3.2). In that conceptualisation, such a stretch of behaviour consists of a series of Test–Operate elements, a series that ends, or Exits, when the ultimate goal of that behaviour is reached. The considerations presented in this work have led me to two different types of 'Test–Operate' elements that can serve as the unit of analysis for stretches of behaviour: an '>> X > Y/report >>' unit and an '>> X/act > ... >>' unit. So, what we have to do is to look at stretches of reports and at stretches of acts. First we look at act tasks, then we consider report tasks.

With the unit of analysis written as

>> X/act > ... >>,

an important aspect of nearly all overt acts is implied that up to now has not been made explicit. That aspect is that overt acts nearly always result in observable changes in the visual world.[40] The system either effectuates a perceivable positional change of (part of) the system itself as, e.g., in walking or reaching, and/or effectuates a perceivable change in the outer environment as, e.g., in picking an apple or throwing a stone. This aspect of overt acts is expressed in the unit of analysis with the dots, > ... >>; in the period of time indicated by the dots, the effects of the act can be observed and evaluated.

The implication of this property of overt acts for a concatenation of acts becomes clearer in the following expression for a stretch of behaviour:

This 'perception–action' cycle captures the important fact that the visual world invites an act, that the act changes the visual world, that the changed visual world invites another act, that this act effectuates another observable change, etc. So this format expresses the important fact that overt acts, through changing the visual world, invite further acts. It is worthwhile to know here that exactly this expression is also used in, and therefore connects my 'cognitive' theorising with, the 'behavioural' theorising in ecological psychology (see, e.g., Kugler, Shaw, Vincente, & Kinsella-Shaw, 1990; especially their Fig. 17).

This 'perception–action' cycle already captures an important contribution to orderly goal-directed behaviour. To see this, let us look at a stretch of behaviour with an invariant intermediate goal; that is, a stretch of behaviour with a fixed X, e.g., picking all apples from this apple tree or walking this distance of *n* steps. After performing the first 'ballistic' act, i.e., after picking the first apple, that apple has disappeared from the apple tree. So (the position of) that apple has disappeared as a possible visible internal short-term goal for a next 'ballistic' act. Given the intermediate goal of picking all apples, there is no other possibility than to select a next apple as the internal short-term goal for picking. So, in this task and in all other overt tasks controlled or guided by an invariant intermediate goal, the visual world serves as a kind of 'external memory'. That memory forces the system into an appropriate, visual-world-adapted, sequence of 'ballistic' acts that are bound together by an unchanging intermediate goal: e.g., picking all apples, walking home, eating a meal, etc. Of course, that intermediate goal disappears when the intermediate goal is reached, e.g., when all apples are picked, home is reached, and dinner is finished.

It can be argued that the format presented above has some serious drawbacks. One drawback is that this scheme seems to force us to think about extended stretches of intermediate-goal guided overt behaviour as a stroboscopic concatenation of discrete 'ballistic' acts.[41] Another drawback is that saccadic eye movements, which accompany all kinds of overt behaviour, are not explicitly included. These problems are, however, easily eliminated. Consider the following perception–action cycle:

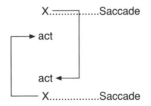

This continuous cycle first expresses that, in ecologically valid situations and possibly only after extended practice, there can be effective action during active perception and active perception during effective action. This cycle also expresses the possibility of selection of the internal short-term goal for a further 'ballistic' act during the performance of an earlier selected act, and of performing a 'ballistic' act while the selection of the next short-term internal goal is already taking place. Moreover, this cycle also expresses the possibility of a continuous adjustment of perception and action, this especially for those who have problems with considering intermediate goal guided actions as a concatenation of 'ballistic' short-term goal guided acts.[42] In this cycle the saccadic eye movements are simply hooked up as described in Chapter 8.

Let us now consider the report tasks. With the unit of analysis written as

$$>> X > Y/\text{report} >>,$$

an incidental aspect of this unit comes too much to the fore. That aspect is that it seems that the external report as such is always of importance for the information processing system. For the system, however, the selection of the relevant object or region and of the relevant attributes or dimensions often suffices. We virtually never report what we see and we only read aloud in exceptional circumstances.[43]

Because overt report is not essential, the 'perception–action' cycle for stretches of 'looking' or 'scanning' behaviour is best characterised with:

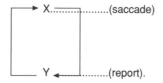

This format captures the important fact that object selection (by state X) and attribute selection (by state Y) are 'internal affairs' that can, but need not, be followed by a saccadic eye movement and/or can, but need not, be followed by the overt expression of the content of state Y.[44]

It will be clear that there is an essential difference between this type of task and the act tasks. Performance of a report task does not usually result in observable changes in the outer visual world. With the invariant intermediate goal of reading this page of text, after reading the first word that word does not disappear from the page. The performance of the internal selective operations by the Intending Mind neither effectuates an observable positional change of (part of) the system itself nor effectuates an observable change in the outer visual environment.[45] This entails that such stretches of behaviour are not unambiguously supported by changes effectuated in the environment. Nevertheless, such stretches of behaviour are under the control of intermediate goals; we search the dark sky until we find a star configuration, we scan the newspaper until we find the information we need, and we read a book from beginning to end, etc. And, because the world 'does not keep the record', the system must have internal means to keep track of where it is on the route towards reaching the intermediate goal. Built-in routines, learned and automated routines, and known routines, are here possibly the 'instruments' that keep the system on track in an unchanging world.[46]

Again, the format just presented possibly has a serious drawback, in so far that it seems to force us to think about an extended stretch of intermediate goal guided internal operations as a series of discrete, non-overlapping, 'X > Y' tasks. This problem is, however, easily remedied. Consider the following 'selection–selection' cycle:

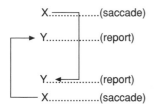

This continuous cycle first expresses that, in ecologically valid situations and possibly only after extended practice, object selection and attribute selection can go on simultaneously. In particular, this cycle expresses the possibility of selecting a next object during attribute selection of the previously selected object, and of some continuation of attribute selection of a previously selected object during the selection of a next object. It is worthwhile to note here that this possibility has already been introduced in Section 8.3, as an alternative for Reichle et al.'s (1998) reading model. Moreover, this cycle expresses the in-principle possibility of a continuous adjustment of object selection and attribute selection – this especially for those who don't like to see the internal operations chopped up into bits and pieces, i.e., those who think in terms of James's (1890/1950) 'stream of consciousness'. Finally, when generalised to auditory information processing, this cycle performs the functions of Broadbent's (1958) filter–channel model and thereby explains how subjects in an experiment select and process the verbal instruction (see Chapter 4, Note 1).

These demonstrations show that the two units of analysis presented in this work are not only applicable to simple laboratory tasks. Via appropriate sequences of simple act and report units with their short-term goals, all interesting intermediate goals, in the laboratory and in real life, can be reached. The 'ballistic' tasks with their short-term goals are just the simple stones that can be used for the complex buildings. Indeed,

> Given a simple unit, complicated phenomena are then describable as lawful compounds. That is the essence of the highly successful strategy called "scientific analysis".
>
> (Miller et al., 1960, p. 21)

These demonstrations also show that the simple tasks used in contemporary experimental psychology – naming a single colour, reading a single letter, making one saccadic eye movement, reaching for a single bar – are not as trivial as is often supposed. These simple tasks are exactly the tasks that can shed light on the detailed way of functioning of the fundamental functional building blocks of human cognition and performance. Indeed, experimental psychologists break up the circles and investigate the segments. But, fortunately, those segments after all appear to be the units of analysis that Wundt, Dewey, Watson, Thorndike, Skinner, and Miller were already looking for.

Notes

1 Because I have never worked in the field of action research, I rely in these sections on the work of experts in this field.
2 Miller et al. (1960) use the word 'attention' sparsely and when they use the word it is applied in another way and has another meaning than in information processing psychology.
3 I return later to the exact format used.
4 For 'direct parameter specification' see Section 2.1.
5 At this point it is of importance to see that saccadic eye movement tasks, as studied in the laboratory, are nearly always '>> X/act > ... >>' tasks. In Chapter 8, this point was possibly obscured by what was said about the relation between the X of >> X > Y >> and the *where* of a saccadic eye movement and between the Y of >> X > Y >> and the *when* of a saccadic eye movement. This point of confusion is easily clarified. Let us briefly return to Reichle et al.'s (1998) reading tasks in Section 8.3. In these, two tasks are performed simultaneously; the subject reads the words and the subject makes saccadic eye movements. It must be clear that it is the X of the reading task and the Y of the reading task that determine the where and the when of the saccadic eye movements. The eye is the slave of the reading sequence >> X > Y >> (see also Figure 8.1). The eye cannot but comply.
6 It turns out here that in this work I am attempting to combine and reconcile Broadbent's (1958) and Miller et al.'s (1960) work. Possibly the title of this work should have been: 'Attention in vision: Perception, communication, and the structure of behaviour'.
7 In this context it is worthwhile to note that my >> X > Y >> conceptualisation, with X in charge of object/region selection and Y in charge of attribute selection, is an attention theory in terms of contents and of associations. The explanatory exercises presented in Chapters 5 and 6 show, in my view, that the >> X > Y >> conceptualisation is at least 'on speaking terms' with the core of the detailed research endeavour and the attention-oriented theorising in the information processing approach.
8 There are more reasons for deleting Test and replacing it by X. One is that it is nearly impossible to see what the Test consists of, what difference is assessed, in report tasks, i.e., in tasks like 'Name the colour of the square' or 'Name the letter indicated by the bar marker' (please ask yourself what that test can consist of or what difference can be assessed with these tasks). It is understandable that internal task performance in these tasks starts with an X for the selection of the relevant object, not that internal task performance starts with a Test when there is no real difference that matters.

Another reason is that, as shown in Chapter 8 and in the partial-report–saccadic-eye movement example just presented, term X can select the required object and simultaneously the parameters for the saccadic eye movement. So, at least for report tasks involving saccadic eye movements, for the saccadic eye movement no term Test is required. The term X, which is already required for adequate report performance, can simultaneously perform the role of the term Test in Miller et al.'s >> Test > Operate >> unit.

Basically the point here is that the term X of >> X > Y/report >> can perform the role of Test in >> Test > Operate >>, but term Test in >> Test > Operate >> cannot perform the role of X in >> X > Y/report >>.

9 It is interesting to note here that Gibson, a 'behaviourist', emphasises the necessity of awareness, while Münsterberg, an introspective psychologist, denies the importance of conscious awareness.

10 That crude dichotomy is sometimes also suggested in the impressive theoretical work of Bridgeman (1992, 1999a) and of Neumann (1989, 1990b). In essence, their theoretical position is that (conscious) awareness is required for verbal report but not for instrumental acts (see Section 2.2 for their theorising; see also further on). With regard to Bridgeman (1999a), Haggard (1999, p. 17) remarks: '. . . are the operations of the motor system accessible to perception? Bridgeman, like most traditional dissociationist accounts, insists that the answer is *no*. Thus Bridgeman seems logically committed to the idea that we know very little about our actions.' Neumann (1990b, p. 212) declares: '. . . according to this view, conscious perception is not a necessary link in the chain that leads from the uptake of stimulus information to the control of action. This would, of course, readily explain dissociations of performance measures from psychophysical data. If response selection does not depend on perceptual experience, there is no reason to expect that the two kinds of measure will necessarily correlate.'

11 As elaborated in Section 2.2, Note 14, these act tasks clearly require the spatial selection of an object or a position, or are under 'attentional control' (i.e., under control of X).

12 It is worthwhile to note that this conceptualisation also provides an adequate starting point for explaining the 'blindsight' phenomena observed with some patients with visual defects. These patients with damage in the occipital cortex report that they see nothing in a (large) part of their visual field, but are nevertheless capable of 'guessing', upon cueing or prompting, the position, direction of movement, and even the shape of stimuli presented in that part of their visual field. In the investigations, the patients first receive an instruction, e.g., 'Whenever you hear a tone, guess and name the position of the light'. In my conceptualisation, this task has to be performed with an intentional sequence >> X > Y/report >> (>> OBJECT > POSITION/report >>). In the patient's experience there is, however, nothing that corresponds with X or OBJECT. The experimenter's cue or prompt serves as a substitute for this lacking experience. In the patient's experience there is also nothing corresponding to Y or position. Information in a module concerned with direct parameter specification for action, e.g., in a module devoted to eye movements (see the EMC in Figure 8.1) or to hand movements (see the HMC in Figure 9.1) that receive information directly from the eye, can serve as a substitute and provide the information required for guessing. (The patients can move the hand or the eyes in the direction of the light; see Weiskrantz, Warrington, Sanders & Marshall, 1974.) *Pace* Dennett (1992, p. 326), in my view these patients are not 'reporting' but 'acting'.

13 At this point it is also worthwhile to return briefly to the analysis of reading, presented in Section 6.1. The important point is that, according to my conceptualisation, the 'muscular'–'sensorial' distinction is not only applicable to

button pushing after extended practice, but also to the reading of words after extended practice. Please remember that in the 'dual-route' model, a word can be read with and without the involvement of term Y. In reading for meaning term Y is always involved. In 'barking to words' no term Y is involved.

14 Dennett (1992, p. 77), a philosopher of mind, who had possibly never heard about the existence of sensorial and muscular reaction times in experimental psychology, argued that a distinction can be made between two types of simple single button-pushing tasks – single button pushing as a report (speech) and single button pushing as an (non-speech) act. With button pushing as a report, the subject informs the experimenter that he has *perceived that*, e.g., there was a light. With button pushing as an (non-speech) act, the subject does not inform the experimenter but simply acts at the moment that the act is called for or is appropriate.

15 It is possibly worthwhile to know that Wundt recognises sensation, perception, and apperception; Wundt's complete theory is a three-stage theory. If one wishes, and I certainly do not, one can argue that this is consistent with my views. Then one has to assume that term X, object selection, transforms sensations into perceptions, and, consistent with what is said in the text, term Y transforms perception into apperception.

16 With act tasks, the correctness of the act can be checked with visual feedback; one can, e.g., see whether the hand is now pointing in the right direction. With report tasks this is impossible; one cannot, e.g., see whether the word 'red' just pronounced is the right word.

17 Bridgeman (1999a, p. 7) even notes that 'Even if both the stimuli and the movements themselves are identical, behavior with a purely instrumental goal might follow different rules from behavior with a communicatory goal.' Lange's (1888) set of experiments, discussed in Sections 2.2 and 9.1, is the classical example here.

18 While Bridgeman's (1992, 1999a) explanation of the behavioural dissociation(s), obtained with cognitive measures and motor measures – in terms of two different neurophysiological/neuroanatomical maps with different spatial properties, a cognitive map and a motor map – is certainly adequate, it is not without theoretical problems. These problems circle around the issue of what is an effective/elegant 'explanation'. What we encounter here is an explanation of two behavioural phenomena (involved in the dissociation) in terms of two 'devoted' structures or systems with properties that explain the dissociation. Similar or related explanations in terms of structures, mechanisms, or channels with required properties, we encountered earlier in, e.g., Broadbent's (1958) theorising (see Section 3.3), in Müller and Rabbitt's (1989) theorising (see Section 6.1), and in Findlay and Walker's (1999) model (see Section 8.2). Clearly, Bridgeman has (some) independent neurphysiological/neuroanatomical evidence on his side (see Section 2.2). Nevertheless, I mistrust this type of 'structures-with-required-properties' explanation. Furthermore, Bridgeman's (1992) explanation only postulates that, but does not really make clear why, the cognitive map suffers from visual illusions but the motor map does not (why not the other way around, why do both not suffer from visual illusions, why not neither one?).

19 It is worthwhile to note that, because both the target and the hand are represented in the HMC, neither eye position information nor further 'coordinate transformations' are required.

20 In my conceptualisation, modules like the EMC and the HMC take care of Neumann's (1990a) 'direct parameter specification'.

21 Wolff (1999b, p. 39) clearly saw the implications of the distinction between code for position and position of code for the issue of the communication between maps, and phrased these implications in an excellent way:

The spatial structure . . . [in P/M] . . . is "meaningless" in the sense that it does not code position or anything else; in other words, it does not have any representational function . . . But "meaningless" does not mean functionless. The anatomical positions separate and distinguish the pieces or elements of information, making it possible to trace them, and, therefore, connect them with the relevant pieces of other maps. Thus, the 'meaningless' spatial structures of the anatomical maps, like interfaces, serve the function of communication between these maps.

22 The classification of tasks is also useful for understanding the symptoms of neurological patients.

Some neurological patients show the symptom of visual apraxia, an inability to reach for and grasp objects appropriately despite being able to identify them . . . In apraxia patients, information in the perceptual pathway is intact, but it is not available to control accurate grasping and reaching.

(Bridgeman, 1999a, p. 4)

In my terminology: These patients can perform >> X > Y/report >> tasks but not >> X/act > . . . >> tasks.

Another, less common group of patients has difficulty with perception and object identification, but can reach for and grasp objects accurately even though the properties of the objects cannot be identified . . . This is a demonstration of a sensorimotor capability using a source of knowledge that is not available to perception.

(Bridgeman, 1999a, p. 4)

In my terminology: These patients can perform >> X/act > . . . >> tasks but not >> X > Y/ report >> tasks.

It is of interest to note that in my conceptualisation both groups of patients can perform object selection (through sequence state X). The difference between the two groups arises after object selection, in selection for action and selection for report, respectively.

23 Because actions are by definition segments of behaviour that are individuated by their goals, there is exactly the same decision problem with regard to actions.

24 Prinz (1997b, p. 265) states that in his theory the linkages between goal codes and motor codes are arbitrary by definition. See Bridgeman (1992, 1999a) in Section 9.2 for a different view; see also later.

25 This action effect principle is derived from observations reported by early introspective psychology, for instance by Lotze, Münsterberg, and James. James (1890/ 1950, Vol. II, p. 521) writes:

It is not the thought of the innervation which the movement requires. It is the anticipation of the movement's sensible effects, resident or remote, and sometimes very remote indeed. Such anticipations, to say the least, determine *what* our movements shall be.

26 Because Prinz (1997b) is mainly concerned with the perception–action coupling, in his theorising this object or region selection required for task performance remains largely implicit. In this respect, Prinz's theorising is like Miller et al.'s (1960), which simply starts with a 'Test'. These theoretical views neglect the existence and importance of object selection.

27 Another function is the evaluation of action success (Prinz, 1997b, p. 253).

28 Prinz (1997b, p. 254) adds:

> In principle, the solution to this problem is to postulate anticipatory goal codes and to assume that they are somehow furnished with the power to elicit movements suited to reach these goals.

In subsequent pages Prinz elaborates this postulate in terms of divergent and convergent fans and concludes:

> The only requirement is that there is a powerful system that is capable of learning the contingencies between movements and their effects . . .
>
> (Prinz, 1997b, p. 255)

> The only requirement one has to add is the assumption that the associations built into this . . . system cannot only be used in the forward direction (i.e., in accordance with the temporal order in which they have been built) but in the backward direction, too.
>
> (Prinz, 1997b, p. 256)

So, after the elaboration, the assumption is still the same assumption (see also Ehrenstein, 1997, and Stins, 1997, for evaluations of Prinz's theory).

29 That this is not a trivial problem becomes clear when Hommel (1997, p. 289) explains how motor patterns and response effects become associated in an experiment.

> In the example, response R produces an effect with three perceivable . . . features, say, an audible click, a kinesthetic sensation . . . , and a visible accuracy feedback . . . As carrying out R will usually be accompanied by all these three events . . . , their codes . . . will be associated with m, the responsible motor pattern. This means that activating any of these codes will increase the activation of and eventually launch m, thereby effecting R.

This, of course, raises the question of who is 'carrying out R' before the associations of perceivable features of R with m are in place. In this theorising, first 'the actor', the 'he or she', has to carry out a substantial number of Rs so that the associations between perceivable features of R and m can be established. Only after that learning, can the 'cognitive system' take over from 'the actor'.

30 It is also not necessary to assume that the system learns associations between the (effector) movements and the (target) goals (that are sometimes reached). It can equally well be assumed that the system learns associations between (target) goals (attractors) and (effector) movements (that are sometimes attracted).

31 It will be clear that, when we neglect the X–SC difference, with regard to report tasks the only remaining difference between Prinz's theorising and my view is in the interpretation of the goal code, GC. In Prinz's theorising, the goal code represents an intended and anticipated event in the outer world. In my conceptualisation, that goal code is already present, albeit implicit, in the (selected) stimulus code, and only has to be extracted or selected and made explicit by sequence state Y. Nevertheless, in my conceptualisation the goal code, i.e., here the colour, also represents and anticipates the event to be realised in the outer world, i.e., here the naming of that colour (the action effect principle). Moreover, with my interpretation, we have a beautiful example of common coding; stimulus code, SC, and goal code, GC, are, by definition, so to say, in a common representational medium; both are simply 'perceived'. With regard to the transition

between the goal code (the selected colour) and the motor code (the overt response), Prinz's view and my view completely agree. The linkage between these two codes is completely arbitrary (see Sections 4.2, 6.1, and 6.4).

32 Here I distinguish between the goal of the system as a whole (having the apple) and the target of the effector(s) that, as means, are used to attain that goal. The target of the hand is 'that apple there'. The goal of the whole system is 'to have that apple here'.

33 It will be clear that this view is very close to Gibson's (1979) view on 'affordances'.

34 As stated, in Prinz's (1997b) theorising there is nothing corresponding to an object or region selection mechanism; [SC] is simply given. There are therefore only two positions left for instruction/task effects, [GC] and [MC]. In my conceptualisation, the stimulus code, [SC], is selected (by sequence state X). So, in my conceptualisation [SC] already reflects task/instruction effects.

35 It is worthwhile here to consider again in detail the conceptualisation of the generation of saccadic eye movements, presented in Section 8.1, Figure 8.1. In that conceptualisation, the EMC is a module with current eye position in the centre. The required eye position is 'triggered' or 'aroused' on another position in the EMC. That 'activated' position 'attracts' the eye. For me it is not clear how to specify the to-be-executed movement starting with [Current Position]. It seems that with that starting point a 'subject' is required.

36 It is worthwhile here to consider again in detail the conceptualisation of a pointing movement, presented in Section 9.2, Figure 9.1. In that conceptualisation, the HMC is a module with current hand position on a position. The position required for the hand action is 'triggered' or 'aroused' on another position in the HMC. That activated position attracts the hand. The movement to be executed equals: [Goal Position] minus [Hand Position]. For me it is not clear how to specify the to-be-executed movement starting with [Current Hand Position]. It seems that with that starting point a 'subject' is required.

37 It will be clear that, if we neglect the X–SC difference, with respect to act tasks the main remaining difference between Prinz's view and my view again concerns the goal code, [GC]. In Prinz's conceptualisation, a goal code, [GC], representing an intended and anticipated event in the outer world, is required. In my conceptualisation, because the stimulus is selected and devoted action modules take care of the execution, in act tasks no sequence state Y is required for extracting a goal code from the stimulus code. Nevertheless, in my conceptualisation, the selected stimulus/goal code, e.g., that reachable ripe red apple there, represents and anticipates the event to be realised in the outer world (the action effect principle). Because in my conceptualisation the goal code coincides with the stimulus code, we have again here a beautiful example of common coding. The stimulus code and the goal code are, by definition, so to say, in a common representational medium; both are simultaneously perceived as one and the same unit. With regard to the transition between this stimulus/goal code (the object wanted) and the motor code (the overt response) Prinz's view and my view diverge. With Bridgeman (1999a), I assume that the linkage between these two codes is not arbitrary but isomorphic (see Figures 8.1 and 9.1 in Sections 8.1 and 9.2; the connections between P/M and the EMC and the HMC).

38 It is interesting to know that this interpretation deviates considerably from Prinz's (1997b) interpretation of what is going on in this task. In my interpretation the subject's goal is to report the colour to the experimenter. In Prinz's view

> In the laboratory task, it is indeed the case that the goal and the movement virtually coincide. In a key-pressing task, there is no goal on top and beyond the movement. Rather, the goal resides, as it were, *in the movement itself*.
>
> (Prinz, 1997b, p. 258)

39 At this point it is worthwhile to consider, as a kind of 'free gift', a choice-reaction task with the two colours and the two keys, as described above, and to imagine an experiment in which, in addition, the position of the light is varied. The light can appear on the left and on the right. The position of the light is irrelevant for task performance and the subjects are instructed to ignore it. The subjects have to perform exactly the same choice-reaction task as before; they have to press the left key when the light is red and the right key when the light is green. In this variation, the (irrelevant) position of the light and the (relevant) position of the key can correspond (right–right and left–left) and the (irrelevant) position of the light and the relevant position of the key can differ (left–right and right–left). What is to be expected?

    In my conceptualisation, intentional sequence state Xv selects the stimulus with all its attributes, so the attribute position (left or right) is also selected. That selection suffices for triggering the hand via the HMC in an act task. However, the system is not performing an act task but a report task, so the HMC is not yet 'switched in'. For performing the 'report' task, the intentional sequence moves to state Yv, receives the colour, and generates the required key (left key or right key). Then the HMC is 'switched in' (act!). Now the HMC receives two position signals, one from the selected stimulus (delivered by Xv) and one from the generated key (delivered by Key/act). When these two signals coincide, fast acting is to be expected. When the two signals differ, delayed acting through interference is to be expected. In the latter case, state Xv creates a problem that can be solved by processes originating from and following state Yv (voluntary selection through state Yv; see also the Stroop task in Section 6.2 for a similar problem and solution).

    The task just described is called the Simon task and the effect just predicted is called the Simon effect. The task has been used in numerous investigations and the effect is readily obtained (see Hommel, 1997, and Prinz, 1997b, for overviews). Space and time do not allow me to go further into the results obtained with various intriguing variations and modifications. One important result deserves to be mentioned however. Hommel (1993) showed that what is generated in the transition between the report part and the act part of the choice-reaction task is completely determined by the task instruction. Phrased the other way around, Hommel showed that the choice-reaction task is an important task for finding out what 'goal codes' or 'action concepts' subjects can generate given a task instruction.

40 Saccadic eye movement is a special case for at least two reasons; for the system making the saccadic eye movement the clarity of the visual world changes, and for a system observing the system that makes the saccadic eye movement the position of two eyes in a head in the world changes.

41 'A skilled motor performance usually runs on continuously in time, and it is not obvious where it should be dissected into discrete stimuli and responses. It is not only that both the stimulus and the response are continuous functions of time; the problem is further complicated by the fact that the consequences of the responses are fed back and modify the stimulus' (Miller, 1964, pp. 200–201).

42 'What we have is a circuit, not an arc or broken segment of a circle. This circuit is more truly termed organic than reflex, because the motor response determines the stimulus, just as truly as sensory stimulus determines movement' (Dewey, 1896, p. 363).

43 See Neumann (1990a) on the importance of selection in vision for 'updating the internal representation'.

44 It is worthwhile to see that this cycle combines the X/act and Y/report units as specified in Section 9.1 for the partial-report – saccadic eye movement task.

45 Of course, this is true when we look only at the 'internal affairs' and neglect accompanying eye, head, etc., movements.

46 It cannot be excluded that, in one way or another, the saccadic eye movement system plays a role in keeping track. A phenomenon that is presently under investigation is Posner and Cohen's (1984) 'inhibition of return'. The eye is inclined not to return to a position previously visited. Theoretical alternatives for 'inhibition of return' are 'inhibitory tagging' (Klein, 1988) and 'visual marking' (Watson & Humphreys, 1997). Possibly of relevance here is also that a saccadic eye movement has two effects, an increase in clarity and detail of the newly fixated and a decrease in clarity and detail of the formerly fixated (see Section 7.1). This has as a result that the *perceived world* changes with each change of fixation.

Epilogue

E.0 Introduction

By introducing an Intending Mind with intentional sequences composed of units of analysis as internal representations of task instructions, I have added a number of degrees of freedom to the standard explanations of the information processing approach. And by deleting/neglecting the assumption of limited capacity in vision and by removing subjects with spotlights or zoom lenses, I have subtracted a number of degrees of freedom. With the overall explanatory scheme resulting from this addition and deletion, it was possible to provide a starting point for adequate explanations for the results obtained in a great variety of selective-attention-in-vision tasks, for report tasks (see Chapters 5 and 6) as well as act tasks (see Chapters 8 and 9). For explaining performance in these tasks, no autonomous, unanalysable 'higher' mechanisms appeared to be required. The operations of the Intending Mind during task performance appeared as determinate as Broadbent's (1987) type-writers.

Of course, ultimately the adequacy of the resulting explanatory scheme has to be demonstrated with theory-guided experimentation, not with post hoc explanations. In other words, my main task is finished and I am now at the point where I have to stop my theoretical enterprise and simply have to sit and wait for further developments in the field of visual information processing and selection. That was indeed what I attempted to do. But, while sitting and waiting, a great number of theoretical ideas – let me call them philosophies – occurred to me. Nearly all these philosophies hinted at a much broader range of applicability of intentional sequences composed of units of analysis than I had formerly thought of. In what follows some of these philosophies, related to and relevant for the issue of how the Intending Mind uses Visual Perception for task performance, are presented and elaborated.

In Section E.1, I briefly turn to the experimental psychologies of the past. In these psychologies subjects, and sometimes rats and pigeons, participated, that used their visual perception in the performance of tasks. What I attempt to show is that the differences between these psychologies concern not so much the data but the theoretical intuitions and stories behind and above the data. When these intuitions and stories are left behind, something like an accumulation of knowledge about the use of visual information for task performance within experimental psychology can be discerned.

In Section E.2, some aspects of the theoretical status of terms like 'subject', 'person', 'agent', 'I', 'me', and 'you' are briefly considered in the context of the theory presented in this work. The problem of the theoretical status of these terms is, of course, the problem of what entities, contents, processes, or functions these terms refer to. With regard to this issue, Descartes and Hume defined the extreme positions. It is argued that with the distinction in the Intending Mind between content and function, and with the help of James (1890/1950), a decent intermediate position can be found.

In Section E.3, some of the problems circling around the concepts 'freedom' and 'free will' are briefly considered. Here we touch, of course, upon the general question of how people at a certain moment in time come to perform one or another task or action. With regard to this issue, Hobbes, concerned with freedom, and Reid, fostering free will, defined the theoretical battlefield. It is argued that experimental psychology has been successful in pushing these complicated issues out of its field of empirical inquiry and theoretical speculation. The model of free choice, introduced by Dennett (1979), is described and elaborated in order to bring these issues back in.

In Section E.4, the general mind–body problem and some of the problems circling around the planning, structuring, and executing of goal-directed behaviour are briefly considered. The main problem considered is that of how the internal, conscious, deliberating, and deciding mind can define and reach goals in the outer, physical world. This problem, which is basically that of the hierarchical structure of behaviour described by Miller et al. (1960), I simply neglected in Section 9.4, which was concerned with *the structure of behaviour*. It will appear that, with the information provided earlier, a rather complete and detailed answer to this planning and structuring question can be given.

E.1   Experimental psychology

From the preceding chapters it will be clear that I now pretend to have the core of a theory of the use of Visual Perception for task performance, and that the core of this core consists of an Intending Mind whose operations can be captured in terms of two units of analysis, an

>> X > Y/report >> unit

for report (name and read) tasks and an

>> X/act > . . . >> unit

for act tasks (see Section 9.4 for extensions and generalisations). I have no principled objections against minor variations of these units. For instance, I have no problems with an >> X > seen act >> unit or an >> X > imagined act >> unit. I also have no problems with a >> ... > Y >> unit for reading for meaning. And I also have no problem with a >> WHOLE > PART >> unit for inspecting and scrutinising a scene. More in general, I have no problem with any decent interpretation of X, Y, report, and act, as long as the basic structure of the unit, >> ... > ... >>, remains intact. My conviction is that with the Intending Mind with such units of analysis, an appropriate analysis of all tasks using vision is possible.

In the recent past there have been a number of experimental psychologies. In these psychologies vision was often used for task performance. In this section, I approach these psychologies with Intending Mind using Visual Perception with the two units of analysis as a pair of spectacles. What I attempt to show is that it is indeed possible to clarify and further understand what was happening in these psychologies when looked at with the units of analysis as a filter. I first turn to early introspective psychology, then to gestalt psychology, then to behaviourism, and I end with current information processing psychology or cognitive psychology. Of course, because of space and time, only some brief and global indications are possible.

Early introspective psychology

An important topic within early introspective experimental psychology was that of how to define 'pure' introspective psychology and its relation with physics.

> Wundt ... drew the distinction between immediate and mediate experience ... Avenarius – and thus Kuelpe and Titchener – talked about dependent and independent experience ... Both psychology and physics work immediately with experience, but they regard it in different ways; physics takes the "point of view" of experience "regarded as independent of the experiencing individual," psychology the "point of view" of experience "regarded as dependent upon the experiencing individual." ... Titchener's fundamental theory was that there is a physical point of view, a psychological point of view and perhaps other points of view ... The data of psychology therefore depend upon its point of view, Titchener thought, and the point of view thus becomes all-important in psychology.
>
> (Boring, 1950, p. 417)

So, roughly speaking, the distinction between psychology and physics is in the 'taking' of what is experienced, in 'dealing' with 'inner things' vs 'dealing' with 'outer things'.

In the orthodox Wundt–Titchener psychological point of view, the conviction was that the 'inner things', the experiences psychology had to be concerned with, were immediately given in introspection; having an experience is the same as observing it. And the conviction was that what was immediately given in introspection consisted of compounds of elements (e.g., sensations, images, feelings) with attributes (e.g., quality, intensity, extensity, duration, and clearness or vividness).[1] Here it is not of importance to know how these psychologists arrived at these convictions. It is important to see that these introspective psychologists, who often themselves served as subjects, used their visual perception for performing their self-defined and self-set introspection tasks. And it is also important to see that the basic structure of what they did is captured with the units of analysis

>> COMPOUND > ELEMENT/report >>,

and

>> ELEMENT > ATTRIBUTE/report >>.

The results obtained with these units of analysis in place and operating upon whatever is given in visual perception, formed the body of evidence for the building of further theoretical speculations (with combinations, associations, etc.).[2]

According to Titchener, when a psychologist takes the physical point of view and reports about the outer objects, he or she makes a fatal error – the stimulus error. In Titchener's view, the nature of the outer objects, for instance of the stimulus, is not immediately given but has to be inferred. To report about the nature of the outer stimulus is to report an inference, an interpretation, and inferences and interpretations belong in epistemology, not in psychology (see also Chapter 1).[3] Again, where Titchener got his wisdom from is, in the present context, not important. What is of importance is to see that Titchener noted that many introspective psychologists used the format

>> OUTER OBJECT > ATTRIBUTE/report >>,

in the performance of their introspective task – a format that, in his view, had no place in introspective psychology proper.

Gestalt psychology

With the early experimental introspective psychologists, the gestalt psychologists – Koehler, Koffka, and Wertheimer for instance – shared the convictions that psychology had to be concerned with the 'inner things' and that these 'inner things' were immediately given in introspection.[4] They differed from their predecessors in their conviction that not compounds of elements, but objects as such are given in experience, that objects are the immediately accessible data, and that Wundt's and Titchener's elements are only inferred and invented theoretical entities.

Here it is not of importance to know where the gestalt psychologists got their convictions from. It must be clear, however, that the 'object' conviction, because of its combination with the 'inner experience' conviction, did not make gestalt psychologists 'physicists' in Titchener's sense. These introspective psychologists, who often themselves served as subjects, were not using

>> OUTER OBJECT > PROPERTY/report >>

as the unit of analysis in their self-defined and self-set tasks. Because they were concerned with their immediate subjective experience, the unit of analysis they were working with is more appropriately characterised with

>> INNER OBJECT > PROPERTY/report >>,

or possibly better with

>> GESTALT > CHARACTERISTIC/report >>,

with GESTALT standing for the subjectively experienced wholes and CHARACTERISTIC standing for the attributes deemed important in these wholes (symmetry, continuity, closure, etc.). The results obtained with this unit of analysis in place and operating upon whatever is given in visual perception, formed the body of evidence for building further theoretical speculations (figure/ground, laws of form, field theory, isomorphism, etc.).

Behaviourism

The behaviourists – Watson, Skinner, and Lashley, for instance – completely rejected the assumption that psychology had to be concerned with 'inner things'.[5] In their conceptualisation of psychology there was no place for experienced 'elements' with 'attributes' or for given 'gestalts' with 'characteristics'. Their psychology was concerned with the directly observable, overt objective behaviour. They were 'physicists' in Titchener's sense:

> Psychology, as the behaviorist views it, is a purely objective, experimental branch of natural science which needs introspection as little as do the sciences of chemistry and physics . . . The position is taken here that the behavior of man and the behavior of animals must be considered on the same plane; as being equally essential to a general understanding

of behavior. It can dispense with consciousness in a psychological sense. The separate observation of 'states of consciousness' is, on this assumption, no more a part of the task of the psychologist than of the physicist.

(Watson, 1913, in Vanderplas, 1966, pp. 83–84)

With this starting point and his subsequent practice,

. . . Watson almost single-handedly transformed psychology into an objective biological science, denying the validity of introspective report and showing by example how to work with behavior instead.

(Hebb, 1980, p. 221)

This was a major step in experimental psychology (see also Chapter 1).[6]

From here on issues get a little bit complicated. The reason for this complexity is that in the research endeavour of the behaviourists and of later psychologies two parties are involved and have to be distinguished – a participant/subject, perceiving the world and producing the behaviour, and the psychologist/experimenter, observing the participant/subject and reporting the observed behaviour.

As participants/subjects in their experiments, the behaviourists mainly used rats and pigeons in boxes and in cages. In their confinements, these animals generated a diversity of overt acts or behaviours. In my conceptualisation, what these animals did can be adequately characterised with

$$\gg X/act > \ldots \gg$$

as the basic the unit of analysis (see also Section 9.4). Pavlov showed how, starting with an unconditioned $\gg$ X1/act $> \ldots \gg$ act, a conditioned $\gg$ X2/act $> \ldots \gg$ act can be learned. And Skinner cunningly filled in the 'empty' part, $> \ldots \gg$, of an act unit with a reinforcing event, so shaping and directing the animal's behaviour. In general, it is worthwhile to note here that my unit of analysis for act tasks *is* Pavlov's and Skinner's unit of analysis, albeit under another interpretation.

With regard to naïve observers, Skinner (1972, pp. 140–141) writes that:

. . . one who is unfamiliar with laboratory practice will find it hard to see what is going on in an experimental space. He sees an organism behaving in a few simple ways, in the presence of various stimuli that change from time to time, and he may see an occasional reinforcing event – for example the appearance of food which the organism eats. The facts are all clear, but casual observation alone will seldom reveal the contingencies. Our observer will not be able to explain why the organism behaves as it does.

From this brief description it will be clear that what the naïve observer does when looking around in the laboratory of a behaviourist can be captured with

>> X > Y/report >>

as the basic unit of analysis (see also Section 9.4). Skinner and his colleagues were not naïve, but highly sophisticated observers. They knew better what to observe and they used sophisticated registering apparatus that assisted them in observing what had to be observed. Nevertheless, the difference between a naïve observer and a sophisticated observer is only a matter of degree. It is a difference in relevant background knowledge.

So, what basically happened in the research of the behaviourists was that an experimenter observed an animal that acted. An observer, engaged in a series of

>> X > Y/report >>

tasks, was concerned with an animal in a visual environment engaged in a series of

>> X/act > . . . >>

tasks (see Section 9.4 for generalisations and extensions). The results obtained with the first unit of analysis in place and operating (in the experimenter) upon the results produced in the visual world by the second unit of analysis in place and operating (in the animal), formed the basis for building further theoretical speculations (contingencies, operant conditioning, reinforcement schedules, extinction, etc.).[7]

The information processing approach

The information processing psychologists or cognitive psychologists – and many names can be mentioned here – make optimal use of an important distinction – that between data and theory. With the behaviourists they share the point of view that only objective observable behaviour, 'outer things', can count as data in experimental psychology. They are 'physicists' in Titchener's sense. Moreover, in the report tasks their subjects have to report 'outer things'; subjects are induced to commit Titchener's 'stimulus error' (see also Chapter 1). They deviate from the hard-core behaviourists – Watson and Skinner – in their assumption that in their theories and explanations, 'inner things' can and have to play an important role.[8] In preceding chapters many examples of the way of working in the information processing approach were presented. Here, to complete my brief history of experimental psychology, the following rough characterisation suffices.

Information processing psychologists always use human subjects for producing the relevant behavioural data. Sometimes act tasks are used (see Part III). Especially in the early days of the approach, however, but also still nowadays, mainly report, name and read, tasks were and are used. In these report tasks – and here I restrict myself to report tasks – subjects are first instructed about what they have to read or name.[9] Then they are confronted with a series of visual worlds, and show how fast and well they can do what they have to do. As shown in Chapters 5 and 6, what these subjects do can be adequately characterised with

>> X > Y/report >>

as the basic unit of analysis (see also Section 9.4).

The information processing psychologists are sophisticated observers. They know what aspects of the objective overt behaviour to observe and they use sophisticated presentation and registration apparatus that assists them in observing what has to be observed (mainly latencies and percentages correct). With regard to the use of perception for task performance, what basically happens in most of the research in the information processing approach is that an experimenter observes (aspects of the registered) behaviour of a subject who observes and reacts to (aspects of) a visual world. An experimenter/observer, engaged in a series of

>> X > Y/report >>

tasks, is concerned with a subject in a visual environment, engaged in a series of

>> X > Y/report >>

tasks (see also Section 9.4). The results obtained with the first unit of analysis in place and operating (in the experimenter) upon the results produced (in the visual world) by the second unit of analysis in place and operating (in the subject), form the basis for a building of further theoretical speculations (filtering, attention as a spotlight, limited capacity, two stage perception, etc.).[10]

One outcome of this extremely brief and heavily biased history of experimental psychology is that we meet time and time again the same basic formats, mainly the >> X > Y/report >> format and sometimes the >> X/act > . . . >> format, albeit embedded in completely different theoretical contexts and leading towards completely different theoretical interpretations and constructions. When looked at through the pair of units of analysis as spectacles, it appears that, as far as the use of visual perception for task performance is concerned, what is basically happening within experimental psychology over the last hundred years is unchanging. And of course, because all experimenters and all 'subjects' used their visual perception for task performance, that is the outcome to be expected with an adequate view on the use of visual information for task performance.

What changed over the years are the 'stories' behind and based on the use of visual information for task performance. And, of course, there is much more between heaven and earth than the use of visual perception for task performance. Within the history of experimental psychology we find behind and above the use of visual information for task performance, highly complicated 'views' or 'stories' that, like religions, lead to energetically defended convictions: What has to be observed and what has to be reported in experiments are 'elements with attributes!', 'gestalts with characteristics!!', 'animals that act!!!', 'subjects that report!!!!'. And what has to be explained, reported, and communicated in scientific reports is 'the compounding of sensations!', 'the analysis of wholes!!', 'the contingencies selecting behaviour!!!', 'the role of attention in perception!!!!'.

Indeed,

> The difference between what was done in the Leipzig laboratory in the 1880s and in the Berlin laboratory in the 1920s [and in the Hopkins laboratory in the 1920s and in the Cambridge Laboratory in the 1960s, etc.] depended on the difference in the investigators' motivations, and each of these motivations was part of the enthusiasm of an in-group fighting for recognition of its new view of the truth.
>
> (Boring, 1950, p. 611)

But motivation is a topic I am not inclined to be concerned with.

However, when we abstract from and suppress the religions and motivations, it becomes apparent that there is more accumulation of knowledge within experimental psychology than is generally thought, and that much more integration is possible.

- The important contribution to our current knowledge of early introspective psychology, especially of James and Kuelpe and associates, has become clear, I hope, in Part I of this work. That psychology showed that, for the explanation of task performance, two representations are required, one for the task to be performed and one for the information required for task performance.
- The important contribution of the gestalt psychologists lies in their rejection of 'sensationalism' and their emphasis on 'objects' and 'wholes'. Their phenomenological analyses support and reinforce James's and Kuelpe's points of view with regard to objects as givens in visual perception and contribute to our knowledge of properties and characteristics of objects and background in Visual Perception.
- The contribution of behaviourism is primarily, but certainly not exclusively, methodological. Behaviourism not only transformed psychology

into an objective science, the findings produced with instrumental conditioning and operant conditioning also contribute substantially to our knowledge of the environmental factors that can trigger an act in real-life act tasks.

From this history, the information processing approach to perception and cognition has learned what the important questions are and how these questions can appropriately be tackled in laboratory experiments. That is why the experimental work of the approach has resulted in a substantial and impressive amount of reliable and valid data that allow, constrain, and deserve an appropriate, integrative, theoretical framework.[11]

E.2   The subject and I

In the Prologue, I stated that my plan was to eliminate 'the self' with 'free will' from the theorising in the information processing approach. And, in Section 1.3, I repeated that my aim was to replace 'the subject' – also appearing as the 'agent', the 'person', 'I', 'you', 'she', and 'he' – by a decent information processing entity, an entity that could do the causal work that the 'selves with free wills' or 'the subjects as autonomous agents' are assumed to do in most current information processing theories. To achieve my aim, in my theorising I replaced this spook by an Intending Mind with a Verbal Intention or intentional sequence, which interacts with the contents in Visual Perception. And, as shown in various chapters, with this replacement the need for a 'ghost in the machine', intervening in and controlling the stream of information processing in visual information processing experiments, has indeed disappeared.

In my view, for experimental psychology as a science, the replacement of 'the self' and 'the subject' by an Intending Mind as specified in the preceding chapters is a welcome result. When stepping outside experimental psychology as a science, however, the replacement of 'the self' and of 'the subject' by this Intending Mind might at first sight appear as nothing less than a severe degradation, a strong humiliation, of human beings. The Intending Mind as specified is a rigid machine that stamps its way step after step through its visual information processing task. Everybody is convinced about the existence of a much richer inner self, about the existence of a free and autonomous inner agent, about the existence of an inner I with responsibility and dignity. This intuition and conviction is not captured by the theoretical concept of Intending Mind as elaborated up to now. And this state of affairs means that the question has to be asked, and answered, of whether the Intending Mind can indeed be regarded as a suitable and decent replacement for 'the self' and 'the subject', for that which we refer to and indicate with the terms 'I', 'you', and 'she' and 'he'. To answer this question let us first turn to some selected pieces of the literature about the 'I' and the 'you' in order to find out what these terms can mean or refer to.

With regard to the inner self, the I in me and the I in you, in the earlier literature two opposing views can be found – an 'existentialist' view and a 'nominalist' view. With René Descartes (1596–1650) I can introduce the existentialist view and with David Hume (1711–1776) I can introduce the nominalist view.

Descartes – well-known from his 'I think, therefore I am', '*Cogito ergo sum*' – firmly and honestly believed that human beings, himself included, are compounds, made of two completely different substances – one, a divisible substance, *res extensa*, consisting of the material body, the other, an indivisible substance, *res cogitans*, consisting of an immaterial soul. In Descartes' view, bodies are simply automata or machines. Animals are just machines and human beings are animals with a soul. The body and the soul interact in the pineal gland in the brain. The body informs the soul via nerves with 'delicate threads' and the soul can control the body via nerves with 'animal spirits'. In Descartes' view, the soul that perceives, reasons, understands, wishes, wills, imagines, remembers, and feels, is rational and free. In Descartes' philosophy, this immaterial soul is the I and

> This I (that is to say, my soul by which I am what I am), is entirely and absolutely distinct from my body, and can exist without it.
>
> (Descartes, 1641, p. 190)

So, in Descartes we find a strong defender of the position that in all of us an immaterial self or I exists, an active thinking *res cogitans* that can function and has to function as a rational and free inner agent.

Hume – well-known for his empiricism and scepticism – cannot find such an I or self in himself.

> For my part, when I enter most intimately into what I call *myself*, I always stumble on some particular perception or other of heat or cold, light or shade, love or hatred, pain or pleasure. I never can catch *myself* at any time without a perception, and never can observe anything but the perception . . . If anyone, upon serious and unprejudiced reflection, thinks he has a different notion of *himself*, I must confess I can reason no longer with him . . . He may, perhaps, perceive something simple and continued which he calls *himself*; though I am certain there is no such principle in me. But setting aside some metaphysicians of this kind, I may venture to affirm of the rest of mankind that they are *nothing but a bundle or collection of different perceptions*, which succeed each other with an inconceivable rapidity, and are in a perpetual flux and movement.[12]

So, in Hume we find a strong defender of the position that nothing in our experience and knowledge corresponds with or points at the existence of an I or a self. In Hume's view, words like I and you are empty names.

Several famous authors have tried to reconcile these two opposing views. Kant, for instance, invented for this purpose a knowable, deterministic 'empirical ego' and an unknowable, free 'transcendental ego'. In my view, and for reasons that will soon become apparent, James (1890/1950, 1892/1948) came up with the most appropriate and productive combination.

In one of the first pages of his lengthy chapter 'The Consciousness of Self', James (1890/1950) writes:

> ... in everyone, at an early age, the distinction between thought as such, and what it is 'of', or 'about', has become familiar to the mind ... Almost anyone will tell us that thought is a different sort of existence from things, because many sorts of thought are of no things – e.g., pleasures, pains and emotions; others are of non-existent things – errors and fictions; others again of existent things, but in a form that is symbolic and does not resemble them – abstract ideas and concepts; whilst in the thoughts that do resemble the things they are 'of' (percepts, sensations), we can feel, alongside of the thing known, the thought of it going on as an altogether separate act and operation in the mind.
>
> (James, 1890/1950, pp. 296–297)

It will be clear that in this description we encounter again the distinction captured by the concept 'intentionality', the distinction between 'mind knowing' and 'thing known' or 'thought thinking' and 'thing thought' (see Chapter 1). From this distinction I derived, as special instances for explaining what happens in visual information processing experiments, the distinction between Intending Mind and Visual Perception – Intending Mind is my particular variety of 'mind knowing' and Visual Perception is one of the providers of 'thing known'.

In subsequent pages of his chapter, James (1890/1950) applies this distinction between 'mind knowing' and 'thing known' to the self. And, after more than 70 pages of careful deliberations and hesitations, he summarises the implications of the concept 'intentionality' as applied to the self and formulates a distinction that is of crucial importance.

> We may sum up by saying that personality implies the incessant presence of two elements, an objective person, known by a passing subjective Thought and recognized as continuing in time. *Hereafter let us use the words* ME *and* I *for the empirical person and the judging Thought.*
>
> (James, 1890/1950, p. 371)

Miller (1964, p. 75) paraphrases and thereby explains:

> In every person's stream of consciousness there is a dichotomy between the *me* and the *not-me*; at the same time it is *I* who am aware of this dichotomy ... James divided the self into *I* the knower and *me* the

known. The *me* is simply an object like any object we might be conscious of, although it is obviously of supreme interest . . . The *I* that knows its own ideas cannot itself be one of those ideas. In addition to the ideas that are known, therefore, there must be an active ego that knows them, relates them in the stream of consciousness, and is the source of whatever unity and organization they possess.

In the chapter 'The Self' in the book *Psychology*, James (1892/1948) also needs fewer deliberations and fewer hesitations. He simply starts that chapter with the assumption

> . . . that the total self of me, being as it were duplex, partly known and partly knower, partly object and partly subject, must have two aspects discriminated in it, of which for shortness we may call one the *Me* and the other the *I*.

So, for James 'mind knowing' is the *I* and a subset of 'things known' is the *Me*. In that chapter he therefore subsequently treats successively

> . . . the self as known, or the *me*, the 'empirical ego' as it is sometimes called; and of . . . the self as knower, or the *I*, the 'pure ego' of certain authors.
>
> (James, 1892/1948, p. 176)

Let us also first turn to the *Me* and then to the *I*.

With regard to the *Me*, James (1890/1950, p. 400) remarks:

> The nucleus of the '*me*' is always the bodily existence felt to be present at the time . . . Whatever other things are perceived to be *associated* with this feeling are deemed to form part of that me's *experience*; and of them certain ones . . . are reckoned to be themselves *constituents* of the me in a larger sense, – such are the clothes, the material possessions, the friends, the honors and esteem which the person receives or may receive. This me is an empirical aggregate of things objectively known.

So, the *Me* is close to the Humean self. It consists of a subset of all that is experienced, perceived, known, and remembered, the subset that I can call mine, e.g., my perceived hand and face, my known position and possessions, and my remembered past and hoped-for future. In visual information processing experiments, experimenters are neither concerned with nor interested in this empirical *Me*. In the experiments proper they do not ask the subjects about their health, history, or housing. Consequently, in this work I also did not have very much use for this rich and structured empirical *Me*. So it is not too surprising that in my analysis only a rather meagre 'subject' or 'self' remained.[13]

With regard to the *I*, James (1890/1950, pp. 400–401) remarks:

> The I which knows [the things objectively known] cannot itself be an
> aggregate, neither for psychological purposes need it be considered to
> be an unchanging metaphysical entity like the Soul, or a principle like
> the pure Ego, viewed as 'out of time'. It is a *Thought*, at each moment
> different from that of the last moment . . .

This *I* is not that far from the Cartesian I. This, however, is mainly because
this *I* is hardly accessible to introspection because, being always concerned
with or directed at an object, it is never experienced as such – it is always
'filled' and never 'empty'.[14]

It will by now be clear that, to answer the question of whether my Intending Mind can indeed be regarded as a decent replacement for 'the self' and
'the subject', we have to concentrate on James's *I*, James's 'mind knowing'
or 'thought thinking'. And the question to be answered is that of whether
my Intending Mind with an intentional sequence developing in time is a
decent version of James's *I*.

To answer this question, it is worthwhile to start with a 'fundamental
underlying banality'.

> The fundamental, underlying banality, of course, is the fact that once a
> biological machine starts to run, it keeps running twenty-four hours a
> day until it dies. The dynamic "motor" that pushes our behavior along
> its planned grooves is not located in our intentions, or our Plans, or our
> decisions to execute Plans – it is located in the nature of life itself. As
> William James says so clearly, the stream of thought can never stop
> flowing. We are often given our choice among several different Plans,
> but the rejection of one necessarily implies the execution of some other.
> (Miller et al., 1960, p. 64)

The fundamental underlying banality is, of course, that when a subject
enters the laboratory to participate in a visual information processing
experiment, what is entering the laboratory is a never-stopping stream
of thought. The experimenter, with verbal instruction and visual stimuli,
intrudes into and changes, i.e., determines and directs, this stream of thought.
Because the instruction is a verbal instruction, the stream of thought
becomes temporarily a verbal stream of thought. And, because the experimental world is made up of visual stimuli, that verbal stream of thought
is of such a form and content that it can interact with Visual Perception.
In short, my Intending Mind is nothing more or less than one particular
instantiation of James's *I*, of James's 'mind knowing' or 'thought thinking'.
It is that instantiation of James's *I* that the experimenter requires and
induces for the purpose and for the duration of his or her visual information processing experiment.

That my Intending Mind is indeed one variety of, one particular temporary instantiation of James's (1890/1950) *I*, becomes more clear when we compare some characteristics of his *I* with some properties I ascribed to my Intending Mind. What follows is what James has to say about the *I* in four instalments, each followed by a brief comment.

James introduces this *I* as follows:

> If the stream [of our personal consciousness] as a whole is identified with the Self far more than any outward thing, a *certain portion of the stream abstracted from the rest* is so identified in an altogether peculiar degree, and is felt by all men as a sort of innermost centre within the circle . . . Compared with this element of the stream, the other parts, even of the subjective life, seem transient external possessions, of which each in turn can be disowned, whilst that what disowns them remains.
>
> (James, 1890/1950, p. 297)

In my conceptualisation of the Intending Mind, the instruction-induced intentional sequence – a stream with states X, Y and > . . . >> – is a central element of total internal task performance, a sort of centre within the circle, compared to which the other parts, the objects (selected by X), the attributes (selected by Y), and the feedback (selected during > . . . >>), seem transient external possessions, of which each in turn can be disowned, whilst that which disowns them remains.

In James's view,

> Probably all men would describe it in much the same way up to a certain point. They would call it the *active* element in all consciousness; saying that whatever qualities a man's feelings may possess, or whatever content his thought may include, there is a spiritual something in him which seems to *go out* to meet these qualities and contents, whilst they seem to *come in* to be received by it.
>
> (James, 1890/1950, p. 297)

Here it is worthwhile to remember that my units of analysis, >> X > Y/report >> and >> X/act > . . . >>, are active elements. Moreover, state X goes out to meet contents whilst in report tasks some qualities of those contents come in and are received by term Y, and in act tasks feedback comes in and is received in the 'empty' interval > . . . >>.

In James's view, the *I*

> . . . is the home of interest . . . It is the source of effort and attention, and the place from which appear to emanate the fiats of the will.
>
> (James, 1890/1950, p. 298)

Here it is worthwhile to remember that in my content theory of attention the Intending Mind, consisting of $>> X > Y$/report $>>$ units and/or $>> X$/act $> \ldots >>$ units, is the source of effort and attention and therefore has to be interpreted as the place from which appear to emanate the fiats of the will.

And, according to James,

> A physiologist who should reflect upon it in his own person could hardly help, I should think, connecting it more or less vaguely with the process by which ideas or incoming sensations are 'reflected' or pass over into outward acts . . . for it plays a part analogous to it in the psychic life, being a sort of junction at which sensory ideas terminate and from which motor ideas proceed, and forming a kind of link between the two.
>
> (James, 1890/1950, p. 298)

Here it is worthwhile to remember that in my Intending Mind the X/act parts and the Y/report parts of the units of analysis are the junctions at which 'sensory ideas' terminate and from which 'motor ideas' proceed – these parts are the links between perception of the world and action in the world.

According to James (1890/1950) there is no need for psychology to look for a further or deeper or more fundamental *I*:

> . . . the special natural science of *psychology* must stop with the mere functional formula. *If the passing thought be the directly verifiable existent which no school has hitherto doubted it to be, then that thought is itself the thinker*, and psychology need not look beyond.
>
> (James, 1890/1950, p. 401)

In my conceptualisation, for the purpose and the duration of the experiment James's thinker becomes, is, and behaves as my Intending Mind. So, for the duration and purpose of the experiment my Intending Mind *is* the subject, the agent, the I, the you, the she, and the he to which most information processing theories refer. In experimental psychology a richer person or agent than my Intending Mind is not required. For a richer and more decent person or agent experimental psychology has to leave the laboratory with its simple tasks and needs to look beyond.

E.3   Freedom and free will

When reading a newspaper, watching TV, and studying a book, time and time again one meets words like 'freedom', 'free will', and 'free choice', and closely related and connected words like 'autonomy', 'responsibility', and 'dignity'. Here is one example. In searching Boring's *A History of Experimental Psychology* for the preparation of section E.1, I found:

Every man finds that the obvious thing about his own mind is 'what he wants to do,' and when he comes to interpret the minds of others they appear to be similar. Effort and volition and freedom are everywhere apparent when mind is in question ...

(Boring, 1950, p. 467)

Of course, this is not just an example. This quotation also makes clear where the need for the set of words just listed basically comes from: Freedom and volition and effort are everywhere apparent when the mind is in question.

It may very well be that, as Boring (1950) surmised, every person finds that the obvious thing about his or her own mind and the minds of others is that they are free agents, and that, through effort and volition, they can be the master of their fate and the captain of their soul.[15] It may very well be that every person finds that with the concepts freedom, effort, and volition a decent and acceptable explanation can be provided for the general problem of how people at a certain moment in time come to select and perform one or another task or action. But even then, two possibilities have to be distinguished. The first is that every person is right in thinking that he or she is a free agent because that is indeed what he or she is. The second is that every person is wrong in thinking that he or she is a free agent because that is not what he or she is. Within philosophy and psychology both possibilities have been seriously considered. Let us have a brief look at part of an important historical dispute to sharpen our appreciation of the two opposing points of view (see Watson, 1995, for an excellent introduction and for further details).

In the materialistic/mechanistic universe of Thomas Hobbes (1588–1679), there was no real place for an inner agent with a free will.[16] In his conceptualisation – known in detail from *Of Liberty and Necessity* (1651) – voluntary actions are necessitated, just as all other events in nature are. In his view, voluntary actions originate in the will, where the will is conceived as an 'appetite', the object and strength of which are given by physiological and psychological conditions that, in their turn, have to be understood by incipient motions necessitated by material processes. So, in Hobbes's (1651, p. 207) view

... when first a man hath an *appetite* or *will* to something, ... the cause of his *will*, is not the *will* itself, but *something* else not in his own disposing.

Nevertheless, according to Hobbes free agency is possible. Just because

Liberty is the absence of all the impediments to action that are not contained in the nature and intrinsical quality of the agent. (p. 206)

A free agent is he that can do if he will, and forbear if he will. (p. 208)

In Hobbes's view, freedom and materialistic/mechanistic determination can go together.[17] Hobbes is a compatibilist (see the Prologue).

It will be clear that this kind of free agency – conceived as the power to do as one wills, with the will completely determined by the 'appetites' – is not the kind of free agency churches and bishops are satisfied with (see Note 16). Some hundred years later, in 1788, Thomas Reid (1710–1796), a Presbyterian pastor, severely attacked Hobbes's point of view in his *Essays on the Active Powers of Man*. In this work, Reid declares

By the liberty of a moral agent, I understand a power over the determination of his own will. (p. 323)

In Reid's view, if we have no power over the will, we have no power whatever, so there must be an agent outside the will that determines what is going to be willed. Reid is a libertarian (see the Prologue).

Watson (1995, p. 177) describes the two opposing positions better than I can:

[According to Reid] When a person is free in acting, the person determines the will that is expressed in the conduct. This determination is the most basic exercise of agency, and without it, none of our movements would exemplify active power. In contrast, Hobbes's reductionist programme . . . implies that 'an intelligent being is an inert, inactive substance, which does not act but is acted upon' . . . Hobbes can allow for only passive powers; the power to be moved by external powers.

So, in Hobbes's view, the will simply wills what it has to will given the internal and external circumstances. In Reid's view, a 'moral agent' or an 'intelligent being' can intervene in this willing and determine what is willed.

At this point it is first of all worthwhile to see that the main theoretical work I have presented was neither explicitly concerned with nor implicitly hindered by issues pertaining to free will, freedom, and related topics. The reason for this fortunate state of affairs has, in my view, to be found in the fact that the part of experimental psychology I was concerned with has been successful in removing this tricky issue from its field of view – the field of empirical investigation and theoretical speculation. As a clue to how my experimental psychology was capable of evading this issue, it is worthwhile to consider the following description of task performance which can be taken as a caricature of what is involved in task performance in the experiments of the experimental psychology with which I was concerned:

There are you at the supermarket, wanting a can of Campbell's Tomato Soup, and faced with an array of several hundred identical cans of Campbell's Tomato Soup, all roughly equidistant from your hands. What to do? Before you even waste time and energy pondering this trivial problem, let us suppose, a perfectly random factor determines which can your hand reaches out for . . . This has never been a promising vision of the free choice of responsible agents, if only because it seems to secure freedom for such a small and trivial class of our choices. What does it avail me if I am free to choose *this* can of soup, but not free to choose between buying and stealing it?

(Dennett, 1979, p. 291)

The important point here is, of course, that a distinction can and has to be made between *action selection* and *action execution*. In this description, the buyer/stealer has already selected the shopping and can-picking action from among a set of alternative actions, from, e.g., the set going to the shop and buying a can of soup, staying home and watching TV, and going to the beach and swimming. It is only the execution of a minor, molecular 'ballistic' act part of an already selected major, molar total action that is considered here.[18]

In the experiments of the information processing approach, task *selection* or action *selection* is not the task of the subject. The experimenter determines what task or action is going to be performed. What remains for the subject is task *execution* or action *execution*. As shown earlier, that task execution or action execution can be described with units of analysis for 'ballistic' acts and reports of the form >> X/act > . . . >> and >> X > Y/ report >>. The resulting description is, however, more a description of how one of several hundred identical cans of Campbell's Tomato Soup is picked than of how the decision between stealing or buying is made. So, the information processing approach has been capable of leaving the tricky issues circling around concepts like freedom and free will outside its field of inquiry by structuring its experimental world in a, for scientific purposes, adequate and productive way. In that world, however, the approach is only capable of studying the minor choices of human subjects with regard to task and action execution. The major choices of responsible agents with regard to task and action selection remain unconsidered.[19]

To elucidate the concepts freedom and free will not only the minor but especially the major choices have to be considered. Dennett (1979) proposed a model for these major choices. To see what my conceptualisation has to say in this regard, it is worthwhile to consider Dennett's model in some detail. According to Dennett,

A realistic model of such decision-making just *might* have the following feature: When someone is faced with an important decision, something in him generates a variety of more or less relevant considerations bearing on the decision. (p. 293)

... a consideration-generator ... produces a series of considerations, some of which may of course be immediately rejected as irrelevant by the agent (consciously or unconsciously). Those considerations that are selected by the agent as having a more than negligible bearing on the decision then figure in a reasoning process, and if the agent is in the main reasonable, those considerations ultimately serve as predictors and explicators of the agent's final decision. (p. 295)

Dennett recounts a great number of convincing recommendations for his suggestion that this type of human decision making involves a 'generation' procedure as just described. One important recommendation is, for instance, that it permits education and information to make a difference.[20] For me and in the context of the present work the most important recommendation lies, however, in the simple accidental fact that Dennett describes his model as 'a process of ... generation and test' (p. 296) and as a 'generate-and-test procedure' (p. 297). Of course, this characterisation invites me to character- ise the essence of his model with

>> GENERATE > TEST >> >> GENERATE > TEST >>
>> GENERATE > TEST >> etc.,

or with

>> GENERATE/test > ... >> >> GENERATE/test > ... >>
>> GENERATE/test > ... >>.

In other words, Dennett's characterisation invites me to introduce and elabor- ate a third unit of analysis for molar action selection, a >> GENERATE > TEST >> unit or >> GENERATE/test > ... >> unit, with GENERATE, TEST and test standing for internal operations that, as such, are not dir- ectly confronted with the outer reality (the precise format of the unit is not of importance here; in the next section I return to this issue).

At this point it is not of importance to know how a sequence composed of these units of analysis generates its alternatives and considerations, tests its alternatives and considerations, and ultimately arrives at an action choice. Given the generally accepted point of view in science and philosophy that the case for determinism is convincing, it is appropriate to regard these processes as completely determined. It is of importance, however, to see that what we meet here again is what I prefer to call the Intending Mind. Now, however, the Intending Mind is not concerned with the use of visual information for the details of task performance. Now the Intending Mind is concerned with, engaged in, the internal generation and evaluation of possible courses of action and the choice of the most appropriate action alternative.

As just stated, it is appropriate to regard the processes of or in the Intending Mind concerned with action selection as completely determined. For the Intending Mind, however, that is not really relevant. In my conceptualisation, the Intending Mind is the *I* (see Section E.2). That *I* can be concerned with the visual world, the auditory world, the remembered world, and with many worlds more, but is now concerned with the world of viable action alternatives. In my conceptualisation there is no further 'active agent', 'moral agent', or 'intelligent agent' as in Reid's and Dennett's conceptualisations. What we thus have here is a determined Intending Mind or *I* that, as an active agent, generates and evaluates the set of viable action alternatives and determines/chooses what action is going to be performed.

Because this *I*, through and in its operation over time, generates and evaluates the set of alternatives and determines/chooses the future course of action, this *I*, when reflecting upon itself and upon its operations, can rightly have the impression that it can determine its future course of action. The *I* cannot otherwise than completely agree with the considerations, evaluations, and choices of the Intending Mind because the *I* coincides with, simply *is*, the Intending Mind. In this sense the *I*, experienced as a generating, evaluating and deciding empirical *me*, can and has to regard itself as a free internal agent. Upon reflection, Hobbes's machine driven by 'appetites' cannot otherwise than regard itself as Reid's agent with free will.

Of importance is here in addition that there is nothing that shows the Intending Mind or *I* that it is not free in arriving at and making the choice that is ultimately made. An example might make this clear. Consider a man sitting in a room contemplating a set of viable action alternatives. Assume that the intentional sequence the Intending Mind of that man runs through is approximately:

>> HOME tv/test > . . . >>
>> SHOP tomato soup/test > . . . >>
>> BEACH swim/test > . . . >>
>> SHOP tomato soup/test > . . . >>
>> SHOP/test > . . . >>
>> X/act > . . . >>.

In this series, the first four units of analysis are the viable molar action alternatives that are considered and evaluated. The >> SHOP/test > . . . >> unit is the ultimate determination or molar action choice and >> X/act > . . . >> is the first unit of analysis of the factual execution of the selected action, say, the unit of analysis for the molecular 'ballistic' act of turning in the direction of the door.[21]

The important point to see here is that only *after* the molar alternative, >> SHOP/test > . . . >>, is selected, does the actual external reality come in and play its role. That reality will inform the man in one or more molecular 'ballistic' >> X/act > ... >> units about the feasibility of the selected action. The outer world will, for instance, teach him whether he can go out or not. When the door can be opened and he can leave the room, one or more >> X/act > ... >> units will inform him about this state of affairs. When the door is locked and he cannot open it, one or more >> X/act > ... >> units will tell him that he cannot go out. So, reality teaches him in the stepwise *execution* of the selected action in one or more >> X/act > ... >> units where the boundaries of his freedom are. The *molar actions* considered and evaluated and the *choice of the molar action*, however, are as such never confronted in this way with the outer reality. The alternatives, tests and choice of alternative are simply 'passing by' in the Intending Mind. Molar actions are only internally selected and evaluated and not, as the molecular 'ballistic' acts, confronted with the external world. So, there is no reason whatsoever for the man to think that, within the limits of the situation he was in, he was not free in choosing the molar action >> SHOP/test > ... >>.

Taken all together, with regard to freedom and free will my conceptualisation leads me to the following conclusions.

- First, within the limits of a given situation, the Intending Mind, the *I*, completely determines/chooses, and therefore can completely determine/choose, its future course of action, and is therefore in this sense an agent with free will.[22]
- Second, there is no evidence stemming from the outer world that indicates or teaches the Intending Mind that within the limits of a given situation it cannot determine/choose its future course of action.
- Third, only in the stepwise execution of a selected action as a series or cycle of molecular 'ballistic' acts – that is, only in the confrontation of the outcome of the determination/choice process with the actual outer world – are the limits of freedom experienced.

The nature of the molar action evaluation and choice processes in the Intending Mind, plus the fact that these processes are never confronted with the actual outer reality, shows that we can maintain and defend the position that we are free and responsible 'inner agents' – even while there is no single convincing scientific argument in favour of this position and all evidence points at determinism.

E.4   The mind–body problem

My starting point in this work was simply that visual perception exists and that the mind exists – that is, they exist as subjectively experienced and as patterns of activation over neurons in regions in the brain. One implication of this starting point was that I had to assume and to accept the possibility that the Intending Mind, as subjectively experienced, and Visual Perception, as subjectively experienced, can be causally involved in task performance.

I had to assume and accept the possibility that the experienced Intending Mind and the experienced Visual Perception are not merely epiphenomena, not merely irrelevant and ineffective shadows.

The idea that Visual Perception as subjectively experienced and Intending Mind as subjectively experienced are causally involved in task performance is an idea that suits me well. Basically my conviction is that some spark of 'subjectivity' or 'mentality' must have appeared somewhere in the course of evolution as a biological accident. That spark must have conferred on its owner some survival and reproductive advantages. Subsequently, evolutionary pressure must have expanded and developed that accidental spark with the result that we now experience and use that elaborated accident that we indicate with clumsy terms like our 'consciousness' or our 'mental life', or 'Visual Perception as subjectively experienced' and 'Intending Mind as subjectively experienced'.

With regard to this conviction I find James at my side. For James (1890/ 1950) it is

> ... quite inconceivable that consciousness should have *nothing to do* with a business which it so faithfully attends. And the question, 'What has it to do?' is one which psychology has no right to 'surmount,' for it is her plain duty to consider it. (p. 136)

What consciousness does for its 'owner' is, according to James,

> ... bringing a more or less constant pressure to bear in favor of *those* of its performances which make for the most permanent interests ... just such pressure and such inhibition are what consciousness *seems* to be exerting all the while. (p. 140)

Specifying in general terms what consciousness does for its owner is one thing. Specifying in detail how consciousness does what it does is, however, quite another. Nevertheless, a theory that pretends to have something to say about how the mind uses visual perception for task performance must have something to say about these details. So, let us start with the general problem and then try to proceed to the details.

The general mind–body problem is the problem of how the subjective phenomena experienced in or through the mind can have an effect via the objective brain and body in the outer world. In other words, when we concern ourselves with the general mind–body problem

> What we want is to understand how such nonphysical things as *purposes, deliberations, plans, decisions, theories, tensions*, and *values* can play a part in bringing about physical changes in the physical world.
>
> (Popper, 1966, p. 15)

How the subjective, conscious, deliberating, and deciding mind can have any effect in the objective, outer, physical world is, of course, the core problem of any theory concerned with the question of how people use their visual perception in the performance of tasks. And it is this core problem that we now have to consider in detail.

With the information provided in preceding sections, for 'act' tasks we can arrive at a rather detailed and complete picture of how the Intending Mind, as subjectively experienced, and Visual Perception, as subjectively experienced, can have their effects in the outer physical world.[23] This is so because, with the information provided, we are now in a position to see where exactly the problem is. Two pieces of information provided earlier are essential:

- The first relevant piece of information is that we have already met Popper's nonphysical things, his purposes, deliberations, plans, decisions, theories, tensions, and values. We have already met such nonphysical things in terms of units of analysis of the Intending Mind in Section E.3, the section concerned with freedom and free will. There my argument was restricted to the considerations and evaluations – Popper's deliberations – and the ultimate choices of an action alternative – Popper's decisions – that are involved in free will. In my conceptualisation, the deliberations and decisions involved in free will, as well as the other processes referred to by Popper, are all and only operations of and in the Intending Mind. These operations lead to the internal selection of one or another molar action. Neither these operations nor the internal selection of the molar action are ever confronted with the outer reality. Only in the execution of the selected molar action as a series or cycle of molecular 'ballistic' acts does the outer world come in. Only in the execution of the selected action as a series or cycle of $>> X/act > \ldots >>$ units does the Intending Mind bring about physical changes in the physical world and is informed about the physical changes it brought about.

- The second piece of relevant information is that I have already provided an answer to the question of how the conscious Intending Mind can bring about physical changes in the physical world in the execution of a selected act task. In Section 9.2, I argued that the Intending Mind can bring about these effects with the molecular units of analysis for 'ballistic' acts, the $>> X/act > \ldots >>$ units. In each of these units of analysis the subjective Intending Mind can steer the objective executive brain/body via the objective anatomical positions of selected codes. In act tasks, in each unit of analysis the anatomical position of the code is the intermediary that allows a selected perceived position to reach and manipulate an intended objective position in the physical world.

With these two pieces of information in place and understood, it is not difficult to see what problem in my conceptualisation still remains to be considered. Section E.3 was concerned with aspects of the question of how in the Intending Mind, from among a number of alternatives, a molar action is selected. The general mind–brain problem is the problem of how that selected molar action in the Intending Mind can have physical effects in the outer world. In my conceptualisation a selected molar action as such exerts no effects in the outer world. Only molecular 'ballistic' units of analysis, >> X/act > . . . >>, can do that. So, in my conceptualisation the general mind–brain problem is solved when it is made clear how a selected molar action is chopped up into a series of molecular acts. In my conceptualisation the general mind–brain problem reduces to the problem of how a selected molar action is translated or transformed into a series of molecular 'ballistic' acts. And exactly here Miller et al. (1960) provide important information about how to proceed.

In *Plans and the Structure of Behavior*, Miller et al. (1960) are explicitly concerned with the hierarchical organisation of behaviour, i.e., with the fact that behaviour is organised simultaneously at several levels of complexity. They declare:

> . . . molar units [of behavior] must be composed of molecular units . . . a proper description of behavior must be made on *all levels simultaneously* . . . For example, the molar pattern of behavior X consists of two parts, *A* and *B*, in that order. Thus X = *AB*. But *A*, in turn, consists of two parts, *a* and *b*; and *B* consists of three, *c*, *d*, and *e*. Thus X = *AB* = *abcde*, and we can describe the same segment of behavior at any one of the three levels . . . we do not want to pick one level . . . the complete description must include all levels. (p. 13)

In their Test-Operate-Test-Exit, i.e., TOTE theorising, Miller et al. (1960, p. 32) try to realise their ambition – a description including all levels – by allowing the operational components of TOTE units, the Os, to be TOTE units. They are very well aware that this method of retaining the same pattern of description for the higher units as for the lower units may be confusing. They therefore consider an example: Hammering a nail in a piece of wood. The details of their procedure are not yet of importance here. Of interest is the hammering result they end up with. That result is listed in the following adapted quotation (Miller et al., 1960, p. 34):

> [T] Test nail. (Head sticks up.)
> [T] Test hammer. (Hammer is down.)
> [O] Lift hammer.
> [T] Test hammer. (Hammer is up.)
> [T] Test hammer. (Hammer is up.)
> [O] Strike nail.
> [T] Test hammer. (Hammer is down.)
> [T] Test nail. (Head sticks up.)
> [T] Test hammer.
> And so on . . .

What, in my view, this quotation first of all shows is that Miller and colleagues are poor carpenters. They spend most of their time with testing (T), and almost completely forget to strike the nail (O). (I wonder how Miller, Galanter, and Pribram eat soup from a soup-plate with a spoon.) What, in my view, this quotation also shows is that Miller et al. made an error in selecting the molecular 'ballistic' act. In their view, lifting the hammer (↑) and striking the nail (↓) are separate 'ballistic' acts. In my view, in this example the 'ballistic' act is either striking-plus-lifting (↓ ↑) or lifting-plus-striking (↑ ↓). But if that is the case, and given the considerations presented in Sections 9.1 and 9.4, Miller et al.'s example can then also be summarised with

with X standing for the selection of the top of the nail as an attractor and act for either striking-plus-lifting (↓ ↑) or for lifting-plus-striking (↑ ↓). In other words, if my choice of 'ballistic' act is correct here, Miller et al.'s hierarchical example simply reduces to one particular instance of my general conceptualisation of the generation of a stretch of behaviour with an invariant intermediate goal (see Section 9.4). In Section 9.4, I even went one step further and elaborated this cycle in such a way that continuous task performance and the hook-up of saccadic eye movements were also accounted for.

So, in Section 9.4 I dealt with Miller et al.'s (1960) example. In my view, however, hammering a nail, picking apples, or eating soup are not the most interesting and appropriate examples of hierarchically structured real-life behaviour. Fortunately, from Miller et al.'s theorising an important hint can be derived about how to conceptualise more interesting hierarchically structured behaviour. Please remember that in their theory these authors realised their ambition – a description of behaviour at all levels – by allowing the operational components of their TOTE units to be TOTE units. Close inspection of their text and example shows that this expansion strategy amounts to the simple rule that in each TOT the O can be replaced by TO, i.e., the rule O → TO (see also Miller et al., 1960, Ch. 2, footnote 11).[24] So, allowable sequences of test, T, and operate, O, components are, for instance,

TOT
TTOT
TTTOT
TTOTTOTT . . . (see the hammering a nail example above)
TTTTTTTTTOT.

In the present context the last type of sequence in particular, when interpreted as an

        XXXXXXXXXX/act > . . .

sequence, is of interest for the planning and execution of hierarchically
structured goal-directed behaviour. The following example serves to make
clear what I mean.

Suppose that I am at home in the kitchen and I suddenly decide that I
now need a can of Campbell's Tomato Soup (see Section E.3 for this decision). I am now here, in this kitchen, and that can of soup is now there, on
that shelf in that shop in that square at the end of that street in that nearby
city. In this situation, with me now here in the kitchen and not in the
position to see that can, there is no molecular 'ballistic' >> CAN/act > . . . >>
unit, or cycle of these units, that can deliver me the can. For this unit to
perform its job, controlling the picking of the can, I have first to manoeuvre
myself in front of the shelf. In this situation however – I am in the kitchen
and not in the position to see that shelf – there is no molecular >> SHELF/
act > . . . >> unit, or cycle of these units, that can guide me to this shelf. For
this unit to perform its job, controlling my walking to the shelf, I have first
to take care that I arrive, in one way or another, in the shop. In this situation however – I am still in the kitchen . . . – there is no molecular >> SHOP/
act > . . . >> unit, or cycle of these units, that can bring me to the shop.
I have first to drive to the square and park my car there. In this situation,
etc., etc. . . . I have first to walk in the direction of the kitchen door. And,
surprise, I am in the position to see that door and now there is a molecular
unit of analysis, or better, cycle of units of analysis, of the form >> DOOR/
act > . . . >> that can guide my walk to the kitchen door.

This drama, this explication of the planning of can-stealing behaviour,
can be summarised with

    >> CAN/test > . . . >>
      >> SHELF/test > . . . >>
        >> SHOP/test > . . . >>
          >> SQUARE/test > . . . >>
            >> ETC/test > . . . >>
              >> . . . /test > . . . >>
                >> DOOR/act > . . . >>,

with each 'test' indicating that the attractor, the X in each >> X/test > . . . >>
unit, cannot be reached with one molecular unit of analysis, or a cycle
of such units of analysis. Of course, this drama can also be summarized
with

    CAN SHELF SHOP SQUARE ETC . . . DOOR/act > . . . ,

and this is Miller et al.'s (1960) TTTTTTTOT sequence, interpreted as an XXXXXXX/act > . . . sequence (see above). In this conceptualisation the planning of a hierarchically structured goal-directed action consists of the generating and testing of the required series of task-appropriate attractors. In the execution of the action the simultaneous availability of these attractors and the actual position of the actor take care that the intended goal is reached.

Many more interesting things can be said about the planning and execution of hierarchically structured behaviour (see Miller et al., 1960, for valuable suggestions), that, however, is not the issue this section has been about. The topic this section was concerned with was the general mind–body problem. And at this point my detailed answer to Popper's question – how can purposes, deliberations, plans, etc. play a part in bringing about physical changes in a physical world – will be clear. That answer consists of two parts.

Deliberations, decisions, plans, etc., as such never bring about the physical changes in the physical world that Popper is talking about. All the activities mentioned by Popper are internal operations of the Intending Mind that as such never touch or come into contact with the outer world.

Only after the selection of a molar action on the basis of the deliberations, values, purposes, etc., and only during the stepwise actual execution of that selected action through the Intending Mind with molecular 'ballistic' units of analysis, are physical changes in the physical world brought about.

Notes

1 It is interesting to know that Wundt already recognised two 'contributions' to perception, one from the outside and one from the inside. According to Wundt (1907, pp. 31–32, in Miller, 1964),

> All the contents of psychical experience are of a composite character. It follows, therefore, that *psychical elements*, or the absolutely simple and irreducible components of psychical phenomena, are the products of analysis and abstraction . . . As a result of psychical analysis, we find that there are *psychical elements of two kinds* . . . The elements of the objective contents we call *sensational elements*, or simply *sensations* . . . The subjective elements, on the other hand, are designed as *affective elements*, or *simple feelings* . . .

Is this Visual Perception and Intending Mind in its most elementary form?
2 Here, and in what follows, I simply neglect the fact these experimenters engaged in quite a lot of preparatory activity, e.g., building apparatus, preparing stimuli, etc. – i.e., performed a great diversity of >> X/act > . . . >> tasks before being in a position to collect the critical observations.
3 In Chapter 1 we already saw that James (1890/1950) completely disagreed with the compound-element and element-attribute convictions. There were more dissidents, for instance Kuelpe. They anticipated gestalt psychology.
4 Boring (1950, p. 602) remarks with regard to gestalt psychology:

> . . . the phenomenologist seeks to find an *experimentum crucis*, the convincing single demonstration of some observed generality . . . Since phenomenology

deals with immediate experience, its conclusions are instantaneous. They emerge at once and need not wait upon the results of calculations derived from measurements.

5 Watson (1913, in Vanderplas, 1966, pp. 77–78) characterises and rejects early introspective psychology when he states:

> My goal is not "the description and explanation of states of consciousness as such," nor that of obtaining such proficiency in mental gymnastics that I can immediately lay hold of a state of consciousness and say, "this, as a whole, consists of gray sensation number 350, of such and such extent, occurring in conjunction with the sensation of cold of a certain intensity; one of pressure of a certain intensity and extent," and so on *ad infinitum.*

In his view, this early introspective experimental psychology,

> Due to a mistaken notion that its fields of facts are conscious phenomena and that introspection is the only direct method of ascertaining these facts, . . . has enmeshed itself in a series of speculative questions which . . . are not open to experimental treatment (p. 83).

6 The problems behaviourism later encountered had nothing to do with the method, but with the naïve theoretical conviction that animals and human beings could be regarded as simple reflex or Stimulus–Response machines. Watson (1913) was convinced that:

> In a system of psychology completely worked out, given the response the stimuli can be predicted; given the stimuli the response can be predicted.
> (Vanderplas, 1966, p. 77)

Skinner (1972, p. 193) agreed in principle but already saw that issues are somewhat more complicated:

> Man is a machine in the sense that he is a complex system behaving in lawful ways, but the complexity is extraordinary.

Chomsky's (1959) verdict we have already met in the Prologue (see Note 4 there).

7 In the behaviourist's experiments the 'results produced in the visual world' consist not only of what is directly, on-line, observed, but also of off-line records, graphs, lists, etc., that are read, interpreted, and used later on.

8 Within behaviourism Tolman and Lashley are the exceptions (see also Chapter 3).

9 For my interpretation of what happens in act tasks, see under Behaviourism.

10 The 'results produced (in the visual world)' mainly consist of records, lists, graphs, etc.

11 In my view, object selection and attribute selection, in this work captured with >> X > Y/report >>, while not generally recognised as such, is one of the most important contributions of the information processing approach (see also Chapter 3). In 'The Neural Basis of Predicate–Argument Structure', J. R. Hurford (in press) argues that in this object–attribute operation possibly 'a preadaptive platform . . . for the linguistic description of scenes' can be found.

12 From the chapter 'Personal Identity' in *Treatise on Human Nature* (Hume, 1739); taken from James (1890/1950, p. 351).

13 With regard to the empirical ego, i.e., with regard to the objective fact that we all *experience* ourselves as distinct and unique beings, contemporary philosophy of mind has interesting things to say. The general idea is that being a 'self', a 'conscious agent', is a concept, a content just as other contents. Different authors emphasise different contents. Harré (1998), for instance, emphasises the self as the sense of one's location, as a person, in the world, and Dennett (1992), for instance, emphasises the self as a source of personal stories, as a 'centre of narrative gravity'. It will be clear that these interpretations of 'agents' or 'subjects' as mental contents, as thoughts or ideas about oneself and about others, are special cases of, proper subsets of, James's (1890/1950) general empirical ego.

14 This I, or Thought, can be regarded as a pair of tongs that can take hold of everything except itself, or as a basket that can contain everything except itself. Such comparisons make clear why this I, Thought, is not readily accessible to introspection.

15 Taken from W. E. Henley's most popular poem, 'Invictus' (1875), which concludes with the lines

> I am the master of my fate;
> I am the captain of my soul.

16 In England Hobbes became the centre of a controversy over free will and mechanism. In 1651, one of his admirers distributed an unauthorised version of his part of a written exchange with Bishop Bramhall of Londonderry on the problem of free will under the title *Of Liberty and Necessity*. A severe reaction by the bishop was the result. A series of written defences and accusations followed. In 1658 the bishop accused Hobbes of atheism.

17 In Hobbes's conceptualisation, 'Liberty and necessity are consistent . . . the actions which men voluntarily do . . . proceed from liberty, and because every act of man's will . . . proceed from some cause, and that from another cause, in a continual chain, proceed from necessity' (Hobbes, 1651, p. 56).

18 The distinction between molecular and molar behaviour stems from E. Tolman (see also Section 3.2).

> An analysis of action into elements gives you . . . what Tolman called *molecular behavior*. The wholes, on the other hand, are *molar behavior* and in it purposiveness emerges. Men and animals act in respect of ends.
> (Boring, 1950, p. 647)

19 As another clue to how my experimental psychology has managed to evade the tricky issues circling around freedom and free will it is worthwhile to return briefly to the theorising in the perception for action camp. As set out in Chapter 2, the theorists in that camp recognised two forms of selection – the selection of an action and the selection of the object to be acted upon. Of these two selections, however, in my analysis and unit of analysis in Chapter 9 only one remained. In the unit of analysis, $\gg$ X/act $> \ldots \gg$, object selection by X is made explicit but action selection does not show up. What act is selected in /act is fully determined by the experimenter.

20 Dennett (1979, p. 296) writes:

> . . . a moral education, while not completely determining the generation of considerations and moral decision making, can nevertheless have a prior selective effect on the sorts of considerations that will occur. A moral education, like mutual discussion and persuasion generally, could adjust the boundaries and probabilities of the generator . . .

21 It is worthwhile to note that in this sequence of considerations and evaluations in the Intending Mind the I, the agent self, is clearly implicated. The first unit of analysis can be read as >> SHALL I STAY HOME and watch tv?/test > . . . >> and the ultimate choice can be read as >> I GO OUT SHOPPING/test > . . . >>. This shows that equating the Intending Mind with the *I* is not that far-fetched. It also shows that in a sequence of considerations and evaluations an empirical me is intimately involved – the empirical me now here in this position in the room with these opportunities and desires. Harré (1998, p. 4) characterises this empirical me with:

> . . . a sense of one's point of view, at any moment a location in space from which one perceives and acts upon the world, including that part that lies within one's own skin.

22 Of course, anticipated outcomes play a role in the determination/choice process; see the example.

23 In this section I am only concerned with the mind–body problem for 'act' tasks. For 'report' tasks a theory elucidating the origin and development of language is required, a theory I do not touch on. Hurford (in press) provides a good start.

24 Stated otherwise, the rule says that an O has to be followed by a T and that a T can be followed by a T and an O (or an exit).

References

Ach, N. (1905). *Über die Willenstätigkeit und das Denken*. Göttingen: Vandenhoeck & Rupprecht.

Allport, D. A. (1971). Parallel encoding within and between stimulus dimensions. *Perception & Psychophysics, 10*, 104–108.

Allport, D. A. (1980a). Patterns and actions: Cognitive mechanisms are content specific. In G. Claxton (Ed.), *Cognitive psychology: New directions*. London: Routledge & Kegan Paul.

Allport, D. A. (1980b). Attention and performance. In G. Claxton (Ed.), *Cognitive psychology: New directions*. London: Routledge & Kegan Paul.

Allport, D. A. (1987). Selection for action: Some behavioral and neurophysiological considerations of attention and action. In H. Heuer & A. F. Sanders (Eds.), *Perspectives on perception and action*. Hillsdale, NJ: Lawrence Erlbaum Associates Inc.

Allport, D. A. (1989). Visual attention. In M. I. Posner (Ed.), *Foundations of cognitive science*. Cambridge, MA: MIT Press.

Allport, D. A. (1993). Attention and control: Have we been asking the wrong questions? A critical review of 25 years. In D. E. Meyer & S. Kornblum (Eds.), *Attention and performance XIV*. Cambridge, MA: MIT Press.

Allport, D. A., Styles, E. A., & Hsieh, S. (1994). Shifting intentional set: Exploring the dynamic control of tasks. In C. Umilta & M. Moscovitch (Eds.), *Attention and performance XV: Conscious and nonconscious information processing* (pp. 396–419). Cambridge, MA: MIT Press.

Allport, D. A., Tipper, S. P., & Chmiel, N. R. J. (1985). Perceptual integration and postcategorical filtering. In M. I. Posner & O. S. M. Marin (Eds.), *Mechanisms of attention: Attention and performance XI*. Hillsdale, NJ: Lawrence Erlbaum Associates Inc.

Andersen, R. A., Snyder, L. H., Li, C., & Stricanne, B. (1993). Coordinate transformations in the representation of spatial information. *Current Biology, 3*, 171–176.

Angell, J. R., & Moore, A. W. (1896). Reaction time: A study in attention and habit. *The Psychological Review, 3*, 245–258.

Anstis, S. M. (1974). A chart demonstrating variations in acuity with retinal position. *Vision Research, 14*, 589–592.

Averbach, E., & Coriell, A. S. (1961). Short-term memory in vision. *Bell System Technical Journal, 40*, 309–328.

Bacon, W. F., & Egeth, H. E. (1994). Overriding stimulus-driven attentional capture. *Perception & Psychophysics, 55*, 485–496.

Baddeley, A. (1986). *Working memory*. Oxford: Clarendon Press.

Baldwin, J. M. (1896). The 'type-theory' of reaction. *Mind*, *5*, 81–90.

Baylis, G. C. (1994). Visual attention and objects. *Journal of Experimental Psychology: Human Perception and Performance*, *20*, 208–212.

Baylis, G. C., & Driver, J. S. (1993). Visual attention and objects: Evidence for hierarchical coding. *Journal of Experimental Psychology: Human Perception and Performance*, *19*, 451–470.

Baylis, G. C., & Driver, J. S. (1992). Visual parsing and response competition: The effect of grouping factors. *Perception & Psychophysics*, *51*, 145–162.

Becker, W. (1972). The control of eye movements in the saccadic system. In J. Dichans & E. Bizzi (Eds.), *Cerebral control of eye movements and motion perception* (pp. 233–243). Basel: Karger.

Besner, D. (1999). Basic processes in reading: Multiple routines in localist and connectionist models. In R. M. Klein & P. A. McMullen (Eds.), *Converging methods for understanding reading and dyslexia. Language, speech, and communication* (pp. 413–458). Cambridge, MA: MIT Press.

Biederman, I., & Checkosky, S. F. (1970). Processing redundant information. *Journal of Experimental Psychology*, *83*, 486–490.

Boring, E. G. (1950). *A history of experimental psychology*. New York: Appleton-Century-Crofts.

Brain, Lord (1951). *Mind, perception and science*. Oxford: Blackwell.

Brentano, F. (1874). *Psychologie vom empirische Standpunkt*. Leipzig: Felix Meiner [2nd Ed.: Leipzig, 1924].

Bridgeman, B. (1992). Conscious vs. unconscious processes. *Theory & Psychology*, *2*, 73–88.

Bridgeman, B. (1999a). Separate representations of visual space for perception and visually guided behavior. In G. Aschersleben, T. Bachmann, & J. Müsseler (Eds.), *Cognitive contributions to the perception of spatial and temporal events* (pp. 3–13). Amsterdam: Elsevier.

Bridgeman, B. (1999b). Neither strong nor weak space constancy is coded in striate cortex. *Psychological Research*, *62*, 261–265.

Bridgeman, B., Kirch, M., & Sperling, A. (1981). Segregation of cognitive and motor aspects of visual function using induced motion. *Perception & Psychophysics*, *29*, 336–342.

Bridgeman, B., Van der Heijden, A. H. C., & Velichkovsky, B. M. (1994). A theory of visual stability across saccadic eye movements. *Behavioral and Brain Sciences*, *17*, 247–292.

Brindley, G. S., & Merton, P. A. (1960). The absence of position sense in the human eye. *Journal of Physiology*, *153*, 127–130.

Broadbent, D. E. (1952). Listening to one of two synchronous messages. *Journal of Experimental Psychology*, *44*, 51–55.

Broadbent, D. E. (1958). *Perception and communication*. London: Pergamon.

Broadbent, D. E. (1970). Stimulus set and response set: Two kinds of selective attention. In D. I. Mostofsky (Ed.), *Attention: Contemporary theory and analysis*. New York: Appleton-Century-Crofts.

Broadbent, D. E. (1971). *Decision and stress*. London: Academic Press.

Broadbent, D. E. (1982). Task combination and selective intake of information. *Acta Psychologica*, *50*, 253–290.

Broadbent, D. E. (1987). Structures and strategies: Where are we now? *Psychological Research*, *49*, 73–79.

Broadbent, D. E. (1993). A word before leaving. In D. E. Meyer & S. Kornblum (Eds.), *Attention and performance XIV* (pp. 863–880). Hillsdale, NJ: Lawrence Erlbaum Associates Inc.

Broadbent, D. E., & Broadbent, M. H. P. (1986). Encoding speed of visual features and the occurrence of illusory conjunctions. *Perception, 15*, 515–524.

Broadbent, D. E., & Broadbent, M. H. P (1987). From detection to identification: Response to multiple targets in rapid serial visual presentation. *Perception & Psychophysics, 42*, 105–113.

Brown, T. L., Roos-Gilbert, L., & Carr, T. H. (1995). Automaticity and word perception: Evidence from Stroop and Stroop dilution effects. *Journal of Experimental Psychology: Learning, Memory, and Cognition, 21*, 1395–1411.

Bryden, M. P. (1961). The role of post-exposural eye movements in tachistoscopic perception. *Canadian Journal of Psychology, 15*, 220–225.

Bundesen, C. (1990). A theory of visual attention. *Psychological Review, 97*, 523–547.

Bundesen, C., Pedersen, L., & Larsen, A. (1984). Measuring efficiency of selection from briefly exposed visual displays: A model for partial report. *Journal of Experimental Psychology: Human Perception and Performance, 10*, 329–339.

Bundesen, C., Shibuya, H., & Larsen, A. (1985). Visual selection from multielement displays: A model for partial report. In M. I. Posner & O. S. M. Marin (Eds.), *Attention and performance XI*. Hillsdale, NJ: Lawrence Erlbaum Associates Inc.

Butler, B. E., Mewhort, D. J. K., & Tramer, S. C. (1987). Location errors in tachistoscopic recognition: Guesses, probe errors, or spatial confusions? *Canadian Journal of Psychology, 41*, 339–350.

Carpenter, R. H. S. (1988). *Movements of the eyes, 2nd Ed.* London: Pion.

Cattell, J. M. (1886). The time it takes to see and name objects. *Mind, 11*, 63–65.

Cave, K. R., & Wolfe, J. M. (1990). Modeling the role of parallel processing in visual search. *Cognitive Psychology, 22*, 225–271.

Cheal, M. L., & Lyon, D. R. (1991). Central and peripheral precuing of forced-choice discrimination. *Quarterly Journal of Experimental Psychology, 43*A, 859–880.

Cherry, E. C. (1953). Some experiments on the recognition of speech with one and two ears. *Journal of the Acoustical Society of America, 25*, 957–979.

Chomsky, N. (1959). Review of *Verbal behavior* by B. F. Skinner. *Language, 35*, 26–58.

Chun, M. M., & Potter, M. C. (1995). A two-stage model for multiple target detection in rapid serial visual presentation. *Journal of Experimental Psychology: Human Perception and Performance, 21*, 109–127.

Coltheart, M. (1972). Visual information processing. In P. C. Dodwell (Ed.), *New horizons in psychology 2*. Harmondsworth, UK: Penguin.

Coltheart, M. (1978). Lexical access in simple reading tasks. In G. Underwood (Ed.), *Strategies of information processing* (pp. 151–216). London: Academic Press.

Coltheart, M. (1984). Sensory memory – A tutorial review. In H. Bouma & D. G. Bouwhuis (Eds.), *Attention and performance X: Control of language processes*. Hillsdale, NJ: Lawrence Erlbaum Associates Inc.

Coltheart, M., Curtis, B., Atkins, P., & Haller, M. (1993). Models of reading aloud: Dual-route and parallel-distributed approaches. *Psychological Review, 100*, 589–608.

Coltheart, M., Rastle, K., Perry, C., Langdon, R., & Ziegler, J. (2001). DRC. A dual route cascaded model of visual word recognition and reading. *Psychological Review*, *108*, 204–256.

Cowan, N. (1999). An embedded-processes model of working memory. In A. Miyake & P. Shah (Eds.), *Models of working memory: Mechanisms of active maintenance and executive control* (pp. 62–101). Cambridge: Cambridge University Press.

Cowey, A. (1981). Why are there so many visual areas. In F. O. Schmitt, F. G. Worden, G. Adelman, & S. G. Dennis (Eds.), *The organisation of the cerebral cortex*. Cambridge, MA: MIT Press.

Crovitz, H. F., & Daves, W. (1962). Tendencies to eye movement and perceptual accuracy. *Journal of Experimental Psychology*, *63*, 495–498.

Dalrymple-Alford, E. C. (1972). Associative facilitation and interference in the Stroop color–word task. *Perception & Psychophysics*, *11*, 274–276.

Dalrymple-Alford, E. C., & Budayr, B. (1966). Examination of some aspects of the Stroop color–word test. *Perceptual and Motor Skills*, *23*, 1211–1214.

De Bie, J., Van den Brink, G., & Van Sonderen, J. F. (1987). The systematic undershoot of saccades: A localization or an oculomotor phenomenon? In J. K. O'Regan & A. Levy-Schoen (Eds.), *Eye movements: From physiology to cognition* (pp. 85–94). Amsterdam: Elsevier.

De Kamps, M., & Van der Velde, F. (2001). Using a recurrent network to bind form, color and position into a unified percept. *Neurocomputing*, *38–40*, 523–528.

Dennett, D. C. (1979). *Brainstorms: Philosophical essays on mind and psychology*. Hassocks, UK: Harvester Press.

Dennett, D. C. (1992). *Consciousness explained*. London: Penguin.

Dennett, D. C., & Kinsbourne, M. (1992). Time and the observer: The where and when of consciousness in the brain. *Behavioral and Brain Sciences*, *15*, 183–247.

Descartes, R. (1641). *Meditations on first philosophy*. Paris: Michel Soly. [In E. Haldane & G. Ross (Eds.), *The philosophical works of Descartes* (1968). Cambridge: Cambridge University Press.]

Descartes, R. (1650/1973). *Les passions de l'âme. Oeuvres philosophiques de Descartes 3*. Paris: Garnier.

Desimone, R., & Duncan, J. (1995). Neural mechanisms of selective visual attention. *Annual Review of Neuroscience*, *18*, 193–222.

Deubel, H. (1996). Visual processing and cognitive factors in the generation of saccadic eye movements. In W. Prinz & B. Bridgeman (Eds.), *Handbook of perception and action: Vol. I, Perception* (pp. 143–189). London: Academic Press.

Deubel, H., & Schneider, W. X. (1996). Saccade target selection and object recognition: Evidence for a common attentional mechanism. *Vision Research*, *36*, 1827–1837.

Deutsch, J. A., & Deutsch, D. (1963). Attention: Some theoretical considerations. *Psychological Review*, *70*, 80–90.

Dewey, J. (1896). The reflex arc concept in psychology. *The Psychological Review*, *3*, 357–370.

Donders, F. C. (1868/1969). Die Schnelligkeit psychischer Processe. *Reichert's und Du Bois-Reymond's Archiv für Anatomie, Physiologie und wissenschaftliche Medicin*, 657–681. [On the speed of mental processes. *Acta Psychologica*, *30*, 412–431.]

Driver, J. S., & Baylis, G. C. (1989). Movement and visual attention: The spotlight metaphor breaks down. *Journal of Experimental Psychology: Human Perception and Performance*, *15*, 448–456.

Duncan, J. (1980). The locus of interference in the perception of simultaneous stimuli. *Psychological Review, 87*, 272–300.

Duncan, J. (1983). Perceptual selection based on alphanumeric class: Evidence from partial reports. *Perception & Psychophysics, 33*, 533–547.

Duncan, J. (1984). Selective attention and the organization of visual information. *Journal of Experimental Psychology: General, 113*, 501–517.

Duncan, J. (1985). Visual search and visual attention. In M. I. Posner & O. S. Marin (Eds.), *Attention and performance XI* (pp. 85–106). Hillsdale, NJ: Lawrence Erlbaum Associates Inc.

Duncan, J. (1993a). Similarity between concurrent visual discriminations: Dimensions and objects. *Perception & Psychophysics, 54*, 425–430.

Duncan, J. (1993b). Coordination of what and where in visual attention. *Perception, 22*, 1261–1270.

Duncan, J. (1996). Cooperating brain systems in selective perception and attention. In T. Inn & J. L. McClelland (Eds.), *Attention and performance XVI* (pp. 549–578). Cambridge, MA: MIT Press.

Duncan, J., Martens, S., & Ward, R. (1997). Restricted attentional capacity within but not between sensory modalities. *Nature, 387*, 808–810.

Duncan, J., Ward, R., & Shapiro, K. L. (1994). Direct measurement of attentional dwell time in human vision. *Nature, 369*, 313–315.

Dyer, F. N. (1973). Interference and facilitation for color naming with separate bilateral presentation of the word and color. *Journal of Experimental Psychology, 99*, 314–317.

Egeth, H. E., & Dagenbach, D. (1991). Parallel versus serial processing in visual search: Further evidence for subadditive effects of visual quality. *Journal of Experimental Psychology: Human Perception and Performance, 17*, 551–560.

Egeth, H. E., & Yantis, S. (1997). Visual attention: Control, representation, and time course. In J. T. Spence, J. M. Darley, & D. J. Foss (Eds.), *Annual review of psychology, Vol. 48* (pp. 269–297). Palo Alto, CA: Annual Reviews Inc.

Ehrenstein, A. (1997). Commentary on Prinz. In B. Hommel & W. Prinz (Eds.), *Theoretical issues in stimulus–response compatibility* (pp. 269–272). Amsterdam: Elsevier.

Engel, F. L. (1977). Visual conspicuity: Visual search and fixation tendencies of the eye. *Vision Research, 17*, 95–108.

Eriksen, B. A., & Eriksen, C. W. (1974). Effects of noise letters upon the identification of a target letter in a nonsearch task. *Perception & Psychophysics, 16*, 143–149.

Eriksen, C. W. (1990). Attentional search of the visual field. In D. Brogan (Ed.), *Visual search*. London: Taylor & Francis Ltd.

Eriksen, C. W. (1995). The flankers task and response competition: A useful tool for investigating a variety of cognitive problems. *Visual Cognition, 2*, 101–118.

Eriksen, C. W., & Collins, J. F. (1969). Temporal course of selective attention. *Journal of Experimental Psychology, 80*, 254–261.

Eriksen, C. W., & Hoffman, J. E. (1972a). Some characteristics of selective attention in visual perception determined by vocal reaction time. *Perception & Psychophysics, 11*, 169–171.

Eriksen, C. W., & Hoffman, J. E. (1972b). Temporal and spatial characteristics of selective encoding from visual displays. *Perception & Psychophysics, 12*, 201–204.

Eriksen, C. W., & Hoffman, J. E. (1973). The extent of processing of noise elements during selective encoding from visual displays. *Perception & Psychophysics, 14,* 155–160.

Eriksen, C. W., & Lappin, J. S. (1967). Independence in the perception of simultaneously presented forms at brief durations. *Journal of Experimental Psychology, 73,* 468–472.

Eriksen, C. W., & Rohrbaugh, J. W. (1970). Some factors determining efficiency of selective attention. *American Journal of Psychology, 83,* 330–342.

Eriksen, C. W., & Schultz, D. W. (1978). Temporal factors in visual information processing: A tutorial review. In J. Requin (Ed.), *Attention and performance VII.* Hillsdale, NJ: Lawrence Erlbaum Associates Inc.

Eriksen, C. W., & Steffy, R. A. (1964). Short-term memory and retroactive interference in visual perception. *Journal of Experimental Psychology, 68,* 423–434.

Eriksen, C. W., & St. James, J. D. (1986). Visual attention within and around the field of focal attention: A zoom lens model. *Perception & Psychophysics, 40,* 225–240.

Eriksen, C. W., Webb, J. W., & Fournier, L. R. (1990). How much processing do nonattended stimuli receive? Apparently very little but . . . *Perception & Psychophysics, 47,* 477–488.

Eriksen, C. W., & Yeh, Y. Y. (1985). Allocation of attention in the visual field. *Journal of Experimental psychology: Human Perception and Performance, 5,* 583–597.

Estes, W. K. (1978). Perceptual processing in letter recognition and reading. In E. C. Carterette & M. P. Friedman (Eds.), *Handbook of perception, IX.* New York: Academic Press.

Estes, W. K., & Taylor, H. A. (1964). A detection method and probabilistic models for assessing information processing from brief visual displays. *Proceedings of the National Academy of Sciences USA, 52,* 46–54.

Exner, S. (1868). Ueber die zu einer Gesichtswahrnehmung nöthige Zeit. *Sitzungsberichte der kaiserlichen Akademie der Wissenschaften zu Wien, mathematisch-naturwissenschaftliche Classe, 58, Band 2,* 601–632.

Felleman, D., & Van Essen, D. (1991). Distributed hierarchical processing in the primate cerebral cortex. *Cerbral Cortex, 1,* 1–47.

Fera, P., Jolicoeur, P., & Besner, D. (1994). Evidence against early selection: Stimulus quality effects in previewed displays. *Journal of Experimental Psychology: Human Perception and Performance, 20,* 259–275.

Fernandez-Duque, D., & Johnson, M. L. (1999). Attention metaphors: How metaphors guide the cognitive psychology of attention. *Cognitive Science, 23,* 83–116.

Findlay, J. M., & Walker, R. (1999). A model of saccade generation based on parallel processing and competitive inhibition. *Behavioral and Brain Sciences, 22,* 661–721.

Flanagan, O. (1991). *The science of the mind, 2nd Ed.* Cambridge, MA: MIT Press.

Fodor, J. A. (1998). *Concepts: Where cognitive science went wrong.* Oxford: Clarendon Press.

Folk, C. L., & Egeth, H. E. (1989). Does the identification of simple features require serial processing? *Journal of Experimental Psychology: Human Perception and Performance, 15,* 97–110.

Folk, C. L., Remington, R. W., & Johnston, J. C. (1992). Involuntary covert orienting is contingent on attentional control settings. *Journal of Experimental Psychology: Human Perception and Performance, 18,* 1030–1044.

Fox, L. A., Shor, R. E., & Steinman, R. J. (1971). Semantic gradients and interference in naming color, spatial direction, and numerosity. *Journal of Experimental Psychology, 91,* 59–65.

Fraisse, P. (1969). Why is naming longer than reading? *Acta Psychologica, 30,* 96–103.

Francolini, C. N., & Egeth, H. E. (1980). On the non-automaticity of "automatic" activation: Evidence of selective seeing. *Perception & Psychophysics, 27,* 331–342.

Fryklund, I. (1975). Effects of cued-set spatial arrangement and target–background similarity in the partial-report paradigm. *Perception & Psychophysics, 17,* 375–386.

Garfield, J. L. (2000). The meanings of "meaning" and "meaning": Dimensions of the sciences of mind. *Philosophical Psychology, 13,* 421–440.

Garner, W. R. (1974). Attention: The processing of multiple sources of information. In E. C. Carterette & M. P. Friedman (Eds.), *Handbook of perception, II.* New York: Academic Press.

Gathercole, S. E., & Broadbent, D. E. (1984). Combining attributes in specified and categorized search: Further evidence for strategy differences. *Memory & Cognition, 12,* 329–337.

Gatti, S. V., & Egeth, H. E. (1978). Failure of spatial selectivity in vision. *Bulletin of the Psychonomic Society, 11,* 181–184.

Gholson, B., & Hohle, R. H. (1968). Verbal reaction times to hues vs hue names and forms vs form names. *Perception & Psychophysics, 3,* 191–196.

Gibson, J. J. (1941). A critical review of the concept of set in contemporary experimental psychology. *Psychological Bulletin, 38,* 781–817.

Gibson, J. J. (1960). The concept of the stimulus in psychology. *American Psychologist, 15,* 694–703.

Gibson, J. J. (1979). *The ecological approach to visual perception.* Boston: Houghton Mifflin.

Glaser, M. O., & Glaser, W. R. (1982). Time course analysis of the Stroop phenomenon. *Journal of Experimental Psychology: Human Perception and Performance, 8,* 875–894.

Glaser, W. R. (1992). Picture naming. *Cognition, 42,* 61–105.

Glaser, W. R., & Düngelhoff, F. J. (1984). The time course of picture–word interference. *Journal of Experimental Psychology: Human Perception and Performance, 10,* 640–654.

Goodale, M. A., & Milner, A. D. (1992). Separate visual pathways for perception and action. *Trends in Neuroscience, 15,* 20–25.

Gould, J. D. (1973). Eye movements during visual search and memory search. *Journal of Experimental Psychology, 98,* 184–195.

Grandison, T. D., Ghirardelli, T. G., & Egeth, H. E. (1997). Beyond similarity: Masking of the target is sufficient to cause the attentional blink. *Perception & Psychophysics, 59,* 266–274.

Green, M. (1991). Visual search, visual streams, and visual architectures. *Perception & Psychophysics, 50,* 388–403.

Guitton, D., Buchtel, H. A., & Douglas, R. M. (1985). Frontal lobe lesions in man cause difficulties in suppressing reflexive glances and in generation of goal directed saccades. *Experimental Brain Research, 58,* 455–472.

Güzeldere, G. (1996). Ist Bewusstsein die Wahrnemung dessen, was im eigenen Geist vorgeht? In T. Metzinger (Ed.), *Bewusstsein, Beiträge aus der Gegenwartsphilosophie* (pp. 397–422). Paderborn: Schöningh.

Haber, R. N. (1966). Nature of the effect of set on perception. *Psychological Review*, 73, 335–351.

Haber, R. N., & Hershenson, M. (1974). *The psychology of visual perception*. London: Holt, Rinehart & Winston.

Hagenaar, R., & Van der Heijden, A. H. C. (1986). Target–noise separation in visual selective attention. *Acta Psychologica*, 62, 161–176.

Hagenaar, R., & Van der Heijden, A. H. C. (1997). Location errors in partial-report bar-probe experiments: In search of the origin of cue-alignment problems. *Memory & Cognition*, 25, 641–652.

Haggard, P. (1999). The new dissociationism: Implications for action. In G. Aschersleben, T. Bachmann, & J. Müsseler (Eds.), *Cognitive contributions to the perception of spatial and temporal events* (pp. 15–18). Amsterdam: Elsevier.

Hall, D. C. (1974). Eye movements in scanning iconic imagery. *Journal of Experimental Psychology*, 103, 825–830.

Hallett, P. E. (1978). Primary and secondary saccades to goals defined by instructions. *Vision Research*, 18, 1279–1296.

Harms, L., & Bundesen, C. (1983). Color segregation and selective attention in a nonsearch task. *Perception & Psychophysics*, 33, 11–19.

Harré, R. (1998). *The singular self: An introduction to the psychology of personhood*. London: Sage Publications.

Harris, C. S., & Haber, R. N. (1963). Selective attention and coding in visual perception. *Journal of Experimental Psychology*, 65, 328–333.

Hebb, D. O. (1966). *A textbook of psychology*. Philadelphia, London: W. B. Saunders Company.

Hebb, D. O. (1980). A behavioral approach. In M. Bunge (Ed.), *The mind–body problem, a psychobiological approach*. Oxford: Pergamon.

Henderson, J. M. (1992). Visual attention and eye movement control during reading and picture viewing. In K. Rayner (Ed.), *Eye movements and visual cognition* (pp. 260–283). New York: Springer.

Henderson, J. M., & Ferreira, F. (1990). Effects of foveal processing difficulty on the perceptual span in reading: Implications for eye movement control. *Journal of Experimental Psychology: Learning, Memory, and Cognition*, 16, 417–429.

Henderson, J. M., Pollatsek, A., & Rayner, K. (1989). Covert visual attention and extrafoveal information use during object identification. *Perception & Psychophysics*, 45, 196–208.

Henderson, J. M., Weeks, P. A., & Hollingworth, A. (1999). The effects of semantic consistency on eye movements during complex scene viewing. *Journal of Experimental Psychology: Human Perception and Performance*, 25, 210–228.

Henson, D. B. (1978). Corrective saccades: Effect of altering visual feedback. *Vision Research*, 18, 63–67.

Hobbes, T. (1651). *Of liberty and necessity* [F. Woodbridge (Ed.), *Hobbes selections* (1930). New York: Scribner's].

Hodgson, T. L., & Müller, H. J. (1995). Evidence relating to premotor theories of visuospatial attention. In J. M. Findlay & R. Walker (Eds.), *Eye movement research: Mechanisms, processes and applications* (pp. 305–316). New York: Elsevier.

Hoffman, J. E. (1975). Hierarchical stages in the processing of visual information. *Perception & Psychophysics*, 18, 348–354.

Hoffman, J. E. (1998). Visual attention and eye movements. In H. Pashler (Ed.), *Attention*. Hove, UK: Psychology Press.

Hoffman, J. E., & Subramaniam, B. (1995). The role of visual attention in saccadic eye movements. *Perception & Psychophysics, 57*, 787–795.

Hommel, B. (1993). Inverting the Simon effect by intention: Determinants of direction and extent of effects of irrelevant spatial information. *Psychological Research, 55*, 270–279.

Hommel, B. (1997). Toward an action-concept model of stimulus–response compatibility. In B. Hommel & W. Prinz (Eds.), *Theoretical issues in stimulus–response compatibility* (pp. 281–320). Amsterdam: Elsevier.

Hooge, I. T. C., & Erkelens, C. J. (1996a). Control of fixation duration in a simple search task. *Perception & Psychophysics, 58*, 969–976.

Hooge, I. T. C., & Erkelens, C. J. (1996b). Adjustment of fixation duration in visual search. *Vision Research, 38*, 1295–1302.

Hume, D. (1739). *Treatise on human nature, Vols. I & II* [1740: Vol. III]. London: John Noon.

Humphreys, G. W. (1981). Flexibility of attention between stimulus dimensions. *Perception & Psychophysics, 30*, 291–302.

Humphreys, G. W., Price, C. J., & Riddoch, M. J. (1999). From objects to names: A cognitive neuroscience approach. *Psychological Research, 62*, 118–130.

Hurford, J. R. (in press). The neural basis of predicate–argument structure. *Behavioural and Brain Sciences.*

Husserl, E. (1907). *Ding und Raum* (unpublished MS). [Published in 1957 in *Husserliana, Vol. XVI.* Den Haag: Nijhoff.]

Intraub, H. (1985). Visual dissociation: An illusory conjunction of pictures and forms. *Journal of Experimental Psychology: Human Perception and Performance, 11*, 431–442.

Jaensch, E. R. (1929). *Grundformen menslichen Seins.* Berlin: Otto Elsner.

James, W. (1890/1950). *The principles of psychology.* New York: Dover.

James, W. (1892/1948). *Psychology.* Cleveland, New York: The World Publishing Company. [*Psychology: The briefer course* (1961). New York: Harper & Row.]

Javal, E. (1878). *Annales d'oculistique*, 1878, 1879. [In Woodworth, R. S. (1938). *Experimental psychology.* New York: Henry Holt & Company.]

Johnston, W. A., & Dark, V. J. (1986). Selective attention. In M. R. Rosenzweig & L. W. Potter (Eds.), *Annual review of psychology, Vol. 37* (pp. 43–75). Palo Alto, CA: Annual Reviews Inc.

Johnston, W. A., & Hawley, K. J. (1994). Perceptual inhibition of expected inputs: The key that opens closed minds. *Psychonomic Bulletin and Review, 1*, 56–72.

Jonides, J. (1980). Towards a model of the mind's eye's movement. *Canadian Journal of Psychology, 34*, 103–112.

Jonides, J. (1981). Voluntary versus automatic control over the mind's eye's movement. In J. B. Long & A. D. Baddeley (Eds.), *Attention and performance IX.* Hillsdale, NJ: Lawrence Erlbaum Associates Inc.

Jonides, J. (1983). Further toward a model of the mind's eye's movements. *Bulletin of the Psychonomic Society, 21*, 247–250.

Kahneman, D. (1973). *Attention and effort.* Englewood Cliffs, NJ: Prentice Hall.

Kahneman, D., & Chajczyk, D. (1983). Tests of the automaticity of reading: Dilution of Stroop effects by color-irrelevant stimuli. *Journal of Experimental Psychology: Human Perception and Performance, 9*, 497–509.

356   *References*

Kahneman, D., & Henik, A. (1981). Perceptual organization and attention. In M. Kubovy & J. R. Pomerantz (Eds.), *Perceptual organization* (pp. 181–211). Hillsdale, NJ: Lawrence Erlbaum Associates Inc.

Kahneman, D., & Treisman, A. M. (1984). Changing views of attention and automaticity. In R. Parasuraman & P. R. Davies (Eds.), *Varieties of attention*. New York: Academic Press.

Kahneman, D., Treisman, A. M., & Burkell, J. (1983). The cost of visual filtering. *Journal of Experimental Psychology: Human Perception and Performance, 9*, 510–522.

Kandel, E. R. (1985). Processing of form and movement in the visual system. In E. R. Kandel & J. H. Schwartz (Eds.), *Principles of neural science, 2nd Ed.* (pp. 366–383). New York & Amsterdam: Elsevier.

Kaptein, N. A., Theeuwes, J., & Van der Heijden, A. H. C. (1995). Search for a conjunctively defined target can be selectively limited to a color-defined subset of elements. *Journal of Experimental Psychology: Human Perception and Performance, 21*, 1053–1069.

Keele, S. W., Cohen, A., Ivry, R., Liotti, M., & Yee, P. (1988). Tests of a temporal theory of attentional binding. *Journal of Experimental Psychology: Human Perception and Performance, 14*, 444–452.

Klein, G. S. (1964). Semantic power measured through the interference of words with color-naming. *American Journal of Psychology, 77*, 576–588.

Klein, R. M. (1980). Does oculomotor readiness mediate cognitive control of visual attention? In R. S. Nickerson (Ed.), *Attention and performance VIII* (pp. 259–276). Hillsdale, NJ: Lawrence Erlbaum Associates Inc.

Klein, R. M. (1988). Inhibitory tagging facilitates visual search. *Nature, 324*, 430–431.

Klein, R. M., Kingstone, A., & Pontefract, A. (1992). Orienting of visual attention. In K. Rayner (Ed.), *Eye movements and visual cognition* (pp. 46–65). New York: Springer.

Koenderink, J. J. (1990). The brain a geometry engine. *Psychological Research, 52*, 122–127.

Kowler, E., Anderson, E., Dosher, B., & Blaser, B. (1995). The role of attention in the programming of saccades. *Vision Research, 35*, 1897–1916.

Kramer, A. F., & Hahn, S. (1995). Splitting the beam: Distribution of attention over noncontiguous regions of the visual field. *Psychological Science, 6*, 381–386.

Kroese, J., & Julesz, B. (1989). The control and speed of shifts of attention. *Vision Research, 23*, 1607–1619.

Kuelpe, O. (1904). Versuche über Abstraktion. In F. Schumann (Ed.), *Bericht über den 1 Kongress für Experimentelle Psychologie* (in Giessen, Lahn, vom 18. bis 21. April 1904) (pp. 56–68). Leipzig: Barth.

Kuelpe, O. (1912). Uber die moderne Psychologie des Denkens. *Internationale Monatschrift für Wissenschaft, Kunst und Technik, June*, 1070 ff.

Kuelpe, O. (1922). *Vorlesungen über Psychologie, 2nd Ed.* Leipzig: Hirzel.

Kugler, P. N., Shaw, R. E., Vincente, K. J., & Kinsella-Shaw, J. (1990). Inquiry into intentional systems: I. Issues in ecological physics. *Psychological Research, 52*, 98–121.

LaBerge, D. (1995). *Attentional processing: The brain's art of mindfulness.* Cambridge, MA: Harvard University Press.

LaBerge, D., & Brown, V. (1989). Theory of attentional operations in shape identification. *Psychological Review, 96*, 101–124.

LaBerge, D., & Samuels, S. J. (1974). Toward a theory of automatic information processing in reading. *Cognitive Psychology, 6*, 293–323.

La Heij, W., Helaha, D., & Van den Hof, E. (1993). Why does blue hamper the naming of red? *Acta Psychologica, 83*, 159–177.

La Heij, W., Van der Heijden, A. H. C., & Plooy, P. (2001). A paradoxical exposure duration effect in the Stroop task: Temporal segregation between stimulus attributes facilitates selection. *Journal of Experimental Psychology: Human Perception and Performance, 27*, 622–632.

La Mettrie, J. O. (1748/1912). *L'homme machine [Man a machine]*. Leiden: La Salle.

Lange, L. (1888). Neue Experimente über den Vorgang der einfachen Reaktion auf Sinneseindrucke. *Philosophische Studien, 4*, 479–510.

Lashley, K. S. (1951). The problem of serial order in behavior. In L. A. Jeffress (Ed.), *Cerebral mechanisms in behavior: The Hixon symposium* (pp. 112–146). New York: John Wiley & Sons.

Lawrence, D. H. (1971). Two studies of visual search for word targets with controlled rates of presentation. *Perception & Psychophysics, 10*, 85–89.

Logan, G. D. (1978). Attention in character-classification tasks: Evidence for the automaticity of component stages. *Journal of Experimental Psychology: General, 107*, 32–63.

Logan, G. D. (1985). Skill and automaticity: Relations, implications and further directions. *Canadian Journal of Psychology, 39*, 367–378.

Logan, G. D. (1995). Linguistic and conceptual control of visual spatial attention. *Cognitive Psychology, 28*, 103–174.

Logan, G. D., & Zbrodoff, N. J. (1999). Selection for cognition: Cognitive constraints on visual spatial attention. *Visual Cognition, 6*, 55–82.

Lotze, R. H. (1846). Seele und Seelenleben. In R. Wagner (Ed.), *Handwoerterbuch der Physiologie (Vol. 3)*, (pp. 142–263). Braunschweig: Vieweg.

Lotze, R. H. (1852). *Medicinische Psychologie oder Physiologie der Seele*. Leipzig: Weidmann.

Luck, S. J., & Vogel, E. K. (1997). The capacity of visual working memory for features and conjunctions. *Nature, 390*, 279–281.

Lycan, W. G. (1996). Consciousness as internal monitoring. In N. Block, O. Flanagan, & G. Güzeldere (Eds.), *The nature of consciousness*. Cambridge, MA: MIT Press.

Mach, E. (1885). *Die Analyse der Empfindugen*. Jena: Fischer.

MacLeod, C. M. (1991). Half a century of research on the Stroop effect: An integrative review. *Psychological Bulletin, 109*, 163–203.

MacLeod, C. M. (1992). The Stroop task: The "gold standard" of attentional measures. *Journal of Experimental Psychology: General, 121*, 12–14.

MacLeod, C. M., & Dunbar, K. (1988). Training and Stroop-like interference: Evidence for a continuum of automaticity. *Journal of Experimental Psychology: Learning, Memory, and Cognition, 14*, 126–135.

Mandler, J. M., & Mandler, G. (1964). *Thinking: From association to gestalt*. New York: John Wiley & Sons.

Marx, M. H. (1951). *Psychological theory: Contemporary readings*. New York: Macmillan.

McClean, J. P., Broadbent, D. E., & Broadbent, M. H. P. (1982). Combining attributes in rapid serial visual presentation tasks. *Quarterly Journal of Experimental Psychology, 35*A, 171–186.

McConkie, G. W., Kerr, P. W., Reddix, M. D., & Zola, D. (1988). Eye movement control during reading: I. The location of initial fixations on words. *Vision Research, 28*, 1107–1118.

McConkie, G. W., & Rayner, K. (1975). The span of the effective stimulus during a fixation in reading. *Perception & Psychophysics, 17*, 578–586.

McConkie, G. W., & Rayner, K. (1976). Asymmetry of the perceptual span in reading. *Bulletin of the Psychonomic Society, 8*, 365–368.

Meiran, N. (1996). Reconfiguration of processing mode prior to task performance. *Journal of Experimental Psychology: Learning, Memory, and Cognition, 22*, 1423–1442.

Meiran, N. (2000). Modeling cognitive control in task-switching. *Psychological Research, 63*, 234–239.

Merikle, P. M. (1980). Selection from visual persistence by perceptual groups and category membership. *Journal of Experimental Psychology: General, 109*, 279–295.

Merikle, P. M., & Gorewich, N. J. (1979). Spatial selectivity in vision: Field size depends upon noise size. *Bulletin of the Psychonomic Society, 14*, 343–346.

Mewhort, D. J. K., Campbell, A. J., Marchetti, F. M., & Campbell, J. I. D. (1981). Identification, localization, and "iconic memory": An evaluation of the bar-probe task. *Memory & Cognition, 9*, 50–67.

Mewhort, D. J. K., Johns, E. E., & Goble, S. (1991). Early and late selection in partial report: Evidence from degraded displays. *Perception & Psychophysics, 50*, 258–266.

Miller, G. A. (1964). *Psychology: The science of mental life.* London: Hutchinson & Co.

Miller, G. A., Galanter, E., & Pribram, K. H. (1960). *Plans and the structure of behavior.* New York: Holt, Rinehart & Winston.

Milner, A. D., & Goodale, M. A. (1993). Visual pathways to perception and action. In T. P. Hicks, S. Molotchinkoff, & T. Ono (Eds.), *Progress in brain research, Vol. 95* (pp. 317–337). Amsterdam: Elsevier.

Milner, A. D., & Goodale, M. A. (1995). *The visual brain in action.* Oxford: Oxford University Press.

Mitterer, H., La Heij, W., & Van der Heijden, A. H. C. (2003). Stroop dilution but no word-processing dilution: Evidence for attention capture. *Psychological Research, 67*, 30–42.

Monsell, S., Yeung, N., & Azuma, R. (2000). Reconfiguration of task-set. Is it easier to switch to the weaker task? *Psychological Research, 63*, 250–264.

Moore, C. M., Egeth, H., Berglan, L., & Luck, S. (1996). Are attentional dwell times inconsistent with serial visual search? *Psychonomic Bulletin and Review, 3*, 360–365.

Morrison, R. E. (1984). Manipulation of stimulus onset delay in reading: Evidence for parallel programming of saccades. *Journal of Experimental Psychology: Human Perception and Performance, 10*, 667–682.

Morton, J. (1969). Interaction of information in word recognition. *Psychological Review, 76*, 165–178.

Morton, J., & Chambers, S. M. (1973). Selective attention to words and colours. *Quarterly Journal of Experimental Psychology, 25*, 387–397.

Müller, H. J., & Rabbitt, P. M. A. (1989). Reflexive and voluntary attention: Time course of activation and resistance to interruption. *Journal of Experimental Psychology: Human Perception and Performance, 15*, 315–330.

Münsterberg, H. (1889). *Beiträge zur experimentellen Psychologie, Heft 1*. Freiburg: Akademische Verlagsbuchhandlung Mohr. [Reprinted in H. Hildebrandt & E. Scheerer (Eds.), *Frühe Schriften*. Berlin: Deutscher Verlag der Wissenschaften.]

Müsseler, J., Van der Heijden, A. H. C., Mahmud, S. H., Deubel, H., & Ertsey, S. (1999). Relative mislocalization of briefly presented stimuli in the retinal periphery. *Perception & Psychophysics, 61*, 1646–1661.

Nakayama, K., & Mackeben, M. (1989). Sustained and transient components of focal visual attention. *Vision Research, 29*, 1631–1647.

Neisser, U. (1967). *Cognitive psychology*. New York: Appleton-Century-Crofts.

Neisser, U. (1976). *Cognition and reality*. San Francisco: Freeman.

Neumann, O. (1987). Beyond capacity: A functional view of attention. In H. Heuer & A. F. Sanders (Eds.), *Perspectives on perception and action*. Hillsdale, NJ: Lawrence Erlbaum Associates Inc.

Neumann, O. (1989). Kognitive Vermittlung und direkte Parameterspezifikation. Zum Problem mentaler Repräsentation in der Wahrnehmung. *Sprache & Kognition, 8*, 32–49.

Neumann, O. (1990a). Visual attention and action. In O. Neumann & W. Prinz (Eds.), *Relationships between perception and action: Current approaches* (pp. 227–268). Heidelberg, New York: Springer.

Neumann, O. (1990b). Direct parameter specification and the concept of perception. *Psychological Research, 52*, 207–215.

Neumann, O. (1991). *Konzepte der Aufmerksamkeit*. Habilitationsschrift, Ludwig-Maximilians-Universität, München.

Neumann, O. (1996). Theories of attention. In O. Neumann & A. F. Sanders (Eds.), *Handbook of perception and action, Vol. 3* (pp. 299–446). London: Academic Press.

Neumann, O., Van der Heijden, A. H. C., & Allport, D. A. (1986). Visual selective attention: Introductory remarks. *Psychological Research, 48*, 185–188.

Nissen, M. J. (1985). Accessing features and objects: Is location special? In M. I. Posner & O. S. M. Marin (Eds.), *Attention and performance XI*. Hillsdale, NJ: Lawrence Erlbaum Associates Inc.

Norman, D. A., & Shallice, T. (1986). Attention to action: Willed and automatic control of behavior. In R. J. Davidson, G. E. Schwartz, & D. Shapiro (Eds.), *Consciousness and self-regulation, Vol. 4* (pp. 1–18). New York: Plenum Press.

O'Regan, J. K. (1984). Retinal versus extraretinal influences in flash localization during saccadic eye movements in the presence of a visible background. *Perception & Psychophysics, 36*, 1–14.

Osaka, N. (1977). Effect of refraction on perceived locus of a target in the peripheral visual field. *Journal of Psychology, 95*, 59–62.

Palmer, S. E. & Kimchi, R. (1986). The information processing approach to cognition. In R. J. Knapp & L. C. Robertson (Eds.), *Approaches to cognition: Contrasts and controversies*. Hillsdale, NJ: Lawrence Erlbaum Associates Inc.

Pashler, H. E. (1984). Evidence against late selection: Stimulus quality effects in previewed displays. *Journal of Experimental Psychology: Human Perception and Performance, 10*, 429–448.

Pashler, H. E. (1998). *The psychology of attention*. Cambridge, MA: MIT Press.

Perry, R. B. (1921). A behavioristic view of purpose. *Journal of Philosophy, 18*, 85–105.

Phaf, R. H., Van der Heijden, A. H. C., & Hudson, P. T. W. (1990). SLAM: A connectionist model for attention in visual selection tasks. *Cognitive Psychology*, *22*, 273–341.

Plaut, D. C., McClelland, J. L., Seidenberg, M. S., & Patterson, K. E. (1996). Understanding normal and impaired word reading. Computational principles in quasi-regular domains. *Psychological Review*, *103*, 56–115.

Poincaré, H. (1902). *La science et l'hypothese*. Paris: Flamarion.

Poincaré, H. (1905). *La valeur de la science*. Paris: Flamarion.

Pollatsek, A., & Rayner, K. (1990). Eye movements and lexical access in reading. In D. A. Balota, G. B. Flores d'Arcais, & K. Rayner (Eds.), *Comprehension processes in reading* (pp. 143–163). Hillsdale, NJ: Lawrence Erlbaum Associates Inc.

Pollatsek, A., & Rayner, K. (1999). Is covert attention really unnecessary? *Behavioral and Brain Sciences*, *22*, 695–696.

Popper, K. R. (1966). *Of clouds and clocks*. St. Louis: Washington University Press.

Posner, M. I. (1978). *Chronometric explorations of mind*. Hillsdale, NJ: Lawrence Erlbaum Associates Inc.

Posner, M. I. (1980). Orienting of attention. The VIIth Sir Frederic Bartlett Lecture. *Quarterly Journal of Experimental Psychology*, *32*, 3–25.

Posner, M. I., & Badgaiyan, R. D. (1998). Attention and neural networks. In R. W. Parks, D. S. Levine, & D. L. Long (Eds.), *Fundamentals of neural network modeling* (pp. 61–76). Cambridge, MA: MIT Press.

Posner, M. I., & Cohen, Y. (1984). Components of visual attention. In H. Bouma & D. G. Bouwhuis (Eds.), *Attention and performance X: Control of language processes* (pp. 531–556). Hillsdale, NJ: Lawrence Erlbaum Associates Inc.

Posner, M. I., Nissen, M. J., & Ogden, W. C. (1978). Attended and unattended processing modes: The role of set for spatial location. In H. L. Pick & I. J. Saltzman (Eds.), *Modes of perceiving and processing information*. Hillsdale, NJ: Lawrence Erlbaum Associates Inc.

Posner, M. I., & Snyder, C. R. R. (1975). Facilitation and inhibition in the processing of signals. In P. M. A. Rabbitt & S. Dornic (Eds.), *Attention and performance V*. New York: Academic Press.

Posner, M. I., Snyder, C. R. R., & Davidson, B. J. (1980). Attention and the detection of signals. *Journal of Experimental Psychology: General*, *109*, 160–174.

Posner, M. I., Walker, J. A., Friedrich, F. J., & Rafal, R. D. (1984). Effect of parietal lobe injury on covert orienting. *Journal of Neuroscience*, *4*, 1863–1874.

Prinz, W. (1987). Ideo-motor action. In H. Heuer & A. F. Sanders (Eds.), *Perspectives on perception and action* (pp. 47–76). Hillsdale, NJ: Lawrence Erlbaum Associates Inc.

Prinz, W. (1990). A common coding approach to perception and action. In O. Neumann & W. Prinz (Eds.), *Relationships between perception and action: Current approaches* (pp. 167–203). Berlin: Springer.

Prinz, W. (1997a). Perception and action planning. *European Journal of Cognitive Psychology*, *9*, 129–154.

Prinz, W. (1997b). Why Donders has led us astray. In B. Hommel & W. Prinz (Eds.), *Theoretical issues in stimulus–response compatibility* (pp. 247–267). Amsterdam: Elsevier.

Proctor, R. W. (1978). Sources of color–word interference in the Stroop color-naming task. *Perception & Psychophysics*, *23*, 413–419.

Rauk, M., & Luuk, A. (1980). Identification and detection of spatial position in one-dimensional pattern. In *Problems of cognitive psychology* (*Acta et Commentationes Universitatis Tartuensis, 522,* 143–163). Estonia: Tartu State University, Department of Psychology.

Raymond, J. E., Shapiro, K. L., & Arnell, K. M. (1992). Temporary suppression of visual processing in an RSVP task. An attentional blink? *Journal of Experimental Psychology: Human Perception and Performance, 18,* 849–860.

Raymond, J. E., Shapiro, K. L., & Arnell, K. M. (1995). Similarity determines the attentional blink. *Journal of Experimental Psychology: Human Perception and Performance, 21,* 653–662.

Rayner, K. (1995). Eye movements and cognitive processes in reading, visual search, and scene perception. In J. M. Findlay, R. Walker, & R. W. Kentridge (Eds.), *Eye movement research: Mechanisms, processes and applications* (pp. 3–22). North Holland: Elsevier.

Rayner, K., McConkie, G. W., & Erlich, S. (1978). Eye movements integrating information across fixations. *Journal of Experimental Psychology: Human Perception and Performance, 4,* 529–544.

Rayner, K., & Pollatsek, A. (1989). *The psychology of reading.* Englewood Cliffs, NJ: Prentice Hall.

Rayner, K., Well, A. D., & Pollatsek, A. (1980). Asymmetry of the effective visual field in reading. *Perception & Psychophysics, 27,* 537–544.

Reichle, E. D., Pollatsek, A., Fisher, D. L., & Rayner, K. (1998). Toward a model of eye movement control in reading. *Psychological Review, 105,* 125–157.

Reid, T. (1788). Essays on the active powers of man. Edinburgh.

Remington, R. W. (1980). Attention and saccadic eye movements. *Journal of Experimental Psychology: Human Perception and Performance, 6,* 726–744.

Rizolatti, G., Riggio, L., Dascola, I., & Umilta, C. (1987). Reorienting attention across the horizontal and vertical meridians: Evidence in favor of a premotor theory of attention. *Neuropsychologia, 25,* 31–40.

Roberts, R. J., Hager, L. D., & Heron, C. (1994). Prefrontal cognitive processes: Working memory and inhibition in the antisaccade task. *Journal of Experimental Psychology: General, 123,* 374–393.

Rogers, R. D., & Monsell, S. (1995). Costs of a predictable switch between simple cognitive tasks. *Journal of Experimental Psychology: General, 124,* 207–231.

Rosch, E. (1978). Principles of categorization. In E. Rosch & B. B. Lloyd (Eds.), *Cognition and categorization* (pp. 27–48). Hillsdale, NJ: Lawrence Erlbaum Associates Inc.

Rose, D., & Halpern, D. L. (1992). Stimulus mislocalization depends on spatial frequency. *Perception, 21,* 289–296.

Rosenthal, D. M. (1996). A theory of consciousness. In N. Block, O. Flanagan, & G. Güzeldere (Eds.), *The nature of consciousness.* Cambridge, MA: MIT Press.

Ryle, G. (1949). *The concept of mind.* London: Hutchinson.

Saraga, E., & Shallice, T. (1973). Parallel processing of the attributes of single stimuli. *Perception & Psychophysics, 13,* 261–270.

Scheerer, E. (1984). Motor theories of cognitive structure: A historical review. In W. Prinz & A. F. Sanders (Eds.), *Cognition and motor processes* (pp. 77–98). Berlin & Heidelberg: Springer.

Scheerer, E. (1986). The constitution of space perception: A phenomenological perspective. *Acta Psychologica, 63,* 157–173.

Scheerer, E. (1992). *Orality, literacy, and cognitive modeling.* Bielefeld: Zentrum für interdisziplinäre Forschung. [Expanded version of a paper presented at the conference on Biological and Cultural aspects of Language Development.]

Scheibe, K., Shaver, P. R., & Carrier, S. C. (1967). Color association values and response interference on variants of the Stroop test. *Acta Psychologica, 26,* 286–295.

Schneider, W. X. (1999). Visual-spatial working memory, attention, and scene representation: A neuro-cognitive theory. *Psychological Research, 62,* 220–236.

Schneider, W. X., & Deubel, H. (1995). Visual attention and saccadic eye movements: Evidence for obligatory and selective spatial coupling. In J. M. Findlay, R. Walker, & R. W. Kentridge (Eds.), *Eye movement research* (pp. 317–324). Amsterdam: Elsevier.

Schweickert, R. (1983). Latent network theory: Scheduling of processes in sentence verification and the Stroop effect. *Journal of Experimental Psychology: Learning, Memory, and Cognition, 9,* 353–383.

Seidenberg, M. S., & McClelland, J. L. (1989). A distributed developmental model of word recognition and naming. *Psychological Review, 96,* 523–568.

Seiffert, A. E., & DiLollo, V. (1997). Low-level masking in the attentional blink. *Journal of Experimental Psychology: Human Perception and Performance, 23,* 1061–1073.

Shapiro, K. L., Raymond, J. E., & Arnell, K. M. (1994). Attention to visual pattern information produces the attentional blink in rapid serial visual presentation. *Journal of Experimental Psychology: Human Perception and Performance, 20,* 357–371.

Shepherd, M., Findlay, J. M., & Hockey, R. J. (1986). The relationship between eye movements and spatial attention. *Quarterly Journal of Experimental Psychology, 38*A, 475–491.

Shiffrin, R. M., Diller, D., & Cohen, A. (1966). Processing visual information in an unattended location. In A. F. Kramer, M. G. H. Coles, & G. D. Logan (Eds.), *Converging operations in the study of visual selective attention.* Washington, DC: American Psychological Association.

Shiffrin, R. M., & Schneider, W. (1977). Controlled and automatic human information processing: II. Perceptual learning, automatic attending, and a general theory. *Psychological Review, 84,* 127–190.

Shiu, L., & Pashler, H. (1994). Negligible effect of spatial precuing on identification of single digits. *Journal of Experimental Psychology: Human Perception and Performance, 20,* 1037–1054.

Singer, M. H., Lappin, J. S., & Moore, L. P. (1975). The interference of various word parts on color naming in the Stroop test. *Perception & Psychophysics, 18,* 191–193.

Skavenski, A. A. (1990). Eye movement and visual localization of objects in space. In E. Kowler (Ed.), *Eye movements and their role in visual and cognitive processes* (pp. 263–287). Amsterdam: Elsevier.

Skavenski, A. A., Haddad, G., & Steinman, R. M. (1972). The extraretinal signal for the visual perception of direction. *Perception & Psychophysics, 11,* 287–290.

Skinner, B. F. (1957). *Verbal behavior.* New York: Appleton-Century-Crofts.

Skinner, B. F. (1972). *Beyond freedom and dignity.* Toronto/New York/London: Bantam/Vintage.

Smythies, J. R. (1994a). Shipwreck of a grand hypothesis. *Inquiry, 37,* 267–281.

Smythies, J. R. (1994b). Requiem for the identity theory. *Inquiry, 37*, 311–329.

Snodgrass, J. G. (1984). Concepts and their surface representations. *Journal of Verbal Learning and Verbal Behavior, 23*, 3–33.

Snyder, C. R. R. (1972). Selection, inspection and naming in visual search. *Journal of Experimental Psychology, 92*, 428–431.

Sperling, G. (1960). The information available in brief visual presentations. *Psychological Monographs, 74(11)* (whole no. 498).

Sperling, G., & Reeves, A. (1980). Measuring the reaction time of a shift of visual attention. In R. S. Nickerson (Ed.), *Attention and performance VIII* (pp. 347–360). Hillsdale, NJ: Lawrence Erlbaum Associates Inc.

Sperling, G., & Weichselgartner, E. (1990). *Episodic theory of visual attention*. Paper presented at the meeting of the psychonomic Society, New Orleans, November 1990.

Stelmach, L. B., Campsall, J. M., & Herdman, C. M. (1997). Attentional and ocular movements. *Journal of Experimental Psychology: Human Perception and Performance, 23*, 823–844.

Stevens, J. K., Emerson, R. C., Gerstein, G., Kallos, T., Neufield, G., Nichols, C., & Rosenquist, A. et al. (1976). Paralysis of the awake human: Visual perceptions. *Vision Research, 16*, 93–98.

Stigler, R. (1910). Chronophotische Untersuchungen über den Umgebungskontrast. *Pflüger's Archiv für die gesamte Physiologie, 134*, 365–435.

Stins, J. F. (1997). Commentary on Prinz: Action codes or informationally guided movements? In B. Hommel & W. Prinz (Eds.), *Theoretical issues in stimulus–response compatibility* (pp. 273–278). Amsterdam: Elsevier.

Stroop, J. R. (1935). Studies of interference in serial verbal reactions. *Journal of Experimental Psychology, 18*, 643–662.

Taylor, J. G. (1975). *The behavioral basis of perception*. Westport, CT: Greenwood Press. Originally published in 1962 by Yale University Press, New Haven.

Teichner, W. H., LeMaster, D., & Kinney, P. A. (1978). Eye movements during inspection and recall. In J. W. Senders, D. F. Fisher, & R. A. Monty (Eds.), *Eye movements and the higher psychological functions*. Hillsdale, NJ: Lawrence Erlbaum Associates Inc.

Theeuwes, J. (1991). Exogenous and endogenous control of attention: The effect of visual onsets and offsets. *Perception & Psychophysics, 49*, 83–90.

Theeuwes, J. (1992). Perceptual selectivity for color and form. *Perception & Psychophysics, 51*, 599–606.

Theeuwes, J. (1993). Visual selective attention: A theoretical analysis. *Acta Psychologica, 53*, 93–154.

Theeuwes, J., Atchley, P., & Kramer, A. F. (2000). On the time course of top-down and bottom-up control of visual attention. In S. Monsell & J. Driver (Eds.), *Attention and performance XVIII: Control of cognitive processes*. Cambridge, MA: MIT Press.

Theios, J., & Amrhein, P. C. (1989). Theoretical analysis of the cognitive processing of lexical and pictorial stimuli: Reading, naming and visual and conceptual comparisons. *Psychological Review, 96*, 5–24.

Titchener, E. B. (1895a). Simple reactions. *Mind, 4*, 74–81.

Titchener, E. B. (1895b). The type-theory of the simple reaction. *Mind, 4*, 506–514.

Titchener, E. B. (1896). The "type-theory" of the simple reaction. *Mind, 5*, 236–241.

Titchener, E. B. (1898). The postulates of a structural psychology. *The Philosophical Review, 7,* 449–465.

Tolman, E. C. (1932). *Purposive behavior in animals and man.* New York: Appleton-Century-Crofts.

Tolman, E. C. (1936). Operational behaviorism and current trends in psychology. Proceedings of the Twenty-fifth Anniversary Celebrating Inauguration of Graduate Studies. Los Angeles: University of South California Press. [Reprinted in M. H. Marx (Ed.), *Psychological theory: Contemporary readings.* New York: Macmillan, 1951]

Tolman, E. C. (1959). Principles of purposive behavior. In S. Koch (Ed.), *Psychology: A study of a science; Study I: Conceptual and systematic; Vol. 2: General systematic formulations, learning and special processes* (pp. 92–157). New York, Toronto, London: McGraw-Hill.

Treisman, A. M. (1960). Contextual cues in selective listening. *Quarterly Journal of Experimental Psychology, 12,* 242–248.

Treisman, A. M. (1964). Verbal cues, language, and meaning in selective attention. *American Journal of Psychology, 77,* 206–219.

Treisman, A. M. (1969). Strategies and models of selective attention. *Psychological Review, 76,* 282–299.

Treisman, A. M. (1988). Features and objects: The fourteenth Bartlett memorial lecture. *Quarterly Journal of Experimental Psychology A, 40,* 201–237.

Treisman, A. M. (1990). Variations on the theme of feature integration: Reply to Navon (1990). *Psychological Review, 97,* 460–463.

Treisman, A. M. (1993). The perception of features and objects. In A. Baddeley & L. Weiskrantz (Eds.), *Attention: Selection, awareness, and control* (pp. 5–35). Oxford: Clarendon Press.

Treisman, A. M., & Gelade, G. (1980). A feature integration theory of attention. *Cognitive Psychology, 12,* 97–136.

Treisman, A. M., Kahneman, D., & Burkell, J. (1983). Perceptual objects and the cost of filtering. *Perception & Psychophysics, 33,* 527–532.

Treisman, A. M., & Sato, S. (1990). Conjunction search revisited. *Journal of Experimental Psychology: Human Perception and Performance, 16,* 459–478.

Treisman, A. M., & Schmidt, H. (1982). Illusory conjunctions in the perception of objects. *Cognitive Psychology, 14,* 107–141.

Tsal, Y., & Lamy, D. (2000). Attending to an object's color entails attending to its location: Support for location-special views of visual attention. *Perception & Psychophysics, 62,* 960–968.

Tsal, Y., & Lavie, N. (1988). Attending to color and shape: The special role of location in selective visual processing. *Perception & Psychophysics, 44,* 15–21.

Tsotsos, J. K. (1990). Analyzing vision at the complexity level. *Behavioral and Brain Sciences, 13,* 423–445.

Tulving, E. (1985). How many memory systems are there? *American Psychologist, 40,* 385–398.

Turing, A. M. (1936). On computable numbers, with an application to the Entscheidungsproblem. *Proceedings of the London Mathematical Society, 42,* 230–265.

Underwood, N. R., & McConkie, G. W. (1985). Perceptual span for letter distinctions during reading. *Reading Research Quarterly, 20,* 153–162.

Van der Heijden, A. H. C. (1981). *Short-term visual information forgetting*. London: Routledge & Kegan Paul.

Van der Heijden, A. H. C. (1989). Probability matching in visual selective attention. *Canadian Journal of Psychology, 43*, 45–52.

Van der Heijden, A. H. C. (1992). *Selective attention in vision*. London: Routledge.

Van der Heijden, A. H. C. (1993). The role of position in object selection in vision. *Psychological Research, 56*, 44–58.

Van der Heijden, A. H. C. (1995). Modularity and attention. *Visual Cognition, 2*, 269–302.

Van der Heijden, A. H. C. (1996a). Visual Attention. In O. Neumann & A. F. Sanders (Eds.), *Handbook of perception and action: Attention, Vol. 3* (pp. 5–42). London: Academic Press.

Van der Heijden, A. H. C. (1996b). Two stages in visual information processing and visual perception? *Visual Cognition, 3*, 325–361.

Van der Heijden, A. H. C., & Bem, S. (1997). Successive approximations to an adequate model of attention. *Consciousness and Cognition, 6*, 413–428.

Van der Heijden, A. H. C., Hagenaar, R., & Bloem, W. (1984). Two stages in postcategorical filtering and selection. *Memory & Cognition, 12*, 458–469.

Van der Heijden, A. H. C., Kurvink, A. G., De Lange, L., de Leeuw, F., & Van der Geest, J. N. (1996). Attending to color with proper fixation. *Perception & Psychophysics, 58*, 1224–1237.

Van der Heijden, A. H. C., Müsseler, J., & Bridgeman, B. (1999). On the perception of position. In G. Aschersleben, T. Bachmann, & J. Müsseler (Eds.), *Cognitive contributions to the perception of spatial and temporal events* (pp. 19–37). Amsterdam: Elsevier.

Van der Heijden, A. H. C., Van der Geest, J. N., De Leeuw, F., Krikke, K., & Müsseler, J. (1999). Sources of position-perception error for small isolated targets. *Psychological Research, 62*, 20–35.

Van der Heijden, A. H. C., & Van der Velde, F. (1999). Cognition for selection. *Visual Cognition, 6*, 83–87.

Vanderplas, J. M. (1966). *Controversial issues in psychology*. Boston: Houghton Mifflin Company.

Van der Velde, F., & de Kamps, M. (2001). From knowing what to knowing where: Modeling object-based attention with feedback disinhibition of activation. *Journal of Cognitive Neuroscience, 13*, 479–491.

Von Helmholtz, H. (1866). *Handbuch der physiologische Optik, Vol. 3*. Leipzig: Voss.

Von Helmholtz, H. (1871). Ueber die Zeit welche nötig ist, damit ein Gesichtseindruck zum Bewusstsein kommt. *Berliner Monatsberichte, June 8*, 333–337.

Von Helmholtz, H. (1894). *Handbuch der physiologischen Optik*. Hamburg, Leipzig: L. Vos.

Von Holst, E., & Mittelstaedt, H. (1950). Das Reafferenzprinzip (Wechselwirkungen zwischen Zentralnervensystem und Peripherie). *Naturwissenschaften, 37*, 464–476. [English translation: (1980). The reafference principle. In C. R. Gallistel (Ed.), *The organization of action*. New York: Wiley.]

Von Holst, E., & Mittelstaedt, H. (1971). The principle of reafference: Interactions between the central nervous system and the peripheral organs. In P. C. Dodwell (Ed.), *Perceptual processing: Stimulus equivalence and pattern recognition*. New York: Appleton-Century-Crofts.

Von Wright, J. M. (1968). Selection in visual immediate memory. *Quarterly Journal of Experimental Psychology, 20*, 62–68.

Von Wright, J. M. (1970). On selection in visual immediate memory. *Acta Psychologica, 33*, 280–292.

Walker, R., Husain, M., Hodgson, T. L., & Kennard, C. (1998). Saccadic eye movements and working memory deficits following damage to human prefrontal cortex. *Neuropsychologia, 36*, 1141–1159.

Walker, R., Kentridge, R. W., & Findlay, J. M. (1995). Independent contributions of the orienting of attention, fixation offset and bilateral stimulation on human saccadic latencies. *Experimental Brain Research, 103*, 294–310.

Ward, R., Duncan, J., & Shapiro, K. (1996). The slow time-course of visual attention. *Cognitive Psychology, 10*, 79–109.

Warren, R. M., & Warren, R. P. (1968). *Helmholtz on perception: Its physiology and development.* New York: John Wiley & Sons.

Watson, D. G., & Humphreys, G. W. (1997). Visual marking: Prioritizing selection for new objects by top-down attentional inhibition of old objects. *Psychological Review, 104*, 90–122.

Watson, G. (1995). Free will. In J. Kim & E. Sosa (Eds.), *A companion to metaphysics* (pp. 175–182). Oxford: Blackwell.

Watson, J. B. (1913). Psychology as the behaviorist views it. *The Psychological Review, 20*, 158–177.

Watson, J. B. (1936). J. B. Watson. In C. Murchison (Ed.), *A history of psychology in autobiography, Vol. 3* (pp. 271–281). Worcester, MA: Clark University Press.

Watt, H. J. (1904). Experimentelle Beiträge zu einer Theorie des Denkens. *Archiv. Für die gesamte Psychologie, vol. 4.* Leipzig: Engelmann.

Watt, H. J. (1905–1906). Experimental contribution to a theory of thinking. *Journal of Anatomy & Physiology, 40*, 257–266.

Weichselgartner, E., & Sperling, G. (1987). Dynamics of automatic and controlled visual attention. *Science, 238*, 778–780.

Weiskrantz, L., Warrington, E. K., Sanders, M. D., & Marshall, J. (1974). Visual capacity in the hemianopic field following a restricted occipital ablation. *Brain, 97*, 709–728.

Wertheimer, M. (1923/1958). Untersuchungen zur Lehre von der Gestalt, II. *Psychologische Forschung, 4*, 301–350. [Principles of perceptual organization; Abridged translation by M. Wertheimer in D. C. Beardsly & M. Wertheimer (Eds.) (1958). *Readings in perception* (pp. 115–135). Princeton, NJ: Van Nostrand.]

Wienese, M., La Heij, W., Van der Heijden, A. H. C., & Shiffrin, R. M. (2000). Perceptual inertia: Spatial attention and warning period? *Psychological Research, 64*, 93–104.

Wolfe, J. M. (1994). Guided search 2.0: A revised model of search. *Psychonomic Bulletin & Review, 1*, 202–238.

Wolfe, J. M. (1996). Extending guided search: Why guided search needs a preattentive "Item map". In G. D. Logan, M. G. H. Coles, & A. F. Kramer (Eds.), *Converging operations in the study of attention* (pp. 247–270). Washington, DC: American Psychological Association.

Wolfe, J. M., Cave, K. R., & Franzel, S. L. (1989). Guided search: An alternative to the feature integration model for visual search. *Journal of Experimental Psychology: Human Perception and Performance, 15*, 419–433.

Wolff, P. (1987). Perceptual learning by saccades: A cognitive approach. In H. Heuer & A. F. Sanders (Eds.), *Perspectives on perception and action* (pp. 249–274). Hillsdale, NJ: Lawrence Erlbaum Associates Inc.

Wolff, P. (1999a). Space perception and intended action. In G. Aschersleben, T. Bachmann, & J. Müsseler (Eds.), *Cognitive contributions to the perception of spatial and temporal events* (pp. 41–63). Amsterdam: Elsevier.

Wolff, P. (1999b). Function and processing of "meaningless" and "meaningful" position. In G. Aschersleben, T. Bachmann, & J. Müsseler (Eds.), *Cognitive contributions to the perception of spatial and temporal events* (pp. 39–42). Amsterdam: Elsevier.

Woodworth, R. S. (1938). *Experimental psychology.* New York: Henry Holt & Company.

Wundt, W. (1907). *Outlines of psychology* [C. H. Judd, trans.]. Leipzig: Wilhelm Engelmann.

Wundt, W. (1912). *Introduction to psychology* [R. Pinter, trans.]. London: George Allen.

Wurtz, R. H., & Mohler, C. W. (1976). Organization of monkey superior colliculus: Enhanced visual response of superficial layer cells. *Journal of Neurophysiology, 39*, 745–765.

Wylie, G., & Allport, D. A. (2000). Task switching and the measurements of "switch costs". *Psychological Research, 63*, 212–233.

Yantis, S., & Egeth, H. E. (1999). On the distinction between visual salience and stimulus-driven attentional capture. *Journal of Experimental Psychology: Human Perception and Performance, 25*, 661–676.

Zeki, S. (1992). The visual image in mind and brain. *Scientific American, 267*, 68–77.

Zeki, S. (1993). *A vision of the brain.* Oxford: Blackwell Scientific Publications.

Author index

Subject index